W9-APB-438

SHEA'S CHARLEVOIX.

Bienville

GOVERNOR OF LOUISIANA

HISTORY

AND

GENERAL DESCRIPTION

OF

NEW FRANCE

BY

THE REV. P.F.X. DE CHARLEVOIX, S.J.

TRANSLATED, WITH NOTES, BY JOHN GILMARY SHEA

IN SIX VOLUMES

VOLUME VI

LOYOLA UNIVERSITY PRESS
CHICAGO 13, ILLINOIS

NEW YORK:
JOHN GILMARY SHEA
1870

Yours truly
J B A Ferland Ptre

PREFACE.

To give completeness to this edition of Charlevoix, I have, in the Addenda et Corrigenda, not only rectified some errors, but have also introduced references to all works on Canadian History published while it was in progress.

Before issuing my last volume, I must also express my deep sense of obligation to the many friends who have aided me in my researches while preparing for and completing it, students in the same field of historical investigation. Among these I would name the Hon. Jacques Viger, the Abbé Faillon, Mr. Faribault, and in an especial manner the Abbé Ferland, who have all passed from amongst us, and the Rev. Father Felix Martin, S. J., the Abbés Laverdiere and Casgrain of Quebec, the Abbé Bois of Maskinonge, Rev. Mr. Daniel of Montreal, Dr. E. B. O'Callaghan, Mr. Francis Parkman, the Hon. H. C. Murphy and Mr. George H. Moore, whose services will long, I trust, be given to the cause of History.

CONTENTS.

BOOK XXI.

Various opinions as to Louysiana. Condition of Louysiana in 1700. Coppermine among the Sioux. Remarkable observations. Description of the mine. Settlement of Maubile and Isle Dauphin. Slow progress of the colony. Arrival of a Commissaire Ordonnateur. Dauphin Island ravaged by a pirate. Cession of Louysiana to Mr. Crozat. Establishment of a Superior Council. The Spaniards refuse to allow trade between Louysiana and Mexico. Overland expedition of St. Denys to Mexico. He is imprisoned at Mexico. His adventures. He refuses to enter the Spanish service. He renders a service to the Spaniards. His marriage with a Spanish lady. The English endeavor to debauch our Indians. Irruption of Indians into Carolina. La Motte Cadillac forms an alliance with several nations. Treachery of the Natchez. The Messrs. de la Loire escape. The chief of the Tonicas refuses to enter the plot. Bienville sent to demand satisfaction. He encamps at the Tonicas. What occurred between him and the Natchez. He makes peace with them. Settlement among these Indians. Fort built at Natchitoches. State of Louysiana commerce in 1716. Crozat's propositions and complaints. He surrenders his privilege to the King. His Majesty transfers it to the Western Company on certain conditions. Mr. de l'Epinai, Governor of Louysiana. His reception by the Indians. The port of Isle Dauphin closes. Commencement of New Orleans. A ship enters the Mississippi. Arrival of the first concessions. St. Joseph's Bay occupied by the French and almost immediately abandoned. Description of Pensacola. Its fort taken from the Spaniards. The French who convey the Spanish garrison to Havana arrested there. The Spaniards prepare to recapture Pensacola. They arrive in sight of the bay. Capture of the fort. The Spaniards defeated near Mobile. Serigny summoned to surrender the Philippe. Repulse of the Spaniards at Dauphin Island. They fortify Pensacola. Arrival of Mr. de Champmêlin with a squadron. Preparations for attacking Pensacola. The squadron enters the bay. Capture of the fort at the Point, and of the Spanish ships. Fort San Carlos taken and its garrison prisoners of war. The enemy's loss. Cruelty of the Spaniards to their French prisoners. Mr. de Champmêlin's reprisals. The fort at Pensacola in part demolished. Presents made to the Indians. New tidings of the approach of a Spanish squad-

ron. De Champmêlin sails for France. Mr. de Saujon arrives. Serigny's departure. Arrival of two royal vessels. De St. Denys at Natchitoches. First tidings of peace. Unsuccessful enterprise at St. Bernard's Bay. Pensacola restore d to Spain. Headquarters transferred to New Orleans. English intrigues. Fidelity of the Choctaws. Cause of the desertions. Hurricane and its effects. The Chickasaws ask peace. Hostilities of the Natchez. The Illinois all unite on the Micissipi. The Natchez make peace with the French.

BOOK XXII.

Introduction of the Capuchin Fathers into Louysiana. Missionaries to the Indians thought of. Jesuits sent. Perrier, Commandant-General of Louysiana. He asks aid in vain. Indian conspiracy against the French. How it was thwarted. Treachery of the Choctaws and confidence of the French. All those settled at Natchez killed or taken by the Indians. The same happens at the Yazoos. Causes of the death of Father Souel. A missionary attacked by the Yazoos and saved almost miraculously. Activity of Perrier on hearing of the massacre at Natchez. How he is informed of the general plot against the French. Discouragement of the whole colony. Singular conduct of the Choctaws. They arm against the Natchez. Perrier puts the French settlements in a state of defence. Disposition of the several Indian tribes. The French army assembles at the Tonicas. Insolent proposals of the Natchez. The Choctaws, commanded by Mr. le Sueur, gain a great advantage over them, but do not end the war, because they do not act in concert with the French. De Loubois besieges the Natchez in their forts. They make a sortie and clear the trench. They are repulsed by the Chevalier d'Artaguette. What saved the besieged. They give up the French prisoners and the siege is raised. Fort built at the Natchez. The Chevalier d'Artaguette commandant. Insolence of the Choctaws. The Chickasaws in vain tempt the fidelity of our allies. The English as unsuccessful. The Natchez renew their raids. Perrier negotiates with the Choctaws. Reinforcements arrive from France. De Loubois attacks the Indians in their forts. They make a sortie and clear the trench. Repulsed by the Chevalier d'Artaguette. What saves the besieged. They give up the French prisoners. Siege raised. Fort built at Natchez. The Chevalier d'Artaguette in command. Insolence of the Choctaws. English equally unsuccessful. The Natchez renew their raids. Perrier treats with the Choctaws. Arrival of reinforcements from France. The army marches. Its order. The Natchez attack a periagua, killing or wounding sixteen French. Indocility of our Indian allies. The army in sight of the enemy. They ask peace. They give up all the negroes captured from the French whom they still hold. They continue to parley. The Head Chief, his presumptive successor and another chief, come into the camp. They are secured. One of the chiefs escapes and induces several to follow him. Others surrender to the French. Most of them escape. Our Indians refuse to pursue them. The French army decamps. Forces of the Natchez after this siege. The Chief of the Tonicas allows himself to be surprised and killed by the Natchez. Several Natchez killed in different actions. Others be-

siege de St. Denys at Natchitoches. Their defeat. Forces of the Chickasaws Their intrigne to excite our negroes to revolt. The latter conspire against us The plot discovered. They are punished. The Arkansas and Illinois refuse to league with the Chickasaws. Conditions on which the India Company cedes Louysiana back to the King, who confides the government to Mr. Perrier. That Governor returns to France. Bienville succeeds him. Commencement of the Chickasaw war. Noble action of a Jesuit and skillful retreat of an officer sixteen years of age.

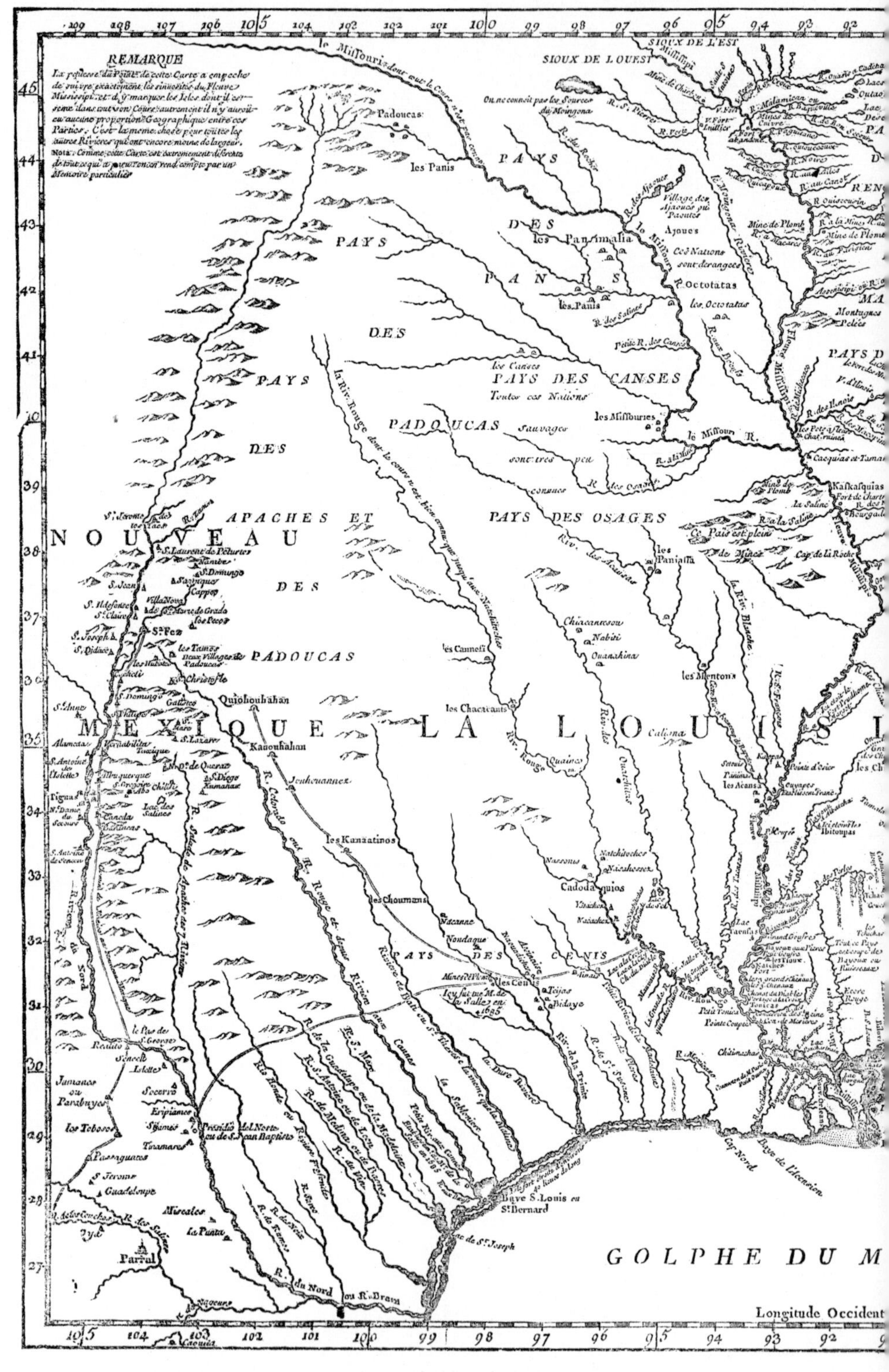

REMARQUE
SIOUX DE L'EST
SIOUX DE L OUEST
Padoucas
les Panis
PAYS DES PANIS
les Panimalia
Ajoues
Octotatas
les Octotatas
DES
PAYS DES CANSES
Toutes ces Nations
les Missouries
le Missouri R.
PADOUCAS
PAYS DES OSAGES
APACHES ET
NOUVEAU
DES
PADOUCAS
MEXIQUE
LA LOUIS
Kaskasquias
Cap de la Roche
les Paniassa
Chiacansesou
Nabiti
Ouanakina
les Cannesi
les Chacacants
les Mentons
Quiohouhahan
Kanouhahan
Jouhouannez
les Kanaatinos
les Choumans
Natchitoches
Cadodaquios
PAYS DES CENIS
les Cenis
Teijas
Bidaye
S.t Fez
Parral
Los Tobosos
Presidio del Norte ou de S.t Jean Baptiste
Baye S.Louis ou S.t Bernard
GOLPHE DU M
Longitude Occident

CARTE DE
LA LOUISIANE
COURS DU MISSISSIPI ET
PAIS VOISINS
Dediee a M. le Comte de Maurepas, Ministre et
Secretaire d'Etat Commandeur des Ordres
du Roy
Par N. Bellin Ingenieur de la Marine 1744
ECHELLES
Lieues communes de France de 25 au Dégré
Lieues Marines de France et d'Angleterre de 20 au Degré
LAC HURON
I. Manitoualin
LAC MICHIGAN
LAC ONTARIO
LAC ERIE
La longue Pointe
Ancien Pais des Hurons
PAYS DES MIAMIS
PENSILVANIE
Philadelphie
VIRGINIE
CAROLINE
GEORGIE
FLORIDE
PRESQU'ISLE DE LA FLORIDE
Montagnes des Apalaches
PAYS DES CHAOUANONS
CHERAQUIS
Cheraquis
Baye de Laware
Chesapeack
C. Charles
Cap Henri
Passe de Curritucé
Albemarle
C. Hatteras
Cap Lookout
C. Fear
la Longue Baye
C. Carreret
Charles Town
James Town
I. Ossabaw
I. St. Catherine
I. Sapola
I. du Petit S. Simon
I. du Grand S. Simon
I. Jekill
I. Wése
R. S. Augustin que les Anglois appellent R. St. Jean
S. Augustin
I. Matance
I. Mosquites
Cap Canaveral
Caye d'Anclote
B. du St. Esprit
B. de Carlos ou de S. Jean Ponce
Fort Palachuicala
Bafton
Cap Cod
R. Merimac
Cap Anne
Paris

BOOK XXI.

WHAT often befalls two classes of persons befell Louysiana. The one class, with acknowledged and superior merit, for some inexplicable reason, never succeed in obtaining their due meed of justice, or in displaying their talents, remaining useless and obscure, while possessing every requisite for attaining the highest reputation and rendering the most essential services to the state.

1700–25.

Various opinions as to Louysiana.

The other class, from the fact that too favorable an opinion was formed of them at first, or an imaginary merit attributed to them instead of a real one, are rejected in spite of solid merit, being compelled to bear the penalty of the hasty judgments formed in regard to them. Unless I am much deceived, my readers will themselves apply this to the province with which I close my History.

We have seen that the Spaniards under Ferdinand de Soto had, at great expense, attempted to settle Florida; that their commander spent the whole last year of his life in exploring both banks of the Micissipi, called by his historian, Garcilaso de la Vega, the Cucagua; that neither he nor his successor, Moscoso, took any steps to found a colony; and that, for a long time after, men seemed to be ignorant in Spain that one of the greatest rivers in the world ran through Florida, watering a delightful country, with a healthy and temperate climate, the possession of which would secure to the Catholic King all the Gulf of Mexico.

The French, after discovering all the known course of this same river, seemed to pay scarcely any greater atten-

1700–25. tion to the advantages to be derived from it; nearly thirty years glided by in this indifference; at last the proximity to the mines of New Mexico, and those published as having been discovered in Louysiana itself, having aroused our nation from this lethargy, the kingdom in less than three years sent out more men, money and material to found a settlement in that part of America, than had left France for any one of our colonies in the New World since the days of Francis I.

But when it was evident that this country produced neither gold nor silver, and that it was not easy to make the wealth, which New Spain possessed within it, flow in Louysiana, the province suddenly fell under general censure: no one regarded the fertility of the soil, or the productions it would yield with moderate toil, nor the importance of establishing a naval station on the Gulf of Mexico. The treasures brought from France disappeared; men died of want, although they had all requisite to live in opulence, or else they dispersed on all sides, as we shall see in the sequel of this history.

Condition of Louysiana in 1700.

When d'Iberville left it, in April, 1700, Louysiana had no French settlements except those of some Canadians, in Illinois, a fort near the mouth of the Micissipi, which lasted only till 1705, and another at Biloxi on the sea shore. Mr. de Sauvole commanded in this latter, which was the headquarters. The former had been intrusted by d'Iberville to his brother de Bienville and the Sieur Juchereau de St. Denys,[1] his wife's uncle, a man much esteemed by the Indians, and a fluent speaker of the languages of several nations. He had also, on parting, given orders to his kinsman, le Sueur, to proceed to the Sioux country

[1] Louis Juchereau de St. Denys, whom Mr. Daniel, (Nos Gloires, i., p. 207,) supposes to have been called Barbara, was a son of Nicholas Juchereau, Sieur de St. Denys. According to the recent work of the Abbé Tanguay, Dictionnaire Genéalogique, p. 328, he was born at Quebec, Sept. 18, 1676. The exact time of his death I have not ascertained. Le Page du Pratz, i., p. 178, refers to his manuscripts, but they are not now known, and elsewhere the latter author speaks of the grief of the Indians at his death. Ib., p. 301–2.

with twenty men, establish a post there and take possession of a copper-mine, which le Sueur had discovered.[1] 1700.

Copper-mine among the Sioux.

This detachment started towards the end of April, (1700,)[2] ascended the Micissipi to St. Anthony's Falls, entered St. Peter's River,[3] forty leagues up which they found another river emptying on the left, and which has been called Rivière Verte, (Green River,)[4] because earth falling from the mine gives it that color. Le Sueur could sail up this river only about a league, finding it covered with floating ice, although it was only the end of September. This compelled him to throw up at that spot a kind of fort[5] to pass the winter, which proved extremely severe, and lasted till the beginning of April.

Remarkable observation.

The writer who gives an account of this voyage, states a circumstance which is worthy of notice. He says that having run out of provisions, they made up for it by hunting buffaloes; that to preserve the flesh of these animals, they quartered them, and for want of salt, left them in the air, where they soon spoiled; that at first they found it very hard to accustom themselves to this food, which gave them all diarrhœas and fevers, with such a loathing for it,

---

1 There are two accounts of Le Sueur's Voyage, that in Penicaut, Annale Veritable, ch. ii., § 2, here followed by Charlevoix, and that in Bénard de la Harpe, Journal Historique, pp. 38–70; Early Voyages up and down the Mississippi, pp. 87–112.

Le Sueur was a Canadian and a kinsman of d'Iberville. In 1693 he was at Chegoimegon, maintaining peace between the Chippewas and the Sioux. N. Y. Col. Doc., ix., p. 570. He built a fort in the west in 1695. In 1697 he was in France and got permission to work mines he had discovered, but on his way to Canada was captured by the English. On recovering his liberty, he sailed to Canada with a new commission, but meeting difficulties, went back, and in 1699 proceeded to Louysiana. After his voyage up to Minnesota, he returned to France in 1702. Some years after, while again on his way to Louisiana, he died at sea. La Harpe, p. 21. Early Voyages up, &c., pp. 89–91.

2 Le Sueur arrived in Louisiana on Dec. 7th, 1699, with 30 miners.

3 Sept. 19th. La Harpe, p. 52. Early Voyages, p. 91.

4 Penicaut, ch. ii., § 2. La Harpe says Rivière Bleue, as Charlevoix does in his Journal, p. 397. It is now called Blue Earth River, or Mankato; see Owen's Survey of Wisconsin, Iowa and Minnesota, p. 486.

5 At 44° 13′ N. La Harpe, p 53. Early Voyages, p. 101. It was one league up the river, on a point of land.

1700. that they could not even bear the smell; but their stomach gradually became so adapted to it, that at the end of six weeks there was not one among them who did not eat ten pounds a day and drink four bowls of soup; that far from being affected by it, they became quite fat, and not one was sick.[1]

Description of the mine. As soon as April came, le Sueur proceeded to the mine, which was only two miles and a quarter distant, and in twenty-two days he got out thirty thousand pounds of ore; he picked out four thousand of what seemed richest and sent it to France. The spot worked by him is at the beginning of a mountain which is ten leagues long, and all apparently of the same character. It is on the bank of the river, does not produce a single tree, and is constantly enveloped in mists, even in the finest weather. The soil where the ore is extracted is green, and you can scratch the copper with a knife; but you must first take off a kind of crust as hard as rock, black and burned like coal by the vapor issuing from the ore. Many rather interesting incidents, too long to detail here, but still more, want of funds prevented le Sueur from pushing this enterprise.[2]

Settlement of Maubile and Isle Dauphine. The next year d'Iberville made a third voyage to Louysiana, and began a post on Maubile River. He even laid the foundations of a fort to which de Bienville, (who became commandant on de Sauvole's death,) soon after transferred all that there was at Biloxi, abandoning the latter post.[3] In 1702 d'Iberville returned for the fourth time and erected on Massacre Island storehouses and barracks, because as that island had a port, it was much easier to land goods brought from France there, than to send them on sloops to Fort Maubile.[4] It was at this time

---

[1] Penicaut, ch. ii.

[2] Ib., ch. iii., § 1. La Harpe makes him bring down 2,000 quintals of blue and green earth, p. 38.

[3] D'Iberville with de Serigny arrived in Dec., 1701, in the Renommée, 50, and Palmier, 44, and a brigantine. He put in at Pensacola and sent orders to Bienville to evacuate Biloxi and begin a post at Mobile. Bénard de la Harpe, p. 37. The new fort was completed by March, 1702. Ib. p. 71. D'Iberville sailed back in June, 1702. Penicaut, ch. 4.

[4] The port was closed by the sea before 1718. Le Page du Pratz, i., p. 38. Bénard de la Harpe says nothing of Iberville's voyage in

also, that the island received the name of Dauphin Island.[1] It was gradually settled, and some years after, a fort was built there with larger storehouses, so that it became insensibly the head-quarters of the colony.[2]

Slow progress of the colony.

The settlers depended for subsistence on what came from France and what could be obtained from the Indians. They quarrelled and then made peace with some tribes; many Indians were induced to settle in the neighborhood of Maubile, where they cleared quite a large tract, and always lived harmoniously with the whites. Others, like the Apalaches, came there of their own accord, preferring the French to the Spaniards, among whom they had long been settled; but these last excepted, to whom for a time a missionary was assigned, no more suitable steps were taken to gain the Indians of these parts to Christ, than were adopted to give a solid foundation to the French colony.[3]

1702; although Pénicaut states it, ch. 4, § i., but he is somewhat confused, making Sauvolle die after the departure of d'Iberville and le Sueur, (April, 1702. La Harpe, p. 70–2,) while Bénard de la Harpe says he died Aug. 22, 1701.

A memoir of d'Iberville in 1702, Archives de la Marine, Louisiane, Portef. ix., gives his reasons for the founding of Mobile. The population of the place was 139. Sauvolle left a Journal from May 3, 1699, to Aug. 1701, which Mr. French has published in his Louisiana Hist. Coll., iii., pp. 223–240.

[1] Pénicaut, ch. 4. Isle Surgère at the same time took the name of Ship Island.

[2] Settlers removed to the island from Mobile in 1707. Pénicaut, ch. 9; and Gravier in 1708 mentions the fort as projected, Letter, p. 17. It was built in 1709 by Capt. La Vigne Voisin. Pénicaut.

[3] The Apalaches were a tribe from Florida, among whom the Spanish missionaries had labored successfully. They were all Christians, and the chiefs could read and write. Exposed, however, to the English and Alibamas, they retired to Mobile in the latter part of 1705. Bienville gave them lands and seed. A Rev. Mr. Huet became their pastor. Penicaut, ch. 7, § 6. Father Gravier in 1708 says, however, that this clergyman, whom he calls Huré, had not then learned the language. Lettre sur les Affaires de la Louisiane, p. 8. The missions founded by the Seminary of Quebec among the Tonicas, Natchez, Taensas, Alibamons &c., had not been very successful. Two missionaries, Rev. Messrs. St. Cosme and Foucault were killed, and others withdrew, Rev. Mr. Davion being the last, and he finally abandoned the Tonicas about 1716. The Jesuit Father Limoge labored for a time among the Oumas. See Shea, Catholic Missions, 439–44, also Early Voyages up and down the Mississippi, pp. 45–86.

1710–25. Indeed, there could scarcely be said to be a colony in Louysiana, or at least it did not begin to take shape till the arrival of Diron d'Artaguette as Commissaire Ordonnateur in 1708. This magistrate's first care was to enable the settlers to cultivate the soil, which seemed quite fertile along Maubile River, so that they might not be obliged to wander about, living by hunting or with the Indians whenever the ships from France were late in bringing provisions, as it happened on several occasions.[1]

Arrival of a Commissaire Ordonnateur.

But success did not crown his hopes. Around Maubile there is only a mere surface of good soil, and moreover, wheat can never ripen there well on account of the fogs, which produce rust. They made up for this for some time by raising tobacco, which succeeded better.[2] D'Artaguette, in a letter dated January 10th, 1711, says that Maubile tobacco was esteemed above the Virginian.

He added that in the month of September of the preceding year, an English corsair had ravaged Dauphin Island, plundered and burned the houses and stores, wreaked unparalleled cruelties on the people to force them to tell where they had hidden their money, and that the damage done to the King and to individuals amounted to eighty thousand francs,[3] whence he concluded that it was absolutely necessary to fortify the island. The Commissaire reasoned well according to the prevailing idea, which was to plant the

---

[1] The Aigle, Capt. de Noyant, arrived Feb., 1707, to find them hunting or living on the Indians; yet brought over many families to settle, and implements, as well as two priests, de la Vente and la Maire. D'Artaguette arrived 10th Feb., 1708. Pénicaut, ch. 10. Bénard de la Harpe, p. 106.

In 1704, Lousiana, including the garrison, contained 180 men, comprising 27 families, occupying 80 houses and 190 acres of cleared land. Document, Archives de la Marine, Portef. 1, No. 40. Twenty girls of good character, selected by the Bishop of Quebec, were sent out in 1704. Gayarré, Hist. de la Louisiane, i., p. 76.

[2] The first fort at Mobile was on a site so badly selected that it was overflowed in 1709, and a new fort was erected and occupied the next year. Pénicaut, ch. 11, 12.

[3] Bénard de la Harpe, p. 107, says this Jamaica corsair landed 60 men, and did damage to the extent of 50,000 livres, but says nothing of the cruelties. Lediard details the operations of Commodore Littleton's squadron at Jamaica in 1709 and 1710, but is silent as to this attack, probably the act of a privateer.

colony away from the Micissipi River, because Isle Dauphin was the only port where ships could unload, but from what had occurred, it would have been a much wiser conclusion that the best course would be to transfer settlers and storehouses to the Micissipi, as they were subsequently obliged to do.[1]

Louysiana ceded to Crozat.

D'Artaguette returned to France the same year, and gave the court a great deal of light as to Louysiana. Some years before, de Muys, major of the forces in Canada, and heretofore mentioned, had been appointed Governor of Louysiana, but that officer dying on the way, the King appointed as his successor the Sieur de la Motte Cadillac,[2] and in the instructions given him it was stated, that the King, having deemed proper to grant to the Sieur Crozat the monopoly of the Louysiana trade for sixteen years, with an absolute right in perpetuity to him and his heirs in the mines, veins and minerals, discovered and worked on the conditions laid down in his Letters Patent, the King wished the Governor to examine on the arrival of every one of said Sieur Crozat's ships, whether the condition of carrying out six unmarried young men or women by each ship was complied with.[3]

Establishment of a Superior Council,

The King added that the Sieur d'Artaguette, commissaire in said country, having returned to France, he had selected the Sieur Duclos[4] to perform the duties of Commissaire Ordonnateur; that as there was as yet no judicial officer in Louysiana, and it was at present impos-

---

[1] For dispatches of Bienville, Boisbriant, La Salle, see Gayarré, Hist. de la Louisiane, i., p. 77–82.

[2] Gravier, Lettre sur la Louisiane, p. 7. Nicholas Daneaux de Muy, Knight of St. Louis and Captain, born at Beauvais in 1651, married Margaret Boucher in 1676. He served at Chambly, in Frontenac's Onondaga expedition, and in Newfoundland. He came out in the Renommée, (Gravier, Lettre, 1708,) to examine charges against Bienville, and if necessary send him as a prisoner to France. Gayarré, Hist. de la Louisiane, i., p. 82. He died however, at Havana. As to la Motte Cadillac, see ante iv., p. 264; v., p. 160, &c. His Louisiana administration showed him as unfit as he had been at Detroit. He was appointed Governor of Louisiana, May 6, 1710.

[3] See Letters Patent to Crozat, dated Sept. 14, 1712. French Louisiana Hist. Collections, iii., p. 38, n. These say ten men or women.

[4] Louisiana Hist. Coll., iii., p. 66, 80.

1712-25. sible to create judges there as in other colonies, the population being so small, he had nevertheless deemed it best to establish a Superior Council there for three years, to judge all matters, civil and criminal; to compose this council, he selected the Governor and Commissaire Ordonnateur jointly, and one clerk; that by their conduct in discharging the judicial powers vested in them, he would decide either to continue and increase the powers of the Council or abandon it.[1]

The Spaniards refuse to allow trade between Louysiana and Mexico.

Meanwhile, de Crozat had recommended de la Motte Cadillac, whom he had made a partner in his trade, to send detachments towards the Illinois to discover mines; and towards the Spaniards of Old and New Mexico, to open trade with those two provinces. I have spoken in my Journal[2] at length on the former of these two enterprises, which kept all France in suspense for several years, and at last came to nothing.

Nor was the second more successful. Scarcely had La Motte Cadillac landed at Dauphin Island,[3] before he dispatched the ship that had brought him to Vera Cruz; but this voyage was useless. Mr. de la Jonchere[4] who commanded the vessel, could not obtain the Viceroy's permission to sell his cargo; the Viceroy presented him some cattle and provisions that he needed, and then required him to set sail at once.[5] The Governor hoped to succeed better in a second attempt made overland with the same

[1] This Council was permanently established in 1716. *Charlevoix.*

[2] Journal, p. 393. In 1719 de Lochon was sent to the Marameg to work a supposed silver-mine; he got some poor lead, and in disgust returned to France. The Western Company then sent one Antonio, a Spanish prisoner, who pretended to find silver. The matter was then taken by La Renaudiere, and a brigade of royal miners, who failed utterly. In June, 1721, Renaud, acting for a private company, found a vein of lead two feet thick. Ib.

[3] He came early in 1712 in the Baron de la Fosse, a 40 gun vessel, Capt. de la Jonquière. Pénicaut, ch. xiv., § 1. Bénard de la Harpe, p. 110.

[4] Pénicaut and Bénard de la Harpe write de la Jonquière. An officer of the same name, James Peter de Tafanell, Marquis de la Jonquière, was Governor of Canada from 1747 to 1752, N. Y. Col. Doc., x., p. 250.

[5] The Spaniards acted thus to please the English, to whom they had granted the Assiento Company

view, but it met with about the same result as the former.[1] 1712-25.

Overland expedition of de St. Denis to Mexico.

This expedition he confided to the Sieur de St. Denys,[2] and it could not have been placed in better hands. The Governor gave him ten thousand francs' worth of goods, and agreed with him that they were to be stored among the Natchitoches, an Indian tribe on Red River, with whom de Bienville and this same Saint Denys had formed an alliance in 1701, and of which some members had, within a few years, settled on the Micissipi, near the Colapissas.

Saint Denys, deeming it expedient to take these Natchitoches with him, proposed it through Pénicaut, a ship-carpenter. This man had accompanied le Sueur to his copper-mine: he had made several other excursions on the Micissipi, and understood almost all the Indian languages of Louysiana. He himself had brought the Natchitoches to the Colapissas, and had no difficulty in persuading them to return to their former abode with de Saint Denys.

But the Colapissas, who had received them with great humanity, and who had found them not useless, were so offended to see them depart without even any apology, that they pursued them, killed seventeen, and carried off a great many of their women and children. The rest escaped through the woods and reached de Saint Denys, who was awaiting them at Biloxi. He set out with them, and passing through the village of the Tonicas, induced the chief of that nation to follow him with fifteen of his best hunters.[3]

On arriving at the village of the Natchitoches, situated on an island in Red River, forty leagues from its mouth

---

by the treaty of March 26, 1713. Bénard de la Harpe, p. 113.

1 Pénicaut, Relation, ch. 13.

2 St. Denys styles himself, in a declaration made at Mexico June 22, 1715, Captain of Fort St. Jean, near Mobile, though he makes it really 40 leagues from that place.

3 Pénicaut, Relation, ch. 14, § 1. Bénard de la Harpe, p. 116, says he set out Aug. 23, 1714, with 30 Canadians, or rather, 24. Declaracion de Don Luis de San Denis, Mexico, June 22, 1715. Le Page du Pratz, Histoire de la Louisiane, i., p. 10, says the expedition was induced by a letter from the Recollect Father Ydalgo, asking aid to establish a mission among the Asinais, but he evidently confounds the expedition itself with the service he rendered as subsequently stated.

1712-25. on the Micissipi,[1] he built some houses for the Frenchmen whom he intended to station there; he induced some other Indians to join the Natchitoches, assuring them that he would never forsake them, and he distributed among both, agricultural implements and seed to sow. He then selected twelve of the Frenchmen whom he had brought along, and some Indians, and leaving Red River, which is not navigable above the Island of the Natchitoches, took his route westward.

After twenty days' march he reached the Assinais,[2] neighbors of the Cenis, if they are not the Cenis themselves,[3] and quite near the spot where de la Sale was killed. But the fact is, that these Indians did not recollect to have ever before seen Frenchmen, or know any other Europeans than some Spaniards, who went naked like themselves and lived miserably. The Assinais gave de Saint Denys guides, and he travelled one hundred and fifty leagues further to the southwest, before reaching the first Spanish settlements.

At last he found, on the banks of a great river, a fort which bore the name of San Juan Bautista, and Presidio del Norte. He was well received by the commandant, Don Pedro de Vilescas,[4] who took him to his quarters, as well as Medard Jallot, his valet de chambre, surgeon, and Pénicaut, and assigned lodgings for the rest of his party. After some days' rest, Saint Denys began negotiations with Don Pedro; he told him that he came in behalf of the Governor of Louysiana to propose opening a regulated trade with that colony, under such conditions as he should propose.

The Spanish commandant replied that he could do noth-

[1] The Declaracion makes it 40 leagues from Mobile to Fort St. Jean, 40 leagues from that to Red River, and then 80 leagues to Natchitoches.

[2] The Declaracion makes it 40 leagues.

[3] Pénicaut, Relation, ch. xiv., § 4-5. The Assinais are the Cenis. See ante vol. iv., p. 78. Bénard de la Harpe says he reached the Assinais Nov. 15.

[4] Charlevoix here follows Pénicaut. Bénard de la Harpe, p. 129 and le Page du Pratz, ii., p. 12, call him Captain Don Diego Raimond. He was really Don Domingo Ramon.

1710–25.

ing without the permission of the Governor of Caouis,[1] his immediate superior, to whom he at once dispatched an express to receive his orders. Caouis is sixty leagues from Presidio del Norte on the route to Mexico. The Governor, having read Vilescas' letter, sent twenty-five horsemen for Saint Denys, and after examining his passport, told him that it was necessary for him to go and see the Viceroy at Mexico. Saint Denys agreed, but did not set out till the next year with Jallot, and on starting from Caouis, wrote to the French whom he had left at Presidio del Norte to return to Natchitoches.[2]

He is imprisoned at Mexico

It is two hundred and fifty leagues from Caouis to Mexico; Saint Denys made the journey guided by an officer and escorted by twenty-four horsemen. On reaching the capital of New Spain,[3] he was taken before the Viceroy, to whom he presented his passport. The Viceroy read and returned it, and without listening to him even, sent him to prison. There he remained three months, and would perhaps have never recovered his liberty, if some French officers, who were in the service of the Catholic King, who knew d'Iberville intimately, and knew also that Saint Denys was uncle to d'Iberville's wife, had not interceded in his behalf.[4]

His adventures. He refuses to enter the Spanish service.

He was then released; the Viceroy even gave him three hundred dollars and a commodious lodging, and often invited him to his table. The more he knew Saint Denys, the more he esteemed him; at last he spared no effort to induce him to give up service in a poor colony for that of New Spain. He told him that several of his countrymen had already set him the example and found no reason to repent. Some of these officers even pressed him earnestly to follow the course they had adopted, and in which they found complete satisfaction.

---

[1] Pénicault writes Caouïl—meaning Coahuila.

[2] Pénicault was sent back. Relation ch. xiv., § 4–5.

[3] He arrived June 25, 1715. Bénard de la Harpe, p. 129. Le Page du Pratz, § i., p. 14, says 5th. F. de Alencastre, Noroña y Silva, Duque de Linares, was viceroy 1711–6.

[4] Declaracion de Don Luis de San Denis y Don Medar Jallot, naturales de la Nueva Francia, taken before Gerardo Mora, Mexico, June 22, 1715, MS.

1710–25. Saint Denys held no rank in Louysiana, serving only as a volunteer; here he was offered a company in the cavalry, an offer to tempt a Canadian officer without means; he refused it, however, and in spite of all they could say, adhered to his refusal. The Viceroy told him that he was already half a Spaniard, as he sought the hand of the daughter of Don Pedro de Vilescas, and was to marry her on his return to Fort San Juan.

Saint Denys replied: "I cannot dissemble, since your excellency is informed that I love that lady, but I had not indulged the hope of winning her as my wife." "You will obtain it," said the Viceroy, "if you accept the offer I have made, and I give you two months to consider it." At the end of that time he sounded him again, and finding him inflexible, dismissed him, placing in his hands a purse of a thousand dollars, saying that it was for his wedding expenses. "I hope," he added, "that Doña Maria will be more fortunate than myself in persuading you to remain in New Spain. As for establishing trade with Louysiana, which you have come so far to solicit, it is not possible for me to grant it to you."

He renders a service to the Spaniards.

The next day he sent him a very fine bay horse from his stables, and had him escorted[1] to Caouis by an officer and two mounted men. There he found Jallot awaiting him, his surgical skill having won him very great respect in the country. They proceeded to the quarters of Don Pedro de Vilescas,[2] whom they found in great perplexity. That commandant had just learned that the whole population of four Indian towns, exasperated at the oppression of the Spaniards at Presidio del Norte, had just set out to emigrate elsewhere, and he feared to be held responsible for this desertion, which, moreover, reduced his fort to great extremity, as the garrison owed its subsistence almost entirely to these very Indians.

On imparting his troubles to de Saint Denys, the latter offered to go to the Indians, confident that he could recall

---

[1] He left Mexico Oct. 26, 1715. Bénard de la Harpe, p. 130.

[2] Don Domingo Ramon, according to better authority.

1712-25.

them. Don Pedro embraced him, but warned him of the great risk of going alone.; Saint Denys replied that he felt no fear, and at once with Jallot mounted his horse. He soon overtook the Indians, whose baggage, men [1] and children rendered the march very slow. As soon as he perceived them at a distance, he put his handkerchief on a rod as a flag, then advanced towards the chiefs, who awaited his approach.

He showed them, using the Spanish language, to what dangers they would be exposed by venturing among tribes that they did not know, but whom he knew to be very unsociable and cruel. He then told them that if they would return to their former abode, he would guarantee, in the name of the commandant, that no Spaniard should ever set foot in their villages unless they approved it, and that in the future they should have only reason to praise the officers and soldiers.

They yielded to his arguments, and Don Pedro was no less surprised than delighted to see his guest return with all the Indians, whose flight would undoubtedly have proved his ruin. He instantly ratified all the promises made by Saint Denys, and they returned to their towns, which the Spaniards were forbidden to enter under pain of death, unless by express permission.[2]

His marriage with a Spanish lady.

After this great service, Saint Denys had no difficulty in inducing Vilescas to give him his daughter in marriage, and the wedding was celebrated with all the Spanish pomp and magnificence that the place permitted. The newly-married pair remained there together six months, when Saint Denys thought that he should no longer delay in returning to report to de la Motte Cadillac the result of

---

[1] This should apparently be women.

[2] Domingo Ramon, Derrotero para las Misiones, July 22, 1716, says he sent out St. Denis, with his (Ramon's) son, June 26, 1716, to the Texas or Asinais Indians, with whom St. Denis had great influence. That he brought in 25 Indians, mostly chiefs, and by embracing the missionaries, made them regard the Spaniards favorably. The chacuano or calumet was then smoked. Bonilla, in his Compendio de los sucesos ocurridos en Tejas desde su Conquista hasta Noviembre de 1772, § 8, also relates this and calls St. Denys "a man worthy of eternal memory."

1712-25. his mission. He set out for Maubile with Don Juan de Vilescas, his wife's uncle, leaving her with child and promising to return as soon as possible for her.[1]

The English endeavor to debauch our Indians.

During the whole course of these negotiations and adventures, the Governor of Louysiana had sent the Sieur de la Loire to the Natchez, with goods to establish storehouses. There he found Englishmen from Carolina, come to induce these Indians, with the Yazous and Chicachas[2] to declare war on other nations, so as to bring in captives, and it was all carried out. They were even suspected of intriguing against us, and la Loire soon after received orders to arrest their officer, who had remained alone among the Natchez.

He obeyed, and the officer was taken to Maubile, where Mr. de Bienville, who commanded there in the absence of Mr. de la Motte Cadillac, regaled him well for three days, after which he permitted him to return. He took his route by Pensacola, where the governor, Don Guzman, also gave him a cordial welcome ; but while endeavoring to reach Carolina through the Alibamons, he fell in with a hunting band of Tomez Indians, who tomahawked him. What then roused these Indians against the English, does not appear, but most of them suddenly rose against them.

Irruption of the Indians into Carolina.

They had a warehouse in a Tchactas (Choctaw) village, which these Indians plundered, murdering all who had charge of it. This was but the commencement of their misfortunes : no sooner was it known among the other na-

[1] Pénicaut, Relation, ch. 17, § 2. He reached Mobile Aug. 25, 1716. Barcia, in his Ensayo Cronologico, makes only an incidental allusion to Saint Denis and his visit, (p. 312, 2,) although he has much relating to Louisiana. Dumont, Memoires Historiques, ii., p. 65, alludes to it briefly. Le Page du Pratz, Histoire de la Louisiane, i., p. 15–6, makes St. Denis help to establish the Spaniards among the Asinais. Father Morfi, in his Memorias, para la historia de la Provincia de Texas, p. 101, says that Don Domingo Ramon set out Oct. 1, 1715, with a party of twelve missionaries, whom he mentions as friends of St. Denis. They founded six missions among the Natchez, Bidaes, Nazones, Nacogdoches, Ays and Adaes. Compare Espinosa, El Peregrino Septentrional Atlante, pp. 251–4 ; Bonilla, Compendio de los sucesos ocuridos en Tejas desde su conquista hasta Noviembre de 1772, MS ; Domingo Ramon, Derrotero para las Misiones, 22 July, 1716, MS.

[2] Yazoos and Chickasaws.

1713-25.

tions what had occurred among the Choctaws, than the Alibamons and several other tribes, with whom we had been almost always at war, formed a league and made an incursion into Carolina, ravaging several settlements and carrying off a number of prisoners, whom they took to Maubile. Bienville ransomed them from the Indians and provided for their support till he found a favorable opportunity to send them home without any risk.[1]

La Motte forms an alliance with several tribes.

De la Motte Cadillac had gone up to the Illinois, and on his return to Maubile, it was announced that a silver mine had been discovered in the country whence he came.[2] I have explained in my journal the whole affair of these pretended discoveries, which so deluded the French, though much more in Europe than in America. There was more reality in a deputation which the Governor received on his arrival at Maubile. A chief highly esteemed in the country, came in to form an alliance with him in the name of several tribes, and at the same time the Alibamons, hitherto our most declared enemies, offered to introduce the French into their village and erect a fort at their own expense. Their offer was accepted, the fort built, and Captain de la Tour took possession with two lieutenants and some soldiers.[3]

Treachery of the Natchez.

Meanwhile, it was perceived that the Natchez were plotting some treachery; they killed four Frenchmen[4] who were travelling with some of their tribe, and prepared to

---

[1] Richebourg, who came in Aug., 1713, in his Memoire sur la premiere guerre des Natchez, (French, La., iii., p. 241,) does not make any English traders killed. See Barcia, Ensayo Cronologico, p. 325, 329.

[2] Renaud, sent in 1719, extracted silver from Illinois lead ore in 1722. Bénard de la Harpe, Memoire, p. 366. Louisiana Hist. Coll., iii., p. 116, n. Dumont, Memoires, ii., p. 73.

[3] Adair, American Indians, p. 159, makes this "mischievous French garrison Alebamah," 40 leagues below Coosa. See Gayarré, i., p. 113. On p. 117, &c., he gives a memoir of the Abbé de la Vente, on the religious condition of Louisiana.

[4] Richebourg, Memoire, p. 242, and the Relation de la Louisianne, (Voyages au Nord, p. 21,) says that the refusal of the calumet by the governor on his way to Illinois, made them imagine he was about to destroy them, and Richebourg ascribes all the trouble to the self-will of Cadillac.

1713-25. do the same to the Messieurs de la Loire, the elder of whom had set out for the Illinois with another party of these savages, while the younger remained in their great village. But one of those who accompanied the former, warned him to be on his guard. He immediately spoke to all the others in private, and without revealing the name of his informant, he promised them a great reward, and gave them his word to keep their secret if they acknowledged the truth.

The Messrs. de la Loire escape.

All declared that at a point six leagues further on, where they would have to run close by the shore to avoid a very dangerous whirlpool, a party of one hundred and fifty of their tribe, armed with muskets, were lying in wait for them, commanded by a chief named le Barbu, and that he would infallibly be slain there. This avowal of eight men, all stating the same thing, induced la Loire to turn back; but as he had every reason to believe that there was a general conspiracy among the Natchez, he was filled with anxiety in regard to his brother.

Penicaut, who accompanied him, offered to rescue him from the great village of the Natchez, and adopted these steps to effect his design. The whole party having arrived about an hour and a half before nightfall at the Natchez landing, Penicaut went ashore alone, telling la Loire to wait for him till midnight, and that if he did not appear by that time, to give him up for dead; in which case his only course would be to push on. He then advanced towards the cabin of the younger la Loire, which was a league distant, carrying only his gun, powder-flask and a few balls.

As he approached the village, some Natchez, who perceived him, ran to tell la Loire that a Frenchman was coming; he came out to see who it was, and recognizing Pénicaut, asked tidings of his brother and the reason of his coming. Penicaut told him that he had fallen sick; but once in his cabin, he told him to send for the Great Chief of the Natchez, who came at once. Penicaut told him that six of the eight Natchez who had started with the Sieur de la Loire and him, to go to the Illinois, hav-

ing fallen ill, they had been forced to turn back; that they were all at the landing, and he begged him to send thirty Indians early in the morning to unload the canoe and transport the goods to the warehouse. 1713-25.

This the Great Chief promised, and he added that Mr. de la Loire had done well to go no further, as he had been very anxious about him on account of the Yazoos, a treacherous tribe, hostile to the French. Penicaut made no reply, and manifested absolute confidence in the chief; but when the latter retired, he informed la Loire of the motive of his coming, and showed him that he must think only of escaping, and that there was not a moment to lose. This was no easy matter, la Loire told him, as three Indians slept in his room; but Penicaut reassured him, and was sanguine of success.

When it was really night, they lay down, and the Indians first fell asleep; Pénicaut would have stabbed them, but la Loire prevented him, thinking it not easy to kill three men before one of them might have a chance to cry out. Penicaut then gently opened the door and let out la Loire, who had taken the precaution of loading his gun. A few minutes later he glided out himself, double locked the room on the outside and ran after his companion, whom he soon overtook. As they approached the landing, they met the elder la Loire, who had begun to be alarmed; they embarked at once, and dismissed the eight Natchez after liberally rewarding them.[1]

The chief of the Tonicas refuses to enter their plot.

About ten o'clock in the morning they reached the Tonicas, and while they were there, they saw three Natchez arrive, whom the Great Chief, furious at the escape of the la Loires, sent to the chief of the Tonicas, to induce him to massacre all the French who were in his village. The Tonica, who was an upright man, a sincere friend of the French, was indignant at such a proposal.[2] He would have tomahawked the man who dared make it,

---

1 Pénicaut, Relation, ch. 16, § 2–3.

2 Richebourg represents the Tonicas as having accepted presents from the Natchez, p. 242.

1713-25. as his sole answer, had he not been restrained by Mr. Davion, who was a missionary in his village.

Mr. de Bienville sent to demand satisfaction.

The Messrs. de la Loire continued their journey, and reached Maubile, where all were surprised to see them back, and still more to learn the reason of their return. Mr. de la Motte Cadillac thought that this treachery of the Natchez should not be allowed to go unpunished, and raised a party of a hundred men, soldiers and settlers, under the command of Mr. de Bienville, King's-lieutenant, with whom he associated Mr. de Pailloux, major in the army, Captain de Richebourg, Lieutenant du Tisné and the two brothers who had just escaped from the Natchez.[1] As they passed before the Bay of the Tonicas, they noticed a bag hanging from the branch of a tree on the river side, and in this bag they found a letter from Mr. Davion, who, ascertaining that they would pass by there without stopping, informed them that a Frenchman named Richard, on his way from the Illinois, had been taken by the Natchez; that these savages, after plundering him of all his goods, had taken him to their village, cut off his feet and hands, and cast him, still living, into a mudhole.[2]

They encamp at the Tonicas.

Up to this time, Mr. de Bienville had imagined that the Messrs. de la Loire had been seized with a mere panic; the perusal of this letter disabused him. He did not
1716. even deem himself strong enough to march direct upon the Natchez; he entered the Bay of the Tonicas, built a fort, and sent du Tisné with twenty men to the Great Chief of the Natchez, to tell him that he had some matters to impart to him, and that he begged the chief to meet him at the Tonicas. Du Tisné returned the next day and informed de Bienville that the Great Chief would soon follow him. He did not, however, leave his village, but sent to the French commandant some subaltern chiefs, with about twenty-five men.

---

[1] The King had ordered Bienville, with 80 men, to begin a fort at Natchez. La Motte Cadillac would give him only Richebourg's company of 34 men. Richebourg, p. 242.

[2] They reached the Tonicas, April 23. Richebourg, p. 242. See Charlevoix, Journal, pp. 431–4.

1713-25.

What occurred between him and the Natchez.

As soon as Bienville perceived their canoe in the distance, he raised five flags on the river bank, erected a number of tents, and beat all his drums to make them believe that he had at least six hundred men. The Indians disembarked and entered the fort with as much confidence as though the affair were a mere visit. They then presented to the commandant a calumet of peace, but he refused it, which so startled those savages, that they gave themselves up for lost. Bienville told them, with an angry air, that he had come to exact satisfaction for the murder of the five Frenchmen which they had committed; that he wished them either to deliver up the murderers, or at least bring in their heads.

What he demanded, was, they replied, not in their power; but if he so desired, they would send some of their party to their Great Chief, to notify him of the commandant's intentions. He consented on condition that all the others should remain his prisoners, and he at once had them conveyed to a cabin, where a strict watch was kept over them.[1] Those who went to the Natchez soon returned and presented to the commandant the head of a man[2] whom the Great Chief had put to death, but who really was not one of the murderers. Bienville asked them whether they intended to make game of him, and added that he must have the heads of the culprits, especially the head of a chief whom he had named expressly.

The envoys replied that this chief was the nephew of the Sun, who would sooner see his whole village perish than sacrifice that young man, the bravest of all his nation; that besides, he had among those detained by him, the four murderers of the French, and might bring them to justice. Bienville at once had them brought up: they

---

[1] Richebourg, (p. 245,) gives this differently. He says the Great Sun, Little Sun and the Stung Serpent came to Bienville, who detained them and put them in irons. The Little Sun was allowed to go back for the heads of the murderers. He brought, May 14, three, one of them of a warrior not implicated.

[2] Bienville insisted on the head of Oyelape, or White Earth.

1713-25. attempted to deny the fact, but were convicted, and their brains dashed out with clubs. Among them was one chief so notorious throughout the country for his cruelties and acts of treachery, that all the nations had long desired his death.[1]

He makes peace with them.

This expedition ended, a consultation was held on the most expedient course in the actual conjuncture, and it was unanimously decided, that as the Natchez, if driven to extremes, were able to interrupt the navigation of the river and all communication with the Illinois, it was better to profit by the terror which we had succeeded in inspiring, to make an advantageous peace with them, and to offer as a favor the following conditions:

1. That they should erect at their own expense, and in a place to be assigned in their great village, a fort with storehouses and barracks necessary for the garrison and the storekeepers to be established there. 2. That they should restore all the goods taken from the French, and make full reparation for all the other losses which they had caused. 3. That the Great Chief's nephew, of whom complaint was made, should not appear in the village, under the penalty of having his head broken. These articles were read to the deputies, who approved them, and Mr. de Pailloux was dispatched with twenty men to have them ratified by the Great Chief.[2]

He entered the village with drums beating and ensign unfurled; the whole tribe, who loved the French, came out to meet him, and received him with great acclamations. He went directly to the Sun's cabin and presented to him the conditions of peace: the chief accepted them, and said that he simply awaited Mr. de Bienville's orders to begin work on the fort: and on this reply, which was communicated to the commandant, he came up from the

---

[1] Evidently alluding to le Barbu. Gayarré, i., p. 145; Richebourg, Louisiana H. Coll., iii., pp. 248, 251; two were tomahawked June 9, and two others on the 12th. Ib., p. 251. Relation de Louisianne, (Voyages au Nord, v., p. 21).

[2] Gayarré, i., p. 143; Richebourg, Memoire, Louisiana Hist. Coll., iii., p. 249. They were to kill the White Earth chief as soon as they could lay hands on him.

Tonicas with fifty men to the Natchez, where the Sun, followed by all his towns, received him as he disembarked from his canoe.

Post established among these Indians.

The next day he selected the spot where he wished the fort erected; it was laid out at once, and de Pailloux appointed to superintend the work. It was completed at the end of six weeks, and Bienville, who had returned to his camp at the Tonicas, came up with all the French to take possession. He added quarters for the officers, barracks for the soldiers and magazines both for merchandise and for ammunition and army stores.

The fort was named Rosalie, after Madame de Pontchartrain, wife of the Chancellor, a name, as I have elsewhere observed, already proposed by Mr. d'Iberville for a city which he designed founding at this very spot. The Natchez then sang the calumet to Mr. de Bienville,[1] who spent all the rest of that year, 1714[2] at Rosalie. Before leaving it, he placed the Sieur de Pailloux in command, assigning to him du Tisné as lieutenant. He proceeded at once to Maubile, where he remained only long enough to prepare a great convoy, which he himself conducted to the Natchez.

Fort built at the Natchitoches.

It was about the same time that Mr. de Saint Denys arrived at Maubile, and as the reply which he bore from the Viceroy of New Spain deprived de la Motte Cadillac of all hope of carrying on trade with the Spaniards openly, he thought it his duty to prevent their approaching too closely to us, as they seemed bent on doing; with this view, he dispatched the Sieur du Tisné to build a fort on the Island of the Natchitoches. Scarcely was this fort completed when du Tisné was informed that the Spaniards had established a post among the Assinais, and there was every reason to believe that they designed to push on to the Micissipi, had they not been prevent-

---

[1] August 25. Richebourg, p. 252.

[2] He reached Mobile Oct. 4, and there found a royal order, appointing him to command in the absence of Mr. de l'Epinay, appointed to succeed Cadillac. See also as to this Natchez war, Duclos to the minister, June 7, 1716. Gayarré, i., p. 130.

1712-25. ed. This obliged the Governor of Louysiana to reinforce the garrison of the Fort of the Natchitoches.[1]

State of Louysiana commerce in 1716.

Meanwhile, the exclusive commerce granted to Crozat in 1712, far from accelerating the progress of the Colony of Louysiana, had been prejudicial to it, nor had Crozat derived from it all the benefit he had promised himself. These two things always go together; to acquire wealth by the trade of a colony, it must be peopled, and the inhabitants made consumers of the goods sent there, giving in return. This cannot be attained without great outlay. Those engaged in such enterprises must select carefully the men to whom they confide their interests. Nothing of this was done, and all parties suffered.

To understand well what the sequel of this history obliges me to say on this point, we must go back a little, and state more in detail the actual position of Louysiana, when Crozat obtained the privilege above mentioned, and the position when he renounced that privilege. In 1712 there were in all that province only twenty-eight French families, not half of them engaged in cultivating the soil, or properly styled settlers; the rest were traders, innkeepers and mechanics not permanently settled in any place.

Trade was then conducted only at Maubile and Isle Dauphine, and the only articles were planks, bear, deer and cat-skins and other like furs. The voyageurs or bushlopers, almost all Canadians, went to the Indians, to barter such French goods as they could get, for peltries

---

St. Denys was on good terms with his Spanish neighbors, and as Spanish authorities show, rendered them good service. Bonilla says he facilitated the entrance of the Spaniards into Texas, and by his amiable manners won the Indians, and gave the most constant proofs of his good faith. Yet the Spanish government ordered him to be carried off to Guatemala, and Ramon to be removed from the frontier, a disgrace which the latter escaped by death in 1724, having been killed by the Indians. Bonilla, Compendio, § 8. For his visit in 1716, see Bénard de la Harpe, p. 138, &c. Le Page du Pratz, i., p. 10-23. He reached Mexico May 3, 1717, to claim goods seized, but was put in prison; escaped Sept. 15, 1718, reached Natchitoches 24 Feb. 1719, La Harpe, pp. 145-6.

and slaves, which they then sold to the settlers; these last sold the peltries again to the Spaniards at Pensacola, or the vessels which occasionally came from France, and they employed these slaves in clearing the ground, or sawing planks, for which they found a market sometimes at Pensacola, more frequently at Martinique or St. Domingo. They obtained from these colonies in exchange, sugar, tobacco, cacao and French goods when there had been a long delay in receiving them direct. 1716-25.

They also carried to Pensacola, where the Spaniards had cleared no land, vegetables, Indian corn, poultry, and in general, all the products of their industry which their less ingenious and less laborious neighbors needed. All this brought in a little money, with which they purchased what they were obliged to obtain from abroad: it was not enough to enrich them, but they had quite an easy life. They had also learned that the country would produce tobacco, indigo, cotton and silk, but there were no hands for all these crops; there was no one in the colony who could aid them, or who thought of encouraging them; they did not even know the method of cultivating these plants.

Moreover, the colony was by no means solidly established, so that there was always a fear that the King would abandon it, and all the care and pains they might take would be lost. Many even retired elsewhere, and others remained only because they lacked means to go. It is astonishing that Mr. Crozat, when acquiring the domain of Louysiana with the exclusive right to trade for twenty-five years, did not inform himself of the real state of things, so as to form his plans on these necessary data: but it is quite ordinary on these occasions to distrust the very persons from whom the most correct information can be obtained, and whose experience fits them most to second a new enterprise. It is feared that they will sacrifice the new proprietary's interests to their own, and men do not reflect that the surest way to succeed in such affairs is to interest those who are most versed in it,

1716-36. so that they shall see their own advantage in the success of the enterprise.

This Mr. Crozat failed to do, and he did not understand that nothing can be derived from a country, how good soever it may be, when the settler is not allowed to grow richer. Scarcely had he taken possession of his exclusive trade, when the vessels from the West Indies ceased to appear in Louysiana. At the same time the settlers were forbidden to go to Pensacola, the very source whence all the money came that was current in the colony, or to sell anything whatever except to Crozat's agents, who thus found themselves in a position to put on the colonial products such values as they chose; a power which they did not fail to abuse; at last they rated peltries so low, that the hunters, finding it more profitable to dispose of them in Canada and the English colonies, carried them all there.

By pursuing just the opposite course, Crozat's company would have acquired credit and secured the confidence of the colonists, after which it might have led them to its object, when it had increased their number and induced them to derive from their country all that it could produce. But by cutting them off from the little vein of silver flowing in from Pensacola, by depressing the price of their products and wares, by fettering their commerce, which they understood far better than the company, and the product of which would have flowed back to the company itself, by raising the price of what they were obliged to draw from France, it left them unable to subsist, and still more to make their lands available.

This decline of Louysiana trade and cultivation could not but prove highly injurious to the King also, if we reflect that after the twenty-five years for which Crozat's monopoly was to last, the colony would be found less advanced than it was when granted to him, and his majesty was not compensated by the fifty tons freight which the company was bound to give him on its vessels. The King indeed thus saved the expense of a ship, which he

would have had to send to Louysiana, to carry over all required for the subsistence of the troops; but there was a more natural way of saving this, or rather of meeting this expense by the freight, which the vessel would be sure to find at Saint Domingo. 1716-36.

This would only require the fitting out of a 170 ton frigate every year, or one of those two decked English galleys, which, for all their having a large hold, are still good sailers, and managed by a small crew, on account of the lightness of their movements. In fact, I say nothing here, except after a detailed memoir transmitted at the time to the minister by Mr. Duclos, who, as already noted, succeeded Mr. d'Artaguette in the office of Commissaire Ordonnateur in Louysiana, and who subsequently held the same office at Cap François in Saint Domingo, where he acted so well during the troubles that occurred in that colony in 1723, and who was soon after appointed Intendant of the Leeward Isles.

Crozat saw the damage which his monopoly did to the King's interests sooner than he did the injury he inflicted on the people of Louysiana. This obliged him to make new propositions to his majesty on the 5th of July, 1714, with the view of enabling the officers, soldiers and other employees, whom the King maintained in the colony, to receive their pay more promptly, as well as consignments of goods and munitions, either for public works, or for keeping up the forts, or for the presents annually made to the Indians, and the propositions were accepted. He had some months previously presented other memoirs full of complaints on various topics, and which disclose the fact that great complaints were made in Louysiana against his monopoly. Crozat's propositions and complaints.

His complaints were: 1. That the weakness of the French in that colony drew on them the contempt of the Indians, and left them unable to prevent those savages from constantly making war on each other, the result of which was, that it was impossible to establish any kind of trade in the country, nor consequently to send ships from

1716-36. France without risking the loss of all the expenses of outfit. 2. That the English were coming very near the French, who cantoned on the Maubile River and Dauphin Island, where the lands are worthless, left open to the English all the banks of the Micissipi, where nothing prevented their settling, and then penetrating to New Mexico and New Biscay: this was a general complaint among intelligent persons. 3. That the indifference manifested in France for Louysiana was inexplicable. Mr. Crozat did not hesitate to aver that if the advantages to be derived from it were considered, there was no colony which it was more important for the state to preserve and extend. The maritime commerce, said he, is almost reduced to nothing. Yet it is only by the voyages of merchantmen in time of peace that sailors are formed, whom the King can employ in his naval forces when war is declared. Hence it is, as a general thing, important to extend navigation, and by the different settlements which might be made in Louysiana, there is hope, if the work is seriously begun, that the commerce of that country will in a few years employ a considerable number of ships. So well are the English convinced of the importance of the Louysiana colony, that it is only necessary to ask the Marshal d'Uxelles what he heard them say at Utrecht about our settlement on the Micissippi. Their conduct since that time justifies day by day what the memoir put forward on this point. 4. And this is Crozat's worst complaint, and at the same time his reply to the objections made him that after undertaking with the King to colonize Louysiana and establish there all kinds of trade, of which he admitted it was capable, it was nevertheless in a worse condition than when he took control of it. He complained that they had refused to register his Letters Patent in the Council of that province; that all parties opposed it, and that this opposition was fomented by the officers, accustomed to trade with the Spaniards.[1]

It was apparently in the endeavor to bring the troops to

[1] Dumont, Memoires Historiques, ii., pp. 6–7.

his side that he made to the King the proposals contained in the memoir already mentioned; but as his affairs did not improve after this step, he waited till the term of his privilege expired, in the following year, 1717, and then surrendered it to the King. Then it was that that famous Western Company was formed, which, under the direction of Law, gradually took in hand almost all the internal and exterior commerce of the kingdom, and from the bosom of which sprang the now flourishing India Company," the only one that has succeeded in France since the foundation of the monarchy. The Letters Patent of the former, in the form of an edict, entitled "Establishment of Trade under the name of the Western Company," registered in the parliament on the 6th of September in the same year, declared that his majesty grants to the said company for twenty-five years:

He surrenders his privilege to the King. His majesty transfers it to the Western Company.

1st, The commerce of Canada on condition of extending cultivation and plantations.

2d, To carry on exclusively for the space of twenty-five years, counting from the day of registration, trade in the province and jurisdiction of Louysiana, and in perpetuity all the lands, ports, coasts, harbors and islands which composed that province, to enjoy in all property, seignory and justice, reserving to himself no right or duty, except simple fidelity and liege homage, which the said company shall be bound to render him; and to his successors, at every change of king, with a gold crown weighing thirty marks. And it is well to note here, that by another Enactment of the 27th of said month of September, the Illinois country was detached from the jurisdiction of New France, and incorporated with that of Louysiana.

3d, The power to treat and form alliances in his majesty's name, throughout the grant, with all the nations of the country, not dependent on other European powers, and in case of insult, to declare war against them, treat of peace or truce.

4th, The absolute possession of the mines, and veins opened by it during the term of its privilege.

1716-36. 5th, Permission to sell and alienate the lands within said grant, to erect such forts, castles and strongholds as it shall deem necessary for the defence of the territory granted; to place garrisons there, to raise troops in France with his majesty's concert, and to appoint such governors, majors, officers and others as shall please it, to command the troops.[1]

Mr. de l'Epinai Governor of Louysiana.

Mr. de la Motte Cadillac and Mr. Duclos were no longer in Louysiana when this change took place. Mr. de l'Epinai[2] had succeeded the former, and Mr. Hubert the latter. They had arrived at Dauphin Island[3] in the month of March of that year, and some months after the Western Company appointed Mr. de Bienville Commandant General of all the province. His commission bore date September 20th, but he did not receive it or take possession till the ensuing year. Mr. de l'Epinai had come with three ships, bringing many officers, a great number of soldiers, a supply of ammunition, and provisions and merchandise of all kinds. All was discharged at the storehouses on Dauphin Island except the goods which were in the Dudlow, commanded by Mr. de Golleville, whose orders were to proceed to Vera Cruz to dispose of them. This captain, learning what had befallen Mr. de la Jonchere, who had failed to obtain permission to trade at that port five years before, did not deem it prudent to show himself there: he anchored at Villarica, the ancient Vera Cruz, built by Cortez, and secretly notified the Spanish merchants, who came on board, bought his cargo and paid him in hard cash.[4]

---

[1] Letters Patent to the Western Company, Aug., 1717. Le Page du Pratz, i., p. 47–81. Louisiana Hist. Coll., iii., p. 49–59. Bénard de la Harpe, p. 139. This was the company formed by the famous John Law.

[2] Mr. de Lepinai, appointed by the King Governor of Louisiana, Oct. 8, 1716, was a naval officer, and came over in command of the Paon, which, with the Ludlow, reached Dauphin Island March 9. Relation de la Louisianne ou Mississipi, (Voyages au Nord,) p. 4. Bénard de la Harpe, p. 131. See his Instructions in Gayarré, Histoire de la Louisiane, i., p. 153. Pénicaut, Relation, ch. xix., § 2.

[3] It now dropped its name Isle Massacre for that of Dauphin Island. Dumont, ii., p. 7. Le Gac was Chief Director, and le Maire missionary. Ib.

[4] Pénicaut, Relation, ch. 19, § 3.

1716-36.

His reception by the Indians. The port of Isle Dauphin closes.

Meanwhile, Mr. de l'Epinai was busily fortifying Dauphin Island, where all the storehouses were, and while he was engaged with these cares, twenty-four Indian nations[1] sent deputies to compliment him and sing the calumet to him. But the joy inspired by this general concourse of the nations included in his jurisdiction, was soon dashed by an unforeseen accident which disconcerted his plans and rendered useless all the money just expended on Dauphin Island. Towards the end of August, the mouth of the only harbor on the island was closed by a prodigious collection of sand heaped up there by a hurricane. The island itself was almost entirely inundated, and many of the cattle were drowned.[2]

A new roadstead had to be sought for the ships, and Isle Surgère was selected, afterwards called Isle aux Vaisseaux—Ship Island. It has, however, only one roadstead, a tolerably good one, except when the wind blows from the north, or northwest, but these winds are rare there, and not violent. To protect the ships, a small fort was built on the island, and the Dauphin Island establishment was transferred to Biloxi, north of Ship Island, though ships cannot approach within four leagues of it.

Nothing shows more clearly how we then confined ourselves to the trade that might be carried on with the Spaniards, than this new post: for the soil of Biloxi is no better than that of Dauphin Island, and that post has not even a roadstead for the smaller brigantines. It is inconceivable how they could dream of placing the centre

[1] Pénicault, ch. 19, § 5, names the Choctaws, Taouachas, Apalaches, Tinnsals, Mobilians, Tomes, Gens de Fourches, Capinans, Colapiças, (Aquelon-pissas—nation of men who hear and see. Le Page, i., 46.) Bayagoulas, Oumas, Chaouachas, Natchez, Chicachas, Nassitoches, Yalaas, Alibamons, Canapouces. We may here add some tribes with definitions. Pascagoula, (Bread nation, Le Page, i., 41.) Oufé-ogoulas, (Dog nation,) 2, p. 226. Chactchioumas, (Red crabs,) 2, p. 226. Atacapas, (Men eaters,) 2, p. 231. Oqueloussas, Blackwater, p. 241.

[2] A storm in March choked up the channel, and at the end of April, 1717, a bar 14 fathoms wide and as high as the island was formed, shutting in the Paon and a merchantman. Relation de la Louisianne, p. 9; Bénard de la Harpe, Journal, p. 132. Pénicault, ch. 19, § 4.

1716-36. of a colony on sterile sands, unapproachable to anything but sloops; unable to defend the shipping or be defended by it; yet it was left there for five whole years.

Commencement of New Orleans.

It was, nevertheless, this same year that the foundations were laid of the capital of Louysiana, under the name of New Orleans. Mr. de Bienville having come from Natchez to Maubile to salute the new Governor, told him that he had remarked on the banks of the river a site well fitted for a post, and Mr. de l'Epinai entrusted him with its establishment; he gave him eight salt smugglers, just arrived from France, with carpenters, to build some houses there. He at the same time commanded Captain Blondel to relieve Mr. de Pailloux at Natchez, the latter officer receiving orders to join Mr. de Bienville and aid him in his enterprise, which was not carried out to any great extent at this time. Mr. de Pailloux was made Governor of the rising city. In my Journal I have noted the drawbacks of its situation.[1]

A ship enters the Micissipi.

1718.

In the early part of the following year, they at last thought of sounding the mouth of the Micissipi, to see whether ships could enter with all their cargo on board, and sixteen feet of water were found on the bar. The Neptune,[2] just arrived from France, was at once sent there, and it ascended without any difficulty to New Orleans. It is astonishing, that after this experiment men did not open their eyes to the importance of making it at once the headquarters, and that so many thousand men were left to waste with misery and disease under the pretext that there were not batteaux enough to transport them to their destination, when the very ships that brought them from France might have landed them at New Orleans, and even nearer to their concessions.

---

[1] Pénicaut, Relation, ch. 19, § 7. For the founding of New Orleans, See Dumont, Memoires Historiques sur la Louisiane, ii., p. 39–46; Le Page du Pratz, Histoire de la Louisiane; Charlevoix, Journal, p. 441; Louisiana Hist. Coll., iii., pp. 179–182. Bienville, in February, 1718, left 50 carpenters and convicts to clear the ground and build. It was laid out later by la Tour, the engineer.

[2] Pénicaut, Relation, ch. 20, § 1. The Philippe and the Marie arrived also, but brought few settlers. Dumont, ii., p. 8.

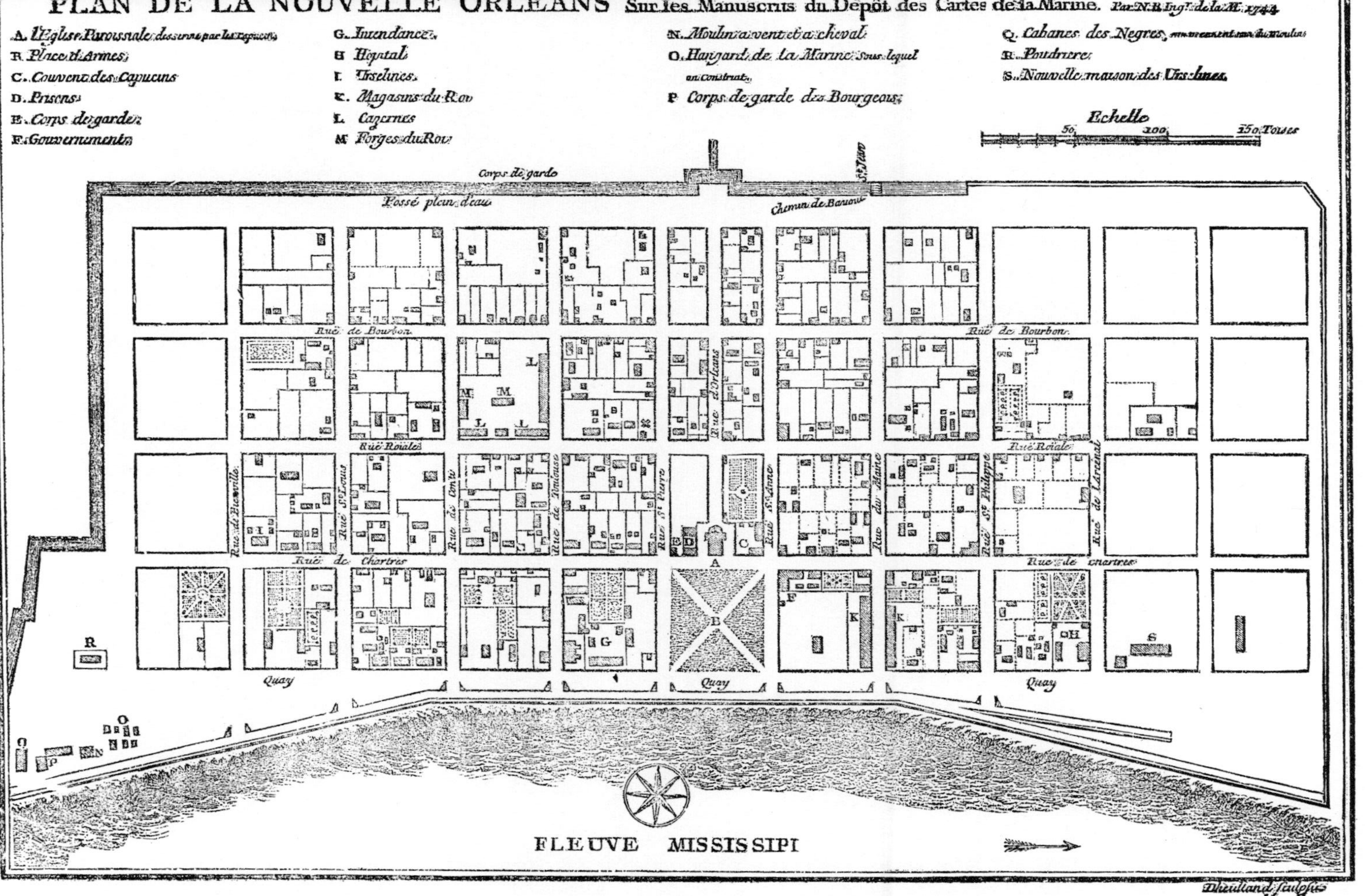
PLAN DE LA NOUVELLE ORLEANS Sur les Manuscrits du Dépôt des Cartes de la Marine. Par N.B. Ingr. de la M. 1744
A. L'Eglise Paroissiale desservie par les Capucins
B. Place d'Armes
C. Couvent des Capucins
D. Prisons
E. Corps de garde
F. Gouvernement
G. Intendance
H. Hopital
I. Urselines
K. Magasins du Roy
L. Cazernes
M. Forges du Roy
N. Moulin a vent et a cheval
O. Hangard de la Marine sous lequel on construit
P. Corps de garde des Bourgeois
Q. Cabanes des Negres
R. Poudriere
S. Nouvelle maison des Urselines
Echelle
50
100
150 Toises
Corps de garde
Fossé plein d'eau
Chemin de Bayou
St. Jean
Ruë de Bourbon
Ruë Roiale
Ruë de Chartres
Ruë de Bienville
Ruë St. Louis
Ruë de Conti
Ruë de Toulouse
Ruë St. Pierre
Ruë d'Orleans
Ruë St. Anne
Ruë du Maine
Ruë St. Philippe
Ruë de l'Arcenal
Quay
FLEUVE MISSISSIPI
Dheulland Sculpsit

1718.

Arrival of the first Conces-sions.

It was in the month of March ensuing that the colony saw the first Concessionaries arrive. The Sieur Dugué de Boisbriand accompanied them, bearing the orders of the King,[1] or rather of the Company, which, under his majesty's good pleasure, had appointed him Commandant at the Illinois, Mr. de Bienville Commandant-General of Louysiana and Director of the Company, and Mr. de Pailloux Major-General. De Boisbriand ascended to the Illinois without delay, taking with him Mr. Diron and the Chevalier d'Artaguette, both brothers of the former Commissaire Ordonnateur; the former was a captain, and ere long was declared Inspector-General of Louysiana; the latter was a lieutenant.

At the same time several Indian tribes, some of which had long seemed hostile to the French, like the Chetimachas, settled on the Micissippi, quite near New Orleans, and as most of these tribes are accustomed to the cultivation of the soil, they cleared large tracts, which was a resource for the city, since the Indians often in need supplied it with provisions. Some of the Concessionaries also sent part of their people up this river, and the advantages they found there for settling permanently, made all who had the general good at heart, regret that the other Concessionaries were prevented from adopting the same course. The uneasiness at first entertained in regard to the English had vanished; all the tribes bordering on the Micissipi lived on very good terms with us, and the only means of arming ourselves against the intrigues of the former and the inconstancy of the latter, was to fortify and people the colony.[2]

In the month of June of this same year, de Bienville took possession of St. Joseph's Bay, fifty leagues east of Dauphin Island.[3] His brother, Mr. de Chateaugué, was

---

[1] Pénicaut, Relation, ch. 20, § 1. The order of the Council of State, directing Mr. de l'Epinai to turn over the government of the colony to Bienville, was dated Oct. 27, 1717. Gayarré, i., p. 157. His only act during his short rule was to pass a prohibitory, and of course unpopular, liquor law.

[2] Pénicaut, Relation, ch. 20; Charlevoix, Journal, p. 394. Le Page du Pratz, i., p. 82.

[3] It still retains the name; it lies E. of Apalachicola, and N. of Cape

1718. entrusted with this expedition, which he carried out without any obstacle; he then erected a stone fort there. The Spaniards had abandoned this post eighteen years before; but the Governor of Pensacola was no sooner informed of this enterprise, than he wrote to Bienville that St. Joseph's Bay belonged to the Catholic King.[1] It was not worth a contest with that crown, and Mr. de Chateaugué, who had taken possession of it, did not doubt for a moment that it would soon have to be abandoned, as in fact it was the next year. The reasons which brought Mr. de Bienville and the Company to this were: 1st, That the post is useless, not only on account of its great distance and want of security for ships there, but chiefly on account of the impossibility of defending the entrance, which is more than a good league in width. 2nd, That it is extremely inconvenient, both in regard to the difficulty of landing reinforcements, for you have to wait for the proper moment, which frequently will not occur for a week, or even a fortnight; and on account of the sterility of the soil, which for more than four leagues around is nothing but bare sand, and on account of the insalubrity of the air, which in all that country is very unhealthy, all our soldiers having been very sick there. This occasioned many desertions, which there was no way to prevent. 3rd, That the vessels are not sheltered there from any wind, and the water to be found there is very bad.

St. Joseph's Bay occupied by the French and almost immediately abandoned.

Description of Pensacola.

What occurred the following year in this colony will suffice to let all judge what we would now be in a position to effect there had men profited by the advantages in

1719.

San Blas. Don Juan Manuel Roldan discovered Chateauguay soon after he entered, and seeing his intention to settle, reported to Matamoros, Governor of Pensacola, who sent him with a letter to Chateaugué, who referred him to Bienville. Roldan then endeavored to induce French soldiers to desert, and 25 actually did, persuaded by Roque, a Spanish captain. La Harpe, p. 141. Capt. de Gousy was left in command of the French fort. Matamoros disapproving of this, wrote to Bienville. Bienville replied May 14, that he acted under orders from court. Barcia, Ensayo Cronologico, pp. 338–9. The French abandoned it May, 1718. La Harpe, p. 142. In 1719 Gregorio de Salinas sailed to reoccupy it, and thus left Pensacola exposed. Ib. p. 347.

[1] Pénicaut, ch. 21, § 1. Bénard de la Harpe.

their hands to establish a powerful colony. In the month of February, 1719, de Serigny arrived in Louysiana with three ships,[1] announced that war was declared with Spain, and showed the orders he had received to take Pensacola. The bay which bears that name was, according to the Spaniards, first discovered by Pamphilo de Narvaez,[2] who landed there in his unhappy Florida expedition.[3] Subsequently, Diego de Maldonado, one of Hernando de Soto's captains, rediscovered it and gave it the name of Port of Anchusi.[4] In 1558, Don Tristan de Luna named it Saint Mary's Bay,[5] and in 1693, Don Andres de Pes, General of the Barlovento fleet, having gone to explore it, added to the last name that of Galve, in honor of the Count of Galve, then Viceroy of Mexico.[6] Accordingly among Spaniards, the bay is known only under the name of Santa Maria de Galve. And the name of Pensacola, that of the native inhabitants of the spot, who have been destroyed by other Indians, is retained by the province, to which the Spaniards assign a very great extent.[7] 1719.

Its fort taken from the Spaniards.

In 1696, Don Andres de Arriola having been appointed first Governor of this province, proceeded to take possession, and on the Bay of Santa Maria de Galve, built a fort with four bastions, which he styled Fort San Carlos; with a church and some houses;[8] and the place was in

---

[1] Pénicaut, ch. 21, § 1. Bénard de la Harpe.

[2] Smith's Cabeza de Vaca, p. 64; Ensayo Cronologico, p. 299.

[3] Pamphilo de Narvaez landed at Espiritu Santo, now Tampa Bay. Smith's Cabeza de Vaca, p. 58; although Siguenza supposed him to have landed at Pensacola. Barcia, Ensayo Cronologico, p. 308. As to his Expedition, see Smith's Cabeza de Vaca, Albany, 1871; Oviedo's Relation in Historical Magazine, II. ii., pp. 141, &c.

[4] Barcia, Ensayo Cronologico, 308, 299 The fact is not mentioned by the Knight of Elvas or Biedma.

[5] Barcia, Ensayo Cronologico, 33.

[6] Ib. 299, 308. This Viceroy was Gaspar de Sandoval, Silva y Mendoza, Count of Galve, Nov., 1688, to Feb., 1696. Alaman, Disertaciones, iii., pp. 41–3.

[7] The Indians were hostile to the Spaniards, killing them under the very guns of the fort, and keeping up a blockade. Relation de la Louisianne, p. 19. The French land force was commanded by Captains de Chateaugué and de Richebourg. Dumont, ii., p. 10.

[8] Barcia, Ensayo Crono., p. 316. Fort Siguenza on Santa Rosa Island, was begun in 1718. Ib., p. 342.

1719. this state in 1719, when Mr. de Serigny laid siege to it; the Western Company having seized the opportunity of the rupture between the two crowns to obtain the only port there is in all the northern coast of Florida, from the Bahama Channel to the Micissipi. De Serigny began by convening a great council of war, the decision of which was, that Messrs. de Bienville and de Chateaugué, his brothers, should summon to Maubile all the Indian allies, all the French settlers, voyageurs and concessionaries, and lead them overland to Pensacola, while the three vessels,[1] after taking on board a hundred and fifty soldiers, should enter the bay. All this was carried out with great secrecy and diligence.

On the 14th of May, at ten o'clock in the morning, Mr. de Serigny entered the bay: Don Juan Pedro de Matamoros,[2] Governor of Fort San Carlos, who was not in a condition to resist, had just sent to Don Gregorio de Salinas, Governor of St. Joseph, to ask him for assistance; but he had no time to receive it. Serigny began by opening a brisk fire, and, although it lasted five hours, the Spaniards pretend to have had only one man killed.[3] The fire having ceased, the Governor sent an infantry captain to know from the French commandant, the cause of so unforeseen a hostility. De Serigny sent this officer back with a French captain, who informed Don Juan that war had been declared and published in France on the 14th of January, and summoned him to surrender the place. The Governor, by the advice of his council, asked till next day to answer, and he obtained the delay; but then reflecting that with the hundred and sixty men

[1] A Spanish author reckons four vessels. *Charlevoix.* Bienville sailed from Dauphin Island May 13, in a sloop with 80 men; Serigny in the Philippe; with the Comte de Toulouse, Capt. Mechin, and Maréchal de Villars, Capt. the Chev. de Grieu. Bienville to Minister, Oct. 20, 1719, in Gayarré, Hist. de la Louisiane, i., p. 168 Laval, Voyage, p. 103. Dumont, Memoires, ii., pp. 9–12. Bénard de la Harpe, p. 148.

[2] Juan Pedro Matamoros, born at Granada; entered the army in 1696; distinguished himself at Tarifa, Ceuta and at Gibraltar, where he was wounded. He was appointed Governor of Pensacola Feb. 18, 1717. He was taken to France, and did not reach Spain till 1720. Barcia, Ensayo Cronologico, 330, 363.

[3] Barcia, Ensayo Cron., p. 349.

whom he had, with no hope of receiving in season the reinforcements he had solicited, it was impossible to resist six hundred men who attacked him by sea, and seven hundred who were coming by land, he deemed it prudent to try and obtain favorable terms, rather than risk the consequence of a useless resistance. Hence, the same day, before the expiration of the term granted him, he capitulated on the following conditions : 1719.

1st, That two vessels should be furnished him, provisioned to go to Havana. 2nd, That the Spaniards should take with them neither arms nor munitions of war. 3rd, That all hostilities should cease for a week after the departure of the garrison, and in case of their putting back, for a week more.[1]

As soon as this capitulation was signed by the two commandants, the garrison on the 15th marched forth and encamped outside. Mr. de Chateaugué entered with three hundred men, and began by making an inventory of all he found there. On the 18th of June, the Governor of Pensacola sailed for Havana with four hundred Spaniards on the Comte de Toulouse and the Marechal Villars, commanded by Mr. Méchin and the Chevalier de Grieu.[2] These two ships were attacked off the coast of Cuba by English privateers, who, not perceiving the superiority of their antagonists until they were so engaged that they could not easily escape, sent to apologize to the commandants for mistaking them for Spaniards.[3] This might be ; but it is well known that such mistakes are so common with the English, that we would be justified in not always overlooking them.

Meanwhile, Don Gregorio Guaço, the commander at Havana, had just sent out a fleet under Don Alphonso Carrascosa de la Torre, to expel the English from Fort

---

[1] Bienville to minister, Oct. 20, 1719. Laval, Voyage, p. 103 ; Dumont, Memoires Historiques, p. 11 ; Barcia, Ensayo Cronologico, p. 349, gives the articles in full ; Pénicaut, Relation, ch. 21. Le Page du Pratz, i., pp. 93–5.

[2] The prisoners were sent under the charge of Capt. de Richebourg. Dumont, Memoires, p. 11. Le Page du Pratz, i , p. 95.

[3] Barcia, Ensayo Cronologico, p. 350.

1719. St. George,[1] in Carolina, promising himself nothing less than the conquest of all that province. Some time after he discerned the two French frigates, and at once dispatched a barque to Don Alphonso, to order him to attack them. The French commandants, on their side, seeing a whole fleet bearing down upon them, wore ; but the wind suddenly falling, they took heart from the fact that as they carried the Governor and garrison of Pensacola, the capitulation of that place should serve as a safe conduct. The memoir which I found on this affair in the Dépôt de la Marine, says that the Spanish commandant demanded that the French should restore to him all those of his nation who were on their ships ; that they refused, and that on this refusal, the fleet turned towards Havana and obliged them to enter the port with it, though they did not wish to go in. The Spanish historian avers, on the contrary, that Carrascosa put a guard on board the two French frigates, and entered Havana with his fleet and the two prizes to receive his general's orders.[2]

The French who conduct the garrison to Havana arrested there.

Be that as it may, Don Gregorio Guaço, postponing the Carolina expedition to some other season, thought he should begin by recapturing Pensacola ; he even thought it his duty to reinforce his fleet with all the garrison of that place, with a hundred and fifty men drawn from the forts at Havana, and with a number of volunteers, whom the hope of conquering all Louysiana, enticed to take part in this expedition. He retained the two frigates to employ them in conveying the French to San Domingo and Cumana, and to carry to those two cities the provisions of which they stood in the greatest need. He at the same time dispatched to the Marquis de Valero,[3]

The Spaniards prepare to recapture Pensacola.

[1] De l'Isle, on a map of the period, has St. George or New London. Wilton or New London was on the Edisto. Carroll, ii., p. 453.

[2] Barcia, Ensayo Cronologico, p. 351 ; de Richebourg was put in prison and his soldiers in irons. Dumont, ii., p. 12. Laval, Voyage, pp. 104–5. Bienville to minister, Oct. 20, 1719, refers to the documents forwarded by de Serigny, to prove the bad faith of the Span iards in seizing these vessels. Pénicaut, ch. 21. Le Page du Pratz, i., p. 95.

[3] Baltasar de Zuñiga, Marquis de Valero, Duke of Arion, 1716–1722. Alaman, iii., p. 52.

1719.

Viceroy of Mexico, a light barque, to beg him to order Don Francisco Cornejo, commandant of the Barlovento Fleet, who was then at Vera Cruz, to proceed to join Carrascosa at Pensacola as soon as he heard of that commandant's arrival in Florida. The Viceroy had anticipated him: informed of the capture of Pensacola by the Governor of Saint Joseph, and warned by a Franciscan Father, who was in that place when it surrendered to de Serigny, that the French had undertaken its capture only with the view of penetrating to New Mexico, he had at once dispatched couriers to all the ports of New Spain, with orders to all vessels and mariners whom they met, to proceed to Vera Cruz. He had at the same time made a levy of men on all sides, and had no embarrassment except to find shipping enough to embark all this force, when Don Francisco Cornejo entered the port of Vera Cruz with five men-of-war of the Barlovento Fleet. The Viceroy ordered him to prepare to sail to Pensacola, but as Cornejo was on the point of starting, the Viceroy sent him a countermand, to defer his departure till he had given him a reinforcement.

They arrive in sight of the bay.

Meanwhile, the change in the destination of the Havana fleet had not been to the taste of all who had embarked in it, and more than four hundred deserted before it sailed out of port. This mishap did not disconcert the Governor; he trusted that the valor of those who remained faithful to him would make up for numbers, and contented himself with embarking sixty grenadiers of his garrison in place of the deserters. On the 29th of June,[1] Don Alphonso Carrascosa set sail, having in all only eight hundred and fifty men, including regulars, volunteers and marines on twelve vessels, three frigates, and nine bilanders. As soon as he was in sight of Saint Joseph, he sent Lieutenant-Colonel Don Bruno de Cavallero to the Governor of the fort, Don Gregorio de Salinas, to learn from him the actual situation of the French at Pensacola. The Governor replied that two deserters from

---

[1] Barcia Ensayo Cronologico, p. 353, says July 29, not June.

1719. that fort had assured him that Mr. de Chateaugué had made no repairs there, nor even collected material for the purpose; that Santa Rosa Island and Point Siguença were abandoned, and that the French commandant, he had no doubt, would be obliged to surrender at the first summons.

On this report, Carrascosa ran up to within half a league of Pensacola Bay,[1] and anchoring during the night, sent off a detachment of a hundred men, who, without meeting any resistance, took possession of Point Siguença, which is the western extremity of Santa Rosa Island. Fifty soldiers of the garrison of Pensacola immediately came in and surrendered,[2] assuring them that they had only to show themselves, to become masters of the fort; that all the French who were shut up there were good servants of the King of Spain, and would open the gates as soon as they appeared. This garrison had been very badly selected; it was composed entirely of deserters, salt smugglers, forced emigrants to Louisiana and other like rubbish, whom it was imprudent to collect in too large a body. The Spanish commander himself also entered the bay in a sloop, to inspect the real state of affairs. He saw two frigates, and had perfect leisure to examine them; reconnoitred the fort at his ease, as the cannon fired at him did not reach. Returning to Point Siguença, he ordered all the bilanders to enter the port, and as soon as they came to anchor, they opened a cannonade on the frigates and fort. The two frigates replied briskly, but this did not prevent one of them being boarded and taken. The crew of the other set fire to it and retired within the fort, which was at once invested by all the bilanders.

---

[1] Charlevoix here follows in the main Barcia, but Dumont, Memoires, ii., p. 13–4, says that the Spaniards kept their own vessel outside of Santa Rosa Island, and that the Duke de Noailles, which they had treacherously captured, sailed in under French colors, and in answer to the French hail, said she was commanded by Richebourg. Then she opened fire and was joined by the other.

[2] Chateaugué was left with only about twenty.

The firing was vigorous on both sides all day, but not very effective. In the evening, Don Bruno Cavallero sent to summon Mr. de Chateaugué to surrender as a prisoner of war, with all his garrison, declaring that if he waited till his batteries were planted, he would give quarter to none. He asked till ten the next morning to decide, and this was granted; but the Spanish commandant occupied with strong detachments all the passes by which the Indians could come to the relief of the French. Chateaugué was bent on resisting to the last extremity, but his soldiers all unanimously declaring that they would not fight against the Spaniards, he was forced to surrender, and at the hour designated, he obtained these terms: That he should march out of his fort with all the honors of war, and be conveyed to Spain. Then almost all the French enlisted in the Spanish troops, except some who were thrown into the holds of vessels, tied hand and foot. The Governor, his lieutenant, the Director of the Company and all the officers, were paroled, while the vessel was fitting out to convey them to Havana.[1] That same day Carrascosa took possession of the fort, which he found well supplied with munitions and merchandise: he restored Don Juan Pedro Matamoros as Governor, and left there a sufficient garrison.[2]

1719.

Capture of the fort.

On the 25th of August he dispatched Captain Don Francisco Mendez to the Viceroy of New Spain, to bear tidings of the success of his enterprise, and that officer found Don Francisco Cornejo still at Vera Cruz with his squadron. The Marquis de Valero, charmed to learn that Pensacola had returned to the rule of his royal master, at once ordered Cornejo to set sail and to add to his squadron the ships just arrived from Havana under the command of Don Francisco Guerrero, in order to expel the French entirely from the Gulf of Mexico. Carrasco-

---

Dumont says that he was arrested and made a prisoner in violation of the capitulation, Memoires, ii., p. 15.

Barcia, Ensayo Cronologico, pp. 353–4. Bienville to minister, Oct. 20, 1719. Laval, Voyage, p. 106: Bénard de la Harpe, p. 150. Pénicaut, ch. 21, § 3. Le Page du Pratz, i., p. 96–7.

1719. sa, on his side, was not a little embarrassed in appeasing a mutiny of his men, especially of the volunteers, malcontent at not being allowed to plunder the property of the French. The means adopted to allay the tumult was to surrender to them a hundred and sixty negroes belonging to the Western Company, who had taken refuge in an Indian town; he made them some other presents also, and they seemed satisfied.[1]

Spaniards defeated near Maubile.

He then thought of reducing Dauphin Island, and sent a detachment of three hundred picked men, including several Frenchmen,[2] giving the command to Captain Don Antonio Mendieta,[3] with instructions to approach the island as near as possible, in order to reconnoitre the number of soldiers and Indians who defended it. Don Antonio fulfilled his task very well. He found the Philippe, commanded by Mr. de Serigny, in the roadstead, supported by four good batteries.[4]

He visited the whole coast, although under fire from all quarters; and estimated the number of the French and their allies at two thousand. He then entered Maubile River, and approached Fort St. Louis, capturing five boats loaded with provisions which he saw coming out; but the French in his party having landed opposite an isolated house[5] in the fields, and begun to plunder it. Mr. de Vilinville, sent by de Bienville to de Serigny with a reinforcement of French and Indians, discovered them. He first detached fifteen Indians, who cut off their route; others proceeded to hide flat on the ground, at a place which they would have to pass in their flight; these did not show themselves till the enemy was within gun-shot, when with a yell they began the fight. The enemy, taken between two fires, made but a feeble resistance. Fifteen were killed on the spot; eighteen surrendered as prison-

[1] Barcia, Ensayo Cron., p. 355.

[2] Barcia mentions Mr. Roque as the leader of these traitors.

[3] In the Gran Diablo. Dumont, Memoirs, ii., p. 16. Le Page du Pratz, i., p. 98.

[4] The Philippe was anchored in the Trou du Major. Dumont, Memoires, ii., p. 16.

[5] The house of de Miragouïne, a Canadian. Dumont, Memoires, ii., p. 17. They took 20,000 livres worth of goods sent there for safety. Bénard de la Harpe, p. 154.

1719.

ers; the rest took to the water to reach their brigantine, and some of them were drowned. The prisoners were all French deserters; Vilinville sent them to Mr. de Blainville, who, for want of hangmen to run them up, tomahawked seventeen, and sent the eighteenth to de Serigny, who hung him.[1]

Serigny summoned to surrender the Philippe.

While this was going on in Maubile River, Don Estevan Berroa set sail with the Maréchal de Villars and another ship,[2] with orders to attack the Philippe, and to land on Dauphin Island all Mendieta's detachment, and a number of soldiers whom he had taken on board for that purpose; to burn the town if possible, so as to drive off the Indians and force them to leave the island; in a word, to do all that prudence might suggest as best for the service of the King, his master. He also bore a summons addressed to the Captain of the Philippe, in these terms:

SIR: I send you my boat to summon you to surrender, and not injure your vessel; otherwise, I will treat you as incendiaries, and show no quarter to any one. I will not even spare Mr. de Chateaugué, your brother, or your friend, who is in my power with the garrison of Pensacola, it being the will of my King, Philip, to treat with all rigor those taken with arms in their hands; while those who surrender, shall meet all possible leniency, and receive all the aid they need.[3]

Mr. de Serigny replied[4] that the Spaniards might attack him when they pleased, and that he was ready to receive them. In fact, besides the sixty men under the

---

[1] Bienville to the minister, Oct. 20, 1719. Bénard de la Harpe, p. 155, evidently confounds Vilinville and Bienville. Pénicaut, ch. 21, § 4, says the Indians were Mobilians. Barcia makes all the Spaniards killed on the field, p. 355.

[2] The Santo Christo del Buen Viage, Barcia, p. 356, an English vessel captured by the Spaniards off the coast of Cuba. La Harpe, p. 155.

[3] This letter, dated On board the Nuestra Señora de Vicuña, Aug. 13, 1719, 10 a. m., and signed by Antonio de Mendieta, was received by Capt. Diourse of the Philippe. Bénard de la Harpe, p. 152–3.

[4] He expressed his contempt for the bravado of this letter. Ib.

1719. Sieur de Vilinville, who joined them most seasonably, a great many Indians had flocked to him from around Maubile; Mr. de Saint Denys brought in all the Biloxi Indians, and the Concessions sent him every man able to bear arms. Thus Berroa soon perceived that it would not be easy to succeed in his enterprise. As soon as he joined Mendieta, he learned from that officer that the island was daily filling up with French and Indians, all well armed, and a landing was nowhere practicable.

Repulse of the Spaniards at Dauphin Island.

He nevertheless attempted a descent on the little Isle Guillory, which is almost connected with Dauphin Island; but this detachment found Canadians and Indians there, who repulsed them, killing more than thirty men.[1] Two days after, the commandant having embarked on the Maréchal de Villars, and hoisted the great royal standard of Spain, appeared with another ship, a great flibustier boat, carrying ten guns, and with seven sloops. He approached Dauphin Island, and the next day the two ships anchored within gun-shot of the Philippe. The sloops, which were all filled with soldiers, and the great boat at the same time, entered the port, as if with the design of cannonading the town, and under favor of their guns, effecting a landing; but they found all the French and Indians in such an attitude, that they durst not attempt anything. They renewed the same manœuvre for fourteen days in succession, sometimes at one place, and sometimes at another, and were everywhere forced to draw off without doing anything. Yet there were on the whole island only two hundred Indians, and fewer Canadians and volunteers, on whom Mr. de Serigny could depend. The soldiers, to the number of eighty men, were of the same stamp as those who had deserted at Pensacola, and he had to distrust them as much as he did the enemy.

What most incommoded the Spaniards, was the cannon of the Philippe, which was anchored within pistol-shot of the land, and a barbette battery, which de Serigny had

---

[1] They were commanded by Trudeau, a Canadian. Bénard de la Harpe, Journal Historique, p. 156.

planted on the island, and which prevented their vessels from approaching near enough to the shore to favor their landing. At last, on the 26th, they weighed anchor and sailed back to Pensacola. The extent of their loss could not be precisely ascertained, but there was every reason to deem it considerable. Their greatest error was their lack of persistence, for had they continued to blockade Dauphin Island for never so short a time, they would infallibly have taken it. The besieged had been sleeping on the sand for three weeks, and could scarcely stand any longer; most of them were actually sick.[1]

They fortify Pensacola.

During this time the general had not been idle or free from trouble. He had wisely deemed it necessary to build a fort at the point of Santa Rosa Island, to defend the entrance to the harbor; and on this he employed all the negroes he had succeeded in taking from the French. What most retarded these works was the frequent alarms given to Fort St. Charles by the Indians; and when the Governor wished to make sorties upon them, these Indians leaped, says the Spanish historian, like goats on the mountain top, where it was impossible to follow them. This, with the first information which Carrascosa received from Don Estevan Berroa, as to the impossibility of taking the Philippe and landing on Dauphin Island, finally convinced him that he required a larger force to put an end to this war. A brigantine detached from Vera Cruz had assured him that the great reinforcement promised him would soon arrive; he expected provisions from Havana; the fort at Point Siguença was almost finished, as well as a fifteen gun battery that was to command the entrance of the harbor; they were diligently laboring to make Fort St. Charles proof against any insult; but hunger began already to be sensibly felt, and sickness began to spread.

The hope of receiving the supplies, announced as very near at hand, for a time sustained the troops, but as the

---

[1] Bienville to the minister, Oct. 29, 1719; Bénard de la Harpe, pp. 155–8. Barcia, Ensayo Cronologico, p. 357.

1719. disease spread, and no relief appeared, many advised that the country should be abandoned before the mortality increased, because, if the French came with a new force, it would avail little to be well fortified, when want of provisions would force them to surrender. Men even began to think, ere long, that the expected succors were lost, it not being probable that the Viceroy of Mexico and the Governor of Havana would have neglected to send them at the time they had set, and some said openly that their departure should no longer be delayed, as they had only just provisions enough to carry them to Havana.

The general was so fortunate as to succeed in quelling this incipient mutiny, but he was soon after notified that five sail had been seen near Dauphin Island; that the captain of a bilander had sent his longboat to reconnoitre them, and that this boat, having gone too near, had been detained.[1] There was then no doubt that they were French ships, and this opinion was confirmed by the fact that for three days past not a band of Indians had been seen near Pensacola. This led to the conclusion that these savages had joined the French troops to invest the fort by land, while the ships attacked by sea. The Governor of San Carlos, the first to receive this tidings, thought it the best expedient to burn the fort to prevent the French from establishing themselves there, and to carry to the fort on Siguença Point all his artillery and munitions. But as he was almost alone in this opinion, he bade the general do what he deemed best for the King's service.[2]

Arrival of Mr. de Champmêlin with squadron.

The next morning the captain of another bilander assured the general that the ships which he had seen were merchantmen of from twenty to twenty-six guns at the most, but it was soon after reported to him, that six men-of-war were in sight to the southeast. He at first took it for Cornejo's squadron, but was soon undeceived, and it was evident that they were French vessels.[3] Carrascosa re-

[1] Barcia, Ensayo Cronologico, pp. 357–9. Dumont, ii., p. 19.

[2] Barcia, Ensayo Cron., p. 359.

[3] Champmêlin had arrived at Dauphin Island, Sept. 1, with the Hercules, 60, Capt. de Gouyon;

solved to make at least a bold front; he sent Don Bruno Cavallero with a hundred men to the still unfinished fort on the Point; he proceeded in person with his frigate to the midst of the channel, where he lay to under several anchors. He ordered the two other frigates and the Maréchal de Villars, having reinforced them with a hundred men, to do the same thing, and draw up in line of battle, leaving only one side free at Fort Siguença; he drew all his other vessels up in line, and sent word of all to the Governor of San Carlos. The latter, on his side, had at once made out the ships to be French, because the moment they turned to approach the mouth of the harbor, he was attacked by a large body of Indians, with Frenchmen, as he judged, among them. 1719.

In fact, the Count de Champmêlin, commanding the squadron, having arrived in sight of Dauphin Island on the 31st of August, anchored the next day in the roadstead of that island with five men-of-war and two of the Company's ships. He met in the channel two Spanish bilanders, cruising there to cut off communication between the island and Maubile, but on sighting his squadron, they set sail for Pensacola. On the other hand, Mr. de Serigny, before communicating with Mr. de Champmêlin, had notified Mr. de Bienville to assemble the Indians with all the French he could find, and march with them to Dauphin Island; this done, he proceeded to salute the Count de Champmêlin and report to him the position of affairs. A few days after, Bienville arrived, and on the fifth the general held a great council of war. It was there decided that de Bienville should invest the fort at Pensacola by land with the four or five hundred Indians, and that Mr. de Serigny should remain with Mr.

Mars, 56, Capt. de Roquefeuille; Triton, 54, Capt. de Vienne; the Union, 48, Capt. de la Mancilliere-Gravé and the Marie, Capt. Japy or Chappy, bearing 28 officers and 800 men. La Harpe, p. 159. Dumont, ii., p. 18. On the 7th Sept., 1719, he sailed for Pensacola, leaving the Marie, but taking the Philippe. He landed the soldiers and Canadians from Dauphin Island at Rio Perdido. Dumont, ii., p. 21. Le Page du Pratz, i., p. 100.

1719. de Champmêlin, to serve as his guide along the coast and entering the harbor.[1]

Preparations for attacking Pensacola.

On the seventh, Dardennes, a Canadian, who had been sent to Pensacola to endeavor to reconnoitre the condition of the place, reported that he had counted eight vessels at anchor off St. Rosa Island, the masts lowered and the yards sheered up; that he had perceived a number of tents on the island and many men walking there; that the fort at Pensacola seemed to him in very good condition; that the bastion on the northeast, and curtain on the north had been entirely restored, and that the garrison durst not sally forth by day or night, such was their fear of the Indians. On the tenth, some Apalaches, also returning from a scout, brought in a Spaniard, but he was a galley slave, from whom no information could be obtained. Finally, on the twelfth, de Bienville came aboard the flagship with a troop of Canadians, to receive Mr. de Champmêlin's last orders, and on the night between the thirteenth and fourteenth,[2] the general signalled to weigh anchor with three King's ships, two of the Company's frigates, the Union and Philippe, and a small bark to aid in landing, in case of need.

The Western Company had recently sent to Louysiana two hundred and fifty men of the late levies; these were distributed among the King's vessels. Bienville's orders were to proceed by sloop to Rio Perdido with the soldiers and volunteers to join the Indians whom the Chevalier de Longueville[3] was to bring thither, and whom he in fact found there. Bienville then detached a body of French and Indians to harass the garrison of Pensacola, and prevent any one from leaving the fort. This was punctually carried out.

In fine, on the 15th, before sunrise, the squadron weighed anchor; and on the 16th in the evening, it an-

---

[1] Bienville to the minister, Oct. 20, 1719, in Gayarré, i., p. 171. Pénicaut, Relation, ch. 21, § 5.

[2] Dumont, evidently in error, says seventh, in his Memoires, ii., p. 21.

[3] Relation de la Louisianne, p. 27–8. Dumont, ii., p. 21.

1719.

The squadron enters the bay.

chored in seven fathoms, south of Pensacola, about two cannon-shot from the bar, as Mr. de Champmêlin wished to examine in person whether there was sufficient water on the bar for the King's ships, the two largest of which, namely, the Hercules, his flagship, and the Mars, drew nineteen feet. The Canadians declared that they would pass with ease; but several Spanish and French pilots maintained that he would not find more than eighteen feet of water. On the morning of the seventeenth the general ordered all the sloops and boats of the squadron to go and sound the bay; Mr. de Vienne, the Chevalier de Goyon and Mr. de Serigny embarked, and nowhere found less than twenty-two feet, but the tide was high and Mr. de Champmêlin still hesitated to risk the King's ships. Mr. de Serigny pledged his head that he would take them in, and the whole council of war favored the projected passage.[1]

Capture of the fort at the Point, and of the Spanish ships.

In fact, though the tide was quite low when the squadron got under weigh, it found twenty-one feet of water everywhere except in one spot, where the Hercules, by not exactly following the channel, touched slightly, but without sustaining any injury. The ships Comte de Toulouse, Maréchal de Villars, St. Louis, and a small frigate of eighteen guns, were anchored with a spring upon the cable,[2] just within the entrance of the harbor, under the guns of the fort at the point of Santa Rosa Island or Siguença, which had fourteen mounted, and nearer the shore lay seven bilanders, armed with from eight to fourteen guns. The squadron entered wind astern, with the topsails on the cap, in order to have time to cannonade the ships and fort at the point. These latter fired first on the King's ships, which showed only the bow, being obliged to wear, so that they were for a time unable to reply, but when they came within good musket-shot

[1] Dumont says, p. 22, that the Hercules was piloted in by an old Canadian named Grimeau, who the next year received Letters ennobling him. Bénard de la Harpe, 161–3. Pénicaut, Relation, ch. 21, § 5, MS.

[2] With a rope made fast to the cable.

1719. of the enemy's vessels, and when to anchor with a spring on the cable would have required a starboard tack, that is, turning to the right, the fire became very warm on both sides and lasted two hours. The Spanish historian counts six hours' combat, including, apparently, all the time that his nation's ships were firing on ours; he adds that the Indians and Canadians kept firing all night on Fort San Carlos; that the fire at the entrance of the port was kept up till the fort at the point was entirely demolished, and only two frigates in fighting condition, and that which bore the Spanish general sinking; that then Mr. de Champmêlin, touched to see so many brave men perish, sent to tell Don Alphonso Carrascosa to surrender, which he did. Don Bruno also surrendered with the remnant of the garrison of the fort on the point.[1]

Fort San Carlos taken, with its garrison prisoners of war.

This done, the French general sent to summon the Governor of Pensacola to surrender as a prisoner of war with all his garrison, in default whereof, there should be no quarter for any one. Matamoros said that he would answer in two days. Mr. de Bienville, who had five hundred Indians and a hundred and fifty Canadians, had already refused to make terms with him, and he felt that if Mr. de Champmêlin allowed Bienville to storm the place, as he threatened through Mr. de Lille, his first lieutenant, he could never hold out, yet he allowed de Lille to depart without a reply; but his officers, to whom he imparted the summons, forced him to recall that officer. He told him that he surrendered, and lowered his flag. Mr. de Champmelin showed great courtesy to all the officers, and told them that he had never yet seen so gallant a defence; it was indeed conducted with great ardor and valor.[2]

---

[1] Barcia, Ensayo Cronologico, p. 360. Dumont and Le Page du Pratz on the contrary, say, p. 23, that the great fort San Carlos fired only one gun, and surrendered for fear of falling into the hands of Saint Denis and his Indians, who were investing him. He says the Spaniards fled between decks, and had not courage to venture out to haul down their flag.

[2] Charlevoix here generally follows Barcia, but La Harpe says, p. 163, that Champmêlin received Don Alphonso courteously, but that Matamoros was disarmed by a sailor,

1719.

The enemy's loss.

The next day Mr. de Champmêlin sent his long boat with one of his officers and an officer of the Spanish general, to order the commanders of the bilanders, which had run ashore at the head of the bay, to bring them back to the port; but only French prisoners were found on board, the Spaniards having escaped to St. Joseph,[1] as a brigantine and periagua did at the commencement of the action. The same day the Spanish garrison marched out of Fort San Carlos, and the officers, disarmed, were sent on the ships; but they were allowed to retain their clothing and all private property. Mr. de Champmêlin chose to have in his vessel, the general, the Governor of Pensacola, Don Bruno Cavallero, Don Estevan Berroa, and Don Antonio Joseph Martinez.[2] But as the number of other prisoners, whom Bienville estimates at fifteen hundred, and Mr. de Serigny at twelve hundred, greatly embarrassed the squadron and would have famished it; six hundred were sent to Havana on the St. Louis. No one doubted that the enemy must have had many killed and wounded, yet only sixty in all were found, and on our side there were only six or seven.[3]

Cruelty of the Spaniards to the French prisoners. Mr. de Champmelin's reprisals.

Early in the morning of the 24th, a brigantine was perceived, which, without mistrusting, entered the port; it was commanded by Andrew Gonzales, bringing from Havana the provisions so long expected at Pensacola. Mr. Champmêlin seized it and found wherewith to relieve all his men, who needed it extremely. Gonzales was also bearer of several letters, of which the general delivered only such as he deemed proper. By the same channel, Mr. de Bienville received one from Mr. de Chateaugué, who informed him that the Governor of Havana refused to furnish provisions to him, as well as to the officers and

---

and reproached by de Champmêlin with his lack of courage, telling him that he was unfit to be an officer.

[1] Dumont, p. 24–5, charges that the Spaniards before running off laid a train so as to fire the magaine and blow up this bilander, the Gran Diablo, with the French prisoners on board.

[2] Bienville to the minister, Oct. 20, 1719. Barcia, Ensayo Cronolo gico, p. 360.

[3] The fort was given up to the Indians to plunder. Pénicaut, ch. 21.

1719. sailors who were prisoners with him, and that the latter were forced to carry stone or enlist in Spanish ships, to have wherewith to sustain life.[1] Mr. de Champmêlin bitterly reproached the Spanish General and officers with this; but he did not think it right to take any other vengeance than by treating kindly all the prisoners of their nation in his hands. He nevertheless thought it his duty to write to the Governor of Havana; he then sentenced the French taken arms in hand against the King; the most guilty were hanged, the rest condemned to the galleys.[2]

The fort at Pensacola in part demolished

The only question left was whether the fort at Pensacola should be preserved. There was no lack of soldiers to garrison it, but most of them were wretches who had deserted from the army in France, or taken by force; and past experience showed how little dependence could be placed on their fidelity. It was therefore resolved to demolish two bastions on the land side, preserving only the two facing the port, and to leave there an officer, two sergeants, twenty soldiers and twelve Indians.[3] On the third of October, the frigate Duke de Noailles arrived at Pensacola and delivered to the Count de Champmêlin letters, by which he was ordered to winter with his squadron in Louysiana, inasmuch as information had reached the Court of France that a strong squadron had left Spain for the Gulf of Mexico; but the condition in which his ships and crews were, rendered this order impracticable.

On the eleventh a Spaniard, sole survivor of the crew of a storeship of twenty-four guns, intended to revictual St. Joseph's Bay, stated that he had sailed from Vera Cruz sixteen days previously; that he had left there five men-of-war, carrying each from fifty to seventy guns; two frigates and three bilanders, with a great number of land troops, who were preparing to come and seize all the posts occupied by the French in Louysiana. On the

---

[1] Bienville to the minister, citing Chateaugué's letter. Gayarré, i., p. 172.

[2] Ib. Dumont, Memoires, ii., p. 26. Bénard de la Harpe, p. 165.

[3] Bienville to the minister, Oct. 20, 1719. The officer left was Lieut. Delisle, of the navy. Dumont, ii., p. 28. Le Page du Pratz, i., p. 103.

13th, at three o'clock in the afternoon, a ship hove in sight, and at the same time they brought to the general another Spaniard, who had been found on Santa Rosa Island. This man told him that he had come from Vera Cruz in the ship then in sight; that he and two others had been sent ashore in the boat, which had been lost; that his comrades were drowned, and that he had escaped by swimming. Soon after, the ship fired three guns, as if to recall the boat, and the longboat was seen putting off. It landed at Point Siguença, with casks to take in water. It was captured, and those in it said that they had sailed from Vera Cruz thirty-five days before, and that their ship was loaded with stores, and a reinforcement of a hundred men for Pensacola; that the northeast wind had detained them at Dauphin Island, and that they had endeavored to take in water there, but had been prevented. 1719.

The next morning the ship, which had anchored outside the bay, fired a gun to recall its longboat, but as it did not return, she lay to where she was till eleven o'clock. But then a violent southeast wind forced her to enter and anchor. The Count de Champmêlin hoisted his flag. This ship was commanded by Don Francisco de la Peña, one of the captains of the Barlovento Fleet. As soon as he saw the French flag he lowered his, and the general sent to demand the letters which he had from the Viceroy.[1] He gave them and they confirmed all that was already known of the designs of the Spaniards. This information did not alter at all the resolution to depart which Mr. de Champmêlin had formed, as sickness was increasing in his ships. The Mars, however, had orders to remain till its crew recovered from the pestilence, which had not left the ship from the time of its arrival in America. The Maréchal de Villars and the Comte de Toulouse were not in a seaworthy condition, and were also obliged to remain.

---

[1] The vessel thus captured was the Chico. Barcia, p. 361. The captain threw his letters overboard, but they were recovered by a French soldier. Dumont, ii., p. 27. Bénard de la Harpe, p. 167.

1719. These arrangements made, Mr. de Champmêlin's next thought was to reward the Indians for the zeal they had displayed for the French nation since the commencement of this war. Mr. de Saint Denys, who was greatly beloved by these tribes, received orders to assemble them, and he made them chant the calumet in honor of the general, who attended with all his officers. He then addressed them in the general's name, exhorting them to remain ever attached to the French, whose superiority over their enemy they had just witnessed. When he had ended his address, presents were distributed to all in the King's name, and they were sent off highly pleased.

Presents made to the Indians

New tidings of the approach of a Spanish squadron.

On the 21st,[1] as the squadron was about to set sail, a bilander was seen endeavoring to enter the bay, wind astern. It was seized, and the captain declared that he had cleared from Vera Cruz eighteen days before in company with a 44 gun ship, and three others of thirty, eighteen and twelve guns, and another bilander; that three ten gun ships had remained in port, the pestilence having broken out among the crews; that General Cornejo in person was in the largest ship; that it was his design to join the Governor of Pensacola, to aid him in conquering all that was still left to the French in Louysiana, and that he supposed Dauphin Island and Fort Maubile already in the power of his Catholic majesty; that moreover, a gale having separated his bilander from the squadron three days after its departure from Vera Cruz, he did not know what had become of it.

De Champmêlin sails for France. Mr. de Saujon arrives.

This news decided Mr. de Champmêlin to remain some days longer at Pensacola, awaiting the Spanish squadron, but as it did not appear, he hoisted sail and started for France again.[2] It is probable that Cornejo, having learned by the way the capture of Pensacola, and the

[1] Oct. 21 the fleet left Pensacola after burning the forts and houses, having only sub-Lieut. Terrisse with a few soldiers and Indians. Bénard de la Harpe, p. 167.

[2] With the Hercules, Mars, Triton, Union and Maréchal de Villars. Barcia, p. 362. He reached Brest, Jan. 3, 1720. After he sailed in Nov., 1719, the fort at Old Biloxi was restored. Dumont, ii., p. 34. Pénicaut, ch. 21, MS.

presence of the French fleet there still, did not deem it prudent to engage a squadron much stronger than his own. Be that as it may, de Champmêlin had scarcely sailed when the Chevalier de Saujon arrived in Louysiana with a new squadron,[1] and his presence contributed in no slight degree to prevent anything being undertaken by the Spaniards. He then wished to go to St. Joseph's Bay and capture that post; but this was not the opinion of Mr. de Bienville, who had taken possession of it the year before, and soon after abandoned it on account of its uselessness and the difficulties of defending it, or approaching it, or sheltering vessels there, and especially on account of the sterility of the country, which is adapted to no natural products. Mr. de Serigny, too, remarked that the famine which threatened the colony would prevent any delay in the departure of the Company's ships, which it was intended to use on this expedition, and on which he saw himself compelled to send back many of the people to France. Mr. de Saujon did not insist, and as there was no longer anything to detain him in America, he sailed for France.[2] 1719.

1720. Departure of de Serigny and arrival of two royal vessels.

De Serigny followed soon after: he set sail June 27, 1720,[3] and on reaching Brest he learned that the King had appointed him captain of ships of the line; a reward well merited by his valor, his good conduct, and the zeal with which he had served his prince from childhood; having never been promoted to any rank in the navy till

[1] Laval, Voyage, p. 97; De Vallette-Laudun, Journal, p. 234. Escorting the Mutine, Capt. de Martonne, one of the Company's ships, (Dumont, ii., p. 36,) and the Duc de Noailles. (La Harpe, p. 220.) Soon after the whole establishment on Dauphin Island was removed to Old Biloxi. Dumont, p. 37. The arrival of Concessionaries and a fire at Old Biloxi, led to a new establishment at New Biloxi. Ib., p. 38–43. La Harpe, p. 220, gives as his vessels the Achille, 62; Capt. de Laujon, (Saujon); Content, 60, Capt. de Rochambeau; Mercure, 56, Capt. de Gabaret. They arrived Feb. 28, 1720.

[2] He sailed May 4th. De Vallette Laudun, Journal, p. 235. Laval, Voyage, p. 97. Bénard de la Harpe, p. 222.

[3] On the Amazon, Capt. St. Villiers, which sailed with the Victoire, la Jaille. De Vallette Laudun, p. 235. Pénicaut says with the Comte de Toulouse and Maréchal de Villars, ch. 22.

1720. he had distinguished himself by some signal action or in some important service. Three days after his departure, two of the King's vessels, the Toulouse and the Henry, which had sailed from Toulon under the command of Messrs. de Valette[1] and de Cafaro, arrived in wretched plight at the roadstead off Dauphin Island. The Jesuit Father Laval, royal professor of hydrography at the port of Toulon, was on board, having come to make observations in Louysiana, and especially to fix the longitude of the mouth of the Micissipi;[2] but the pestilence having broken out on both vessels, Mr. de Cafaro died on the voyage;[3] the chaplains were not able to attend the sick, who were very numerous; accordingly, that religious, feeling that science is only an accessory to a man of his profession, thought the duty of his ministry paramount to any good to be expected from his astronomical observations: he did not go to the Micissipi, although he was only fourteen leagues distant from it: he did not leave the crews, employing in his observations only the moments he stole from sleep. This conduct elicited high praise from the prince who presided in the Navy Council.[4]

De St. Denys at the Natchitoches.

Meanwhile, the Fort of the Natchitoches was always maintained, and some detachments of concessions had advanced in that direction, in hopes of acquiring wealth by trade with the Spaniards, a chimerical hope, which prevented their adopting surer methods of making a solid settlement elsewhere, and which finally ruined them. Towards the close of this year de Bienville received orders from court to send back Mr. de Saint Denys,[5] whom the

---

[1] De Vallette Laudun, author of "Journal d'un Voyage fait en 1720." La Haye, 1768. Each of 66 guns. Laval, p. 1. La Harpe, p. 223, says July 1 arrived the Comte de Toulouse, 64, Capt. de Vatet, *vice* de Cafaro, and the St. Henri, 70, Capt. Domce.

[2] Father Anthony Laval published in 1728 his Voyage de la Louisiane, 4°. Mariette, Paris.

[3] De Vallette Laudun, p. 195. Ferdinand de Caffaro, brother of the Marquis de Caffaro, (Barcia, p. 363,) died June 11. B. de la Harpe, p. 223.

[4] Chateaugué and other prisoners taken at Pensacola, were brought back to Mobile June 15. Ib. p. 224.

[5] St. Denys had settled at Biloxi with his colonists and slaves, and had commanded the Indians in the late operations. He was made, in consequence, captain in the army and Governor of Fort Natchitoches. Pénicaut, ch. 22.

1721.

King had honored with the brevet of Captain, and the Cross of Saint Louis, on the high testimony which Mr. de Champmêlin had rendered in his favor in the Council of the Navy. He set out at the commencement of the following year with a reinforcement of troops and munitions, and his wife soon joined him there. Mr. de Chateaugué, who had proceeded from Havana to France, also returned at the same time, with the rank of King's Lieutenant, and resumed command of Fort Saint Louis at Maubile. Finally, de Bienville again established the headquarters of Louysiana at Biloxi, and fixed his residence there, with the greater part of the troops and the Directors of the Company, of which he was the presiding officer.

First tidings of peace.

No further fears were entertained of the Spaniards, because from the preceding year while Mr. de Valette was still at Dauphin Island, positive information had come that two Spanish ships of sixty-six and sixty-seven guns, commanded by two commodores, and which were to join the Vera Cruz fleet to surprise Pensacola, had received counter orders at Havana, and that this change was caused by a suspension of hostilities between the two crowns. The court of Madrid feeling, no doubt, that the restitution of Pensacola would be one of the articles of the treaty of peace then negotiating, thought it needless to incur useless expense, and the result was as she had foreseen.[1]

Unsuccessful enterprise at St. Bernard Bay.

It was a favorable opportunity to establish the concessions, who did not cease to arrive from France, and who, well managed, would in a few years have peopled both banks of the Micissipi up to the Illinois; but the sole aim of the Directors of the Company was to get near the Spaniards, and prevent their settling in our vicinity. This same year de Bienville formed the design of secur-

[1] Pensacola was restored to the Spaniards in Dec., 1722. Alexander Wauchop, an Irish officer who had reached the rank of captain of a frigate, arrived there Nov. 26 in the frigate Grande Holandesa to take possession. Charlevoix, Journal, p. 481; La Harpe withdrew the French garrison to Mobile. Journal, pp. 346–7.

1721. ing St. Bernard's or Saint Louis Bay, but he did not select the right man for the enterprise. This man entered the Magdalen River, which he met on his way, and ascended it five or six leagues. He found the Indians on their guard all along, resolved not to suffer any strangers in their country. He told them that he came to form an alliance with them, and to improve their condition, but they answered that they were satisfied as they were, and preferred their liberty to all the advantages offered them. The officer, however, found means to allure some of their chief men on board, where he retained them. He at once set sail and brought them to Biloxi. De Bienville sharply censured this treacherous act, and sent the Indians home; but the next year he learned that the Spaniards from Vera Cruz had built a fort in Saint Bernard's Bay.[1]

Towards the end of May, 1722,[2] a Spanish brigantine, carrying twenty-two guns and two hundred and fifty men,

---

[1] The Viceroy of New Spain, in June, 1718, sent Don Dionisio Perez Ballones to occupy Espiritu Santo, or St. Bernard's Bay; (see Charlevoix, Jour., p. 452,) but he was unable to enter the channel. Barcia, Ensayo Cronologico, p. 342. The West India Company was very urgent in its orders to occupy the bay, and the King, Nov. 16, 1718, issued an order, but the colonial authorities merely sent a coaster under Berranger to explore it. La Harpe, p. 233, 235. On the 10th of August, 1721, Bienville sent La Harpe in the Subtile, Capt. Berranger, with 20 soldiers to occupy it. Ordres, &c. Ib., p. 257. He entered a bay at 28° 20,′ Aug. 27, (p. 263,) and took off nine natives, (p. 275.) Pénicaut, ch. xxiii. The real St. Bernard's, or Espiritu Santo, was occupied by Martin de Alarcon in 1718. Ib., 275. For the Spanish occupation, see Don Juan Antonio de la Peña, Diario del Viage del Marques de San Miguel, MS.; Bonilla, Compendio de los Succesos ocuridos en Texas, MS.; Morfi, Historia de Texas, MS. We here lose Pénicaut, who sailed to France Oct. 3, 1721, to obtain medical treatment for his eyes, and a pension for his relief after 22 years' services.

[2] Barcia cites among his authorities, Situacion del Presidio de Santa Maria de Galve, escrita por su Gobernador, el Coronel Don Juan Pedro Matamoros, MS. Diario de lo acaecido en las Perdidas y Restauracion del Presidio de Santa Maria, Prision, y Libertad de los Españoles, desde el dia 14 de Maio de 1719, hasta 3 de Junio de 1720, by the same, and Relacion de la Expedicion, hecha por los Franceses en el Puerto y Presidios de Santa Maria de Galve a Pençacola y Restauracion por las Armas de España, &c., escrita por Don Alfonso Carrascosa de la Torre. Barcia's work was printed July, 1722, and has nothing as to the restoration of Pensacola.

arrived from Vera Cruz at Biloxi. It was commanded by Don Agustin Spinola, and brought over the Sieur Walcop,[1] an Irishman, captain of a man-of-war in the service of the King of Spain, as bearer of the treaty of peace concluded between France and the Catholic King, one of the articles of which restored Pensacola to the Spanish crown. This peace was celebrated at Biloxi, where I was at the time, with great demonstrations of joy, apparently very sincere on both sides.[2]

1722.

Pensacola restored to Spain.

As soon as the brigantine set sail again, that is to say, towards the middle of June, they began transferring to New Orleans all the goods in the Western Company's storehouses at Biloxi, because the Council had ordered the headquarters to be established there, only a detachment with an officer to remain at Biloxi. The troops had already begun their march to the capital, but all did not follow the route assigned to them. A company of Swiss, with their captain at their head, having embarked in a small coaster with a quantity of provisions and munitions, steered with ensigns spread towards Carolina, where they were very well received. Only two officers with a sergeant and some women remained in Louysiana, and even their clothes had been carried off by the others.[3]

Headquarters transferred to New Orleans.

This was not the only desertion by which the English colonies as well as Havana profited.[4] Louysiana, accord-

[1] Alexander Wauchop. La Harpe, p. 325. Charlevoix in his Journal, p. 481, says a brigantine of 14 guns, 150 men. The Wauchops, though officers of the Irish Brigade, were Scotch. Bourke's regiment, commanded by Francis Wauchop, passed from the French to the Spanish service in 1715. See O'Callaghan, Irish Brigade, pp. 151-2; Military Memoirs of the Irish Nation, p. 193.

[2] Charlevoix, Journal, p. 481. Charlevoix arrived at New Orleans Jan'y 5th, 1722. Journal, p. 438: La Harpe's date (p. 285,) is evidently wrong. Although the Mercure had represented New Orleans as containing 800 houses, he found a hundred rude huts, a storehouse, and two or three good houses. During his stay he effected a reconciliation between Bienville and Hubert, the Commissaire Ordonnateur. La Harpe, p. 287.

[3] June 12, the Swiss company, commanded by Mr. Brandt in the absence of Capt. Wouverdelik, while in the Elizabeth rose against the captain, Lasou, and forced him to take them to Havana; Bénard de la Harpe, p. 331; but they really reached Carolina; the Spaniards refusing to receive them, p. 348. Charlevoix, Journal, p. 483.

[4] The garrison of Fort Toulouse among the Alibamons mutinied,

1722. ingly, declined daily, and it was high time to send from France wherewith to repair its losses. The English, on their side, enriched by our spoils, and informed of our weakness, thought it a favorable opportunity to regain our Indians, who had handled them so roughly. The first whom they attempted were the Tchactas (Choctaws), exaggerating our poverty, to persuade them that they need expect nothing in future from us, and making them the most alluring offers if they would renounce our alliance and join them.

English Intrigues.

Fidelity of the Choctaws.

It was a great temptation for Indians, partly convinced by their own eyes of what was told them, and only too conscious that our last successes had produced no solid result. It is moreover certain, that if this nation, the most numerous in all Louysiana, had been gained by the bait of the proffered advantages, all our other allies would have followed their example, more especially as those who were most attached to us were not in a condition to stem the torrent; but the Choctaws, on this occasion, displayed a disinterestedness and a fidelity of which the most civilized nations cannot always boast; they themselves informed de Bienville of the proposals made to them, and that commandant found them in a disposition towards the French from which he thought he could expect everything.

Cause of the desertions.

The English were not, however, unanimous in regard to the great number of French taking refuge among them. Some even possibly feared to see them multiply too rapidly in their colonies; it is at least certain that the Governor of Carolina, writing to Mr. de Bienville, to inform him of the arrival of the Sieur Brandt[1] and his Swiss company, advised him to inform the court of

killed their captain, Marchand, and started for Carolina, but were pursued by Sieur Villemont with a party of Indians, and nearly all killed. Gayarré, i., p. 181.

[1] Bienville to the Minister, 1 Feb., 1723. Gayarré, i., p. 198. This year, June 4, 250 Germans arrived under the Swedish Chevalier d'Arensbourg, sent out by John Law to settle on his Concession on the Arkansas. After his fall they came down and settled near New Orleans. New Orleans was laid out by the Sieur le Blond de la Tour, Brigadier and Chevalier of St. Louis, the chief of a troop of engineers sent over. Dumont, ii., pp. 39, 46. La Harpe, p. 251.

France of this great disorder, which would infallibly soon draw down utter ruin on his colony. But all that happened should have been anticipated; that colony having been settled almost entirely by people sent over by force, or Concessionaries who did not find there what they had been led to expect; for soon the only thought of either was to get out of it; numbers died of misery or disease, and the country was emptied as rapidly as it had filled. 1722.

For their part, the deserters everywhere adduced the necessity to which they were driven, of providing for themselves elsewhere, by the refusal to give them the very necessaries of life. Some even wrote to the Regisseurs of Louysiana [1] in terms that showed how much the step they had just taken cost them; and this was still more clearly evinced by what happened in the month of August of this same year. One Duclos, commanding a coaster with a very rich cargo, was met by a party of these deserters, who merely took from him some provisions and liquors, without touching his merchandise. On his expressing his surprise, they replied that they were not robbers, but decent men, whom necessity forced to seek life in other nations, since their own let them perish with hunger. The most malcontent were the soldiers, who received absolutely nothing but bread, while meat was distributed to the Company's workmen, and even to the criminals, who were quite frequently employed by the settlers.

Hurricane and its effects.

To crown the misfortunes, on the 12th of September, at ten in the evening, there rose on the Micissipi a hurricane, which lasted in all its fury till noon on the following day, and was felt as far as Natchez in one direction, and Biloxi in the other. At New Orleans, the church, hospital and thirty houses or log huts were thrown down; all the other edifices were injured. No lives were lost, but some of the sick in the hospital were wounded. A number

---

[1] On the 15th of April in the preceding year, the King had by an Arrêt appointed four Commissaries, all Councillors of State for the Regimen of Louysiana and the Western Company, and the rendering of the accounts. *Charlevoix*. Two Commissaries, du Sausoy and de la Chaise, arrived in the Venus in 1722.

1722. of boats, periaguas, canoes and sloops were crushed in the port; three ships anchored there were very much damaged, and found themselves high ashore on the bank of the river, which had risen eight feet. In the settlements above and below the city there was not a building standing. Biloxi suffered even more; all the houses and stores were overthrown, and as the sea overflowed its bounds, a part of that post was inundated. The coasters which were in the roadstead were driven on the islands, or on the mainland. There was even one, the captain of which alone escaped with a cabin boy, having spent twenty-four hours on the yard-arm; the rest of the crew were drowned. Several periaguas, coming down to New Orleans loaded with provisions and poultry, were wrecked. The vegetables that were mature were destroyed, and the continual rains which came on spoiled a good part of what was still green.[1]

The Chickasaws ask peace.

Meanwhile, the war with the Chicachas (Chickasaws) still continued, although it was confined to some surprises,[2] which compelled travellers to proceed with caution. These Indians even themselves were the first to grow weary of it at a time when they might have given us great trouble. Two Canadians, father and son, having fallen into their hands, were well treated by them, and the chiefs begged them to write to de Bienville that if he would restore them to favor, they would release the prisoners at once. They did more, they proceeded to the Sieur de Grave, commandant at the Yazoos, presented the calumet to him, and solicited peace, which he did not deem it wise to refuse.

---

[1] Dumont, Memoires, ii., p. 48–50. Le Page du Pratz, i., 174. Bénard de la Harpe, p. 339. After laying out New Orleans, la Tour and de Pauget, his second engineer, in 1722 built a fort on piles at the Balize, to guard the entrance and aid the shipping. Ib., pp. 57–9. La Tour died soon after. Ib., p. 114. See Le Page du Pratz, i., p. 159. This balize was swept away into the river, and a new one built by Ulloa in 1768. Louisiana Hist. Coll., v., p. 29, n.

[2] They surprised Sergeant Riter and his family near the Yazoo post. Dumont, pp. 84. This author calls it the first Indian hostility against the French. See La Harpe, p. 305, 330. Le Page du Pratz, ii., p. 282–7.

1722.

Hostilities of the Natchez.

But the colony, though relieved as far as this tribe was concerned, not only the bravest in all Louysiana, but also the most to be feared in consequence of its relations with the English, soon saw that it could depend on the fidelity of the Natchez only so long as they kept on their guard against that naturally treacherous nation. In fact, these savages no sooner perceived that the French, engaged in other affairs, paid less attention to their doings, than they renewed their outrages, and displayed all their ill will, of which it will be soon seen the authorities were not sufficiently on their guard.

The Illinois all unite on the Micissipi.

At the same time sad tidings came from the Illinois. Mr. de Boisbriand, warned that the (Illinois) of the Rock and of Pimiteouy were besieged by the Foxes, had embarked with the Chevalier d'Artaguette and the Sieur du Tisné, both captains, several other officers and a detachment of a hundred men, to hasten to their deliverance, and had ordered forty Frenchmen and four hundred Indians to march by land to Pimiteouy and await him there; but when each division had got about half way, they learned that the Foxes had retreated with a loss of more than a hundred and twenty of their men. This success did not, however, prevent the Illinois, although they had lost only about twenty men, with some women and children, from leaving the Rock and Pimiteouy, where they were kept in constant alarm, and proceeding to unite with those of their brethren who had settled on the Micissipi; this was a stroke of grace for most of them, the small number of missionaries preventing their supplying so many towns, scattered far apart; but on the other side, as there was nothing to check the raids of the Foxes along the Illinois River, communication between Louysiana and New France became much less practicable.

Some time after they received a very severe check from the Sieur de Saint Ange, the officer at Fort Chartres in the Illinois, who, having drawn a large body of them into a kind of ambuscade, cut them almost all to pieces; other less numerous bands met the same fate soon after; but

1722. their fury increased as their forces diminished, and communicated it so fully to the new enemies they raised up against us, that the whole course and neighborhood of the Micissipi was infested with Indians with whom we had never had any difficulty, and who gave no quarter to any French whom they could well surprise or attack.

The Natchez make peace with the French.

Several Natchez came out openly against us,[1] and what most embarrassed de Bienville was the fact that the brother of the Great Chief was at their head. To make a lasting arrangement with this nation, it would have been necessary to have this man, who was the author of all the evil, given up to the Governor by his own brother, and there was no way to drive the latter to it. The wisdom and firmness of the Sieur Delietto, who commanded at that post, extricated de Bienville from this difficulty. That commandant so adroitly worked on the mind of the Great Chief, as to bring him to resolve to go in person and put his brother at the discretion of the general, who, on his side, generously pardoned an humbled enemy and gained him. Great marks of confidence were given on both sides, and this good understanding would to all appearance have been durable, had Mr. Delietto lived longer. He was already dead when I reached Natchez at the close of the year 1722, and the good understanding, it seemed to me, was still perfect between the French and Indians. A little more distrust and precaution on the side of the former, would undoubtedly have deprived the latter of the very thought of regarding them differently, and prevented the evils of which we shall soon speak.

[1] A quarrel arose between a sergeant and some Indians about a debt, and the guard in trying to restore peace, killed a chief's son and wounded some others. Bénard de la Harpe, p. 343. Le Page du Pratz, i., p. 180–3. To avenge this, Guenote, one of the Directors of the St. Catharine Concession at Natchez, was wounded, and la Rochelle, a soldier, murdered. Dumont, ii., pp. 94–5. Troops were sent up under the Sieur Payon, in four batteaux; but the Stung Serpent, then Great Chief, fined three villages to make reparation. These villages in retaliation began killing the cattle and horses of the settlers. Bienville went up with a French and Indian force, but after a fight at one cabin, the Natchez of the Apple Village fled, and Bienville burnt the town, which stood near Second Creek. On their giving the heads of Old Hair, chief of the Apple Village, and of a negro, Bienville made peace. Ib., ii., pp. 96–113. Le Page du Pratz, i., pp. 197–206.

BOOK XXII.

BOOK XXII.

IT is not easy to say what had hitherto prevented their affording the colonists settled in the different parts of Louysiana the spiritual succors so necessary to new settlements, even on the ground of sound policy. However, on my return from America in the commencement of the year 1723, I found the court and the Company equally surprised at the destitution in which I showed this rising colony to be in this essential point, and the Directors of the Company made it their most pressing duty to remedy this great disorder. They cast their eyes on the Capuchin Fathers, and having obtained several, distributed them in the quarters where there were the greatest number of French dwellings.[1]

1723.

Introduction of the Capuchin Fathers into Louysiana.

It was no less important to have missionaries among the Indians amid whom we were settled. We have seen that the salvation of these tribes was always the main object which our kings kept in view before all else, wherever they extended their dominion in the New World, and the experience of nearly two centuries had taught us that the surest means of binding the natives of the country to us,

Missionaries to the Indians thought of.

---

[1] In 1724 Bienville received orders to return to France; Mr. de la Tour to take command till Mr. de Boisbriant, Governor ad interim, returned from Illinois. He embarked on the Bellona in 1725, but she sank in the Trou du Major; he then went in the Gironde. Before going, Bienville in March published the celebrated "Code Noir," or "Black Code." See it in Gayarré, i., p. 203; Louisiana Hist. Coll., iii., p. 89. Bienville presented a memoir in his defence: Gayarré, i., p. 219; but was removed, as was his brother Chateaugué, King's Lieutenant, while Captain and Ensign de Noyan, his nephews, were cashiered and sent to France, p. 221.

1725. was to gain them to Christ. Nor could it moreover be unknown that even independent of the fruit which the evangelical laborers might produce among them, the mere presence of a man, venerable by his office, understanding their language, able to observe their conduct, and able by gaining the confidence of some to learn their designs, is often better than a garrison, or may at least supply its place, and give the governors time to take steps to defeat their plots. The example of the Illinois, who had since 1717 been incorporated with the government of Louysiana, was sufficient to show how important it was not to leave the other nations any longer without missionaries.[1]

Jesuits sent.

The India Company saw this, and in the year 1725 applied to the Jesuits, a great number of whom offered themselves for this new mission. But as the Superiors could not grant permission to all to devote themselves to it, and there were not enough to give some to all the tribes, the commandant and directors thought best to place the first who arrived in positions where there were no Capuchins, whence it happened that the Natchez, the very people whom it was most important to enlighten, had none, and the fault thus committed was not perceived till it was irreparable.[2]

Ursulines.

Provision was at the same time made for the education of the young French girls at the capital and its vicinity, by bringing over Ursulines from France; and to avoid multiplying establishments in a colony which scarcely be-

[1] Chicagou, chief of the Illinois, and some chiefs of the Missouris, Osages and Otoptatas went to France in 1725. Father de Beaubois presented them to the India Company. Postman, London, Jan. 27, 1726. See Dumont, ii., pp. 74–78; Bossu, i., p. 161–2.

[2] After Fathers du Ru and Dongé, (ante, iv., p. 129, n.,) came F. Joseph de Limoges, who entered the order Sept. 24, 1686, came over in 1698, founded a Baiogoula mission, and returned to France in 1703. Martin's list in Carayon; Jouvency, Hist. Soc. Jesu, p. 223. Under the arrangement now made, F. Nicholas de Beaubois, who had been some years in Illinois, became Superior, and was joined in 1726, by FF. Paul du Poisson, Mathurin le Petit, John Dumas, and John Souel; and in 1727 by FF. Alexis de Guyenne, René Tartarin, and Stephen d'Outreleau. Martin's List. Of the labors of this Jesuit mission, we have only the Letters of du Poisson, and le Petit in the Lettres Edifiantes, (Kip's Jes. Missions, pp. 29, &c.); a few letters in the Louisiana Documents, and the Banissement

gan to take form, these same religious were entrusted with the care of the hospital.[1] 1726.

In the month of October, 1726, Mr. Perrier, lieutenant of a ship of the line, was appointed Commandant-General of Louysiana[2] in place of Mr. de Bienville, who returned to France. Although everything seemed quiet in the country, the new commandant soon saw the necessity of having more troops than he found there. The better he knew the Indians, the more convinced he became that they could never be made permanent allies till we had securely prevented their being our enemies, and that our neighbors could be delivered from the temptation of urging them to conspire against us, only by garrisoning all the posts in such a way as to have no fear of them. Nevertheless, I do not find that he pressed the Company to send him any reinforcements before the year 1729; but in the month of August of that year, he asked for two or three hundred good soldiers.

Perrier Commandant-General of Louysiana.

It was somewhat late; nevertheless, he not only did not obtain what he asked, but in one of his letters of March 18th, in the following year, he complains that in their answer they charge him with wishing an increase of troops only to have more men under his command, or to

He asks aid in vain.

des Jésuites de la Louisiane," published by F. Carayon, Paris, 1865. There is a contemporary tribute to them in the "Relation de la Louisiane ou Mississippi écrite à une Dame par un officier de Marine," in Voyages au Nord, v., p. 25. Of the Capuchin mission there is no published account.

[1] See Treaty with Ursulines, Sept. 13, 1726. Gayarré, i., p. 223. For Brevet of King, Sept. 18, 1726, and an account of the first nuns, see Tranchepain, Relation du Voyage des Premières Ursulines à la Nouvelle Orleans et de leur etablissement en cette ville, New York, 1859. Life of St. Angela Merici, p. 200–219. They reached New Orleans Aug. 7, 1727.

[2] Perrier had distinguished himself in reducing Fort d'Arguin in Africa. Le Page du Pratz, iii., p. 325. This author, as well as Dumont, eulogizes him, ii., pp. 123–5. See his Instructions. Gayarré, i., p. 224. He was made Lieut.-Gen'l for his services against the Natchez. Le Page du Pratz, iii., 325. This year copper coin, struck for Louisiana, was made current, and not only legal tender, but any stipulation for payment in gold or silver made penal. Edict, Oct. 31, 1726. Gayarré, i., p. 228. This copper coin bore on one side two L en sautoir, and on the other, Colonies Françoises. It was struck at Rochelle. Dumont, ii., p. 55. For an account of the paper money previously issued, see Ib., p. 54.

1726. make war and distinguish himself at the expense of the Company. But when he received this letter, he had only too strong evidence to disprove these insulting suspicions, in an event which soon changed the minds of those whose advice had been taken rather than his. In the letter just mentioned, and written from New Orleans, he says: "I have not been astonished that the Company has been assured that troops are not needed in Louysiana, or presents for the Indians, to retain them as our allies; nevertheless, I have seen the men who maintained this absurdity, trembling to the very marrow of their bones, although there is less to be feared here than elsewhere."

In another letter, dated April 1st, in the same year, he adds one thing, which shows that he knew the Indians better than those who boasted most of their knowledge of them. Speaking of these Indians, he says: "We are sure of retaining their good will as long as we give them what they wish; but as they feel that we need them, they multiply their wants in such a way that the English and ourselves are the dupes of these savages, who are much less so than we." What he proceeds to say, that we shall not make them what they ought to be, till after we have thoroughly defeated them, is not, however, true, except when they have given grounds for so treating them; for nothing embitters them more than to make war on them without cause; but there are other means of controlling them. Mr. Perrier was not ignorant of them; and in fact remarks very justly in his previous letter, that the war in which he was engaged had convinced him that to escape the importunity of the Indians, who are always begging, you need only to pretend to do without them. "It is," says he, "the means to make them all wish to follow us. Then, if they are not satisfied, we can tell them that they were not invited. Although it is necessary to bind them to us by presents to avoid war, you must never so far reckon on their fidelity as to think yourself safe from insult."

However, both those who depreciated Perrier with the Company, and Perrier himself, either did not know or did not sufficiently consider that Christianity alone can avert

1726.

from us the dangers to be apprehended from the Indians. The former judged of the Louysiana Indians by those of Canada, where we have seen the Abénaquis and all the Indians domiciliated in that colony enter zealously and heartily, often very disinterestedly, into all that was asked of them, and they did not consider that Christianity alone had brought them to this disposition; the Commandant-General, who had never known any Indians except those whom he had to deal with, did not sufficiently understand that religion, if they could be made to appreciate our Holy Mysteries, would gradually correct the faults of which he complained.

Be that as it may, the tranquillity enjoyed in Louysiana since peace had been granted to the Natchez and Chickasaws, was but a delusive calm which lulled the inhabitants, while there was gathering around them a storm, whose most disastrous effects were averted only by mere chance, saving the country from becoming in a single day the tomb of all the French; but which was fatal indeed to those on whom it burst, and who had no time to shield themselves from it.

Indian conspiracy against the French.

For several years past the Chickasaws, at the instigation of some English,[1] had formed the design of so extirpating the whole colony of Louysiana, that not a single Frenchman should remain. They had managed their scheme with such secrecy that the Illinois, the Acansas and the Tonicas, to whom they had not ventured to impart it, aware of their tried attachment to us, had not the slightest suspicion. All the other tribes joined it; each was to fall on all the settlers marked out for it, and all were to strike the same day and the same hour. Even the Tchactas, (Choctaws,) the most numerous nation on this continent, and at all times our allies, had been won over, at least those on the east, who are called the Great Nation; those on the west, or Little Nation, had taken no part in it, but the conspirators long preserved the se-

[1] As to English intrigues, see 1727. Gayarré, i., p. 232. Baron Perrier to the Minister, Nov. 15, to the same, Ib., p. 254.

1729. cret, and it was only by chance that they discovered it, when already too late to warn all the settlers.

How it was thwarted.

Perrier, learning that the former had had some difficulty with Diron d'Artaguette, King's-lieutenant and commandant at Fort Maubile, invited the chiefs of the whole nation to meet him at New Orleans, with the prospect of giving them complete satisfaction as to all their complaints. They came, and after explanations given by them on the matter which had summoned them, they told the Commandant-General that the nation was delighted at his sending an officer to reside in their country, and at his inviting them to come and see him. They said no more, but returned strongly inclined: 1st. To break their word with the Chickasaws, to whom they had promised to destroy all the settlements depending on Fort Maubile. 2nd. To act so as to enable the Natchez to execute their project. This the Natchez have since reproached them to their face in presence of the French, without their venturing to deny it. We have never doubted that their design was to force us to call upon them, and by this means, profit by what we would give them to secure their co-operation, and by the booty they would take from the Natchez.

Treachery of the Choctaws and confidence of the French.

The Commandant-General was thus unconsciously on the point of seeing one portion of the colony destroyed by enemies whom he did not mistrust, and betrayed by allies on whom he supposed he could depend, and who were in fact one of his great resources, but who wished to profit by our misfortunes. Moreover, it was all the easier for those whom the Chickasaws had won over, to succeed in their project, as no French settlement had any defence against a surprise and sudden attack. There were forts indeed, in some places, but except that at Maubile, they were only stockades, two thirds of which were decayed, and had they been in a state of defence, they could protect from the fury of the Indians only a small number of the nearest dwellings. Everywhere, too, men lay in perfect security, which would have enabled these savages to massacre all the French, even in the best-guarded places,

as happened on the 28th of November at the Natchez, in the manner about to be described: 1729.

All those settled at Natchez killed or taken by the Indians.

Mr. de Chepar, who commanded at that post, had some little difficulty with the Indians;[1] but they apparently carried their dissimulation so far as to persuade him that the French had no more faithful allies. He was in fact so little distrustful, that when on the 27th a vague rumor spread that the Natchez were plotting something against us, he put in irons seven settlers who had come to ask his permission to assemble and take up arms to prevent a surprise.[2] He even carried his confidence so far as to receive thirty Indians into the fort, and as many in and around his house. The others were scattered in the houses of the settlers and the workshops of the mechanics, two or three leagues above and below their village.

The day set for the execution of the general plot had not yet come, but two things induced the Natchez to anticipate it. The first was the arrival just then of some batteaux well stocked with goods for the garrison of that and the Yazoo post, as well as for several settlers, and that they wished to seize them before they were distributed; the second was, that the commandant had received a visit from the Messrs Kolly, father and son, whose concession was at no great distance, and from several other persons of consequence, for they saw at once that by pretending to get up a hunt, to furnish Mr. de Chepar wherewith to regale his guests, they could all arm without exciting any suspicion. They made the proposal to the commandant, who accepted it cheerfully, and they at once proceeded to trade with the settlers to obtain guns, balls and powder, which they paid for on the spot.

---

[1] Dumont writes Chopart. Le Page du Pratz, Chépart.

The little difficulty consisted in his seizing one Indian's ground and cabin, and then ordering the Great Sun to abandon their great village, which he wished for his own use. Dumont, ii., p. 131. Le Page, iii., p. 232.

[2] Le Page du Pratz, iii., p. 253. Dumont mentions only two, Macé and Papin, ii., p. 140. Le Page du Pratz says that the first put in irons was a soldier, sent by the Female Sun, Bras Piqué, a strong friend of the French, to warn Chépart, iii., p. 242–253.

1729. This done, early on Monday, the 28th, they scattered through the dwellings, announcing that they were about to start for the hunt, careful to outnumber the French everywhere. They then sang the calumet in honor of the commandant and his company, after which each returned to his post, and a moment later, at a signal of three musket-shots fired successively at the door of Chepar's quarters,[1] they began the massacre at the same time everywhere. The commandant and the Kollys were the first killed; there was no resistance except at the house of Mr. de la Loire des Ursins,[2] Chief Commissary of the India Company, where there were eight men.[3] They fought well; eight Natchez were killed there, and six Frenchmen, the other two escaped. Mr. de la Loire had just mounted his horse; at the first noise he heard, he endeavored to return to his house, but was intercepted by a party of Indians, against whom he held out for some time, till he fell dead, pierced by many wounds, after killing four Natchez. Thus these savages lost at this point twelve men; but that was all their treachery cost them.[4]

Before executing their plot, they had made sure of several negroes, among whom were two commanders. These had persuaded the rest that under the Indians they would be free; that our women and children should become their slaves, and that there was nothing to fear from the French of the other posts, as the massacre would be carried out simultaneously everywhere. It seems, however, that the secret had been confided only to a small number, for fear of its taking wind. Be that as it may, two hundred men perished in this way almost in an instant. Of all the French who were at this post, the

[1] Chopart's house is said to have been just below Fort Rosalie, on a point jutting out into the river. Louisiana Historical Collections, v., p. 71.

[2] The eldest of the brothers, mentioned in the preceding Book. He had been in command at Natchez. The unfortunate appointment of his successor, enabled the Natchez to succeed. Perrier to the Minister, Mar. 18, 1730. Gayarré, i., p. 242.

[3] Dumont says three men and one woman.

[4] Le Page, iii., pp. 255–6. Dumont, ii., pp. 134–144, says that Chopart was not killed till late; as the Natchez nobles despised him, they sent a Puant chief to brain him with a club.

most populous of all, only about twenty escaped, and five or six negroes,[1] most of them wounded. One hundred and fifty children, eighty women, and almost as many negroes, were taken.[2] The Jesuit Father du Poisson and Mr. du Codere, commandant at the Yazoos, who happened to be at the Natchez, also perished. 1729.

The former had started from his Arkansas mission for some business that required his presence at New Orleans. He arrived at the Natchez quite late on the 26th, intending to set out again the next day, after saying mass. Unfortunately for him, the Capuchin father, who exercised parochial functions at that place, was absent, and Father du Poisson was requested to sing high mass and preach, it being the first Sunday of Advent, and he consented. In the afternoon, as he was on the point of embarking, he was informed that there were some sick persons at the point of death; he attended them, administered the last sacraments to some, and deferred one till next day, as his case was not so urgent, and it was already quite late. The next day he said mass, and then carried the Viaticum to the sick man, to whom he had promised it, and it was after performing this duty of charity that he was encountered by a chief, who seized him around the body, threw him to the ground, and chopped off his head with an axe. Mr. du Codere, who happened to be near, had already drawn his sword to defend him, when another Indian, whom he had not seen, shot him down.[3]

During this massacre, the Sun, or Great Chief of the Natchez, was calmly seated under the tobacco shed of the India Company. The head of the commandant was first brought to him, then those of the leading Frenchmen,

---

1 Dumont, Mem., ii., pp. 148–152.

2 They killed Madame Papin, Mme Macé, and some others. Dumont, ii., p. 153. Dumont's wife was taken, and his account is based in part on her statements.

3 Lettres Edifiantes—Kip's Jesuit Missions, pp. 286–7. Le Page du Pratz, iii., p. 257. Father Paul du Poisson belonged to the Province of Champagne, and had entered the order in 1712. He came to Louisiana in 1726, and was killed at Natchez, Nov. 28, 1729. F. Martin's List in Carayon's Chaumonot, pp. 207, 214.

1729. which he caused to be arranged around the first; then all the others in heaps. The bodies were left unburied, to be devoured by the dogs and birds of prey. These savages spared only two Frenchmen, who might be of some service to them; one was a tailor, and the other a carpenter.[1] They did not ill treat the negro and Indian slaves who surrendered without offering any resistance; but they ripped up the pregnant women, and butchered almost all those who had children at the breast, because they annoyed them by their cries and tears. All the other women were made slaves, and treated with the utmost indignity.

As soon as they were sure that there were no more men left in the country, they began to plunder the houses, stores, and the boats in the port. The best treated of all were the negroes, because they wished to sell them to the English in Carolina; and to dispel any hope the women and other slaves might entertain of ever recovering their liberty, they assured them that what had just occurred before their eyes, had happened all through the colony, and that not a single Frenchman was left in Louysiana, where the English would at once come to take their place. Some had, nevertheless, escaped to the woods, where they suffered greatly from cold and hunger. There was one who at night ventured to come out, in order to warm himself at a house which he saw. As he approached, he heard the voices of Indians, and deliberated whether to enter; he made up his mind at last to do so, preferring a violent and speedier death to the slower one which seemed inevitable in his actual condition. But he was agreeably surprised by the welcome the Indians gave him. They were Yazoos, who, after comforting him, gave him food and covering, as well as a periagua to escape to New Orleans. Their chief even commissioned him to assure Mr. Perrier that he had nothing to fear from his tribe, which would always remain faithfully attached to the French, and that he was about to start with his troop to warn all the

[1] Dumont says le Beau, a tailor, and Mayeux a carter, (chartier,) whom they employed in removing the French goods to their village, ii., pp. 155–6. Le Page du Pratz, iii., p. 260 corresponds.

French whom he might meet coming down the river, to be on their guard.[1] 1729.

This man found the capital in great alarm; news of the massacre had already reached it by the first who had escaped, and great fear was entertained for the French settlers among the Yazoos. On his testimony they were somewhat relieved, but this did not last long. On the 11th of December, the Jesuit Father Souel, who was missionary to the Yazoos, then mingled in the same village with the Corrois and Offogoulas, when returning in the evening from visiting the chief of the Yazoos, received several musket-shots as he was crossing a river, and expired on the spot. His murderers at once ran to his cabin to plunder it. His negro, recently baptized, and who lived quite piously, attempted to defend himself with a woodcutter's knife, and even wounded an Indian, but he was at once pierced with thrusts.

The same happens at the Yazoos.

Father Souel was much beloved by these Indians, but they rebelled at his constantly reproaching them with the infamous sin which brought destruction on Sodom, and to which they were greatly addicted; and there is every probability that this was the main cause of his death; for although the Yazoos and Corrois had already resolved to exterminate all the French, the very men who had slain the missionary reproached themselves with his death as soon as their blood cooled. They however soon recovered their natural ferocity, and began to cry that as the Chief of the Prayer was dead, no Frenchman must be spared.

Causes of the death of Father Souel.

Early the next morning they proceeded to the fort, which was only a league from their village. On seeing them approach it was supposed that they were coming to chant the calumet to the Chevalier des Roches, who commanded in the absence of du Codere; for although it

Fidelity of the Offogoulas.

[1] For this massacre, the contemporary accounts are Perrier's dispatch, March 18, 1730, in Gayarré, i., pp. 242–251. Father le Petit to Father d'Avaugour, July 12, 1730, in the Lettres Edifiantes—Kip's Jesuit Missions, pp. 265–312. Carayon, Documents Inédits, xiv., pp. 22–4. Adair, History of American Indians, pp. 353–4.

1729. is only forty leagues by water and fifteen by land from the Natchez to the Yazoos, no information had reached the latter post of what had occurred nearly a fortnight before in the former. The Indians were accordingly allowed to enter the fort, and when it was least expected, they rushed on the French, who were only seventeen in all; they had not even time to attempt to defend themselves, and not one escaped. These savages spared the lives only of four women and five children, whom they made slaves. One of Father Souel's murderers at once put on his cassock, and in this attire proceeded to announce to the Natchez the massacre of all the French settlers on their river.[1] The Corrois joined them in this expedition. The Offogoulas were then on a hunt; on their return they were strongly urged to enter the plot; but they steadily refused, and withdrew to the Tonicas, whom they knew to be of all the Indians the most inviolably attached to the French.

A missionary attacked by the Yazoos and saved almost miraculously.

Some suspicion of this last calamity was already entertained at New Orleans, when the arrival of the Jesuit Father Doutreleau,[2] missionary to the Illinois, dispelled all further doubts. This religious had taken the period of his Indians' winter hunt to come down to the capital, and

1730. there arrange some affairs connected with his mission. On the first day of the year 1730, he wished to say mass at Father Souel's, being ignorant of his death; but as he feared that he would not get there till after noon, he resolved to celebrate the Holy Mysteries at the mouth of the Yazoo River. While he was making ready, a periagua of Indians arrived at the same spot; when asked to what nation they belonged, they replied that they were

[1] Father le Petit to Father d'Avaugour, July 12, 1730, in the Lettres Edifiantes—Kip's Jesuit Missions, pp. 289–290; Carayon, Documents Inédits, xiv., p. 23. Dumont, Memoires, ii., pp. 163–4. Le Page du Pratz, iii., p. 264. Father John Souel belonged to the Province of Champagne, arrived in 1726, and was killed December 11, 1729.

[2] Father Stephen d'Outreleau was born Oct. 11, 1693, entered the Society in the Province of Champagne July 27, 1715, came to Louisiana in 1727, and returned to France in 1747. Martin in Carayon, Doc. Inédits, xiv., pp. 121, 128.

Yazoos, friends of the French, and at the same time they cordially offered provisions to the companions of the missionary. A moment after, the latter perceived some wild geese flying overhead; the Canadians never resist the temptation of firing when they see game; these voyageurs had only two guns loaded; they fired both at the geese, and as the father was all vested to begin mass, they did not think of reloading. 1730.

The Indians noted it well, and took their places behind the French, as if they wished to hear the mass, although they were not Christians. As the priest was saying the Kyrie eleison, they fired. Father Doutreleau feeling himself wounded in the right arm, and seeing one of his men fall dead at his feet, knelt down to receive in that posture the death-blow, which seemed inevitable. In fact, the Indians fired three times at him, almost at the point of the muzzle, but nevertheless inflicted no new wound. Then, full of confidence in Divine Providence, whose protection was so clearly shown, he took his chalice and paten, and, attired as he was in his priestly vestments, ran to the spot where his periagua was. His two surviving men had already jumped in, and believing him dead or unable to escape from the Indians, had pulled off.

The missionary waded out to reach them, and as he got into the periagua, having turned his head to see whether he was pursued, received a charge of duck-shot in the mouth. Most of the shot flattened against his teeth, and some entered his gums. He escaped with this, and undertook to steer the periagua; his two men, one of whom had his leg broken by a musket-ball, rowing with all their might. The Indians pursued them for more than an hour, keeping up a constant fire on them; but seeing pursuit useless, which surprised the missionary still more, they regained the shore. It was afterwards ascertained that on arriving at their town, they boasted of having killed a Jesuit and all his boatmen.

Nor was it indeed without difficulty that they escaped, as long as their enemies kept up the stubborn chase; the

1730. two oarsmen were more than once tempted to give up, but encouraged by the missionary, they in turn alarmed the Indians, who, apparently having now neither powder nor balls, threw themselves down flat in their periagua whenever one of the two Frenchmen aimed at them an old musket, that was not even loaded, and they at last disappeared. Our party, delivered from this alarm, dressed their wounds as well as they could, then lightened their periagua by throwing overboard everything not absolutely needed, and keeping only a little raw pork for their subsistence.

On coming opposite Natchez, unconscious of what had occurred there, they ran in towards the landing, intending to rest there and have medical aid; but seeing the nearest houses burned or demolished, durst not land. Some Indians who had discovered them, in vain invited them to approach by making every demonstration of friendship; they passed on as quick as they could. Then the Indians fired several guns at them; but they were already out of reach. They intended also to pass the Bay of the Tonicas without stopping, but with all the exertion in their power, a periagua, sent out to reconnoitre, soon overhauled them. They gave themselves up for lost past all resource, till they heard French spoken in the periagua. Then they lay to, and they recovered entirely from their fright on seeing some Frenchmen who were in the boat.

They were taken ashore, where they found troops assembling to go and punish the Natchez. The officers lavished their attentions on Father Doutreleau, had his wounds dressed by the army surgeon, as well as that of his boatman, whose leg was broken, and after giving them rest and refreshment, they placed him and his two men on a periagua, which they were sending to New Orleans. He promised them to return and serve as their chaplain as soon as his wounds were healed:[1] he kept his word, and did not even wait till his perfect recovery before

[1] He reached New Orleans Jan'y 8, 1730. Perrier to the Minister in Gayarré, i., p. 247.

doing so.[1] But before entering on the account of the expedition prepared against the Natchez, we must describe the effect produced throughout the colony by the tidings of the massacre which these Indians had committed on so large a number of the French. 1730.

Activity of Perrier on hearing of the massacre at Natchez.

Mr. Perrier was informed of it on the second of December.[2] He at once dispatched the Sieur le Merveilleux, a Swiss captain, with a detachment to warn all the settlers on both sides of the river to be on their guard, and to throw up redoubts at intervals, in order to secure their slaves and cattle, and this was promptly executed. He then enjoined the same officer to observe closely the small tribes on the river, and to give arms to no Indians, except when and to whom he should direct. He at the same time dispatched a courier to summon to him two Choctaw chiefs, who were hunting on Lake Pontchartrain. The next day a periagua from Illinois reached New Orleans, bringing a Choctaw, who asked to speak to him in private. He admitted him at once, and this man told him that he was greatly affected by the death of the French, and would have prevented it had he not deemed a falsehood what some Chickasaws had told him, namely, that all the Indians were to destroy all the French settlements, and massacre all the men. "What prevented me," he added, "from crediting this story, was their stating that my tribe was in the plot; but Father, if you will let me go to my country, I will immediately return to render a good report of what I have done there."

How he is informed of the general plot against the French.

Mr. Perrier had no sooner left this Indian than others from the smaller tribes came to warn him to distrust the Choctaws, and he learned almost at the same time that two Frenchmen had been killed in the neighborhood of

---

He apparently went up to the camp at the Tonicas with Baron. Baron to the Minister, 10 April, 1730. Gayarré, i., p. 254. Kip, p. 294. As to his escape, see Father Le Petit's Letter of July 12, 1730, in Lettres Edifiantes; Kip's Jesuit Missions, pp. 291–2. Carayon, xiv., p. 23. Dumont, Memoires, ii., pp. 160–3; Le Page du Pratz, iii., p. 263.

[2] By the Sieur Ricard, store keeper, who escaped. Dumont, ii., pp. 149, 170.

1730. Maubile; that the perpetrators of the murder had not been discovered, but that throughout the district it was said openly that the Choctaws were to attack the fort and all the dwellings. The Commandant-General would gladly have concealed this news from the settlers, who were but too panic-stricken already; but it spread all over in less than no time, and the consternation became so great and so general that thirty Chaouachas, who lived below New Orleans, made the whole colony tremble; this obliged Mr. Perrier to send negroes and destroy them.

On the fifth he adopted the plan of sending the Saint Michael to France, to inform the Court and Company of the condition in which Louysiana was, and ask relief proportioned to its actual need. Two days after, one of the two Choctaw chiefs whom he had sent for, came to tell him that he had dispatched his letter to his nation, and invited all who were enemies of the Natchez to march against them, and that he advised him not to employ the smaller tribes, as he suspected them of being in concert with the Natchez. "I also suspect them," said Mr. Perrier, "but if they are in the plot, it is because they are convinced that you, too, are implicated; however, whether you are or not, I have given good orders everywhere, and I am very glad that you know that the secret has taken wind."

On the first day of January, uneasy at not receiving any dispatches from the Sieur Regis, who by his orders resided among the Choctaws, he dispatched the Sieur de Lusser, a Swiss captain, to ascertain the actual disposition of these Indians, and on the fourth he learned that the Natchez had gone to sing the calumet to them; this confirmed all his suspicions, and threw him into great perplexity.[1] But on the 16th he received a letter from the the Sieur Regis, informing him that immediately after speaking to the Choctaws in his name, they had raised

[1] Perrier to the Minister, March 18, 1730. Gayarré, i., pp. 244–7. Le Petit, (Kip,) p. 295. Dumont, ii., p. 205, makes the attack on the Chaouachas after the Negro Plot, but is evidently wrong.

1730.

the death-cry; that afterwards seven hundred warriors had set out to attack the Natchez, and that a party of a hundred and fifty was to pass to the Yazoos, to intercept all the negroes and French prisoners, whom they wished to conduct to the Chickasaws. The next day he received letters from de Saint Denys, the commandant at the Natchitoches, about whom he was much concerned, as some Natchitoches were seen among the Natchez at the time of the massacre of the French; but he learned by these letters that the wisdom and vigilance of that officer had saved him from the disaster threatening his post.

Discouragement of the whole colony.

He had, however, great difficulty in reassuring the settlers, whom the sad tidings brought in from all parts, almost all with no foundation, but an alarmed imagination, had hurled at once from excessive confidence to as excessive discouragement. He himself felt less sanguine, as he was fully informed that the smaller tribes had been gained by the Chickasaws, and that if the Natchez had not anticipated the day fixed for the execution of the plot, they would have acted simultaneously with them. He also discovered that what had induced the Natchez to precipitate their meditated blow, was their learning that at the very time that the first Choctaw chiefs who had come to New Orleans on his invitation, were on their way thither, a hundred and twenty horses loaded with English goods had entered their country. The Natchez were convinced that these two circumstances were the most favorable to ensure the success of the project; that the two Choctaw chiefs were going to delude the Commandant-General by feigned protestations of fidelity, and that their nation, seeing that an alliance with the English would bring plenty into their country, would not hesitate to keep the promise they had given to fill all on the Maubile River with fire and blood.

Conduct of the Choctaws.

But they were deceived: the Choctaws, from the moment they received the general's invitation through the Sieur Regis, began by declaring that they would not receive the goods from the English till they had learned

1730. what their Father wished to tell them; and on the return of their deputies, they resolved to follow exactly the line of policy which they had long before adopted. Several years before they had wished to destroy the Natchez, and the French had prevented them; they had pretended to enter the general conspiracy only to involve us with our enemies, to whom we had granted peace in spite of them, and thus force us to apply to them to rid ourselves of them, and thus at the same time profit by the spoils of the Natchez and our liberality.

Perrier had not yet well unravelled all the meshes of this self-interested policy, and all that then seemed to him certain, was, that but for the Western Choctaws, the general conspiracy would have taken effect. He accordingly did not hesitate to employ them to obtain redress of the Natchez, cost what it might. Fortunately two of the Company's vessels arrived at New Orleans in the midst of all this, and he did not wish to defer any longer his march against the enemy, convinced that he could not too soon involve the Choctaws, recall the smaller tribes to our interest, or at least overawe them and reassure the settlers. Yet he felt that he ran some risk by beginning the war with such slender forces. "Do not estimate my forces," he said in one of his letters, (March 18, 1720,) "by the step I have taken in attacking the enemy; necessity compelled me. I saw consternation everywhere, and fear increased day by day. In this position I concealed the number of our foes, and treated the idea of a general conspiracy as chimerical, an invention of the Natchez to prevent our acting against them. If I had been at liberty to adopt the most prudent course, I should have held myself on the defensive, and waited for reinforcements from France, lest I should be reproached with having sacrificed two hundred Frenchmen of the five or six hundred whom I may have, for the defence of the lower part of the river. The event has shown that we must not always adopt what is seemingly the most prudent course. We were in a position where violent remedies were required, and it was

necessary to inspire alarm, if we could not do harm. Chance has permitted us to do both, and come honorably out of an affair, the success of which has given us time to understand our position. We have recovered more than two hundred women and children,[1] all our negroes, and brought our enemies to the necessity of abandoning their forts and their lands. If we could have kept our Indians two or three days longer, not a single Natchez would have escaped; their destruction is merely deferred by the measures that I have taken. I do not regard them as our most cruel enemies; the Chickasaws really are; they are entirely devoted to the English, and have managed all the intrigue of the general conspiracy, although they are at peace with us. I have avoided urging the Choctaws to make war on them till I received reinforcements and orders from France, although they asked nothing better; but they are so self-seeking, that it would cost us much to get them to make a move, which I feel convinced they will make of their own accord, from grounds of dissatisfaction of their own."[2]

1730.

They arm against the Natchez.

As on the plan adopted by the General, the most urgent point was to make sure of the Choctaws and other nations nearest to the Fort of Maubile, he made known the first tidings of the Natchez disaster as soon as he received them, to Mr. Diron,[3] who commanded at that post, and by a second letter, which was handed to that officer on the 16th of December, he directed him to sound the Choctaws, to see whether he could depend upon them. The difficulty was to find a man willing to run the risk of putting himself at the mercy of these savages, whose disposition was then doubtful enough, and to whom we could as yet only make promises. Mr. le Sueur,[4] who had

[1] Perrier says 54 women and children, and 100 negroes. Gayarré, i., p. 249.

[2] This is not an extract, but a summary. See dispatch in Gayarré, i., pp. 243–253. As to the missions among the Choctaws and their influence, see Carayon, Documents Inédits, xiv., pp. 17–8.

[3] Diron d'Artaguette died at Cap François in St. Domingo, where he was King's Lieutenant. Charlevoix, Journal, p. 436.

[4] See ante, iv., p. 273*n.*; vi., p. 13*n.*

1730. come when quite young from his native Canada to Louysiana, and had grown up among these tribes, counted enough on the friendship which all the Indians, and these especially, had ever shown him to offer to go to them. His offer was accepted, and he set out from Fort Maubile on the nineteenth. With great toil he visited all the villages; he was well received everywhere, and had no great difficulty in forming the corps of seven hundred warriors of whom I have spoken, and whom he led straight against the Natchez.

On his side, Perrier sent up to the Tonicas two of the Company's vessels. He sent overland warning to all the posts, as far as the Illinois, of what had happened and what he intended to do. He dug a ditch around New Orleans; he placed barracks at its four angles; he organized militia companies for the defence of the city, and as there was more to fear for the settlements and concessions than for the capital, he threw up entrenchments everywhere, and erected forts in the most exposed points; he finally prepared to go and take command of his little army which was assembling in the Bay of the Tonicas. But it was represented to him that his presence was absolutely required at New Orleans; that we were not yet perfectly sure of the Choctaws, and that there was even a fear that the negroes, if these Indians declared against us, would join them in the hope of escaping from slavery, as some had done at Natchez. He accordingly judged it best to confide the expedition to the Chevalier de Loubois, Major of New Orleans, whose valor and experience he knew.[1]

Disposition of several Indian tribes.

The first effect of his preparations was to restore to our side the small Mississippi tribes, who had abandoned it, as Mr. le Sueur regained those around Maubile. We were sure of the affection and fidelity of the Illinois, Akansas,

[1] Diron d'Artaguette to the Minister. Gayarré, i., p. 258. He reproaches Loubois for losing four weeks here in inaction. Le Page du Pratz, iii., p. 267, says he did not think himself strong enough to attack the Natchez without the aid of the Choctaws. He speaks highly of Loubois, and ascribes his inefficiency to ignorance of the country.

Offogoulas and Tonicas; and soon, as I have said, of the Natchitoches, and they all gave striking proofs of it in the course of this war. On the other hand, the Natchez seemed to behold without alarm the storm gathering against them. They did not at first despair of winning over the Tonicas, and on the 9th of December sent to them the Tioux, a little tribe long domiciliated among them, to offer them some of the plunder taken from the French, in order to win them over to their side. They did not succeed in this, but killed two straggling Frenchmen whom they found. 1729-30.

The French army assembles at the Tonicas.

On the 10th, the Sieur le Merveilleux entered that bay with his detachment and some Frenchmen who had joined him. He entrenched for fear of surprise. The following days all the troops arrived, and on the 18th the Chevalier de Loubois entered it with twenty-five additional soldiers.[1] He found the whole army encamped, well entrenched, and in good condition. He had two days previously detached the Sieur Mexplex with five men to obtain tidings of the enemy, and, the better to ascertain their strength, he had ordered him to throw out some proposals of peace; but as he was on the point of landing, he received a volley of musketry, which killed three of his men, leaving him and two others prisoners. The next day the Natchez sent one of these latter to Mr. de Loubois to make proposals also on their side, but they assumed a haughty tone, which revealed great confidence and great contempt for us.

Insolent proposals of the Natchez.

They asked in the first place that we should give as hostage the Sieur Brouttin, who had commanded among them, and the Great Chief of the Tonicas. They then specified, with great detail, all the goods they required for the ransom of the women, children and slaves, whom they had in their hands; and although their demands were exorbitant, they seemed to suppose that we would be only too happy to accept them. It was afterwards ascertained that, adding treachery to insolence, their design was to

[1] Le Page du Pratz, iii., p. 265.

1729-30. butcher the French who brought this ransom, and then sell their prisoners to the English. The soldier was retained and no answer given. They took their revenge the same day by burning with more than savage barbarity the Sieur Mexplex and the soldier left with him.[1]

The Choctaws gain a great victory over them.

On the 27th, le Sueur arrived at Natchez with the Choctaws, and began the attack almost as soon as he came up. He apparently did not yet know that our army was at the Bay of the Tonicas, or was unable to control the selfish impetuosity of his Indians,[2] who wished to have the best part of the booty, and also profit by the prisoners whom they delivered, for the sequel leads us to infer this. Be that as it may, they charged the enemy so fiercely that they killed eighty men, took sixteen women prisoners,[3] delivered fifty-one French women and children, the two mechanics whom the Natchez had spared, and a hundred and fifty negroes and negresses. They would even have pushed their victory further, for it had cost them only two men killed, and some wounded, had not those of our negroes, whom the Natchez had won over, taken up arms on their side, and prevented the Choctaws from carrying off their powder; this would have compelled the enemy to surrender or fly. There can be no doubt that, had this attack been concerted with the Chevalier de Loubois, not a Natché would have escaped.[4]

I cannot exactly ascertain what detained that commandant so long inactive at the Tonicas.[5] He has been

---

[1] Perrier to the Minister, Mar. 18, 1730. Gayarré, i., p. 248. Father Le Petit, (Kip,) p. 295-7. Le Page du Pratz, iii., pp. 275-280.

[2] There is evident confusion as to this date. D'Artaguette to the Minister, Jan'y 10, 1731, (Gayarré, p. 269,) makes it Feb. 27; Dumont, (ii., p. 181,) and Le Page du Pratz, iii., p. 283, make them arrive in February, Dumont says, to the number of 1,600, under de Lery, though Le Page says Le Sueur; but Baron's Journal, (Gayarré, i., p. 255,) under date of Feb. 8, and Perrier's, under date of Jan. 31, (Ib., p. 249,) show that it was Jan'y 27, 1730, as Father Le Petit gives it, (Kip) p. 296).

[3] D'Artaguette says 60 killed, 18 taken.

[4] Perrier to the Minister, Gayarré, i., p. 249. This attack was near the Bayou Sainte Catherine.

[5] D'Artaguette, (Jan'y 10, 1731, says he staid to watch the Choctaws, believing in a general conspiracy. Gayarré, i., p. 269.

1730.

severely blamed for it, and Perrier, in endeavoring to shield him, drew upon himself a part of the censure of some men, whose authority should not, I think, prevail over his. And the misfortune is, that some of those who were loudest in condemning the manner in which the Natchez war was managed, were not more fortunate in the Chickasaw war, and committed nearly the same faults with which they reproached Mr. Perrier and those commanding under him, if faults they were.

De Loubois besieges the Natchez in their forts.

Be that as it may, de Loubois on the 2nd of February marched from the Bay of the Tonicas with two hundred men and some field-pieces; on the 8th he arrived at the Natchez and encamped around the temple. On the 12th the cannon were placed in battery before one of the two Indian forts, and as it was supposed that these preparations, especially after the defeat they had received, would induce them to submit to all exacted of them, they were notified that they might still avoid their total ruin by this submission; but they were found more resolute than ever to defend themselves.[1] Accordingly de Loubois opened next morning with seven cannon; but they were two hundred and fifty fathoms from the fort, and they were so badly handled that, after six hours' constant fire, they had not dislodged a single palisade, which put the Choctaws in a very bad humor, as they had been assured that a large breach would be made in two hours. On the other hand, the insolence and avidity of these Indians, whom nothing could satisfy, and who wasted a part of the munitions given them, disgusted the French commandant as much as the desperate resistance of the Natchez.

On the 15th he again wished to try whether they had not become more tractable; he sent them an interpreter

---

[1] Baron, Journal, (Gayarré, i., pp. 255–6.) Diron d'Artaguette to Minister. Ib., p. 259. Same to same, Jan'y 10, 1731. Ib., p. 269. French supposes the fort to have been on the bluff, just below the bend of St. Catharine's Creek, near the Lynwood plantation. Louisiana Hist. Coll., v. p. 93 n. See Adair, p. 354.

1730. with a flag to summon them; but they received this envoy with a volley of musketry, which alarmed him so that in his fear he threw aside his flag. It would have fallen into the enemy's hands, if a young soldier had not had the courage to go and recover it, exposing himself to the fire of the besieged; an exploit which on his return to camp won his promotion to the rank of sergeant. The same day the Natchez made a sortie, with a view to surprise de Loubois, who was quartered in their temple, but it failed. During the night of the 19th–20th, a trench was opened two hundred and eighty fathoms from the fort, and on the 21st the cannonade was renewed. "If the opening of the trench was so long delayed, this delay," says Mr. Perrier, in one of his letters, "was caused by the ill-will of our soldiers and some other Frenchmen, who thereby prevented the entire destruction of the Natchez."

They make a sortie and clear the trench. They are repulsed by the Chevalier d'Artaguette.

On the 22nd, these Indians made a second sortie, to the number of three hundred,[1] attacking in three places; they surprised, in the trench, an outpost of thirty men and two officers, who all took flight, imagining that they were attacked simultaneously by the Natchez and the Choctaws; they were ready to seize the cannon, when the Chevalier d'Artaguette came up, and although he had only five men with him, he repulsed the enemy, and recovered the trench. We had only one man killed that day. The same day de Loubois ordered forty soldiers, as many Indians, and some negroes, to storm the two forts the next day; but this was not carried out. On the 24th, a battery of four four pounders was planted within a hundred and eighty fathoms, and at the same time they threatened to reduce the besieged to powder, if they did not surrender the prisoners they held. They immediately sent back the wife of the Sieur Desnoyers, to whom they confided their proposals. She was retained and no answer sent.[2]

---

1 Baron, Journal, p. 257, says 200.

2 D'Artaguette to the Minister. Gayarré, i., p. 260. The officer named was his nephew. Baron says nothing of it.

1730.

What saved the besieged.

Perrier pretends that what obliged de Loubois to rest satisfied with saving the prisoners still in the hands of the Indians, without attempting an assault, was, in the first place, because he could not depend upon his troops, especially after seeing them abandon the trench, as they did on the 22nd; in the second place, that the Choctaws were suspected of a design of betraying us; thirdly, that the enemy had spread the report that the Chickasaws and English were coming to their assistance. Meanwhile, on the 25th, the fort most closely invested[1] hoisted a flag. A Choctaw chief[2] at once advanced with a party of his men, to speak to the besieged. "Do you remember, or have you ever seen," said he, "that Indians ever kept the field in such numbers before a fort for two months? Judge by this our zeal for the French. Hence it is useless for you, a mere handful of men compared with us, to refuse any longer obstinately to give up the prisoners whom you hold, for if the French were to fire all their cannon, you would soon be in powder. For our part, know that we are resolved to keep you blockaded here till you submit to what is required of you, if we have to plant grain and settle here."

Perrier assures us, in his letters, that in this parley, or in some other interview, the Natchez reproached the Choctaws in the presence of the French, with having themselves entered the general conspiracy, of which they gave all the particulars.[3]

They give up the French prisoners and the siege is raised.

The fact is, that these Indians hoisted their flag only to make known that they consented to give up the prisoners; but they at the same time declared that we must be satisfied with that, and before all else, the army with its cannon must withdraw to the bank of the river; if not that, they would burn all their prisoners. This last consideration determined de Loubois to do what was asked of him, yet without abandoning his design to prevent the

[1] Fort la Farine. D'Artaguette, p. 260.

[2] Alibamon Mengo.

[3] Dispatch of March 18, 1730. Gayarré, i., pp. 250–3.

1730. escape of the Natchez. On the 25th, the prisoners were given up to the Choctaws, and the army withdrew to the bluff on the riverside, having had during the whole siege only nine men killed and wounded.[1] On the night of the 28th–29th, the Natchez, having succeeded in outwitting the French who had been appointed to watch them, escaped, and this was perceived only when it was too late to pursue them.[2] Thus the sole fruit of this expedition was the rescue of the prisoners, who had next to be ransomed from the Choctaws,[3] and the erection of a fort on the very spot to which they had retired. The Chevalier d'Artaguette,[4] who had extremely distinguished himself in all the engagements, was left as commandant with a garrison, in order to secure the navigation of the river.

It is admitted that the soldiers acted very badly at the siege; that fifteen negroes, who were put under arms, fought like heroes, and that if all the others could have been armed and put in the place of the soldiers, they would have succeeded in storming the besieged works. The settlers, commanded by d'Arembourg and de Laye, also did very well.[5] They cheerfully undertook all the labors, and whatever else was ordered. "These creoles," says Mr. Perrier, "will be good soldiers as soon as they are drilled. In fine, the Natchez were reduced to the last extremity; two days more and we should have seen them with their necks in the halter; but we were every moment on the point of being abandoned by the Choc-

---

[1] Perrier, in one of his letters, says we lost fifteen. *Charlevoix.* He says in the siege and in the detachments. See Gayarré, i., p. 250. Diron d'Artaguette, (Gayarré, i., p. 261,) says 8.

[2] Father le Petit, (Kip,) p. 298 Le Page du Pratz, who describes this siege, vol. iii., pp. 286–292, ridicules the idea of their escaping unperceived with their arms, household utensils, wives and children, and insinuates that the French gave them the opportunity.

[3] They were obtained with great difficulty and at a very high ransom. Dumont, ii., p. 189. Le Page du Pratz, iii., pp. 293–4.

[4] Dumont and Le Page du Pratz say the Baron de Creant, or Crenet.

[5] Dumont's account of this siege is vague. Memoires, ii., pp. 181–8. Most of the families that escaped the massacre, settled at Pointe Coupée. Ib., p. 192. The orphans were taken by the Ursuline nuns. Father le Petit, (Kip's Jesuit Missions,) p. 301.

1730.

taws, who grew very impatient, and their departure would have exposed the French to receive a check, and to behold their women, children and slaves burned, as their enemies threatened."

Insolence of the Choctaws.

Before resolving to make war on the Natchez, the Choctaws had gone to them to enter into some negotiation with them, and they had met with a strange enough reception. They found these Indians and their horses decked with chasubles and antependiums; many wore patens around their necks; drank and made others drink brandy out of the chalices and ciboriums. In a word, they found nothing in the chapel that they had not put to the most profane and sacrilegious use. This highly pleased the Choctaws, who in the sequel, securing this booty, renewed the profanation committed by their enemies, and it was found impossible to rescue all from their hands. Moreover, had these savages rendered the French all the service in their power, by acting in concert with them, their evil disposition always made them most odious to the colony. "There had never yet been seen in all America," wrote a missionary, eye-witness of everything then occurring, "Indians more insolent, more ferocious, more disgusting, more importunate, more insatiable."

However, they were still needed, and had to be managed. The Natchez were not destroyed; they could in future be regarded only as irreconcilable enemies, and it was to be expected that as long as they subsisted, they would do us through themselves and through the enemies whom they would endeavor to raise up against us, all the evil possible to savages, who had no terms to make. The Chickasaws did not yet appear, but we were conscious that they were the authors of the whole trouble, and their engagements with the English left no doubt but that they would be powerfully supported by the latter whenever they thought fit to lift the mask. The sequel only justified these suspicions.

Among the negroes recovered from the Natchez, were some of those who had taken part against us, and these

1730. were punished; the three most guilty were given up to the Choctaws, who burned them with an inhumanity which gave all the other negroes such a horror of the Indians as to make them more docile and more faithful.[1] The Yazoos, Corrois and Tioux, were not more fortunate than the Natchez. The Akansas fell on them and made a perfect massacre; of the two former nations, only fifteen Indians remained, who hastened to join the Natchez; the Tioux were all killed to a man.

The Chickasaws in vain tempt the fidelity of our allies.

About the same time it was discovered that the Chickasaws, after a useless attempt to draw the Akansas and Tonicas into the general conspiracy, had applied also, but with as little success, to the Illinois; these Indians replying curtly, that as they were all Christians, the Chickasaws must never expect to detach them from the French; that they would always place themselves between them and their enemies, who would have to trample over their dead bodies before they could touch one of the French. They soon after learned what had been done at the Natchez and Yazoos, and at once two troops of Mitchigamias and Kaskasquias, led by the two head chiefs of those two Illinois tribes, descended to New Orleans, to bewail the missionaries who had perished in that massacre, and offer the General all who depended on them to avenge the French. Mr. Perrier gave them audience with much pomp, and they spoke as Christians and faithful allies, in a manner that charmed all. Nor did they edify the whole city less by their piety and the correctness of their conduct, and they took leave of the General, promising him to guard well their own country, and all the upper part of the river.

The English as unsuccessful.

Mr. Perrier next learned that the English had earnestly exhorted the Choctaws to declare against us, and supported their solicitations by large presents, and he wrote to the Minister that, placed as he was, he needed a prompt assistance; that the employment of Indians would cost

[1] Father le Petit, Letter, July 12, 1730. (Kip,) p. 301.

much more than the maintenance of troops; that if you employed these Indians, you would be always at the mercy of their caprice and inconstancy; that they got the idea that we applied to them only because we were incapable of making war, and so prevalent had this opinion become among all these nations, that the smallest, petty tribe regarded itself as the bulwark and protection of the colony. That after five or six years, the number of troops might be gradually decreased, as during that time the creoles would multiply and be trained; that then we should have even more Indians ready to side with us when they saw that we no longer needed them. 1730.

For some time the Natchez had not been heard of, but at last tidings came that they were renewing their raids; that they had surprised ten Frenchmen and twenty negroes, and that none had escaped but a young soldier, who had already escaped the great massacre of November 28th, and two negroes. The General then saw that no time was to be lost in rendering that nation utterly incapable of injuring us; and as the intrigues of the English among the Choctaws had increased his anxiety in regard to those Indians, he deemed it imperative to begin by setting his mind at rest in regard to them. He accordingly resolved on having an explanation from the chiefs, and notified them of his wish to have an interview with them at Maubile. He fixed a time when he would go there, and when he judged that they would soon arrive, he left New Orleans, where his presence was less necessary now that reinforcements had arrived from France, as I shall soon explain.

The Natchez renew their raids.

On landing, he found that they had anticipated the day by twenty-four hours. He was even agreeably surprised to see there the Chief of the Caouitas, a numerous tribe, strongly attached to the English, and a Chickasaw chief. He began by inquiring from the Sieur Regis, from Father Baudoin, the Jesuit who was endeavoring to establish a mission among the Choctaws, and from the interpreters, what effect had been produced on the mind of the Indians

Perrier negotiates with the Choctaws.

1730. by the arrival of troops from France; and they told him that most (of the chiefs) had hesitated whether they should attend the conference, for fear some trap should be sprung on them, fully conscious that the French had ground to be dissatisfied with them; but that some of the Western chiefs had answered for the good faith of our nation, adding: "It is the English who corrupt our mind."

Persuaded by this language, they had started for Maubile, which they entered on the 26th of October, to the number of eight hundred men. On the 28th, Perrier, who had arrived on the 27th, began to treat with them, and he had to submit to a hundred and fifty harangues, which took up a week. The substance of all was that the Indians begged him to assure the King of their inviolable fidelity; that they would never forget that he it was who had made men of them, and rendered them a terror to their neighbors; that some rumors unfavorable to the French had indeed circulated in their villages, but that such language came only from some madcaps, and that the chiefs and sachems had not been parties to it; that they begged him not to blame them for it, and to forget the past. This he promised, and spoke to them only concerning the negroes retaken from the Natchez, whom they still kept, although they had pledged their word to bring them into the colony. They replied that they had always intended to bring them back, but that their masters must send for them, because some whom they tried to bring back killed themselves on the way.

Although a good understanding seemed quite well restored between the Eastern and the Western Choctaws, the General nevertheless perceived that they were still somewhat jealous of each other, and as he was much surer of the latter than of the former, he represented to those that it was necessary for them to have a head chief like the others. He added that for this dignity he had cast his eyes on the Chief of the Castachas,[1] whom they

---

[1] A Choctaw tribe. *Charlevoix.*

knew to be a brave and capable man of ancient family. They replied that they approved this choice, and with pleasure accepted this Head Chief at his hands. He showed the warmest friendship to the great Chief, whom he styles in his letters the "Emperor of the Caouitas,"[1] to whom he made a suitable present; it pleased him greatly, and he declared that he would be devoted to the French as long as he lived; that he saw that the advice we gave was always good; that he wished the English thought as they did, as all nations would be the happier for it. 1730.

Mr. Perrier also gave audience to the Chickasaw chief, but adopted a different tone with him. He told him, however, that he was very glad to see him; that when his nation returned to its duty, he would treat it like the rest, and that it depended on them to live calmly and happily; that he was ignorant of none of their intrigues, but that he would resume his paternal feelings for them, when they themselves acted as submissive and obedient children. This man made no reply, but a week after, he asked the Castacha chief to tell the General that they were unhappy, and really worthy of compassion; that since he had withdrawn the French who traded with them, all the northern nations made unrelenting war on them. Perrier told the one who spoke thus to assure that chief that no nation of his province should attack them, as long as they gave him no other cause of complaint, but that he did not answer for the Canada Indians, as they were thoroughly convinced that they were enemies of the French; that they must prove the contrary by unequivocal acts.

The most delicate point on which Mr. Perrier had to treat with the Choctaws, was trade. He knew that they complained loudly of the dearness of our goods, nor was he unaware that the English had promised to furnish their goods at half any price we might set on ours. On the other hand, he was well convinced that if he made the deduction they asked, they would in six months demand another. He thought, however, he might gratify

[1] Called by the Spaniards Chipacafi. Barcia, Ensayo Cronologico, p. 332.

1730. them this once, but on condition that they should trade only with us, and this was in part to avoid being afterwards exposed to new importunities on this point, and in part to show them that the French were sufficient in themselves, and that he did not wish to employ them in the new expedition he was preparing against the Natchez.

Reinforcements arrive from France.

What had rendered the Choctaws so easy to manage was, on the one hand, the arrival of reinforcements from France, which they overrated beyond their actual strength, and on the other the unexpectedly good reception accorded them by Mr. Perrier. The reinforcements had come on the Somme, King's storeship, commanded by Perrier de Salvert, brother of the Commandant-General.[1] He passed the bar of the Micissipi without any difficulty on the 8th of August, low as the waters were, though his vessel, even after discharging a part of the cargo at the storehouses on Isle Toulouse, (or Balise,) drew fourteen feet eight inches of water. On the 15th he anchored before New Orleans, and in a letter which he wrote to the Count de Maurepas, on the 15th of November, he informed that Minister that he found all the inhabitants of the colony in great alarm; that the few troops left his brother, were not good enough to keep all in the line of duty; that the poor recruits sent over by the Company, far from reassuring the colony, had increased the alarm; that out of a hundred men drawn from the regiments, only sixty had arrived, with no explanation of the detention of the others at l'Orient; that his brother had asked six field-pieces, six small mortars, balls and shells, none of which had come; that they would be obliged to use periaguas to transport troops, provisions and munitions, for want of more convenient boats; that the Natchez, joined by some other small tribes, were entrenched in three forts; that their ravages on the river intercepted trade, and that there was no difficulty in seeing whence their support came.

The trifling aid so impatiently expected, was doubtless

---

[1] Both are now post captains. *Charlevoix.*

what had deferred the project of closing the war by storming the intrenchments of the Natchez, as it now required levies of settlers and Indians to make up for it. And it was after giving orders for this, that Perrier proceeded to Maubile to confer with the Choctaws, not to ask those Indians to join him in his expedition, since he was, as we have seen, resolved to act without them, but to prevent their accepting the commercial offers made by the English, and to retain them in our alliance. 1730.

The army marches—its order.

This accomplished, he returned to New Orleans,[1] where he found the army ready to march. His first step was to send the Sieur de Coulonge, a Canadian, to the Akansas, who were to assemble at the French fort at Natchez. The Sieur de Beaulieu embarked with him, with orders to reconnoitre the enemy's condition. On the 9th of December, Mr. de Salvert embarked with two hundred men; including three companies of marines, the rest volunteers or sailors from the Somme.[2] On Monday, the 11th, Mr. Perrier set out with a company of grenadiers, two of fusiliers, and some volunteers. This detachment was also two hundred strong; Captain de Benac commanding the militia, followed on the 13th with eighty men; he was to have a hundred and fifty, but the rest joined him on the way.

On the 20th, the whole force having united at the Bayagoulas, a Colapissa chief arrived there with forty warriors of his tribe. The militia companies were organized at this place, and a company of cadets selected from them, but soon suppressed. Mr. le Sueur had orders the next day to load the demi-galley which he commanded, and to push on to Red River, which he was to ascend; for although it was not precisely known where the Natchez were, they were supposed, beyond doubt, to be on the Black, or River of the Ouatchitas, which empties into the Red ten leagues above its entrance into the Micissipi.

On the 22nd, they set out from the Bayagoulas in this

[1] Perrier to the Minister, March 25, 1731. Gayarré, p. 273.

[2] Perrier as above, says 150 marines, 40 sailors.

1730. order: The army was divided into three battalions, or three squadrons. The marines under de Salvert on the right, the militia under de Benac on the left; the General in the centre, having under him the Baron de Cresnay commandant of the Louysiana troops, the Chevalier d'Artaguette commanding the grenadier company, the Sieur Baron acting as engineer, and the fusileers; a part of the latter were at the French fort at Natchez, whence Mr. de Lusser was to march with them to Red River. The negroes were scattered in different boats, and the Indians, who had not all assembled yet, were to form a corps by themselves.

On the 27th they had made but little progress, as snows and rain had swollen the river and increased its currents, while the fogs were so dense and continual as to force them every moment to stop.

The Natchez attack a periagua, killing or wounding sixteen French.

This day news came that de Coulonges and de Beaulieu had been attacked by the Natchez, and that of twenty-four men in the French batteau, sixteen had been killed or wounded; Beaulieu among the former, and Coulonges among the latter.[1] To crown the disastrous intelligence, it was also reported that the Akansas, weary of hearing no tidings of the French force, had gone home. Perrier halted some time at the Bay of the Tonicas, to assemble the Indians, who had not yet come in; he was blamed for not having arranged to send them on in advance to blockade the Natchez in their fort; but he probably had not sufficient confidence in these Indians to entrust them with a movement on which all the success of the campaign depended. The Canadians, who readily blamed everything that was done, since the colony was no longer governed by one of themselves, judged the Louysiana by the Canada Indians, and in this were mistaken. Perrier might have manœuvred differently if he had had Abénaquis, Hurons, Algonquins and Iroquois to deal with, all Christians, and long domiciliated among us.

That General rejoined the army at the mouth of Red

[1] Perrier to the Minister, March 25, 1731. Gayarré, i., p. 274.

River on the 4th of January, 1731, with several Indians, who now amounted to a hundred and fifty of various nations. He had some days before ordered de Benac to ascend to our Natchez fort to obtain information. He returned on the ninth without having seen anything or heard any intelligence. The same day the Indians and a hundred and fifty volunteers were detached to take the advance under Captain de Laye of the militia, and blockade the Natchez as soon as they were discovered; but this detachment did not proceed far, the Indians not going willingly on this expedition. On the eleventh, they ascended Red River, and at noon the next day they entered the Black. The General had commanded the greatest precaution to avoid being discovered by the enemy; but his orders were unavailing, as the Indians, recognizing no authority and observing no discipline, continued to fire, as usual with them, at all game that showed itself; so that it is rather astonishing that they succeeded in finding the enemy in his fort after so long a march and so little secrecy.

1731. Indocility of our Indian allies.

It was on the 20th of January that they discovered the enemy. Orders were at once given to invest them, and as this was done closely, and they were within speaking distance, the besieged began by invectives. The trenches were opened and skirmishing kept up all day and all night. The next day the mortars and all things necessary for the siege were landed. Some shells were then thrown, which fell inside the fort. The besieged made a sortie, killed one[1] Frenchman and one negro, and wounded an officer, but they were sharply repulsed by Mr. de Lusser. Shells were thrown all through the 22nd, but produced no great result, and the enemy wounded two of our soldiers. However, on the 24th, they hoisted a white flag. Perrier at once raised a similar one at the head of his trench, and soon after an Indian was seen approaching with two calumets in his hand.

The army in sight of the enemy,

The General sent his interpreter to receive him, and when the envoy came before him, he asked for peace,

[1] Perrier says two. Gayarré, i., p. 277. See Le Page du Pratz, iii., pp. 321–5.

1731. offering to surrender all the negroes whom they still had in the fort. Perrier replied that he wished the negroes, but he also required that the chiefs should come to confer with him. The deputy replied that the chiefs would not come, but that if the General had anything to communicate to them, he might advance to the head of the trench, and that the Head Chief would on his side advance to the edge of his fort. Perrier told him to go at all events and get the negroes, and that on his return he would announce his intentions.

They ask peace.

He returned with this reply and in half an hour brought eighteen negroes and one negress. On restoring them to the General, he told him that the Sun would not come out, yet that he asked nothing except to make peace; but on condition that the army should at once retire; that if it adopted this course, he pledged his word that his nation would never commit any hostility against the French, and that he was even ready, if desired, to go and restore his village in its old site. The General replied that he would listen to no proposition till the chiefs came to meet him; that he assured them their lives; but that if they did not come to him that very day, there should be no quarter for any one.

They give up all the negroes captured from the French whom they still held.

The envoy returned with this message, and after a time came back to say that all the warriors, with one accord, refused to let the Sun come out; that this excepted, they were disposed to do anything required. The cannon had just arrived; the General replied to this Indian that he held to his first proposition, and ordered him to notify his people that if they allowed a single cannon to be fired, he would put all to the sword, without sparing even the women and children. This man soon returned with a Natché named St. Côme, a son of the woman Chief, and who consequently would have succeeded the Sun. This Indian, who had at all times been quite familiar with the French, told Mr. Perrier in a very resolute tone, that, inasmuch as peace had been concluded, he ought to dismiss his troops; that he was very sorry for what his na-

They continue to parley

1731.

tion had done against us, but that all should be forgotten, especially as the prime mover in all the mischief had been killed in the first siege during the Choctaw attack.

The Head Chief, his presumptive successor and another chief, come into the camp.

Perrier expressed his pleasure at seeing him, but insisted absolutely on seeing the Head Chief also; that he would no longer be trifled with, and that no Natché must again think of coming to his presence except in company with the Sun, as he would fire on any one advancing to make new proposals; that he accordingly permitted him to return to his fort, but that if the Head Chief did not come forth as soon as he got in, he would reduce the fort to ashes with his bombs. Saint Côme at once took leave of him, and in half an hour was seen coming forth with the Sun, and another called the Flour Chief, (Chef de la Farine.) The last was the real author of the massacre of the French; but Saint Côme had wished to throw the fault on another. They appeared at the moment when preparations were making to attack the fort during the coming night.

They are secured.

Mr. Perrier sent soldiers to meet them and conduct them to his quarters. The Sun told the General that he was charmed to treat with him, and that he came to repeat to him what he had told him through the envoy; that it was not he who had killed the French; that he was then too young to speak, and that it was the ancients who had formed this criminal project. "I am well aware," he added, "that it will always be ascribed to me, because I was the sovereign of my nation, yet I am quite innocent." In fact, it has always been believed in the colony that his whole crime was in not daring to resist his nation, or notify the French of what was plotting against them. Up to that time, and especially before he attained the dignity of Sun, he had never given any grounds to distrust him. Saint Côme, who was likewise not hostile to the French, also cleared him as well as he could; but the other chief merely said that he regretted deeply all that had happened. "We had no sense," he continued, "but hereafter we shall have." As they

1731. stood in the rain, which became more violent, Perrier told them to take shelter in a neighboring cabin, and as soon as they entered, he placed four sentinels there, and appointed three officers to watch it by turns.

He then summoned the Head Chief of the Tonicas and a Natché chief, called the Stung Serpent, (Le Serpent Picqué,) to endeavor by these means to extract some light from his prisoners; but it seems that these two men could elicit nothing new. My authorities do not state whether the Stung Serpent was then in our camp as a friend or as a prisoner, but towards the close of 1721, while I was at the Natchez, I saw that he was regarded as the best friend we had in that nation, and he was said to be a very close relation of the Sun.[1] The commission confided to him by Perrier induces me to believe that he had always remained strongly attached to us.

One of the chiefs escapes and induces several others to follow him.

To return to those who had been arrested: Le Sueur, who was one of the three officers to whom they had been committed, and who understood their language very well, wished to converse with them, but they made him no reply, and he left them to rest, while the other two officers reposed. Half an hour later, these awoke, and he in his turn went to sleep. About three o'clock he was awakened by a loud noise. He sprang to his two pocket-pistols, and perceived Saint Côme and the Sun in the posture of men who are on the point of escaping. He told them that he would blow out the brains of the first who stirred, and as he was alone, the sentinels and other two officers being in pursuit of the Flour Chief, whom they had by their negligence allowed to escape, he called for help. Perrier was the first to run up, and gave new orders to pursue the fugitive, but all in vain.

Early in the morning of the 25th, a Natché approached the camp: he was led into the cabin where the

---

[1] Le Serpent Picqué was detained with the Great and Little Sun during the First Natchez War, ante, p. 29. But Dumont, Memoires Historiques, I., p. 209, says that Le Serpent Piqué or Olabalkebiche died in June, 1725, and Le Page du Pratz makes his death still earlier, i., p. xv. iii p. 27.

1731.

Sun was, and informed him that the Flour Chief had come into the fort; that having awaked his nephew and eight or ten of the oldest warriors, he had told them that the French intended to burn them all; that for his part, he was sternly resolved no longer to remain exposed to fall into their hands, and that he advised them to seek safety with him; that they had followed his advice and escaped with their wives and children; that all the others had deliberated whether to do the same, but had deferred too long coming to a resolution, and day breaking, they saw that escape was impossible. On this, the Head Chief told Mr. le Sueur that the Flour Chief was a usurper, who, although not noble, had seized the place he occupied, which made him the third person in the nation, and gave him absolute power over all whom he commanded.

Others surrender to the French.

In the evening, Mr. Perrier went to see the Sun, and declared to him that he must send orders to all his subjects to come forth from the fort unarmed, with their wives and children; that he would spare their lives and prevent the Indians from illtreating them. He obeyed, and at once sent orders by the Natché who had come to bear the message I have mentioned; but all refused to submit. The wife of the Head Chief came to him the same day, with his brother and some others of his family, and Perrier gave her a hearty welcome, in consideration of the kindness she had shown the French women during their captivity. They were anxious to have the woman Chief, who had even more influence in the nation than the Sun himself. The wife of the Chief went repeatedly to the fort to induce her to come out, but her exhortations were unavailing. About thirty-five men and two hundred women surrendered towards two o'clock in the afternoon; the rest were told that unless they did the same at once, the cannonade would begin, and that as soon as it opened, there should be no mercy for any one. They replied that we might fire when we chose; that they did not fear death. Yet it is certain that there were only seventy warriors at most, remaining in the fort; that they had not

1731. a single chief, and that most of them kept themselves shut up from the fear of falling into the hands of the Indians if they attempted to escape separately, or of being perceived by the besiegers if they all escaped in a body.

Most of them escape.

They were not, however, cannonaded; moreover, the weather was fearful, the rain having been incessant for three days; the besieged trusted that the French would be less careful in watching the passes, and they were not mistaken. About eight o'clock at night, Mr. de Benac sent word to Mr. Perrier that they were escaping. The trenches and all the posts at once were ordered to fire, but the fugitives passed unperceived along a bayou or little river, which ran between the quarter of the militia and that of the Baron de Cresnay; and before it was known, and we entered the fort, they were already far off with their wives and children. Only one woman was found, who had been just delivered of a child, and one man in the act of escaping.[1]

Our Indians refuse to pursue them. The French army decamps.

The next day, the 26th, we endeavored to induce the Indians to pursue these fugitives, but they refused, saying that as they had escaped by our fault, it was our business to pursue them; so that having no longer any enemies to fight, our troops had to think of returning. The same day, all the prisoners were bound; the Sun, his brother, brother-in-law, Saint Côme and all of that family were put on board the Saint Louis. Forty warriors were put in the demi-galley commanded by le Sueur. The women and children, numbering in all three hundred and eighty-seven persons, were distributed among the other vessels. The whole army embarked on the 27th, and on the 5th of February reached New Orleans.[2]

Forces of the Natchez after this siege.

The war was far from being finished. Le Sueur had ascertained from the Head Chief that the whole nation was not by any means in the fort that we had besieged;

[1] Perrier's Dispatch, March 25, 1731. Gayarré, i., p. 272–280, gives this affair mainly as here.

[2] The Sun and other chiefs were sent to St. Domingo and sold as slaves. Bienville saw them there in 1733. Letter, 28 January. Gayarré, i., p. 292.

that it still comprised two hundred warriors,[1] including the Yazoos and the Corrois, and as many youth, who could already in an emergency handle a musket; that one of their chiefs had gone to the Chickasaws with forty men and many women; that another, with sixty or seventy men, more than a hundred women, and a great number of children, was three days journey from his fort, on the shore of a lake; that twenty men, ten women and six negroes were at the Ouatchitas; that a band discovered by the army on the 18th of January, comprised twenty men, fifty women, and many children; that some twenty warriors were prowling around their old village to cut off the Frenchmen; that the Yazoos and Corrois were in another fort three days' march from his; that all the rest had died of hardship or dysentery. We were finally informed that the Flour Chief might have assembled sixty or seventy men, a hundred women, and a great number of children. 1731.

Le Sueur having acquired all this information, proceeded to report it to the General, and told him that if he would allow him to take all the well-disposed men, he believed he could guarantee to master all these separate corps; but he was refused. Perrier had not, perhaps, all the confidence in the Canadians that most of them deserved, and brought up in a service where discipline and subordination are at the highest point, he could not conceive that anything of importance can be effected with militia, who acknowledged no law of war but great bravery and invincible patience in the severest marches and most laborious works. He would doubtless have thought otherwise had he reflected that rules must be adapted according to the enemy's manner of fighting.

However, we were not slow in perceiving that the Natchez could still render themselves formidable, and that the step of sending the Sun and all who had been taken with him to be sold as slaves in St. Domingo, had rather

---

[1] Diron d'Artaguette, June 24. Gayarré, i., p. 281, says 300.

1731. exasperated than intimidated the remnant of that nation, in whom hatred and despair had transformed their natural pride and ferocity into a valor of which they were never deemed capable. In the month of April, the Head Chief of the Tonicas descended to New Orleans, and told Perrier that while he was hunting, four Natchez had come to him to beg him to make terms for them with the French, adding that all, including those who had taken refuge among the Chickasaws, asked to be received and pardoned; that they would reside wherever it was wished, but that they should be glad to be near the Tonicas, and that he came to ascertain his intentions.

The Chief of the Tonicas allows himself to be surprised and killed by the Natchez.

Perrier replied that he consented to their settling two leagues from his village, but not nearer, to avoid all occasion of quarrel between the two nations; but that above all things, he exacted that they should come unarmed. The Tonica promised to conform to this order; yet as soon as he reached home, he received thirty Natchez into his village, after taking the precaution to disarm them. At the same time fifteen other Natchez and twenty women came to the Baron de Cresnay, whom they found in the fort which had been built on their old grounds. A few days after, the Flour Chief arrived among the Tonicas with a hundred men, their women and children, having concealed fifty Chickasaws and Corrois in the canebrake around the village.

The Head Chief informed them that he was forbidden to receive them unless they gave up their arms; they replied that this was indeed their intention, but they begged him to consent to let them keep them some time longer, lest their women, seeing them disarmed, should think themselves prisoners condemned to death. He consented; then food was distributed to their new guests, and they danced till after midnight, after which the Tonicas retired to their cabins, thinking that of course the Natchez would also go to rest. But soon after, that is to say, one hour before day, for it was the 14th day of June, the Natchez, and apparently the Chickasaws and Cor-

1731.

rois, although Perrier's letter says nothing on the point, fell upon all the cabins, and slaughtered all whom they surprised asleep. The Head Chief ran up at the noise, and at first killed four Natchez; but overborne by numbers, he was slain with some twelve of his warriors. His war-chief, undismayed by this loss or the flight of most of his braves, rallied a dozen, with whom he regained the Head Chief's cabin; he even succeeded in recalling the rest, and after fighting for five days and nights almost without intermission, remained master of his village. The Tonicas on this occasion had twenty men killed and as many wounded. They killed of the Natchez thirty-three men, and took three prisoners, whom they burned.[1]

Several Natchez killed in different actions.

Perrier no sooner received this tidings, than he dispatched a detachment, under the command of the Chevalier d'Artaguette, to induce as many Indians as he could to pursue the Natchez. At the same time he ordered the Baron de Cresnay to make sure of all those who had surrendered to him; he obeyed, but his adjutant, to whom he confided them, having allowed them to retain their knives, they sprang, at a moment when it was least expected, on eight muskets which were stacked, and with these kept up a fire till they were all killed, men, women and children, to the number of thirty-seven. Their chief had gone to New Orleans with fifteen of his men; these were arrested and sent to Toulouse Island, where they were put in irons. They found means to break them, but had not time to escape, and were all killed.

Others besiege de St. Denys at the Natchitoches. Their defeat.

Meanwhile the Flour Chief, after the miscarriage of his plot at the Tonicas, proceeded to join those of his nation who had escaped Perrier on the Black River, led them to Natchitoches, where de Saint Denys was with but a few soldiers, and besieged him in his fort. Saint Denys at once sent an express to the Commandant-General to ask

[1] Perrier to the Minister, December 10, 1731, in Gayarré, i., p. 285; Dumont, Memoires, ii., p. 197. He was a Christian, converted and baptized by Rev. Mr. Le Maire. Ib., i., p. 165–6. Le Page du Pratz, iii., pp. 300–302.

1731. relief, and on the 21st of October, Mr. de Loubois set out from New Orleans at the head of sixty men to reinforce him. He had advanced six leagues up Red River, and was only seven or eight days' march from the Natchitoches, when the Sieur Fontaine, sent by de Saint Denys to Perrier, informed him that the Natchez had been defeated; that the Natchitoches had at the outset wished to attack them, but being only forty against two hundred, they had been compelled to retire, and even abandon their village after losing four of their men; that the Natchez had seized the village, and intrenched themselves there; that then de Saint Denys, having received a reinforcement of Assinais and Attacapas, who were joined by some Spaniards, had attacked the enemy's intrenchments and killed eighty-two, including all their chiefs; that all the survivors had taken flight, and that the Natchitoches were in close pursuit.[1]

Forces of the Chickasaws.

So many losses, and especially the loss of the chiefs, reduced the Natchez to a mere tribal band; but there were enough left to harass the settlers of Louysiana, and to interrupt trade. Moreover, it was impossible to dissemble any longer with the Chickasaws, who were not long now in declaring themselves openly, which they had hitherto avoided doing. They numbered a thousand warriors, and eighty or a hundred Natchez might yet join them, to say nothing of the few remaining Corrois and Yazoos. This was enough to plunge the colony back into the panic from which it had not entirely recovered, and it beheld itself on the eve of sustaining a new war, to which its present forces did not promise a speedy termination.

Their intrigue to excite our negroes to revolt.

The Chickasaws, the fiercest and bravest of all the Louysiana Indians, after raising the mask as they had just done at the Tonicas, expected, of course, that we

[1] Diron d'Artaguette, June 24, 1731, says he had 14 Spaniards and 400 Assinais, he gives the French loss, two soldiers, one Spaniard, and many Indians; the Natchez loss, killed and prisoners, 74. Gayarré, i., p. 282. Dumont, ii., pp. 198–200. Le Page du Pratz, iii., p. 272.

1731.

would cease to treat them so considerately. To check us, they had taken steps which led men to believe that their neighbors directed all their movements, and in a very short time we had proofs that were by no means equivocal. They began by sending to New Orleans a trusty negro, to notify all of his race who were among us, that it depended on themselves alone to recover their liberty and live in quiet and plenty among the English.

These latter conspire against us and are punished.

This man managed his intrigues well; he was heard with pleasure by all his race; but Perrier was warned by a negress, a servant in the city, that a plot was formed by a great number of these slaves; that they had agreed to take the time of the parochial High Mass to set fire to various houses in order to occupy apart from each other, all not at church, and then to seize this favorable conjuncture to escape. On this deposition, the Commandant-General arrested a woman who was the mainspring of the conspiracy, and four men, who had been declared the chiefs. They were confronted and convicted; the woman was hung and the men broken alive, and these examples, which showed the rest that their secret had taken wind, was enough to keep the rest in their duty.[1]

The Akansas and the Illinois refuse to league with the Chickasaws.

Meanwhile the Choctaws, of whom a part had been gained by the Chickasaws, had turned a deaf ear to the invitations made by the Sieur Regis in behalf of his general to send three hundred of their warriors against our enemies; but thirty or forty of these last having been killed in an engagement by the French, this little check lost them the alliance of that nation, the only one from whom they had anything to fear or hope: it all united in our favor. Then the Chickasaws again turned to the Miamis, Illinois and Akansas; but they found tribes who were still faithful to their first engagements, and who from the outset dissipated all their hopes of gaining them. The Illinois even gave up to the Commandant-General the three ambassadors whom our enemies had sent them,

[1] Beauchamp to Minister, Nov. 1, 1731. Gayarré, i., p. 284. Dumont, ii., p. 202–4. Le Page du Pratz, iii., pp. 304–317.

1731. and they were put at the discretion of the Choctaws, who burned them at New Orleans itself, and thereby removed all doubt that might yet remain as to their attachment to us.

The India Company cedes Louysiana back to the King, who confides the government to Mr. Perrier.

While these things were going on, Mr. Perrier, who, as he himself states in one of his letters to the Minister, expected to be recalled, because he had been informed that they were working against him in the India Company, was quite surprised to receive a commission, appointing him Governor of Louysiana for the King. On the 22nd of January in this year, the Company had deliberated the question of conveying back to his majesty the grant which had been made to it of that province and the Illinois country and their exclusive privilege, on condition of being empowered to grant permissions to the merchants of the kingdom who might wish to trade there. On the 27th of March, this deliberation was approved by an Arrêt, and Mr. de Salmon, who was discharging at New Orleans the duties of Commissaire Ordonnateur, took possession of the country in the name of his majesty, by Letters Patent of the King, on the 10th of April following.

However, Mr. Perrier had not the time to profit by the measures which he had adopted to push on the Chickasaw War. He preferred the service in which he had been brought up, to expeditions where the risks incurred could not be compensated by the glory that might be acquired, and he was relieved in 1733 by Mr. de Bienville,[1] whom he had succeeded in 1726. The new Governor found himself at once burthened with the Chickasaw War, which had become a much more serious matter than had been at first supposed. This war is not yet terminated, as we cannot flatter ourselves that the peace recently granted them will be durable; moreover, the events which it has furnished for history are so differently related, that it is not yet possible to distinguish the truth amid the clouds in which the friends and enemies of the principal actors have enveloped it.[2]

[1] Le Page du Pratz, iii., p. 397. Bienville and Salmon's Dispatch, May 12, 1733.

[2] For the state of the colony, see Gayarré, i., p. 293.

1736.

Noble action of a Jesuit and skilful retreat of an officer of sixteen years of age.

All the world knows[1] the loss sustained by the colony in 1736, in the persons of the brave Chevalier d'Artaguette and a great number of officers of merit, and the noble action of the Jesuit Father Senat, who preferred to expose himself to the certain peril of being taken and burned by the Chickasaws, as he really was, rather than not assist to their latest breath the wounded who could not retreat or even be transported by those who did. This retreat, which was the work of a young man of sixteen, named Voisin, may be regarded as a masterpiece in point of skill and bravery. Pursued for twenty-five leagues, he lost, indeed, many men, but it cost the enemy dearly, and he besides marched forty-five leagues without food, his men carrying in their arms the wounded who were able to bear transportation. Almost all[2] those who in this affair fell into the enemies' hands, and who were quite numerous, were burned in the most barbarous manner, with the missionary, who was not the only one to exhort the companions of his torture to do honor by their courage and patience, to their religion and their nation. The Sieur de Vincennes,[3] a Canadian gentleman and officer in the army,

---

[1] Charlevoix evidently refers to some publication of the day, probably Drouet de Richarville's Récit, describing the fate of Father Antonine Senat, but I have never been able to find it. Senat refused a horse when offered him, preferring to remain with the dying. Bannissement des Jésuites de la Louisiane, Carayon, Documents Inédits, xiv., p. 24. Dumont, Memoires, ii., pp. 230–1. Adair, History of the American Indians, p. 154, seems to allude to this, and makes Senat's death to have been caused by Indian superstition. He says the English traders tried to save the victims. See p. 354 for his account of the Chickasaw War. This affair was a mere episode in this ill-managed campaign, which Charlevoix does not attempt here to chronicle. See Le Page du Pratz, iii., pp. 401-426. Journal de la Guerre du Micissippi contre les Chicachas en 1739 et finie en 1740 le 1er d'Avril par un Officier de l'Armée de M. de Nouaille. New York, 1859.

[2] Drouet de Richardville, whose three brothers were killed, by the help of the English traders, reached Georgia, where Oglethorpe paid his ransom and gave him a passport, by which he reached Montreal June 10, 1739. Bossu, ii., p. 109, says that Sergeant Louis Gamot was ransomed by the English and was at Charleston in 1750.

[3] D'Artaguette was shot down, and Vincennes was taken while endeavoring to carry him off. The Chick-

1736. shared the glory with him, and won the admiration of his very torturers.

---

asaws burned 20 French on the day of the battle, including Father Senat, d'Artaguette, Vincennes, de Coulonges, de St. Ange, Jr., du Tisné, d'Esgly and de Tonty. De Courcelas, a Louisiana officer, was burned three days later. Récit du Sieur Drouet de Richerville, cited by Ferland, Cours d'Histoire, ii., p. 468. Vincennes has a monument in the post which he founded, and which was sometimes called St. Ange, from an officer who commanded there. From the latter term, apparently, came the name of Ange Gardien, given to the mission. Jouvency, Hist. Soc. Jesu, 233. Carayon, Documents Inédits, xv., p. 15. John Baptist Bissot, Sieur de Vincennes, officer in a detachment of the marine service, was the tenth child of Francis Bissot, and was born at Quebec in January, 1668. Louis Jolliet married his sister, Clara Frances. Vincennes in 1696 married at Montreal, Mary Margaret Forestier, and Tanguay, Dict. Généal., i., p. 56, gives the names of four children. The statement in some Western writers that his name was Morgan is unfounded.

CORRIGENDA ET ADDENDA.

VOLUME I.

The Chronological Tables are all given in Charlevoix's own words without remark. Where they bear on the History of New France they are considered as they occur in the work.

PAGE

27, line 29, for Garcias read Gracias.

51, line 17, Champlain's discovery was in 1609.

105, note 1, add "History of the Gauls since the Deluge," 16○, Paris, 1552.

Note 2, the earliest reference, to Scalve are in Peter Martyr, 1516; Belleforest, 1570; Maginn and Wytfliet. Pontanus, p. 763, makes him sent out by Christian I. of Denmark.

Note 3. For Charles read Richard Biddle.

Note 4, add Ramusio, iii., p. 417.

106, note 1. The earliest printed reference to the Breton discoveries is in Gastaldo's Geografia di Ptolemeo, Venice, 1548, p. 56.

Note 3. The Memoires Chronologiques pour servir à l'Histoire de Dieppe, i., pp. 99–100, make Aubert and John Vérassen sail in 1508; discover, name and ascend the St. Lawrence. It is a work of little authority. The Chronicon of Eusebius, of which I have seen editions printed in 1511 and 1512, allude to these Indians in France. under the year 1508.

107, note 1, The Baron de Leri's voyage seems to rest on the authority of Lescarbot alone, who first mentions it in his second edition. He makes it eighty years before that of the Marquis de la Roche. But the date of the latter is uncertain, (see p. 244;) Bergeron, Traité de la Navigation, 1629; and De Laet, 1633, merely follow Lescarbot. The Hon. H. C. Murphy, whose collection is very rich, can find no allusion to de Leri's voyage in any work issued in the 16th century.

107, note 4. For Thevet, read Belleforest, L'Histoire Universelle du monde, Paris, 1570, col. 253, et seq.

111, notes 4 and 5 are transposed.

129, note 1. Omit to word patent, with my apologies to Mr. Parkman.

143, line 32, and 144, line 30, for "Joanas" read "Ionas."

148, note 2. Biard's Relation in the original edition has Laudouiére.

209, line 13. After "swimming" insert "except the Sieur de la Grange, who was drowned."

229, note 1. The Somme is either the St. Mary's or Saltillo. But the distance to the St. John's is much more than 12 miles. Is it credible that de Gourgues' cannon and the artillery of the second Spanish fort kept up a duel across the mouth of the St. John's, and that Indians swam it?

237, note 1. For "one year after Gourgues death," "read eleven years after de Gourgues' voyage."

245, margin for vogage read voyage.

Note 4. Chauvin sailed in May, 1599. Memoires de Dieppe, i., p. 311.

246, note 1. Chauvin sailed on his second voyage June, 1600, and left 20 men, who perished there, as death prevented his return. Memoires de Dieppe, i., p. 312.

246, note 3, Add "Now published under the care of Messrs. Laverdiere and Casgrain, Quebec, 1871." For the Commander de Chattes, see Memoires de Dieppe, i., pp. 236–314; his tomb has been recently discovered.

248, note 2. The name Arcadia appears on the map "Tierra Nuova" in "La Geografia di Claudio Ptolemeo by

PAGE

Iacopo Gastaldo, " Venice, 1548, and in Porcacchi, Isole Famose, 1570.

249, note 1. Read Denys, i., pp. 58, 105, 126.

Note 2. Add "Charlevoix inverts the order; Novam Scotiam seu Acadiam totam;" see Jefferys' Conduite des François, p. 250, n.

Note 3. Charlevoix is in error. The name Nova Scotia occurs in no treaty prior to that of Utrecht. Mem. des Commissaires, iii., p. 126.

Note 4. "Wrested from France," can apply only to Argal's expedition. Conduite des François, p. 41, n.

250, line 2. For cites, read gives.

Line 7. Add: Note Mem. des Commiss, ii., p. 303.

8. Add: Note, Charlevoix's remarks on Acadia, were violently assailed by Jefferys, in his Conduct of the French, 1754; but were fully defended by Butel Dumont, in the notes to his translation of Jefferys. Conduite des Français, Londres, 1755, 12°. Jefferys was also answered by Grange de Chassieux: "La Conduite des François Justifiée." Utrecht, 1756.

252, note 1. Williamson, History of Maine, i., pp. 81, 188, is in error as to the place where Aubry was lost. He went ashore at St. Mary's Bay, before they got to Port Royal. Compare Lescarbot, 427–438; Parkman's Pioneers, 225.

253, note 4. Nvrvmberg appears in Gastaldo's Ptolemeo, 1548.

Note 7. Omit now Annapolis.

255, note 1. Add Denys, i., p. 41.

268, line 18. For "seal," read "dogfish." *On* the ice is an error of Charlevoix, which I overlooked. Biard, Relation, p, 10, says *under*, Denys, i., p. 148, mentions the ponnamou. The Hon. J. H. Trumbull, who calls my attention to the passage, says it is the tom cod, morrhua pruinosa, the ap8nanmes8 of Rale, (Dict. p. 510,) and the paponaumsu of Roger Williams.

275, line 27. John Alphonse makes the River of Norumbegua to be the Bay of Fundy. Laverdiere's Champlain, 1613.

277, line 10. The gasparot is the alewife, alosa tyrannus. Pereley's New Brunswick Report, 1852.

282, note 2. His epitaph is given in Historical Magazine, iii., pp. 49–50, but H. D. C, are the initials of my late friend, Henry de Courcy, who sent me the note, not part of the inscription as Murdoch supposes.

VOLUME II.

29, note 2. Champlain on his 1627 voyage, (Laverdière's ed., vi., p. 112, n.,) mentions the Ouentouoronons as allies of the Iroquois.

30, note 5. For the Indian name of Three Rivers, Métaberoutine, and its meaning, see Sulte, Histoire des Trois Rivières, p. 20. The first mass was said here July 26, 1615, and a settlement regularly begun in 1617, ib., pp. 35, 38.

44 note 2. Add: Henry Kirke in his First English Conquest of Canada, though he claims the Kirkes to be of English birth, admits that their father, Gervase Kirke, son of Thurston Kirke, of Greenhill, Derbyshire, England, (according to the funeral certificate he cites,) lived nearly forty years at Dieppe, where about 1596 he married Elizabeth Goudin, who bore him David, 1597; Louis, 1599; Thomas, 1603; John, 1606; James, 1616; Elizabeth, who married in Dieppe, and Mary, born 1619; David was knighted by Charles I. in Scotland, July 16, 1633, and, with others, obtained a grant of Newfoundland, Nov. 13, 1637, ib., p. 161. He held it till dispossessed by Cromwell, and died at Ferryland, 1655-6, ib., p. 184; Thomas was killed in 1642, soon after the battle of Edgehill. Lewis was knighted for his services by Charles I., and after the Restoration was made Captain and Paymaster of the Corps of gentlemen at arms, ib., 172–3.

46, note 2. Add: The French King is said to have declared David Kirke and his brothers public enemies,

and to have burnt them in effigy. Kirke's First Conquest, 66–7, citing Colonial Papers, v., no. 37, 49, vi., no. 12.

47, note 2. Add : Kirke in his First Conquest, says July 9 ; but the work is too confused to be of any authority. He makes David fight de Caen before the surrender of Quebec, which he dates Aug. 9.

58, note 1. Add : Charles I. by commission of March 5, 1630, ordered an inquiry as to the goods taken by Capt. David Kirke. First Conquest, pp. 84–5. Kirke resisted, and urged King to retain Quebec, p. 87. This author, p. 88, pretends that the French King promised to pay Kirke £20,000, which seems utterly improbable.

63. Charles I, June 12, 1632, appointed Sir William Alexander, Robert Charlton and William Berkeley commissioners to receive the forts from Capt. Lewis Kirke, and deliver them up to the French. Kirke, p. 89.

64, note 1, line 8, omit 1657.

100, note 5. For the Hotel Dieu of Dieppe, see Memoires de Dieppe, iii., pp. 90–106. Their rule was approved by Archbishop de Harlay, January 3, 1630, and by the Pope, July 7, 1664.

102, note 1. For the Ursulines of Dieppe, see Memoires de Dieppe, ii., p. 132.

126, line 24. For de Manse, read Manse.

Note 4. See concessions in Dollier de Casson, Histoire de Montreal, appendix, pp. 243–250. He makes Maisonneuve arrive the 20, p. 31.

128, note 3. Add : For the Iroquet, see Sulte, Histoire des Trois Rivieres, pp. 11, 18.

146, note. At foot of col. 1, omit from "as to," to "Hunter," and in col. 2, "Father Jogues," to "Dutch," and "and may be," to "E. Canada Creek." For "Greenhalgh describes it," read "Greenhalgh describes Tionondogue." As it stands the note confounds Tionondorogue (Fort Hunter,) with Tionontogue. See both mentioned N. Y. Col. Doc., iv., pp. 81–2. Tionontogue could not have been far from Canajoharie. Brodhead, in his valuable History of New York, vol. ii., p. 129, thinks it was not far from Fort Plain or Palatine. It was burned by de Tracy, removed a quarter of a league further, again removed in 1689, and again burned in 1693.

169. The Relation, 1643, gives the name Tabouret, where Charlevoix has Sabouet ; has Margonne, instead of Margonet, Bordier instead of Verdier. In the list of the Hundred Associates in Du Creux, there is neither Tabouret nor Sabouet, and no Caset, but it has a John Verdier, and a James Bordier.

205, note 2. D'Aillebout died May 31st. 1660. Viger in Dollier de Casson, p. 152.

216, note 2. See, however Sulte, Histoire des Trois Rivières, p. 94; which seems to make it John Godefroy de Linctot as stated by Charlevoix, p. 247, n. He was of Caux in Normandy, came to Canada about 1616 with his brother Thomas, and was one of the founders of Three Rivers. By his wife, Mary Le Neuf de Herisson, he had a large family. He died before 1681. Five of his children were killed and his brother burnt by theIndians. Sulte, pp. 89, &c.

244, note 3. See Lauson's nomination. Dollier de Casson, Appendix p. 265

247, note 2. See addenda to note on p. 216 ; If Charlevoix is right in regard to John Godefroy de Linctot, he errs in making Margaret, wife of James Hertel de Cournoyer, his daughter; she was his granddaughter. Sulte, p. 93. Tanguay, Dict. Gen., i., 274.

251, note 1, line 6. For "governor of" read "commandant at."

258, note 2. Add "He was known among the English as Smit's Jan. Brodhead's New York, ii., p. 116 n."

274, note 2. Insert a period after "lay brother" and read "Garreau was."

275, note 2. Add: "Parish Register of Montreal cited in Dollier de Casson, Appendix, pp.229–230."

VOLUME III.

34, note, col. 1, line 22. Dollier de Casson, pp. 142, 231, gives the date May 26th, or 27th.

40, note 5. Add: F. Peter Bailloquet born 1616. belonged to the Province of Aquitaine, arrived June 25th, 1647. died in Canada June 7th, 1692.

55, note 3. Add : Dollier de, p. 201.

65, note 5. Add : Montreal was transferred to the Seminary of St. Sulpice, March 9th, 1663. Dollier de Casson, p. 173.

72, note 3. Add : Brodhead, ii., pp. 1–36; Cartwright reduced Fort Orange and made a treaty with the Mohawks and Senecas, ib.; p. 46.

73, note 1. Add : Brodhead's New York ii., pp. 205–8.

82, note 4. Add: Fort Richelieu had been left untenanted and was burned by Iroquois in the winter of 1646–7. Dollier de Casson, p. 62.

83, note 1. Add : The map gives the name Saurel, which is also his autograph.

87, note 3. Add: This officer's name is settled by Tanguay, Dict. Géneál., pp. 103, 444, to be Louis de Cauchy, Sieur de Lerolle.

89, note 1. Add : A delegation from Albany demanded why he invaded English territory. Brodhead, ii., p. 103.

90, note 1. Fort St. Anne, on Isle la Motte was built by Capt Pierre, Sieur de la Mothe. Dollier de Casson, Appendix, pp. 238, 255. It was the first white post within the limits of Vermont. St. Anne's day, July 26th, 1666, is doubtless the day of its commencement. See Miss Hemenway's Vermont. Histor. Gazetteer, II., p. 558, &c.

96, note 1. For Ontario read Erie and add: It was published in 1869 by the Montreal Historical Society, with the notes of the late Commander Viger.

98, note 4. Brodhead, ii., p. 127 ; represents Thos. Exton in the privateer Cedar as having captured and burned Forts St. Mary and Du Coudray in Acadia in 1667, but there is no French allusion to it, nor do I find any such forts; they were probably posts of Le Borgne's sons; see N. Y. Hist. Coll. 1869, p. 50–1. Acadia was in the hands of England till July 21–3, 1667, when it was restored to France by the reaty of Breda.

109, note 1. For "Verborem" read "Verborum," line 2, col. 4, dele "Fort Hunter."

110, note 1. See Bishop Laval's instructions. Dollier de Casson, p. 260.

120, note 3. After "given by," read "the French to the tribe whom the Algonquins styled Winnebagoes."

123, note 2. line 6. For "governor" read "commandant." On Maisonneuve's retirement and the temporary commandants in his absence, including Capt. La Mothe, 1669–70. and Perrot subsequently, see Dollier de Casson, pp. 235–239.

139, line 1, supply "surrender."

140, note 5. Guy's settlement was in 1609.

140, note 6. Add : After Lord Baltimore left Newfoundland, Sir David Kirke with others obtained in 1637, a grant of the island, and he took up his residence at Ferryland, see Ante p. 131, n.

164, note 2, omit "the" before Abbé.

175, note 2. Add : see Brodhead's ii., p. 181, n.

176, note 2. Add : See Brodhead's New York, ii., pp. 238–240.

181, note, col. 1, line 3, for Pekitanoni read Pekitanoui.

189, note, col. 2, line 5, supply date 1854.

196, note. Two letters of Frontenac to Andros and one to Brockholts Nov. 18, 1677, Jan. 8, and April 30, 1678.) are in the N.Y. MSS. (English) at Albany. See O'Callaghan's Calendar, ii., pp. 62; 65, 67.

198, note col 2. line 21, for "could" read "would."

208, note 2. Parkman's discovery of the Great West, pp. 173, &c., gives the details of this journey of La Salle. He went up the Illinois and struck across to the mouth of the St. Joseph's on Lake Michigan ; struck across to the Huron and descended it to the Detroit, crossing and striking Lake Erie near Point Pelée, whence he made his way in a canoe to Niagara, and finally reached Fort Frontenac May 7th, after 65 days' toil.

211. De La Barre calls Chambly, Governor of Martinique, N. Y. Col. Doc. ix., p. 122.

212, note 4. Add: The place of F. Ribourde's death must have been about fifteen miles above Starved Rock. Parkman's Discovery, p. 216.

216, note 2, col. 2, line 8 After "next" add: "with the Dutch commander, Abraham Krynssen. Brodhead, ii., p. 126."

274, note 1. See Brodhead, ii., p. 475.

281, note 2, read: Enjalran.

284, note 3. Add : See license to Abel Marion de la Fontaine, April 1st, 1685. N. Y. Eng. Mss. xxiii., p. 106. O'Callaghan's Calendar, p. 136.

285, note 4. For New Irondequois read "now Irondequoit."

286. Add to note 1. In the Register of Quebec, Oct. 16th, 1691, appears Armand Louis de Delorndarce de la Honton, Baron de la Honton et Herlèche, Knight of the order of Our Lady of Mount Carmel, Captain of a detachment of Marine. (Tanguay, Dict. Généal., p. 338.)

287, note, col. 2, read: "Particulier."

292, note 1, read: "Relations."

294, note 2. See Brodhead, ii., p. 510.

298, note 2, for (of) read (N. S.)

VOLUME IV.

12, line 21. For "Seneca" read "Oneida," and in note for Tsonnonthouan read "Onneyouth." For "Hungry Bay" read "Salmon River."

13, note 1. Brodhead, ii., p. 520, note, also rejects La Hontan's account.

15, note 3, for iii., p. 568; read 571, and add to note: See Brodhead, ii., pp. 510, 520, 522.

20, note 1. Add: These memoirs were probably modified by the state of affairs. Brodhead, ii., p. 520.

68, note 3. Add: "According to most recent writers; but see post, p. 82."

82, note 2. For further discussion of this subject see Historical Magazine, Series II., vol. iv., p. 308. For Alonzo de Pes read Alonzo de Leon.

126, note 1. Add: See Brodhead, ii., p. 607; and N. Y. Hist. Coll. 1869, pp. 162-176.

137, note 2, read "hundred."

141. The Chev. Peter d'Aux, Sieur de Jolliet, whose account of his adventures is not now known, was born in 1666. and was a captain of a company detached from the marine service. He did not long survive his Indian captivity and New England imprisonment, dying at Montreal, and being buried in the Recollect Church, April 10th, 1694, Tanguay, i., p. 158.

Line 9, for Provot read Prévot. Tanguay, Dict. Généal., p. 500, gives Provost.

152, note 1. See Vie du P. Chaumonot, p. 93.

154, note 4. Add: Phipps' Journal of Proceedings, says they entered Port Royal River, Friday, May 9, O. S. at 6, P. M.

155, note 1. Add : His fleet comprised the Six Friends; the Porcupine, Capt. Cyprian Southack; the sloop Mary, Capt. John Alden; Mary Ann, Capt. Gregory Sugars; Bachelour, Capt. John Welch, manned by 286 men, and carrying a regiment of foot soldiers numbering 450. Journal, pp. 5, 15.

155, note. Vie du Père Chaumonot, p. 86.

156, note 1. Phipps' Journal, pp. 5-6, says that Petit agreed to surrender the Governor and Priest to come on board, which they performed at the time prefixed: that on the 11th they took possession, the Governor and officers surrendered their swords; the soldiers were guarded to the church, where they were kept as prisoners. He has not a word about terms, though his summons to Menneval ends, "you shall not find me failing in one tittle of my promise."

157, note 1. Phipps is very explicit. "May 12, morning. We cut down the cross, rifled the church, pulled down the high altar, breaking their Images," Journal, p. 6. Chalmers, Political Annals in N. Y. Hist. Soc. Coll. 1868, pp. 53, 88, reproaches him with a violation of all civilized usage in thus treating a place appropriated to the worship of the Deity.

158, note, to §2. Phipps sent Alden to cruise for Perrot May 21, Journal, p. 7. He was directed also to treat with St. Castin and obtain English prisoners in exchange for his daughter, whom Phipps had seized, as well as try and persuade him to go to Boston, which Phipps reached May 30, ib., p. 8.

187. The demoiselle Lalande referred to is in all probability Elizabeth Perrin, wife of John Lalande. She spoke English, as her early life had been spent in New York, where she was baptized in Dongan's time by one of the English Jesuits whom he brought over. See Tanguay, Dictionnaire Génćalogique, pp. 339, 493.

195, Charlevoix has been generally followed in giving the name Crisasy. Yet every document published by Dr. O'Callaghan, in the N. Y. Col. Doc. (vol. ix., pp. 307, 518, 556, &c.) has Crisafy; and de la Potherie, iii., p. 153, and iv., p. 29, Crizafi, and Crisafi. The Abbe Bois kindly sought out the burial entries. The Parish Register of Three Rivers is lost; but in the Index of Interments, he found "Anthony, Marquis de Crisaphée, noted as buried May 12, 1709." The Montreal Register he ascertained gives, March 1, 1696, the burial of the Chevalier Thomas de Crisafy, Knight of Malta. See Tanguay, Dict. Généalogique, i., p. 150, where he gives the name Crisafy. There can be no doubt, therefore, as to the error of the common form.

205, note 1. De la Potherie, i., p. 330.

217, note 7. Add: See examination of La Plante, Aug, 1, 1692, N. Y. Eng. MSS., vol. 38, p. 158.

233, note 3. Add: The narrative of James le Ber de St. Paul (Vie de Mlle le Ber, p. 313) says 300 Canadians, 100 soldiers 230 Indians, with Rev. Mr. Gay, of the Mountain Mission, as chaplain.

245, Add: For a curious account of perhaps the same woman, see Ursulines de Quebec, ii., pp. 149-151.

VOLUME V.

13, line 9, read "seconded." Page 37, line 7, for Freneuse, read Fremeuse.

45, line 24, read "Dugué."

84, note 1. For Vol. III., read soon to be reprinted.

94, note. 1. His body was removed Sept. 11th, 1796, after the burning of the Church of the Recollects, to the Cathedral, and deposited first in the Chapel of Our Lady of Pity, then in the Chapel of St. Anne, the principal chapel on the gospel side. Livre d'Annonces de Mgr Plessis, MS. the citation from which I owe to the Abbé Casgrain, who gives me also the statements of persons who witnessed the removals. See also Tanguay, Dict. Géné., p. 243.

120, note. John Baptist le Moyne de Bienville, 12th son of Charles le Moyne, was born at Montreal, Feb. 28, 1680. He became Post Captain in the navy in 1748, and died at Paris, March 7, 1768.

147. The burial entry has been found by the Abbé Tanguay, Dict. Gén., I., p. 543. Gaspar Soiaga, called the Rat, Chief of the Michilimakinac Hurons, was buried at Montreal, Aug. 3rd, 1701, aged 75.

156, note: Francis de Beauharnois was brother of Charles, subsequently Governor. He was Intendant General of the naval force in 1726, and died in 1746, aged 81, Daniel, ii., pp. 346-7.

199. Simon Peter Denys, Sieur de Bonaventure, Chevalier, Captain of a frigate, &c., was born June 22nd, 1659. son of Peter Denys, Sieur de le Ronde. Tanguay, Dict. Généal., I., pp. 180-1.

227. note 3. Omit 874.

238, note 2. Daniel is evidently wrong. This nobleman was Charles Henry d'Alogny, Marquis de la Grois, captain in the troops. Tanguay, Dict. Généal., I., pp. 153, 167.

INDEX.

Abenaquis, Abenaquinois Indian tribe, i., p. 49; oblige English to leave their river, welcome French, i., p. 273; Father Biart preaches to them, their docility, 273, 278; offer to receive some of Champlain's people, ii., p. 47, n.; ask and obtain a missionary, ii., p. 201; allies of Etechemins and Micmacs, ib.; their character, 202; who comprise the Abenaqui nations, i., p. 276; ii., p. 200; Dreuillette's labors among, p. 202; French ask New England to protect, 215; their utility to New France, 201; Progress of the faith among them, 202; They make war on the Mohawks, iii., p. 45; have to make terms with the English, 211; in Denonville's expedition, 283, n.; account of missions to, 308, n.; at Sillery, ib.; remove to Chaudiere, ib., iv., p. 44 n.; to St. Francis, p. 44 n.; disinclined to be included in treaty of peace with Iroquois, p. 11; surprise an Iroquois-Mohegon party, ib.; English endeavors to detach them from us, 19; their fidelity and disinterestedness. Their services to us. The Canibas, the true Abenaquis, capture Fort Pemkuit from the English, p. 40; pious preparation for the expedition, ib.; their moderation after the capture, 43; offer to lead 200 French to Boston, ib.; other Abenaquis seize fourteen English forts, ib.; Many think of settling in the colony, 44; a party of Abenaquis and Algonquins attack some French and Christian Iroquois, mistaking them for enemies, p. 128; the consequence, ib.; speech of an Abenaqui, 128; on Hertel's expedition, 130; sixty in de Portneuf's New England expedition; joined by others on the warpath, 133; inexperience in siege matters made up by courage, ib.; an Abenaqui gives the commandant at Quebec timely notice of the approach of the English to besiege it, 152; they keep up the war on the English, forty Abenaquis defeat 600 English in open battle, 160; zeal and disinterestedness, 163; tidings they bring to Quebec, 164; reject proposals of Governor-General of New England, 188; result of their New England raids, 191; the King's eulogy on them; his instructions to de Frontenac, 214; in the campaign against Mohawks, iv., p. 233; continue to harass the English, 248; the Governor of New England by threats brings them to treat with him, 255; they raise a party against the English, 256; its success, ib.; intimidated by Governor of New England, reanimated by a missionary and by de Villieu; the latter takes chiefs to Quebec; they renew protestations of fidelity, 259; Abenaquis arrested and massacred by English in violation of the law of nations, iv., p. 273; prepare to take vengeance, 274; accompany de Frontenac in his Iroquois expedition, v., p. 12; the court desires them to be relieved from all fear of Fort Pemkuit, 23; easily deceived by English, ib.; they take a fort near Boston, 78; Frontenac notifies the Governor of New England that he cannot oblige them to give up the English prisoners till theirs are surrendered, 82; kill settlers at Hatfield, v., p. 87; the Governor of New England anxious to secure them, 92; his claims on them, on what based, 97; on what terms they will treat with him, 98; some Abenaquis speak haughtily to the Iroquois deputies, 103; at treaty at Montreal, 111; totem, ib.; new professions of fidelity; they speak well at the general congress, 151; Governor Dudley, when too late, attempts to win them to neutrality, 160; De Beaubassin heads

ABENAQUIS, (*continued.*)
them to ravage New England, ib.; ask aid from Vaudreuil; he sends de Rouville, who surprises the English, kills and takes many, v., 161; they prevent the Iroquois Christians from removing to New York, 164; again surprised; De Montigny goes to their aid, 167; raid into New England, ib.; some settle on Bekancourt river, ib.; advantage of this town, ib.; continue to ravage New England, 191; Abenaquis left unsupported, 194; advantage of their trade with English; retained in our interest by zeal for religion alone, 194; Abenaquis and French in an expedition against New England, 204; others fail to be at the rendezvous, as they had to turn their arms elsewhere, 205; 200 join de Ramezay's force against the English and Iroquois, 218; refuse neutrality and continue to ravage New England, 225; attack Deerfield and Exeter, 226 n.; cool towards us after capture of Port Royal. De Vaudreuil's instructions to their missionaries, 235; dash in near Port Royal, defeat an English party and invest the fort, 238; zeal in defending Quebec, 240; draw English of Port Royal into an ambuscade and kill many, 255; join French and invest Port Royal, ib.; their New England incursions make the Court of England insist on the cession of Acadia, 266; claims of the English over them. What occurred between them and the English on this point, 267; English minister sent to pervert them, 268; make peace at Portsmouth and Arrowsick Island, 267 n.; Governor of New England fails to win them, 269; Charlevoix's loose statement that at first they did not oppose English settlements on the Kinibequi, 269; demand by what right they seize their lands. Reply. Its effect. Ask Vaudreuil whether their country has really been ceded to the English. Relieved by General's reply, 270; English treachery, 271; write to the Governor of New England, 272; the English exhaust their patience by carrying off the Baron de Saint Castin and menacing Father Rasle, 273; hostilities begin, 277; Narantsoak attacked by the English; many Abenaquis and Father Rasle killed, 278; towns ravaged by English, 277 n.; finally left in peace, 281; some settle on Cape Breton, 296; leave the English at peace in consideration of the French, 297; the English fail to gain them. Saint Castin and missionaries more successful in retaining them in our interest. De Vaudreuil's argument on the point to the Minister, 302-3.

ABERCROMBIE, Captain, at siege of Port Royal, v., p. 230, n.

ABREU, DIEGO DE—Discoveries of, i., p. 28.

ABYSSINIA—Early visits to, i., p. 19.

ACADIA—Called on early maps Arcadia, vi., p. 123; by Champlain, Arcadie, i., p. 248 n.; in de Laet, Cadia, ib. n.; derivation, ib.; great American peninsula, p. 49; situation, description, limits, 248; Charlevoix's remarks on attacked and defended, vi., p. 123: fertility, i., p. 250; fish and animals, 268; faults committed, 285; restored to France by treaty of St. Germain, ii., p. 58; Denys' divisions of, i., p. 248; granted to de Razilly, ii., p. 63; resolutions, iii., p. 124; granted by James I. to Earl Stirling, 125; Poutrincourt the younger devises grants in, to La Tour, ib. n.; account of La Tours, 125-7; condition in 1632, division among various proprietaries and governors, 128; civil wars in, 130; captured again by English in 1654, 134; restored to France by treaty of Breda, 138; how far restitution extends, ib.; French neglect, while English profit by, 139; advantageous harbors, etc., 145; visited by Talon, 187; Chambly at, ib.; captured by Dutch (not English, as Charlevoix states), 188; restored, 310; Chambly governor of, ib.; said to have been again taken by English, 211; English inroads, 261; English fortify posts in, 210, 294; De Meulles' report on, 295; what required to secure it and trade, ib.; Census in 1687, ib.; English hostilities, iv., p. 17; what most injured prospects of, 18; conferences at the Court of London in regard to it, 23; what makes them useless, constant danger of English invasion, condition of, when conquered by English in 1690, iv., p. 154; equally neglected by French and English, 214; Villebon made Commandant by the French Court, ib.; condition

when restored to France. The king sends de Fontena there; what he did, v., p. 113; intentions of Court and Bishop of Quebec, 156-7. The Bostonians ravage the coast, 157; Governor Dudley resolves to expel French from Acadia, 191; Queen Anne resolved to have Acadia at any cost, 201; more neglected than ever by the French, ib.; De Subercase proposes a firm settlement there. English profit by fisheries there, 202. Acadia again threatened. De Subercase draws buccaneers there, 225; English bent on reducing it, 226; settlers ill disposed to Subercase, 228; condition of the province after the fall of Port Royal, 233; disposition of the French there, 235; unavailing efforts to recover Acadia, 253-4; ceded in perpetuity to the English Crown; why the English Court persisted as to this cession, 266; its terms, 267; English offer favorable conditions to French settlers to retain them, 296-7; their fate, ib., n.

ACADIANS (FRENCH)--Number included in surrender of Port Royal, v., p. 233, n.; terms, ib.; Nicholson prevents their going to Cape Breton, ib.; English threat to give them up to Indians, 234.

ACADIANS (INDIANS)—Lescarbot and Biart on; attached to France, i., p. 264-5. See GASPESIANS, MICMAKS, SOURIQUOIS, etc.

ACAPULCO—Pretended northern voyage from, to Dublin, i., p. 51.

ACOSTA, JOSEPH DE, Spanish Jesuit—Note on his Historia Natural, i., p. 75.

ACUNHA, TRISTAN D'—Discoveries of, i., p. 26.

ACUNA, CHRISTOPHER DE—Spanish Jesuit, explores and describes Amazon, i., p. 55.

ADAES—Texas Indians, mission among, vi., p. 24, n.

ADARIO—La Hontan's name for KONDIARONK, or THE RAT, which see.

ADOPTION among Indians, iii., p. 16.

ADULTERY—How punished by Sioux, iii., p. 32.

AGARIATA—Mohawk hung, iii., p. 88, n.

AGNIEGUE—Mohawks, ii., p. 190, n.

AGNIER, an Iroquois canton, see MOHAWK.

AGNIER, a Mohawk town, iv., p. 303.

AGONONSIONNI, real name of the Iroquois, ii., p. 189, n.; for other forms, ib.

AGRESKOUE, or ARESKOY—God of Hurons and Iroquois, ii., pp. 109, 143; Jogues refuses meats offered to, 151; his worship abolished, iii., p. 157.

AHASISTARI, EUSTACE, chief of the Attingueenongnahak Hurons; conversion, ii., p. 134; baptism, 136; address to his braves, 136; burnt by Mohawks, 147.

AHIJITES, branch of Texas Indians, iv., p. 80, n.

AHWENDOE (ST. JOSEPH'S)—Now Charity Island, ii., p. 226, n.

AIGRON—Captain of the Belle, one of La Sale's storeships, iv., p. 64; refuses to take a pilot, and loses his vessel, p. 69; suspected of doing it intentionally, ib., n.; de Beaujeu takes him on board his ship to screen him from punishment, 72.

AIGUEFORT, English post, Newfoundland, taken by De Brouillan, v., p. 37.

AIGUEMORTE, LIEUT., killed near Schenectady, iii., p. 89, n.

AIGUILLON, DUCHESS D'—Niece of Cardinal Richelieu, foundress of the Hospital Nuns, Quebec, ii., p. 100.

AILLEBOUT, LOUIS D', Seigneur de Coulonges, brings over settlers for Montreal, ii., p. 130; Governor-General, 203; character, 205; governor of Montreal not as Charlevoix states, of Three Rivers, 206, n.; negotiations with New England, 216; receives fugitive Hurons at Quebec, 235; asked to build prison for Indian drunkards, 243; succeeded by de Lauson, 244; arrests Iroquois murderers, iii., p. 14; makes commercial treaty with Dutch, p. 15, n.; dies at Montreal, 33, n.

AILLEBOUT, MADAME (BARBARA DE BOULOGNE)—Wife of preceding, services of, ii., p. 205, n.

AILLEBOUT, SIEUR D'—Distinguished at capture of St. John, iv., p. 214; v., p. 213.

AILLEBOUT, D'ARGENTEUIL. See ARGENTEUIL, D'.

AILLEBOUT DE MANTET. See MANTET (MANTEHT).

AILLEBOUT DES MUSSEAUX, see MUSSEAUX.

AIRE, D', see HERE, D'.

AKANSAS (AKANSEA, AKAMSCA)—Louisiana Indians, visited by Marquette, iii., p.

AKANSAS, (continued.)
181; comprise the Quappas or Kappas, Ossotteoez or Otsotchoué etc., iv., p. 108, n.; account of, 109, n.; their position, 181; La Sale takes possession of their country, 214; receive Cavelier, 108; give him guides, 109; French sure of their fidelity, vi., p. 79, 94; destroy Sioux, and most of the Yazoos and Corrois, 102; Perrier sends to them to join him at Fort Natchez, 107; they come, but disgusted with delays, go home, 108; Chickasaws unable to turn them against us, 119.

AKO, SIEUR D', see DACAN.

ALARCON, MARTIN DE, occupies Espiritu Santo Bay, vi., p. 66, n.

ALAS, ESTEVAN DE LAS, Spanish officer, intrusted by Pedro Menendez with his affairs, i., p. 184; sends out three vessels, 186.

ALBANEL, FATHER CHARLES, Jesuit, sent by Talon to Hudson Bay to take possession, goes by the Saguenay, i., p. 57; iii., p. 231-3; his adventures at the Mistassins, 232; chaplain on Tracy's expedition, 95, n.

ALBANY—English name of Fort Orange, iii., p. 72; alarm at, and cause, 299; condition of, iv., p. 20; Denonville's advice in regard to, 46; Manteht and St. Helene wish to attack, 122; Fitz John Winthrop's expedition at, 146, n.; Oneidas fly to, v., p. 19, n.; Indian conference at, 84, n.; consternation at, on Walker's shipwreck, 246.

ALBEMARLE, GEORGE MONK, Duke of—Carolina granted to, i., p. 56.

ALBERT DE LA PIERRIA, Captain—Ribaut's commandant at Charlesfort, i., p. 143; explorations of, 144; neglects agriculture, ib.; cruelty provokes mutiny, 145; killed, 146.

ALBERT, FRANCIS, deserter, iv., p. 229; caught and executed, 231.

ALBITES, DIEGO DE, discovers Chagres River, i., p. 29.

ALBUQUERQUE, ALPHONSUS—Discoveries of, i., pp. 25, 27; takes Goa, 27; Malacca, 28.

ALBUQUERQUE, FRANCIS DE—Discoveries of, i., p. 25.

ALDEN, CAPTAIN, at siege of Fort Naxoat, v., p. 30.

ALEGAMBE, FATHER PHILIP, and NADASI JOHN. Notice of their Mortes Illustres, i., p. 81.

ALET, REV. MR., Sulpitian arrives, iii., p. 23.

ALEXANDER VI., Pope, traces line of de markation between Spaniards and Portuguese, i., p. 19.

ALFIADE, v., p. 87, see HATFIELD.

ALFINGER, AMBROSE, German, discoveries of, i., p. 35.

ALGONQUINS (ALGOUMEQUINS, ALGOMMEQUINS)—Indian tribe of Canada, placed by Charlevoix near Quebec, ii., p. 7; their real location, 8; alliance with French, 8; they induce de Champlain to join them in an expedition against the Iroquois, 8, 12-17, 21; success, 17; cruelty, 18; join Champlain at Sorel, 21; more docile than Hurons, 87; maltreat Father Lallemant, 111; defeat an Iroquois party, 121-2; a Christian Algonquin woman forced to cut off Father Jogues' finger, 144; wonderful conversion of an Algonquin chief, 163; make peace, 178; escape of an Algonquin woman, 198; march against Iroquois, 237; defeated, 238; zeal and courage of a young Algonquin slave, 241; exploit of an Algonquin woman, 261; two Christian Algonquin women announce the earthquake of 1663, iii., 57; Algonquins defeat Mohawks and Oneidas, 64, n.; attack Onondaga envoys, 70; prevent Tracy's surprise, 90; an Algonquin woman guides de Tracy, 91; the Algonquins of Three Rivers lose by smallpox, and retire to Cap de la Magdeleine, 153; the Upper Algonquins give great hopes to missionaries and traders, 158; in Denonville's expedition, 283, n.; several tribes of the Algonquin language more closely attached to French, 164; a party of Algonquins and Abenakis attack a French Iroquois party by mistake, iv., p. 128; on Hertel's expedition, 130; march against Mohawks, 233; on Frontenac's expedition, v., p. 13; exploit of thirty young Algonquins, 79; strike a blow at Onondagas, and why, 90; ask for cheaper goods, 143; attire of Algonquin chief at General Congress, 150; his address and history, ib.; accompany a great French war party, p.

ALGONQUINS, (*continued.*)
204; zeal of Algonquins of Montreal Island, p. 240; join in letter to Governor of Massachusetts, 273, n.

ALGONQUINS DE L'ISLE, or of the Island visited by Champlain, ii., p. 24; Tessouat, chief of, ib., n.; see Kichesipirini; ratify peace with Iroquois, 182.

ALIBAMON MENGO, Choctaw Chief, addresses Natchez, vi., p. 99.

ALIBAMONS, Louisiana Indians with other tribes ravage Carolina, and bring prisoners to Maubile, vi., p. 25; build a fort in their village, and put French in it, 25; sing calumet to l'Epinai, 39, n.; Fort Toulouse among, 67, n.

ALIMIBEGONG, see LAKE ALIMIPEGON.

ALIMIBEGUEK—Division of Crees, iii., p. 107, n.

ALKANSAS, see ARKANSAS.

ALLAMIMA, Fox chief, v., p. 263, n.

ALLARD, F. GERMAIN, Recollect, Provincial, subsequent Bp. of Vence, brings several religious to Quebec, and returns to France, iii., pp. 148-9.

ALLIGEWI, perhaps the Arkansas, iii., p. 31, n.

ALLIMACANY—Florida chief, i., p. 163, n.; see 229, n.

ALLOUEZ, F. CLAUDE, Jesuit—Notice of, iii., p. 186; accompanies Ottawas, ill treated, p. 100; his labors and success, ib.; visits Nipissings on Lake Alimipegon, and then keeps on to Chagouamigon, 107-8; visits Quebec, 108; missions in Green Bay, 120; ascends Fox River, ib., n.; accompanies de St. Lusson to take possession of North and West, 168; his address to the Indians, ib.; excursion among Mascoutins, 182; his reception, 184; they try to divert him from going to Outagamis (Foxes), 185; well received, 185; v., p. 132; succeeds Marquette at Kaskaskia, iii., p. 186, n.; said to have settled among Miamis, 186; Allouez and La Salle, 203; goes to St. Joseph's River with Cavelier, iii., p. 186, n.; iv., p. 111; v., p. 132, n.; death, iii., p. 186, n.

ALMAGRO, DIEGO DE, companion of Pizarro, i., p. 34; discovers Chili, 38.

ALMEYDA, LAWRENCE DE, discovers Ceylon and the Maldives, i., p. 26; but not Madagascar, ib.

ALMOUCHIQUOIS—See ARMOUCHIQUOIS.

ALOGNIES, CHARLES HENRY D,' MARQUIS DE LA GROIS, commandant of the forces ordered to support French and Indians besieging Port Royal; countermanded, v., p. 238; dies at sea, captain of a man-of-war, 238, n.

ALONNE, Demoiselle d', taken by Iroquois; informs d'Orvilliers, iii., p. 299; rescued, and returns to Montreal, 306.

ALPHONSE, JOHN, Portuguese or Spanish pilot in the service of Francis I., sent by de Roberval to seek a N.W. passage to India; how far he went, i., p. 130, n., 131.

ALVARADO, one of Melendez' officers, i., p. 208.

ALVARADO, LUIS MUSCOSO DE, Spaniard, descends Mississippi to the sea, i., p. 40.

AMARITON, FRANCIS, exploit of, in Newfoundland, v., p. 161; noticed, 162, n.

AMAZON RIVER discovered and explored, i., p. 55.

AMBERGRIS, in Florida, i., p. 143.

AMBLIMONT, MR. D', relieves Placentia, iv., p. 164.

AMBOYNA, discovered by Portuguese, i., p. 28; taken by Dutch, 50.

AMEDA, or ANNEDDA, the white pine, a cure for scurvy, i., p. 121.

AMERICUS VESPUTIUS, Florentine, received the honor of naming the New World by a stratagem, i., pp. 21, 107.

AMIDAS, PHILIP, English, discovers Roanoke Island, i., p. 45.

AMIKOUEK, or BEAVER INDIANS, same as NEZ PERCÉS iii., p. 120, n.; on Manitouline Island, 166; St. Lusson winters among, ib., n.; at general congress, v., p. 143, n.

AMOURS, LOUIS D', iv., p. 158; Clignancourt, a son of, v., p. 30; see also DE PLAINE.

AMOURS, CHARLOTTE, marries Baron de St. Castin, v., p. 274, n.

AMSTERDAM merchants send ships to Hudson River, ii., p. 10.

ANACHOREMA, Texas Indians, iv., p. 90, n.

ANASTASIA, virtuous Iroquoiss receive Catharine Tegahkouita at La Prairie de la Magdeleine; her employment, iv., p. 290; their close union, ib.; tries to overcome Catharine, 291.

ANAYA, PETER DE, Portuguese, discoveries of, i., p. 25.

ANCHUSI, BAY OF, Pensacola bay so called, vi., p. 43.

ANDAGORON—Mohawk town; Jogues at, ii., p. 144, n.; see vi., p. 125.

ANDARAGUE, ANDAWAQUE—Mohawk town, ii., p. 146, n.; iii., p. 91, n.; see Gandawagué.

ANDASTES (ANDASTOEZ, ANDASTOUEZ, ANDASTOE)—Indians near Virginia, of Huron origin, ii., p. 72; their county, 209, n.; same as Susquehannas and Conestogas, ib., n.; offer to aid Hurons against Iroquois, 209; Huron emigration to, 236; make war on Iroquois, iii., p. 45; 65; at last defeated, ib.; renew war, 151; succes, 158; final overthrow, 174; fate of remnant, 174, n.

ANDATAOUAT—Ottawas, ii., p. 270, n.;

ANDIATAROCTE, or ONJADARACTE—Mohawk name for Lake George, ii., p. 186, n.

ANDRADA, ALONZO DE, account of his Claros Varones, i., p. 81.

ANDRADA, ANTHONY DE, Portuguese Jesuit, discovers source of Ganges and Thibet, i., p. 54.

ANDRADA, FERDINAND DE, in China, i., p. 28;

ANDROS, SIR EDMOND, Commandant in New England, made Governor of New York, iii., p. 308; builds Fort Pemaquid, iii., p. 210, n.; plunders Pentagoët iii., p. 211, n.; iv., p. 15; what New France had to fear from, iii., p. 308; prevents Iroquois sending deputies to the Marquis de Dénonville, iv., p. 14; letter to the Marquis, 15; plunders Acadian French and disavows it, 15.

ANDUSTA, Florida Indian chief, invites French to a feast, i., p. 143.

AÑEZ, GIL, doubles Cape Bojador, i., p. 15.

ANGELIS, JEROME DE, Sicilian Jesuit, visits Yesso, i., p. 53.

ANGO, JOHN, Merchant prince of Dieppe, i., p. 107.

ANGRA DE CINTRA, i., p. 16.

ANIAN, Straits of, i., p. 44.

ANICAN ISLANDS, discovered, i., p. 61.

ANJELRAN, F. JOHN, see ENJALRAN.

ANMESSOUKKANTI, Abenaqui mission, v., p. 167; join in letter to English, 273, n.; see DAMISOKANTIK.

ANNAOTAHA, or ANAHOTAHA, STEPHEN, a Huron, defeats Iroquois in the west, ii., p. 236, n.; at the Long Sault fight, iii., p. 33; abandons French, ib.

ANNANMAC, Seneca chief killed at Michilimackinac, iii., p. 218.

ANNAPOLIS, ROYAL, English name for Port Royal, v., p. 233.

ANNE, Queen of Great Britain, declares war v., p. 156, n.; why she retained Bishop of Quebec, captured at sea, 174; resolved to have Acadia at any cost, 201; thanks Governor of New England ib; promises Governorship of New France to Vesche (Vetch) if he conquers it, 217; plans expulsion of French from Acadia and siege of Quebec, 225; resolved to have Canada, 239; insists on Acadia, and wishes Placentia and Hudson Bay, 266.

ANNE OF AUSTRIA, Queen of France, asks the States General to deliver Father Jogues, ii., p. 157; orders the Governors-General of New France to protect Christian Indians, 217; proposes Father le Jeune as Bishop of Canada, accepts the Abbé de Montigny, Francis de Laval, iii., p. 21.

ANNE OF THE ASSUMPTION, Hospital nun of Dieppe arrives, iii., p. 114.

ANNO BUENO, or Annobon island discovered, i., p. 18.

ANNONTAHA or Kanontaga, Huron chief defeats Iroquois near Montreal, ii., p. 257, n.

ANSCHILD, FREDERIC, Dane, enters Hudson Bay, i., p. 46.

ANSE DES MERES, Phipps runs into, iv., p. 179.

ANTICOSTY, island at mouth of St. Lawrence, situation, names of, i., p. 37; called Assumption by Cartier, 115; not Ascension, ib., n.

ANTILLES discovered, i., p. 19.

ANTONIO DE PORTUGAL, Dom, offer de Gourgues command of his fleet, i., p. 236

ANTOUHONORONS, see ENTOUHONORONS.

AONDIRONONS, neutral tribe attacked by Senecas, ii., p. 210

AOTONATENDIE, on Lake Superior, Tionontatez retreat to, ii., p. 271, n.

APALACHE mountains, Florida French led to believe gold mines in, i., p. 158.

APALACHES, Florida Indians discovered by Narvaez, i., p. 35; account of, vi., p. 15; leave Spaniards to settle at Maubile near French, a missionary given them, ib.; sing calumet to l'Epinai, 39, n.; bring a Spaniard to de Champmêlin, 56,

APALACHINE, or Casine, Florida shrub, the leaves of which dried and boiled make a

Apalachine, (*continued.*) drink used in Florida, i., p. 138, 142, 229; the black drink of the Creeks, 229, n.

Apoyomatzi or Beads of St. Helen i., p. 142.

Appleton, Colonel, at siege of Port Royal. v., p. 191, n.

Arasafa, town in New York taken by English, iii., p. 71 ; probably Esopus, ib.

Arbre Sec, Phips at iv., p. 169.

Archer's Creek, Charlesfort on, i., p. 137.

Areinbourg, Arembourg or Arensbourg, Chevalier d', Swede, brings out German colonists, vi., p. 68, n.; commands settlers in Natchez war, 100.

Arendarronon, or The Rock, a Huron tribe, go to Onondaga, ii., p. 280.

Areskouy, Agreskoué, worshipped by Hurons and Iroquois, ii., p. 109, 143; superseded by Hawenniio, ib., n.; iii., p. 157, n.

Argall, Samuel, expels French from St. Sauveur, i., p. 279; pretext, ib.; ill faith to Saussaye, 280; ruins St. Sauveur and Port Royal, 282 ; Governor General of Virginia claims Manhattan from Dutch, i., p. 283, n.; iii., p. 72 ; his pretended visit to New Netherland, ii., p. 10, iii., p. 72, n.

Argenson, Pierre de Voyer, Viscount d' Governor General of New France; ineffectual pursuit of Iroquois raiders at Quebec, iii., p. 19; disinclined to treat with Iroquois; changes his mind, 37 ; proposes to send F. le Moyne to the cantons to negotiate peace, 38 ; returns to France, ib.

Argenteuil, Peter d'Ailleboust, Sieur d' Lieutenant, notice of, iv., p. 237, n.; goes to Michilimakinac, iv., p. 237; brings a great convoy to Montreal, 241; sent back as lieutenant of Commandant, 242 ; arrives, 279 ; too late at Montreal to join Frontenac's Iroquois expedition v., p. 22; news brought by him, ib.; distinguished at capture of St John, p. 213.

Arguian, Count d', at Quebec, v., p. 181, n.

Arguyn discovered, i., p. 15 ; Perrier distinguished at, vi., p. 77, n.

Arkansas, or Alkansas, a Dacota tribe, iii., p. 31 ; formerly on the Ohio, ib.

Arkansas River, Marquette and Joliet descend to, i., p. 57.

Arlach, d', see Erlach, d'.

Armouchiquois, or Almouchiquois—Canada Indians, country of, i., p. 277 ; character ; retire to New England, ib.; Champlain's account of, ib., n.; 90, n.

Arnaud—Charlevoix's name for Arnold Cornelison Vielé, which see.

Arriola, Don Andres de, first Governor of Pensacola ; builds fort and church, v., p. 118, n.; vi., p. 43.

Arrowsick Island, treaty at, v., p. 267, conference at, 272 ; situation of, 273, n.

Arsikantegou—Abenaquis of. join in letter to Governor of Massachusetts, v., p. 273.

Artaguette, Diron d', Commissaire Ordonnateur in Louisiana ; writes to de Pontchartrain, v., p. 211 ; arrival gives form to colony, vi., p. 16 ; efforts for agriculture, ib.; on Maubile tobacco, ib.; advises fortifying Dauphin Island, ib.; returns to France, 17 ; his two brothers arrive, 41.

Artaguette, Chevalier d', goes to aid Illinois, vi., p. 71; exploit in attack on Natchez, p. 98 ; made commandant of fort erected there, 100 ; death, 121.

Artaguette, Capt. Diron d', brother of preceding, arrives in Louisiana, vi., p. 41 ; King's Lieutenant at Maubile, trouble with Choctaws, vi., p. 80 ; Perrier orders him to sound Choctaws, cited 93 ; dies in St. Domingo, ib., n.

Artieda, Anthony de, Jesuit, explores Amazon, i., p. 55.

Ascension, Jean Alphonse's error as to, i., p. 115.

Ascension Island discovered, i., p. 52.

Ashes, showers of, iii., p. 61.

Askicouanehronon—Huron name for Nipissings, ii., p. 95, n.

Assacambuit, v., p. 207, n. See Nescambouit.

Assembly of Notables convened by de la Barre to consider the Iroquois war, result, iii., p. 224.

Assendasé, Mohawk sachem convert, iii., p. 196.

Assenis, or Assinais—Their country, character, etc., iv., p. 78 ; included under name Texas, p. 80, n.; give La Sale horses, 88 ; reception of Joutel, 98 ; shocked at La Sale's murder and violence of assassins, 103 ; French aid to gain a victory, 104 ; cruelty of women, 105 ; try to keep Joutel from going to the Illinois,

ASSENIS, (*continued.*)
but give him guides, 107; give St. Denys guides, vi., p. 20; Spanish settle among, 31; aid St. Denys against Natchez, 118.

ASSIENTO COMPANY, vi., p. 18, n.

SSINIBOILS (ASSINIPOUALAC)—Indians of the Sioux family, iii., p. 106; meaning of name, ib., n.; Lake of the, i., p. 125; iii., 207, n.; it extent, etc., ib.

ASSONY—Texas tribe called Ayennis by Charlevoix, iv., p. 80; Joutel's party reach, 108, n.; see NASSONIS.

ASSUMPTION—See ANTICOSTY ISLAND, i., p. 37.

ATACAPAS (men-eaters), vi., p. 39, n.; aid St. Denys against Natchez, 118.

ATAOUABOUSCATOUEK BAY, iii., p. 107, n.

ATARONCHRONONS, Huron tribe, ii., p. 109, n.

ATERIHATA, LOUIS, Iroquois of Sault St. Louis, godson of King, iv., p. 199; speech in council before Frontenac, p. 146; proves his fidelity, 199.

ATIRONTA—Huron name of Gabriel Lalemant, ii., p. 225, n.

ATIRONTA, a Huron chief, killed, ii., p. 235.

ATOGWASKWAN, The Great Spoon, Mohawk chief, iii., p. 19.

ATONTRATORONONS, Algonquins, ii., p. 256, n.

ATOTARHO, or TODODAHO, chief sachem of the Iroquois, iv., p. 302, n.

ATSATAION, ASTATAION, CHITSAYON, the Huron death-feast, or farewell banquet, ii., p. 96, n.; 108, n.

ATSENA, or LE PLAT, Huron Bear chief, ii., p. 280.

ATTIGNEENONGNAHAC, (ATTIGNENONHAC,) the Cord, one of the two original Huron tribes so called, ii., p. 72; Ahasistari, chief of, 134, n.; resolves to stay with French, 280, n.

ATTIGOUANTAN, or ATTIGNAOUANTAN, or the Bear, Hurons so called, ii., p. 27, n.; one of the two original Huron tribes, 71; join Mohawks, 280, n,

ATTIKAMEGUES, Canada Indians, near Lake St. Thomas, ii., p. 118; their character, country. Progress of the faith among, p. 118; they attend an audience given to the Iroquois deputies, 178; religious influence of, 243; Father Buteux visits them, 246; almost annihilated by Iroquois, 248; Father Buteux accompanies survivors and is killed, ib.; bravery of women, iii., p. 35; ancient abode, 107; disappear totally after a great mortality in the north, 153; called also Poissons Blancs, or White-fish, ii., p. 118; iii., p. 107; inform Albanel of English, iii., p. 231.

ATINNAOENTEN, or BEARS, Huron tribe, bravery of a corps of, ii., p. 220, n.

ATTIWANDARONK, or NEUTERS, on Niagara River, visited by Father de la Roche Daillon, ii., p. 37, n.; they gave same name to Hurons, ii., p. 151; Hurons take refuge with, ii., p. 236.

AUBERT, THOMAS, a Dieppe pilot, takes Canada Indians to France, i., p. 27; 106; did not discover country by order of Louis XII., ib.

AUBRY, REV. NICHOLAS, priest, lost in Acadia, i., p. 252, n.

AUGIERS, MR. DES, finds three of La Sale's companions on a captured Spanish ship, iv., p. 115.

AUGUELLE, ANTHONY, nicknamed Le Picard du Guay, iii., p. 206.

AULNAY DE CHARNISAY, CHARLES DE MENOU, SIEUR D'—See CHARNISÉ.

AULNEAU, F. PETER, Jesuit, killed at the Lake of the Woods, v., p. 311, n.

AURORA BOREALIS, iii., p. 128.

AUSTRAL LANDS, discovered, i., pp. 26, 53, 64.

AUTHORS, Critical List of, i., p. 67, &c.

AUTMOINS, Acadian Medicine men, i., p. 271.

AUTRAY, SIEUR D', son of John Bourdon, with La Sale, iii., p. 214, n.

AUX, CHEVALIER D'—Charlevoix writes D'EAU, which see.

AVAUGOUR, PETER DU BOIS, BARON D', GOV. of New France, his character, opinion of Canada, iii., p. 38; treats with Garakonthié, 44; solicits aid from King, 52; permits brandy trade out of mere obstinacy, 53; equity, 66; returns to France, 70; killed in Emperor's service against the Turks, ib.

AVENEAU, F. CLAUDE—Jesuit missionary to Miamis of St. Joseph, notice of, v., p. 202, n.; success and character, ib.; driven from his mission by La Motte Cadillac, ib.; restored, 203.

AVILES, Part of Menendez fleet sails from, i., p. 186.

AVISMINDI, CAPTAIN, Report of, iv., p. 188.

AWATANIK, a Nipissing, goes from Green Bay to the Saguenay, *via* Lake Superior and Hudson Bay, iii., p. 30, n.

AYANOS, or CANOHATINNO, Texas Indians, iv., p. 78, n.; 90, n.

AYENNIS, Texas Indians, manners, agriculture, religion, iv., p. 80; probably misprint for Assonis, (Nassonis.)

AYLLON, LUCAS VASQUEZ DE—Discovers Chicora and the Jordan, i., p. 32; extent of his exploration, 134.

AYMALLE, LIEUTENANT, defeats English at Bloody Creek, v., p. 238, n.; 255, n.

AYOLA, Salt springs of, i., p. 22.

AYOLA, JOHN, Spaniard, explores the Paraguay, i., p. 38.

AYS—Texas Indians, mission among, vi., p. 24, n.

AZAMBJUJA, DIEGO DE, Builds Fort St. George, i., p. 18.

AZORES, Biard and companions at, i., p. 283.

BABOUL, an English post in Newfoundland, called also by Charlevoix, REBOU, BAY DE TOULLE; properly BAY OF BULLS, which see.

BACCHUS ISLAND—Cartier's name for Isle Orleans, i., p. 116.

BAFFINS, WILLIAM, discoveries of, i., p. 51; discovers Baffins' Bay, 53.

BAHAMA CHANNEL, cause of shipwrecks in, i., p. 182.

BAHAMOS—Texas Indians, iv., p. 70; see BRACAMOS, HEBAHAMOS.

BAILAI (BAILEY) HENRY, English commandant at Fort Nelson, surrenders to d'Iberville, iv., p. 58.

BAILLEUR, LE—La Motte le Vilin's pilot, i., p. 280, n.

BAILLIF, LE, Huguenot, on English squadron that took Quebec, ii., p. 50; Kertk gives him keys of storehouses, ib.

BAILLIF, FATHER GEORGE LE, Recollect, deputed to the king, ii., p. 33; presents Indian dictionaries, 59, n.

BAILLOQUET, F. PETER, Jesuit—Labors on Gulf and River St. Lawrence, iii., p. 40; notice of, vi., p. 125.

BALDAYA, ANTHONY G., doubles Cape Bojador, i., p. 15.

BALISE, fort built at, vi., p. 70; see 106.

BALLONES, DON DIONISIO PEREZ, fails to enter Espiritu Santo Bay, vi., p. 66, n.

BALSAM LAKE, ii., p. 28, n.

BALTIMORE, LORD, Settles Ferryland in Avalon, Newfoundland, iii., p. 140, n.; succeeded there by Sir David Kirke, vi., p. 125.

BANDA discovered, i., p. 28.

BANTAM conquered by Mascarenhas, i., p. 35.

BAPTISTE, SIEUR, succors Naxoat, v., p. 31.

BAPTISTE, , French privateer, in prison in Boston; harshly treated; Frontenac complains, v., p. 82; Governor of New England wishes to hang him as a pirate, p. 157; saved by threats of reprisal, ib.; not released, p. 82, n.

BARACOA, Jamaica, ravages of French pirates at, i., p. 168.

BARAZA, FATHER CYPRIAN, Jesuit, explores Moxos country, killed, i., p. 57.

BARBIER, or MINIME, GABRIEL, of Montreal, marries in Texas, father of first child born in Texas, iv., p 39, n.; left by La Sale in command of St. Louis, 89.

BARBU, LE, Natché chief, tries to kill de la Loire, vi., p. 26; his cruelty, 30; put to death, ib.

BARCIA, DON ANDRE GONZALES DE—His "Ensayo Cronologico de la Florida," noticed, i., p. 91; pretensions as to Florida, 133; refutes de Thou, 214; criticised by Salazar, 92; edits Garcia, ib.; Leon Pinelo, 94.

BARDOU, BR. ANSELM, Recollect, iii., p. 149, n.

BARENTSZ, WILLIAM, discoveries of, i., p. 46; discovers Spitzbergen, 48.

BARLOW, ARTHUR, discovers Roanoke Island, i., p. 45.

BARNEVELDS' ISLANDS, why so called, i., p. 52.

BARON, SIEUR, Engineer on Perrier's Natchez expedition, vi., p. 108.

BARON, THE—Huron chief—Address at La Prairie, iv., p. 148; treacherously treats with the Iroquois, 270; prevents Hurons going to war, ib.; what Frontenac told him, 272; his intrigues, ib.; settles in New York with several Huron families, v., p. 65.

BARR, CAPT., sent out by Coxe, outwitted by French, v., p. 124.

BARRE, MR. LE FEBURE DE LA, Governor-General of New France, sketch of, iii., p. 216, n.; services in Cayenne and West Indies, ib.; his instructions, 216; arrival, 222; writes to the King against La Sale, ib.; convokes an assembly of Notables, 224; sends decision to the Court, 226; prepares for Iroquois war, 241; sends a deputy, ib.; dispatch to minister, ib.; insolent reply of Iroquois, 242; discovers English intrigues, ib.; seizes Fort Catarocouy and Fort St. Louys, Illinois, belonging to La Sale, 243; how regarded in the colony, 244; why he resolves to attack the Senecas, 245; his arrangements for the campaign, 249; proposals made to him by Onondagas and Senecas, 252; makes peace on dishonorable terms, 253; receives aid from France, 254; King's orders, 255; information sent by F. de Lamberville, 257; recalled, 259; Louis XIV. condemns his regulation in regard to parish priests, iii., p. 25; Denonville's reply to Dongan as to, ii., 284; permits reprisals on La Sale's men, 310.

BARRÉ, NICHOLAS, commandant of Charlesfort, in place of Albert, i., p. 146; destroys fort, and embarks with all for France, 147; sufferings of party till relieved by English, 148.

BARRILLON, French ambassador to Charles II.; complains in vain of English encroachments in Hudson Bay, iii., p. 269; concludes neutrality treaty, 273.

BARROTO, JOHN HENRY, pilot of Andres de Pes, iv., p. 113, n.

BARROW, STEPHEN, English, discovers Nova Zembla, i., p. 42.

BARTHELEMY, young Parisian, starts for Illinois, 107; forced to remain at Arkansas, 109.

BASAN, DON ALVARO DE, galliots commanded by, i., p. 185.

BASANIER, publishes Laudonnière's account, i., p. 72.

BASQUES, early cod fisheries of on the banks of Newfoundland, i., p. 25, 106; pilotois, a Basque word adopted in Canada, ii., p. 13; troublesome in Newfoundland, p. 165.

BASTIDAS, RODERIC DE, discovers Gulf of Uraba, i., p. 24.

BASTON—Charlevoix's mode of spelling Boston. See BOSTON.

BASTON, a soldier, reinforces Lambert Closse, ii., p. 251, n.

BASTONNOIS—General term for English colonists, iii., p. 235, n.; iv., p. 23.

BATAVIA founded, i., p. 53.

BAUDOIN, F. MICHAEL, Jesuit, endeavors to found a Choctaw mission, vi., p. 103.

BAUGY, SIEUR DE, Lieutenant of de la Barre's guards, sent to Fort St. Louis, Illinois, iii., p. 243; repulses Iroquois, 244.

BAUMANOIR, French officer, distinguished at the siege of Quebec, iii., p. 181.

BAURES kill Father C. Baraza, i., p. 57.

BAXTER, REV. JOSEPH, missionary, sent to Kenebec, v., p. 268; controversy with Rale, ib.; retires, 269; notice of, 268, n.

BAY, DE, brother of de la Giraudiere, proposes an arrangement with Denys, iii., p. 137.

BAY OF BULLS—(called in Charlevoix, Bay de Toulle, v., p. 40; Baboul, p. 36; Rebou, p. 173;)—place in Newfoundland, between Renowes and St. John, p. 40; Zephyr (Sapphire) captured at, ib., p. 36; taken by Iberville and Brouillan, 41; Sir John Leake at, 162; captured by French, 173.

BAY OF FUNDY, or FRENCH BAY, description of, i., p. 254; the river of Norumbega, vi., p. 124.

BAY OF THE PUANTS, or GREEN BAY, iii., p. 120.

BAY ST. LAWRENCE—Limits of province of Gaspesie on, i., p. 249.

BAY ST. PAUL, mines at, iii., p. 98.
See CHALEURS BAY, HUDSON BAY, LITTLE BAY, ST. LUKE'S BAY.

BAYAGOULAS, Louisiana Indians, Iberville visits their temple, v., p. 121; the god of, 122; other name of, 123, n.; sing calumet to l'Epinai, vi., p. 39; Limoges missionary to, 76, n.

BAYOU ST. CATHERINE, Choctaws defeat Natchez at, and rescue French prisoners, vi., p. 96.

BEAR TRIBE OF MOHAWKS, F. Jogues killed by, ii., p. 195; of Hurons, 27, 71, 220, 280.

BEAUBASSIN, division of Acadia, English violence at, v., p. 28; English repulsed at, 172.

BEAUBASSIN, LIEUTENANT LA VALLIERE SIEUR DE, inroad into New England, v., p. 160; attacks Wells, &c., 161, n; draws off from Casco, ib., see VALLIERE.

BEAUBOIS, F. NICHOLAS DE, Superior of the Jesuits in Louisiana, takes Chicagou to France, vi., p. 76, n.; brings over missionaries, ib.

BEAUCOURT, CHEVALIER DUBOIS BERTELET DE, sketch of, iv., p. 217, n.; marches against Oneidas, p. 213; defeats Iroquois, 217; fortifies Quebec, 236, n.; probably on Frontenac's expedition, v., p. 13, n.; commands Canadians sent to Newfoundland, 172; ordered to hasten fortifications at Quebec, 237; his labors there, iv., p. 217, n.; Governor of Three Rivers and of Montreal, ib.

BEAUCHENE, MR. DE, i., p. 62.

BEAUHARNOIS, FRANCIS DE, BARON DE BEAUVILLE, Intendant in Canada, v., p. 156, n.; in France, 181; Intendant of Rochelle and Rochefort, p. 254; Pontchartrain urges him to induce merchants to recapture Acadia, ib.

BEAUHARNOIS DE BEAUMONT, brother of preceding, see BEAUMONT.

BEAUHARNOIS, CLAUDE DE, brother of preceding, Napoleon III., descended from, v., p. 310, n.

BEAUHARNOIS, HORTENSE, v., p. 310, n.

BEAUHARNOIS DE LA BOISCHE, CHARLES, CHEVALIER DE and afterwards Marquis de, notice of, v., p. 310; Governor-General of New France, ib.; Begon marries sister of, ib.; sends Verendrye to discover South Sea, v., p. 310.

BEAUJEU (COUNT) DE, notice of, iv., p. 63, n.; commands squadron sent to discover Micissipi, 63; quarrels with de la Sale, 65, vessel lost by his obstinacy, 66; makes La Sale miss mouth of Micissipi, 68; takes captain of storeship on board to shield him from La Sale, 72; sets sail, ib.; at mouth of Mississippi, v., p. 122, n.; question as to bad faith of, ib.

BEAUJEU, DANIEL LIENARD DE, iv., p, 63, n.

BEAULIEU, SIEUR DE, reconnoitres the Natchez, vi., p. 107; attacked and killed, 108.

BEAUMANOIR, commands a detachment, iv., p. 181.

BEAUMONT, MR. BEAUHARNOIS DE, commanding the Heros, reaches Quebec without meeting the English fleet, v., p. 246.

BEAUPORT, militia of, iv., p. 167; farmers of, 176.

BEAUPRÉ, militia of, iv., p. 167; v., p. 13.

BEAUVOIS, LIEUTENANT RENÉ LE GARDEUR DE, notice of, v., p. 12, n.; see BEAUVAIS, TILLY DE and GARDEUR, DE TILLY LE.

BEAUVAIS, LIEUTENANT DE TILLY DE, raises a war party, success, iv., p. 127; commands Indian corps in Frontenac's Iroquois expedition, v., p. 12; confusion as to, ib., n.

BEAVER, faults committed in Canada in regard to, v., p. 286; used as a circulating medium, ii., p. 169, n.

BECHAMEL, Father, French Jesuit, explores Cayenne, i., p. 57.

BEGON, Intendant of Rochefort, orders from the king, iv., p. 24; succeded there by de Beauharnois, v., p. 254; Intendant in the West Indies, iv., p. 66; Commissaire at St. Domingo, ib.; aids La Sale, ib.; ordered to equip ships, iv., p. 275.

BEGON, MICHAEL, son of preceding, Intendant in Canada, v., p. 23, n.; Memoir of Vaudreuil, and of, for peopling Canada, v., p. 301.

BEKANCOURT, RENÉ ROBINEAU, BARON DE, in Seneca expedition, iii., p. 249; said by Charlevoix to have commanded Indian corps in Frontenac's expedition, v., p. 13; de Menneval son to, iv., p. 27.

BEKANCOURT River, Abenaquis settle on, v., p. 167; why, ib.; Iroquois carry off prisoners, iv., p. 142.

BEKANCOURT, Abenaquis town, first on Montesson island, v., p. 167, n.; Portneuf grants land for, ib.; Indians of, on expedtion, v., p. 204.

BELALCASAR, SEBASTIAN, Spaniard, discovers Popayan, i., p. 38.

BELEN, discovered by Columbus, i., p. 25.

BELETRE, SIEUR DE, distinguished in Newfoundland, v., p. 174.

BELLEFOND, MARSHAL DE, urges King to send Frontenac back to Canada, and answers for him, iv., p. 22.

BELLEFONT, brave Canadian, killed in an action between Abenaquis and English, iv., p. 160.

BELLEFONTAINE, SIEUR DE, commandant at the Illinois; receives Cavelier and his party, iv., p. 110.

BELLE ISLE, Strait of, iii., p. 145; v., p. 59; English escape to, v., p. 214.

BELLOMONT, RICHARD COOTE, Earl of, Governor-General of New England, sketch of, v., p. 81, n.; sends back French prisoners to Frontenac, v., p. 80; letter of, 81; pretensions of over Iroquois, ib; Frontenac's reply, 82; holds general Council of the Five Iroquois Cantons, 83; second letter to Frontenac, 85; his reply, 86; false remarks as to missionaries, 90; his pretensions as to several other posts, 91; tries to gain Abenaquis, 92, 97; receives orders from King of England to stop hostilities, 98; prevents Iroquois deputies going to Montreal, 99; tries to thwart peace, 104; Tegannisorens' reply to his envoys, 105; induces Iroquois to accept Protestant missionaries, 106; new efforts to prevent Iroquois making peace with us, 108; puts an Oneida in irons, ib.; threatens to hang Jesuits entering the colony, 112; incenses Indians by his threats, ib.; death of, 81, n.

BELMONT, ABBE VACHON DE, Superior of Seminary of Montreal, cited, ii., p. 250, &c.; founds Mission of the Mountain, iii., p. 117, n.; reply to F. de la Chasse on F. Rasle's death, v., p. 281.

BENAC, CAPTAIN DE, commands militia in Perrier's Natchez expedition, vi., p. 107; receives orders to obtain information, 109; informs Perrier of flight of enemy, 114.

BENEDICTINES—Acadian mission offered to, v., p. 156.

BENEVENT, Abbey of, in France, revenues of conferred on Bishop of Quebec, iii., p. 123.

BENIN, Kingdom of, i., p. 18; de Gourgues authorized to carry slaves from, 225.

BENTIVIGLIO, GUY DE—Nuncio of Pope Paul V. grants faculties to Recollects, ii., p. 25, n.

BENZONI—Novæ Novi Orbis Historiæ, account of, i., p. 71.

BEOTHS, or RED INDIANS OF NEWFOUNDLAND, iii., p. 145, n.

BER DU CHESNE. See Bert.

BER, PETER LE, first Canadian painter, associate of Charon, iv., p. 235, n.

BER, JAMES LE. Journal cited, iv., p. 233; vi., p. 125.

BER, M'LLE LE, the recluse, iv., p. 207; dies, v., p. 303, n.

BERGERES, CAPTAIN DES, Escapes pestilence at Niagara, iii., p. 291, n.; left in a fort in Frontenac's expedition, v., p. 15.

BERMUDA, discovered, i., p. 35.

BERMUDEZ, JOHN, discovers Bermuda, i., p. 35.

BERRANGER, CAPTAIN, misconduct of, vi., p. 66, and n.

BERROA, DON ESTEVAN, attacks Dauphin Island, vi., p. 51; informs Spanish Commandant that it cannot be taken, 52; surrenders, 59.

BERRUYER—Member of the Company of a Hundred, ii., p. 169.

BERSIAMITES—Indians trading at Tadoussac, and instructed in Christianity there, ii., p. 118; p. 243; iii., p. 40.

BERT DU CHESNE, (BER,) JOHN VINCENT LE—Notice of, iv., p. 207; posted with with Indians near Chambly, iv., p. 203; hastens up to meet enemy, 206; mortally wounded, 207; dies, ib.

BERTHIER, CAPTAIN DE, of the Carignan, Salieres regiment, with Sorel, commands rear of army against Mohawks, iii., p. 90; on Denonville's expedition, 283, n.; his batallion gives way, 287, n.

BERTRAND, SIEUR GASPAR—Brave settler at Placentia, leads expedition to Carbonniere Island, v., p. 232; attacks an English frigate, kills the captain, loses his life, ib.

BERWICK, N. H., destroyed, iv., p. 131.

BERWICK'S victory relieves Acadia, v., p. 191, n.

BESCHEFER, F. THIERRY, Jesuit, sent to Orange, iii., p. 87.

BETHANCOURT, JOHN DE, Canary Isands ceded to, i., p. 14.

BETHANCOURT, MACIOT DE, cedes Canaries to Henry, Count of Viseu, i., p. 14.

BIARD, F. PETER, Jesuit, appointed to Acadia, i., p. 260; why stopped at Bourdeaux, 261; sufferings in Acadia, 270; his relation in that country, ib.; Membertou's death, 272; preaches to the Canibas, 273; goes to St. Sauveur, 275; site of his colony, 277; a baptism, ib.; taken to Virginia by Argall, 281; a Frenchman denounces him, 283; how he repaid ill treatment, 284; in England, ib.; death of, ib., n.

BIDAES—Texas tribe, mission among, vi., p. 24, n.

BIENCOURT Chas. DE, son of de Poutrincourt, seeks to avoid taking Jesuits to Acadia, 261–2; treats with Mde de Guercheville, 263; conduct in regard to

BIENCOURT, (*continued.*) Membertou, 272; goes with Biard to Kinibequi, 273; dies in Acadia, iii., p. 125, n.; devises lands to la Tour, ib.

BIENVILLE I, FRANCIS LE MOYNE DE, fifth son of Charles le Moyne de Longueuil, iv., p. 194; killed at St. Sulpice, p. 194; what defeated his war-party, 196.

BIENVILLE II., JOHN BAPTIST LE MOYNE DE, brother of preceding, accompanies his brother d'Iberville to mouth of Mississippi, v., p. 120; put in command of a fort, 123; vi., p. 12; meets English on river, v., 124; Commandant-General, vi., p. 14; abandons Biloxi for Maubile River, ib.; treats English kindly, 24; sent to Natchez, halts at the Tonicas, 28; murderers punished, 30; builds Fort Rosalie at Natchez, 31; made commandant till Epinay's arrival, 31, n.; Commandant-General under the Western Company, 38; selects ground for New Orleans, and is appointed to found, 40; occupies and abandons St. Joseph's Bay, 42; commands Indians at siege of Pensacola, 44; reinforces de Serigny, ib.; ordered to invest Fort Pensacola by land, ib.; harasses garrison, 58; refuses terms to Governor, ib.; dissuades de Saujon from attacking St. Joseph's Bay, 63; ordered by Court to send St. Denys back to Natchitoches, 65; makes Biloxi his headquarters, ib.; attempts to settle St. Bernard's Bay, ib.; sends back Indians treacherously taken, 66; Choctaws report English proposals to, 68; information from Governor of Carolina, ib.; Chickasaws ask peace, 70; marches against Natchez, and exacts reparation, 72, n.; burns a town and makes peace, ib.; ordered to France, publishes Black Code, 75, n.; proceeds to France, 75; reappointed Governor of Louysiana, 120; dies.

BIERRE, Gascon gentleman lost in Gourgues' expedition in Florida, i., p. 236.

BIGOT, FATHER JAMES, Jesuit, (born 1644, died, 1711,) sends word to de Callieres in regard to Abenaquis, v., p. 97; at Quebec, 98, n.; interpreter at the general Council of peace, p. 149; Denonville's remarks on him and his brother, iv., p. 44; Indian labors, v., p. 256.

BIGOT, FATHER VINCENT, Jesuit, (born 1647 died, 1720,) gathers an Abenaqui village near Pentagoët, iii., p. 308; Denonville on, ib.

BIHOREL, one of La Sale's companions, lost, iv., p. 88.

BILOXI, OLD, Mr. d'Iberville builds a fort there, v., p. 123; Sauvolle commandant, vi., p. 12; abandoned, p. 14; restored, 62, n.; establishment at Dauphin Island, removed to, fire at, 63, n.;

BILOXI, NEW, fort built by Bienville, vi., p. 63, n.; headquarters removed to New Orleans and only detachment left at, 67; hurricane at, 69.

BIMINI, fountain of youth on, i., p. 28.

BINNETEAU, F. JULIAN, Jesuit, missionary to the Abénaquis, sends word to Frontenac, iv., p. 239; in Illinois, v., p. 133, n.; notice of, iv., p. 239, n.

BIRD, now FUNK ISLANDS, i., p. 112, n.

BISEAU, MR. DE, French ambassador in England; sends back to France three Acadian missionaries, i., p. 284.

BISHOP—First projects for a Canadian, ii., p. 183, n.; bishop of Quebec, iii., p. 122; depends immediately on Pope, like Bishop of Puy, ib.; revenues, ib.

BISKATRONGÉ, or WEEPERS, Indians, La Salle among, iv., p. 88, n.

BLACK RIVER, Tionontates on, ii., p. 271, n.; iii., p. 31, n.; Mesnard killed on his way to, ib.

BLACK KETTLE, Onondaga chief, envoy at Montreal, iii., p. 303; on the Ottawa, iv., p. 217; defeats St. Michel's party, 218-19; dashes into la Chesnaye, 220; defeated and killed, v., p. 79.

BLAEU, JOHN and WILLIAM, Great Atlas of, i., p. 67.

BLAINVILLE, J. B. CELORON DE, Vilinville sends deserters to, vi., p. 51.

BLANC, JOHN LE, Chief of the Ottawas du Sable, called also TALON, and OUTOUTAGA, speech of, v., p. 143; delivers F. Constantin, 185; speech to Vaudreuil, 188.

BLANC, VINCENT LE, his work, i., p. 79; statement as to a Spanish voyage to the St. Lawrence and Labrador, p. 106.

BLEECKER, JOHANNES, JR., sent to Onondaga, v., p. 138, n.

BLENAC, COUNT DE, Governor-General of French West Indies, de la Barre ordered to co-operate with, iii., p. 216; attacked by English in Martinique, 241; forces them to retire, 244.

BLOME, RICHARD, corrected, ii., p. 10.

BLONDEL, CAPTAIN, Commander at Natchez, vi., p. 40.

BLOODY CREEK, Nova Scotia, English defeated at, v., p. 238.

BLUE EARTH RIVER, copper mines on, vi., p. 13.

BOCHART (QUERBODO)—Mr. DU PLESSIS, Governor of Three Rivers, ii., p. 243; killed by Iroquois, p. 245; his wife, ib., n.

BOESME, BROTHER LOUIS LE, Jesuit, starts with Ottawas, ii., p. 272; abandoned and returns to Quebec, ib.; again goes west, iii., p. 120.

BOIS, REV. MR., army chaplain, arrives, iii., p. 95, n.; on Tracy's expedition, 95.

BOISBRIAND, officer, land grant to, ii., p. 112.

BOISBRIAND, SIEUR DUGUÉ DE, notice of, v., p. 47, n.; captures Kirividi in Newfoundland, 45; left as lieutenant at Fort Bourbon, 58; left in Fort Biloxi, p. 124, n.; goes to Louysiana as commandant of the Illinois, vi., p. 41; Governor ad interim, 75, n. See DUGUÉ, GUÉ.

BOISGUILLOT, Canadian, Denonville's order to, iii., p. 280.

BOISRONDET, SIEUR DE, La Sale's commissary, receives Cavelier, iv., p. 110; accompanies him to Canada, ib.

BOMAZEEN, Abenaqui chief, treacherously seized, iv., p. 273.

BONIFACE, F. FRANCIS, Jesuit, brings several Mohawk Christians into Canada, iii., p. 164.

BONAVENTURE, SIMON DENYS DE, announces succor from France, iv., p. 200; takes English prize into Port Royal, 213; at Quebec, 227; fails to take Pemkuit, 227–8; effect of his arrival in Acadia, 274; defeats the Sorlings, ib., n.; besieges Pemkuit with d'Iberville, v., p. 24; at Placentia, 27; De Brouillan embarks on his vessel, the St. Jean, 39; sails for France, 40; succeeds de Brouillon, v., p. 172; d'Iberville employs him to solicit reinforcement of royal troops, 48; at Port Royal, 197; Subercase leaves him in charge of fort when moving on English, 199.

BONAVISTA—Newfoundland cape and port, named by Jacques Cartier, i., p. 112; English at St. John retire to, v., 44; why not taken by d'Iberville, 45; French ravage all the coast of, 174.

BONIN, FATHER JAMES, Jesuit, returns to Europe, ii., p. 250.

BONREPOS, SIEUR DE, volunteer at Corlar, (Schenectady,) iv., p. 122.

BONTEMS, CAPTAIN, takes a Portuguese ship and rescues two Frenchmen, i., p. 213.

BORDEAUX, Gourgues sails from, i., p. 225; Biard stopped at, p. 261.

BORDENAC, REV. MR., of the Badine; first chaplain of Fort Biloxi, v., p. 124, n.

BORDIER, JAMES, one of the Hundred Associates, ii., p. 169.

BORELLO, CHRISTOPHER, in Japan, i., p. 39.

BORGNE, LE SR., of Rochelle, creditor of de Charnisé, obtains Acadia by a judgment of Parliament, iii., p. 131–2; claims as against la Tour and Denys, violence, ib.; burns la Heve, 133; surrenders Port Royal to English, 134.

BORGNE, LE, JR., taken prisoner to Boston, treats with English, iii., p. 135; exacts tribute from English as Seigneur of Acadia, v., p. 92.

BORIQUEN, original name of Porto Rico, i., p. 19.

BOSTON, built by English on French territory, i., p. 253; Dreuillette and Godefroy sent to, ii., p. 214, 247; La Tour at, iii., p. 131, n.; crew of vessel from, found by Radisson on Bourbon River, 234; return of Phip's fleet to, iv., pp. 189–190; Chevalier d'Aux escapes from, 221, n.; Sir Francis Wheeler's fleet at, 244; outbreak at, 257; squadron at, v., p. 52; English believe French design to take, ib.; abortive project against, 70; de la Valliere and Bruyas at, 98; ill treatment of prisoners at, 157; exchange of prisoners forbidden by Queen. New York militia at, ib.; attempts too late to make Abenaquis neutral; rejoicings at on supposed capture of Port Royal, 160; indignation against General Mark (March,) on this failure, 195; General Court at justifies March, 196; ill treatment of French and Indian prisoners at, 210; great preparations against Canada at, 217; alarmed at de Subercase's activity, 226; Rouville and Dupuys at, 234; preparations at for siege of Quebec, 238; Baron St. Castin treacherously taken to, 274; fear of Rale at,

275; Rev. J. Durand a prisoner at, v., p. 297, n.

Botou, or Ramee Islands, v., p. 300; known in Cartier's time, ib., n.; granted to St. Pierre, ib.

Boucher, Sieur Pierre, Governor of Three Rivers, deputed to the King, iii., p. 52; his work on Canada, i., p. 80; returns with de Monts, iii., p. 53; Boucher de la Perriere, son of, v., p. 47; du Muys marries daughter of, vi., p. 17; Lajemmerais marries granddaughter of, iv., p. 139, n.

Boucherville, Iroquois defeated near, by de la Durantaye, iv., p. 269.

Boularderie, Louis Simon de St. Aubin le Poupet, Chevalier de la, naval ensign wounded at Port Royal, v., p. 199.

Boularderie Island, Cape Breton, v., p. 282, n.

Boulé, Eustace, brother-in-law of Champlain, ii., p. 47, n.; captured by Kertk, 48.

Boulé, Helen, sister of preceding, wife of Champlain, ii., p. 21, n., 88, n.; dies an Ursuline nun, ib.

Boulé, Nicholas, Secretary of the King's chamber, ii., p. 23.

Bourbon River, origin of name, i., p. 59, iii., p. 234; see Port Nelson, Kakiou-kiouay.

Bourdon, Sieur John, chief engineer and procurator of Canada, accompanies Father Jogues to the Iroquois, ii., p. 186; letter to, 195; removed from office and sent to France by de Mésy, iii., p. 74; explores Labrador coast, 230; takes possession of Hudson Bay for the King, i., p. 56, iii., p. 230; his son, d'Autray, with La Sale, iii., 214, n.; sent to Dongan by de la Barre, 248.

Bourgeois, of Beaubassin, waits on commander of English squadron, v., p. 208.

Bourgeoys, Margaret, opens school at Montreal, ii., p. 251, n.; founds the Sisters of the Congregation, ii., p. 250; sketch of, 250–1, n.; death of, v., p. 114, n.; Charlevoix proposed to write life of, ib.

Bourguet, John, member of the Company of a Hundred, ii., p. 169.

Bourgmont, Sieur de, commandant at Detroit, v., p. 184; harshness to Indians, causes Indian outbreak at, ib.; in Louisiana, penetrates to the Comanches, 184, n.

Boursier, Father Daniel, Recollect, taken by English, ii., p. 46.

Boursier, Brother Joseph, Jesuit lay brother, goes to Onondaga, ii., p. 268.

Bouteroue, Claude de, Intendant, sketch of, iii., p. 165, n.; his instructions, iii., p. 120; Colbert's letter to de Courcelle on, 121.

Bouteroue, Mary Dorothy, daughter of preceding, with de Courcelles, sponsors of Garakonthié, iii., p. 153.

Bouvet, Capt., sent to explore Austral land, i., p. 64.

Bracamos, Texas Indians, iv., p. 70, 90, n.; La Salle finds Spanish arms set up among, 80, n.; see Bahamos, Hebahamos.

Bradford, William, Gov. of Plymouth receives Druillettes, ii., p. 214, n.

Braganza, house of succeed to Duchy of Veraguas, i., p. 25.

Braquemont, Robert de, Admiral of France, i., p. 14.

Brandt, Capt., Swiss, deserts with his company and goes to Carolina, vi., p. 67, n.; 68.

Bras Piqué, Female Sun of the Natchez, warns Chepar, vi., p. 81, n.

Bray, de, one of the French colony in Florida, saved by de Gourgues, i., p. 228; reconnoitres Fort San Mathes, 229; called also Debré, ib., n.

Brazil discovered, i., p. 27; Solis discovers the Rio de Janeiro in, 30; the Amazon discovered in, 39; French attempt to colonize, 41–2, 132.

Brazos river, probably crossed by La Salle, iv., p. 88.

Brebeuf, F. John, Jesuit, arrives at Quebec, ii., p. 35; starts for Huron country, compelled to return, 36; returns to Canada after its restoration, p. 64; his Huron voyage deferred, why, 69; his sufferings on the way, 76; Huron's remark to, 79; obtains rain by prayer, 81; at a Huron council, 82; gives his death banquet, 96, n.; baptizes an Iroquois captive at Tondakhra, 105; preaches to Neuters, 152; returns to Quebec, 177; refuses to fly from St. Louis on approach of Iroquois, 219; taken, ib; burnt, 221; his courage and character, 222; sketch of,

Brebeuf, F. John, (*continued.*) ib, n ; works of, ib ; remains removed to Quebec, ib ; head still preserved, ib.

Bremans, Eustace de, young Parisian with La Salle ; his adventures after fall of Fort St. Louys, iv., p. 114.

Bresolles, Mother Judith de, Superior of the Hotel Dieu, Montreal, iii., p. 27.

Bressani, F. Francis Joseph, Jesuit from Rome, captured by Iroquois, ii., p. 171 ; tortured, 172 ; sold to Dutch, who send him to Rochelle, 173 ; returns to Quebec, collects for his torturers 183 ; attacked by Iroquois on his way to the Huron country and wounded, 235 ; at Quebec, ib. ; returns to Italy, 237, 250 ; his work, i., p. 80, ii., p. 174.

Brest, Labrador, iii., p. 145, n.

Brest, v., p. 71, p. 117, n.

Breton, Christopher le, of Havre de Grace, one of Ribaut's men who escaped, i., p. 212, n.

Bretons. When the Breton fishermen began to take cod on the Great Bank, &c., i., p. 25, 106.

Bretonvilliers, Mr., Superior of the Seminary of Montreal, appoints Perrot Governor of that city, iii., p. 123.

Briconnet, Bishop Denys, of St. Malo, blesses Cartier, i., p. 114.

Brigueur, English commandant at Hudson Bay, iii., p. 271.

Brisacier, Abbé, (James Charles,) Letter to Father La Chaise on the liquor trade, iv., p. 230.

Brisay, Mlle de, daughter of Denonville, a nun, iii., p. 258, n.

Britto, Antonio de, discovers Mey Islands, i., p. 34.

Britto, Dominic de, Jesuit, discovers Amazon, i., p. 55.

Broar, Bro. Ambrose, Jesuit, sent to Onondaga, ii., p. 268, n.

Brosse, Peter de la, reduced lieutenant, volunteer in Schenectady expedition, iv., p. 122 ; raises a war party ; its success and accident, p. 127.

Brothers of Charity at Louisbourg, v., p. 296, n.

Brouillan, Mr. de, sketch of v., p. 34; Governor of Placentia, attacked by English, iv., p. 223 ; siege raised, 226 ; to act with d'Iberville in expelling English from Newfoundland, 275 ; character of, v., p. 34 ; expedition against English, 35 ; complains of St. Malo men and they of him, 38 ; at Placentia, disapproves of Carbonniere expedition, 37 ; quarrels with d'Iberville and is reconciled, 38 ; embarks, 39 ; new quarrels and reconciliations, ib ; at the capture of St. John's, 44 ; rudeness to d'Iberville, proposes to hold St. Johns ; but does not, 45 ; returns to Placentia, 46 ; coincides with d'Iberville's going direct to Port Nelson, 54 ; succeeds the Chevalier de Villebon as Governor of Acadia, 157 ; threatens to retaliate in Baptiste's case, 157 ; sends Callieres information from Boston, 157 ; surprised by the English at Port Royal, 170 ; forces them to raise the siege, 171 ; his death, 161, 172, n ; succeeded by Subercase, v., p. 161.

Brouillan, St. Ovide de, nephew of preceding, see St. Ovide.

Brouttin, Sieur, Commandant at Natchez asked as a hostage, vi., p. 95.

Browers' Passage, i., p. 56.

Brulé, Stephen, Huguenot, on English fleet that takes Quebec, ii., p. 50.

Bruyas, F. James, Jesuit, notice of iii., p. 109, n ; missionary to the Iroquois, 109 ; iv., p. 284 ; obstacles to his Oneida mission, iii., p. 158 ; at General Council puts question in Governor's name, iv., p. 253 ; Iroquois asks de Callieres for him, v., p. 94 ; sent to Boston, 98 ; goes to Onondaga, his reception, speech in council, 103 ; returns to Montreal with deputies of two Cantons, v., p. 108 ; why he does not insist in regard to their agreement to admit Protestant missionaries, 107 ; returns to Onondaga at the request of Teganissorens 138 ; success of negotiation, ib. ; interpreter at the General Peace Congress, 150 ; his Radices Verborum Iroquæorum, iii., p. 109, n.

Bry, Theodore de, account of the India Occidentalis of, i., p. 72.

Buenos Ayres, or Villa de la Trinidad, founded by Mendoza, i., p. 37 ; restored by Cabeza de Vaca, p. 40.

Buisson, Sieur du, Commandant at Detroit, insulted by Foxes, v., p. 257 ; calls on our allies, leads them against Foxes ; his conduct in the expedition and its success, 257–260.

BULLION, MADAME DE, gives 60,000 livres, to the Hospital, Montreal, iii., p. 27.

BUNGO, Kingdom of, i., p. 40.

BURIN, BAY OF GRAND, Newfoundland. Its situation. Why Nesmond goes there, v., p. 73.

BURNEFFE, New England orthography of PORTNEUF, which see.

BUSHLOPERS, orders against, iii., p. 194; disorder of, iii., p. 310; prevent settlement of Acadia, iv., p. 16; result of fresh orders against; trouble occasioned by joining Sioux against Miamis, v., p. 64; fresh orders from King against them, v., p. 77; their misconduct force missionaries to abandon Michilimakinac, 182; King grants amnesty to, and Louvigny brings almost all in, 307.

BUTEUX, F. JAMES, Jesuit, obtains narrative from F. Jogues, ii., p. 186; his labors in Northern Canada, 246; returns with a presentment of death, 248; killed by the Iroquois, ib.; sketch of, 249, n.

BUTTE DES MORTS, Foxes invested at, v. p. 306, n.

BUTTON, THOMAS, English, discoveries of, i., p. 51, iii., p. 230.

BYSSIRINIENS, Canada Indians, iii., p. 95. See NIPISSINGS.

CABANAS, French officer, distinguished at siege of Quebec, iv., p. 181.

CABEZA DE VACA, ALVAR NUÑEZ, with Pamfilo de Narvaez, i., p. 34, n; writes account of his expedition, ib.; work translated by Buckingham Smith, ib; founds anew Buenos Ayres, i., p. 40; ascends Paraguay, i., p. 40.

CABOT, OR GABOTO, JOHN, discoveries of, i., p. 20; 105; iii., p. 140.

CABRAL, PERO ALVAREZ, voyages of, i., p. 22.

CABRILLO, JOHN RUYS, Portuguese, names Cape Mendocino, Cal., i., p. 40.

CACAGOUS, Sagamo of Port St. Jean, i., p. 265, n.

CADAMOSTO, LOUIS DE, a Venetian, i., p. 17.

CADILLAC, DE LA MOTTE, succeeds de Louvigny at Michilimakinac; induces Indians to pursue Iroquois, iv., p. 264; action in regard to treacherous Huron chief, 270, policy, 271; anxiety in regard to Indians of his post, 277; his ability; induces Indians to attack Iroquois; what prevented his sending Indians to Frontenac; at Montreal with a large allied Indian force, v., p. 67; sent to Detroit with 100 men, 153; erects Fort Pontchartrain ib., n.; house burnt, 164, n; reply to Ottawa demand for justice on Miamis, 183; last words to Ottawas, before starting for Quebec, ib.; starts back to Detroit, 187; imprudent act on the way, sees and repairs it, 188; Ottawas will not treat with him, but with Governor-General, ib.; receives Vaudreuil's orders, 189; relents towards Miamis, and after promising le Pesant's head to Miamis, pardons him, 190; drives F. Aveneau from the St. Joseph mission, 202; amuses Miamis, and makes a dishonorable peace with them, ib.; marches against them; but is repulsed, and makes terms, 203; Governor of Louysiana, vi., p. 17; his instructions, ib.; attempts to open trade with Spaniards, 18; establishes store-houses at Natchez, 24; arrives at the Illinois, where silver mine said to have been discovered, 25; favorable proposals made to him by various Indian tribes, at Maubile, ib.; sends de'Bienville against the Natchez, 28; precautions to prevent Spaniards approaching us, 31; relieved, and returns to France, 38.

CADIZ, Menendez sails from, i., p. 186.

CAEN, EMERY DE and WILLIAM DE his uncle, Huguenot merchants, acquire rights of the Canada Company, ii., p. 33; Emery left in command at Quebec, 35; William de, arrives at Quebec, 36; ill-treats Jesuits, ib; rebuked by the Duke de Ventadour, Viceroy of New France, 38; suspected of soliciting English to seize Canada, 52; informs Kertk of Roquemont's fleet, 45; Emery taken by English while going to relief of Quebec, 51; returns to Canada and the English restore Quebec to him, 63; trade of the country given him for a year to compensate him for losses, 63.

CAFARO, FERDINAND DE, captain of the Comte de Toulouse, commanding squadron, dies of the pestilence in Louysiana, vi., p. 64, n.

CAFFINIERE, CAPT. DE LA, commands two vessels in the New York expedition, instructions; prize; returns to France, iv., pp. 24–8.

CAHAYNOHOUA, CAHAINIHOUA, or CAHINNIO, Texas tribe, iv., 108, n.

CAHIAGUÉ, a Huron town, Champlain and Hurons start from, to attack Entouohonorons, ii., p. 28.

CAILLE, SERGEANT LA, escapes from mutineers in Florida, i., p. 167 ; sent to Spaniards to capitulate, p. 210.

CALICUT, i., p. 21, 23.

CALIFORNIA, GULF OF, names of, iii., p. 45.

CALIFORNIA, discovered by Cortez and called St. Philip, i., p. 37 ; explored by Kino, 62.

CALIMORE ancient name of Cartagena, i., p. 36.

CALLIERES BONNEVUE, CHEVALIER HECTOR DE, sketch of iii., p. 256, n.; ex-captain in Navarre regiment, 256; governor of Montreal, ib.; leads Denonville's van 286, n.; leads convoy to Catarocouy, 306 ; his project for reducing New York, iv., p. 20 ; temporary governorship of it intended for, 21 ; praise of project, 26 ; condition of Montreal, 29 ; new New York plan, 35; not executed, 36; Frontenac's directions to, 192 ; draws secret from Iroquois deputies, iv., p. 49 ; he sends them to Frontenac, 50 ; Frontenac's orders to, 192; hears of a large Iroquois war party, 202 ; encamps at la Prairie de la Magdeleine to await English and Indians, ib. sends de Valrenes to defend Chambly, 203 ; detained by illness from action at la Prairie, ib.; sends a party against the Iroquois, 217 ; informs Frontenac that they are on the Ottawa, 218 ; Frontenac orders him to give St. Michel an escort, ib.; precautions against Iroquois raid ; instructs party against the Mohawks to take only the women and children prisoners, 234 ; disobeyed, ib.; sends an Oneida chief to the Governor General, 238 ; marches against Iroquois who retire on his approach, 240; management of the Iroquois, 249; Iroquois designs, 250; their defeat, 264; provides for the safety of all the posts, 269; his opinion as to the Iroquois expedition, v., p. 10 ; commands alternately the van and rear guard, 13 ; extricates the French army, from great peril, 14; facilitates the landing of the troops, 15 ; stratagem to prevent Senecas coming to aid of Onondaga, 16 ; commands the left wing of the army, ib.; why mounted, 17; offers to winter in the Iroquis country and assure the conquest, 20 ; advises punishing the Cayugas, 20 ; why it was not done, ib.; Frontenac orders him to send out expedition against Mohawks, his reply, 49; asks Frontenac's orders in regard to Oneidas, and his reply, 50 ; why he cannot accept offers of Christian Iroquois, 51 ; defeats Iroquois plans; 52 ; receives an Oneida deputy at Montreal, 63 ; his advice in regard to maintaining posts, 65 ; argument with Rev. Mr. Dellius on English pretensions, 91 ; distrusts Iroquois deputies ; his reply to their demands, 95 ; sends Courtemanche to France, 96 ; appointed Governor General, his character, 96 ; informed that Governor of New England wishes to negotiate with Abénaquis, his reply, 97 ; receives through King of England orders from the King to stop all hostilities in Canada, and sends a similar one to Governor of New England 98 ; Iroquois congratulate him on his promotion, 99 ; precautions against Iroquois surprise; why he communicates to the Onondagas the King of England's orders to Bellomont, 99 ; his reply to the Ottawas and Iroquois, 101 ; six deputies from two cantons introduced by de Maricourt, 101 ; public audience, ib.; signs a provisional treaty with them, 111 ; sends de Courtemanche and F. Anjelran to the northern and western tribes and his instructions, 111 ; reports state of affairs to de Pontchartrain, 111 ; why he is silent as to Iroquois choice of Protestant or Catholic missionaries, 112; informs de Pontchartrain that vessels were fitting out in England and Holland to settle Louysiana in consequence of Hennepin's work, and that the King of England intended to sends out French refugees, 125 ; Iroquois complain of Ottawa attack on their hunters, his reply, 135 ; remarks to Teganissorens on Detroit, 136 ; gives him French deputies, 138 ; at the congress of the general peace, 143 ; remarks to the Iroquois deputies after signing the treaty, 153 ; silent as to Jesuits, 154 ; threatens Governor of New England with reprisals if he puts Capt. Baptiste to death, 157 ; baffles Iroquois intrigues in the Cantons, 158 ; death, eulogy, 158.

CALLIERES, COUNT FRANCIS DE, brother of preceding, secretary to King. v., p. 96, n.

CANADA COMPANY, formed of St. Malo, Rouen, and Rochelle merchants, ii., p. 25 ; suppressed, 34.

CANADIAN CHARTERS, ii., p. 205, n.

CANADIANS, CANADACOA, Indian tribe, position of, ii., p. 8, n. ; represented now by Nasquapees, ib.

CANADIANS, not litigious, iii., p. 66 ; good faith of ; virtues of, impress new-comers from France, 96 ; disposition of, 260 ; rash, ib. ; fight well in Seneca fight, 289 ; courage of makes up for siege inexperience, iv., p. 135 ; bravery at siege of Quebec made known to King, 174 ; at the battle of La Prairie, 207, march against Mohawks with Indians, 233 ; attached to d'Iberville, v., p. 38 ; feared by de Brouillan ; he attempts to put them under de Muys, 40; their conquests in Newfoundland, 42; why they do not retain their conquests, 48 ; one hundred distinguish, themselves in Newfoundland, 172 ; Port Royal owes its preservation to, 194 ; raids into New England, 225 ; resolution of to defend Quebec, 245 ; result of confining themselves to beaver trade, 286 ; prevented from gulf fisheries, 290 ; distinguished at Dauphin Island, vi., p. 52 ; 150 Canadians at Fort Pensacola, 56 ; imprudence of Canadians with F. Doutreleau, 87 ; Perier unjust to, 115.

CANANOR, i., p. 23.

CANARDIERE, LA, English land at, iv., p. 176.

CANARY ISLANDS, Louis de la Cerda crowned King of, i., p. 14 ; given to John de Bethancourt, ib. ; ceded to Portugal, but restored to Spain, ib., question as to, 17.

CANAPOUCES, Louisiana tribe, sing calumet to l'Epinal, vi., p. 39.

CANAVERAL, shipwrecked French at spared by Menendez, i., p. 222.

CANE RIVER, Texas, iv., p. 90, n.

CANGOXIMA, Japan, i., p. 40.

CANIBAS, real Abénaquis, visited by Champlain, i., p. 49 ; visited by Biard, p. 273 ; some baptized at Sillery, ii., p. 201 ; defeat an English Mohegan force, iv., p. 188 ; ravages, 191 ; besiege and take Pemkuit, iv., p. 40–3; v., p. 25 ; rage on finding a Canibas in irons, 26 ; ordered by Frontenac to stop hostilities, 82, French sure of, 97 ; at Port Royal, 193, see ABENAQUIS.

CANIBEQUI, i., p. 273 ; see KENNEBEC.

CANIBESSINOAKS, meaning of, ii,, p. 201

CANNOHATINNOS, or AYANOS, Texas Indians, iv., p. 78, n, 90, n. ; defeated by Cenis and French, 105.

CANOE RIVER, TEXAS, iv., p. 91 n.

CANONS OF QUEBEC, iii., p. 26.

CANONVILLE, SIEUR DE, informs Provost that he saw English fleet at Tadoussac, iv., p. 152.

CANSES, Louysiana Indians, de Courtemanche prevents Kaskaskias and Ottawas attacking, v., p. 142 ; see KANSAS.

CANTOVA, FATHER DE, describes Caroline Islands, i., p. 63.

CAOUIS, Spanish post, vi., p. 21 ; see COAHUILA.

CAOUITAS, (CREEKS,) Florida Indians, interviewed between Head Chief or Emperor and Perrier, vi., p. 103.

CAPE BATURIER, now Cape Mallebarre, i., p. 253, n.

CAPE BLANC, now Cape Cod, i., p., 253.

CAPE BLANCO, AFRICA, discovered, i., p. 15 ; de Gourgues defeats three negro princes near, p. 226.

CAPE BOJADOR, Portuguese afraid to double, i., p. 14 ; doubled by Añez, 15.

CAPE BONNAVISTA, Newfoundland, Cartier at, i., p. 36.

CAPE BRETON ISLAND, or ISLE ROYALE, discovered, iii., p. 93, n. ; French settlement on, 132 ; missions on, ii., p. 46, 119 ; iii., p. 30, 46, n., 93, n.; attacked by English, iii., p. 93 ; restored to France, 94, n. ; its condition, 132 ; Denys' adventures on, ib. ; Fort St. Pierre on, 133, 137 ; Iberville at, v., p. 27 ; restored by treaty of Ryswick, 93 ; condition, ib. ; taken by Nicholson, 253, n. ; climate, production, ports &c., 282 et seq. ; Raudot's memoir on settlement of, 285 ; when called Isle Royale, 294 ; necessity of colonizing, ib. ; English Parliament inquire why left to France, 301.

CAPE BRULÉ on CAPE BRETON ISLAND, v., p. 284.

CAPE CAMCEAUX, CANSEAU, iii., p. 129.

CAPE CATOCHE, i., p. 30.

CAPE COD, Champlain calls it Cape Blanc, i., p. 49, 253, n.

CAPE CONSOLATION, or ST. AUGUSTINE, i., p. 22.
CAPE CONSOLATION, i., p. 64.
CAPE DESOLATION, i., p. 45.
CAPE DIAMOND, i., p. 50 ; iv., p. 178–9.
CAPE FRANÇOIS, i., p. 42 ; v., p. 118.
CAPE FRANÇOIS, or FRENCH CAPE, so called by Ribaut, i., p. 135, inconvenient, 152.
CAPE OF GOOD HOPE, discovered, i., p. 19.
CAPE GRACIAS Á DIOS, discovered by Columbus, i., p. 24, 27.
CAPE GUARDAFUI, discovered, i., p. 25, 27
CAPE HENRIETTA MARIA, i., p. 54.
CAPE HORN, by whom discovered and named, i., p. 52.
CAPE DE LOREMBEC, on Cape Breton, v., p. 284.
CAPE DE LA MAGDELEINE, given to Jesuits by Abbé de la Magdeleine ; Indian Christians retire to avoid intoxication, iii., p. 55 ; F. Le Moyne dies at, 87 ; iron mines at, 98 ; neglected, 99 ; Indians of Three Rivers retire to, 153.
CAPE MALLEBARRE, situation, why so called, i., p. 253 ; Champlain takes posession in name of King of France, i., p. 49, occupied by English, i., p. 253.
CAPE MENDOCINO, discovered, i., p. 40.
CAPE PINE, N. F., v., p. 163.
CAPE PORPOISE attacked by Abenakis under Beaubassin, v., p. 161, n.
CAPE RACE, early French settlement near, iii., p. 140.
CAPE DES ROSIERS, i., p. 249 ; iii., p. 129.
CAPE ROUGE RIVER, Cartier builds Charlesbourg Royal, on, i., p. 130, n.
CAPE SABLE, in ACADIA, the la Tours at, iii., p. 125, n. ; English repulsed at, 126.
CAPE ST. ANTOINE, Cherokees kill French at, v., p. 307 n.
CAPE ST. CATHARINE, i., p. 18.
CAPE ST. HELENA, i., p. 32.
CAPE ST. MARY'S, (N. F.) English fleet at, iv., p. 223.
CAPE SAN ANTONIO, i., p. 169 ; de Gourgues at, 226 ; La Salle at, iv., p. 67.
CAPE TEMPEST or GOOD HOPE, i., p. 19.
CAPE TIBURON, i., p. 168.
CAPE TOURMENTE, Kerth ravages, ii., p. 44 ; earthquake at, iii., p. 62 ; Villieu at, iv., p. 186.
CAPE DE LA VELA, i., p. 21, 27.
CAPE VERDE discovered, i., p. 16 ; de Gourgues turns from to America, p. 226.
CAPE VERDE ISLANDS, discovered i., p. 17 · ancient name, ib.
CAPE OF THE VIRGINS, i., p. 32.
CAPINANS, Louisiana tribe, sing calumet to l'Epinai, vi., p 39, n.
CAPPE, F. FELIX, Recollect in Acadia, writes to Vaudreuil, v., p. 238.
CAPUCHINS, at Maragnon in Brazil, i., p. 22 ; Canada mission offered to, ii., p. 65, n. ; introduced into Acadia by Comm. de Razilly, iii., p. 128, n. ; and d'Aulnay, 129, n. ; have hospice on the Kennebec, and house at Pentagoët, ii., p. 203, iii., p. 129, n. ; encourage Druillettes, and then ask that he should not return, ii., 202–3, n. ; sent to Louysiana by W. I. Company, vi., p. 75 ; no published account of their labors, 77, n.
CAR, SIR ROBERT, takes Fort Orange, ii., p. 11.
CARAGOUHA, IHONATIRIA, or ST. JOSEPH'S, Huron town, ii., p. 77, n. ; 210, n.
CARANCAGUACES, CARANHUAS, Texas Indians, iv., p. 70, n., 75, n.; see CLAMCOETS.
CARANTOUANIS, probably Susquehannas, ii., p. 71.
CARBONNIERE, English Island and post in Newfoundland, d'Iberville proposes to attack first, v., p. 37 ; de Brouillan opposes, ib. ; difficulty of attacking in winter, 46 ; Costebelle's expedition against, v., p. 231.
CARDENAS Z CANO, GABRIEL, pseudonym of André Gonzales Barcia, i., p. 91.
CARHEIL, F. STEPHEN DE, Jesuit, notice of, iii., p. 109, n. ; 117, n. ; taken to Iroquis by Garakonthié, iii., p. 109 ; his character, 117 ; esteemed in Canada, 118 ; unprofitable labors at Cayuga, ib. ; letter to Frontenac, on western Indians treating with Senecas, iv., p. 54–7 ; esteem of the Rat, a Huron chief for, makes him a zealous Christian, v., p. 146.
CARIGNAN, THOMAS FRANCIS, Prince of, iii., p. 81.
CARIGNAN SALIERES, French regiment, in the war of La Fronde and at Auxerre ; distinguished at St. Godard, sent to Canada on returning from Hungary, iii., p. 81 ; many officers and most of the soldiers settle in Canada, 111 ; some companies return to France, ib. ; grants to officers of, ib. ; Colonel, Henry de

CARIGNAN, (*continued.*)
Chapelas, Sieur de Salieres, iii., p. 81, n. ; Captains, Chambly, 88 ; Sorel, 111–112 ; Rev. Mr. Petit, iv., p. 155, n. ; La Durantaye, iii., pp. 112, 244 ; Lieut. de la Valtrie, iv., p. 237, n. ; Ensign, St. Castin, iii., p. 294.

CAROLINE, LAUDONNIERE's fort in Florida, i., p. 42, 152 ; position, 152, n. ; described, 153 ; Saturiova aids to build, ib. ; error of historians and geographers as to, 152, n., 153 ; no minister at, 165 ; mutiny, ib. ; relieved by Hawkins, 177; Laudonniere demolishes, 176 ; restored by Ribaut, 182 ; captured by Spaniards, 200 ; called San Matheo, 207 ; almost destroyed by fire, 208 ; see SAN MATHEO.

CAROLINA ISLAND, i., p. 63.

CAROLINA, granted to Albemarle, i., p. 56 ; named in honor of Charles II. of England, not of Charles IX. of France, 69 ; Indians commit ravages in and bring many prisoners to Maubile, who are ransomed by Bienville, vi., p. 24 ; Spaniards plan reduction of, 46 ; Swiss company deserts in Louysiana, and goes to, 67.

CARON, F. JOSEPH LE, Recollect, comes to Canada, ii., p. 25, n. ; says first mass, ib. ; goes to Hurons, p. 26 ; returns, p. 29 ; celebrates first marriage, p. 30, n. ; goes to France, p. 30 ; re-visits Hurons, p. 35 ; about to unite with Algonquins, ii., p. 45, n. ; conducts negotiations, 49, n.

CARPENTARIA, i., p. 50.

CARR, SIR ROBERT, ii., p. 11.

CARRASCOSA DE LA TORRE, DON ALPHONSO, see TORRE.

CARRÉ, settler, at head of militia attacks English, iv., p. 181 ; Frontenac permits to carry off two cannon left by enemy, 184.

CARREAU, Gascon gentleman, lost on Gourgues's Florida expedition, i., p. 236.

CARRYING PLACE, v., p. 246.

CARTHAGENA, name given, i., p. 24; settled, 29 ; built by Heredia, 36.

CARTIER, JACQUES, St. Malo pilot, presented to Francis I. to explore America, i., p. 36 ; first voyage, i., p. 36, 74, 111 ; remarks on Newfoundland, p. 111 ; takes possession of Gulf of St. Lawrence, 112; pious preparation for second voyage, p. 114 ; new discoveries, why he gave the name of St. Lawrence to the Gulf of Canada, i., p. 37, 115 ; Jacques Cartier's river, discovers Assumption, or Anticosti, i., p. 37 ; Indians try to divert him from going to Hochelaga, i., p. 37 ; his reception, 118 ; Indians seek cure of disease from him, 119 ; his piety and faith, 120 ; returns to St. Croix, ib. ; attacked by scurvy, ascribes his recovery to white pine, 121 ; his report to the King, ib. ; Charlevoix deems his memoirs of comparatively little value, 122 ; but was misled, ib. ; marvels he relates, 123 ; sent out by de Roberval in 1541; founds Charlesbourg Royal, 130, n. ; visits Hochelaga again, ib. ; abandons fort in 1542, ib. ; meets Roberval at St. John, N. F., ib. ; returns to France, ib. ; sails again in 1543, to take off remnant of Roberval's party, ib. ; birth, marriage, and death of, 131, n.

CARY, MATTHEW, sent to Quebec by Stoughton, to exchange prisoners, v., p. 76, n.

CARY'S SWAN'S NEST, i., p. 51.

CASCADES, Iroquois at, iv., p. 240.

CASCO BAY attacked by Abénaquis under Beaubassin, v., p. 161, n. ; relieved by Southwick, ib. ; see KASKEBÉ.

CASENEUVE, MR. DE, De Gourgues' lieutenant, i., p. 230 ; takes Spaniards between two fires, 231 ; cuts some of them to pieces, ib. ; at San Matheo, 233.

CASET, MR., member of company of a hundred, ii., p. 169.

CASSINE OR CASINE, i., pp. 139, 142, n. ; see APALACHINE.

CASSON, REV. DOLLIER DE, Sulpitian, sketch of, iii., p. 96, n. ; on Tracy's expedition, 95 ; explores Lake Erie, 122, n.

CASTACHAS, Choctaw tribe, their chief made Great Chief of Eastern Choctaws, vi., p. 104.

CASTAÑEDA, FRANCIS DE, Captain of Menendez guard, i., p. 208.

CASTILLA DE ORO, limits of, i., p 27.

CASTILLON, JAMES, member of the company of the Hundred Associates for New France, ii., p. 39.

CASTINE, near Pentagoët, iii., p. 130, n.

CASTRO, FERDINAND DE, sent to the Canaries, i., p. 14.

CATAROCOUY FORT, or FORT FRONTENAC projected by de Courcelles, iii., p. 175

CATAROCOUY, (*continued.*)
built by Frontenac, 176 ; La Salle offers to fortify, 199 ; obtains domain and government of, 200 ; labors on, 202 ; La Salle at, 213 ; importance of, 225 ; seized by de la Barre, 243 ; restored to La Salle, 259 ; projected assembly of five Iroquois Cantons at, 268 ; account of chiefs arrested there, 276 ; Indians seized at, by de Champigny, ib., n.; de Bergers reaches, 291, n. ; English demand dismantling of, 301 ; convoy to, 302 ; Vaillant and Lamberville at ; 303 ; d'Orvilliers commandant at, receives Haaskouaun, ib. ; invested by Iroquois, 305, siege raised, 306 ; convoy sent to, ib. ; the Rat at iv., p. 12 ; demolished by Denonville's orders, 32–4 ; English theory as to, 35, n. ; Iroquois complain of, 45, 49 ; restored, 265 ; built of stone, 267 ; Frontenac at, v., p. 14 ; obliged to leave sick there, ib. ; de la Gemmeraye, commandant, 79 ; Black Kettle killed near, ib. ; King's instructions to de Callieres on, 97 ; Iroquois assured that they will find all they need at, 109.

CATBIRD, ii., p. 72.

CATESBY'S Natural History, noticed, i., p. 92.

CATHARINE OF ST. AUGUSTINE, MOTHER, Hospital nun, account of, iii., p. 112 ; her life by Ragreneau, 113, n.

CATHARINE, THE GOOD, see Tehgahkouita.

CAUGHNAWAGA, N. Y., place of Jogues' death, iii., p. 109, n. ; see GANDAOUAGUE.

CAUGHNAWAGA. Canada, iii., p. 117, n. ; see SAULT ST. LOUIS.

CAVELIER, REV. JOHN, priest of St. Sulpice, Brother of La Sale, accompanies him on his expedition, iv., p. 62 ; wishes Beaujeu to take charge of la Sale's affairs, 67; Beaujeu's reply, ib. ; accompanies la Sale on an excursion, 72 ; starts with la Sale for Illinois, intending to go to France, 89 ; address to his brother's assassins, and their reply, 97 ; resolves to go to the Illinois, 104–5 ; questions Duhaut, ib. ; his reply, ib. ; compelled to follow Hiens to the Cénis, 104 ; starts for the Illinois, 107 ; reaches the Akansas, is well recieved and obtains guides, 108 ; in Illinois, 110; starts, but has to return and winter, ib. ; in Canada, proceeds to France, 111.

CAVELIER, (JOHN BAPTIST,) nephew of La Salle, on his last expedition, iv., p. 62 ; sent to learn fate of frigate, 84 ; reports its loss, 85 ; starts for Illinois, 89, 107.

CAVELIER, MARY MAGDALEN, wife of John Le Forestier and nephew of La Salle, iv. p. 62, n.

CAVELLERO, DON BRUNO DE, LIEUT.-COL. sent to Governor of St. Joseph's Bay, vi., p. 47 ; summons De Chateaugué, 49· surrenders to de Champmêlin, 58–9.

CAYENNE settled, i., p. 54.

CAYUGAS, Iroquois canton, description and peculiarities of, ii., p. 190 ; they ask peace, iii., p. 37 ; peace proposed by a friendly Cayuga chief, iii., p. 71 ; de Mésy's reply, ib. ; solicit peace from de Tracy, 85 ; de Carheil esteemed by, but unable to convert, 117 ; baptism at Quebec of Cayuga chief, 162; begin hostilities, 241 ; de la Barre recommends to minister destruction of Cayugas as worst enemies of the French, 242 ; De la Barre sends it a belt to ask its neutrality in Seneca dispute, 249 ; this canton mediates for peace, 252 ; deputy at Montreal for peace, ib. ; Oureouharé in behalf of this canton, ib. ; Cayuga and Mohawk party met by Bienville, their craft, iv., p. 196 ; deputies at Quebec, embarrassed by Frontenac's questions, 253 ; his declaration to, ib. ; why resolution to destroy not carried out, v., p. 21 ; Oureouharé declares them inclined to peace, 80 ; send no envoys to de Callieres, v,, p. 102 ; but do to Gov. of New England, ib. ; deputies start for Montreal, 108 ; sign treaty at Montreal, 111 ; their totem, ib. ; Joncaire negotiates successfully with, 140.

CEBU founded i., p. 42.

CELEBES discovered, i., p. 28.

CENDRE CHAUDE, Mohawk or rather Oneida chief, Oyenratarihen or Garonhiagué, killed in action with Senecas, had been one of F. de Brebeuf's murderers. Conversion and atonement for that crime, iii., p. 289; instrumental in bringing Catharine Tegahkouita to Canada, iv., p. 288, n.

CÉNIS, ASSENIS OR ASSINAIS, Indians, iv., p. 78 ; situation of their country, character, ib. ; manners, war and treatment of prisoners, 79 ; alliance with la Salle, 88 ; give him, horses, ib. ; receive Joutel, 98; shocked at la Sale's murder, 96; French assist them in war, victory and rejoicings, 104–5 ; cruelty of women, 105 ; divert

CÉNIS, (*continued.*) Joutel from going to Illinois, but give him guides, 107; give guides to St. Denys, vi,, p. 20; Spanish among, 32; aid St. Denys against Natchez, 118; see ASSINAIS.

CEYLON, discovered by Almeyda, i., p. 26.

CHABANEL, F. NATALIS, Jesuit, sketch of, ii., p. 231, n.; ordered to leave Huron town of St. John, ii., p. 230; disappears, conjectures as to his fate, ib.; killed by Louis Honareenhax, 231, n.

CHABOT, PHILIP DE, Count de Buzensais et de Chargni, Seigneur de Brion, Admiral of France, induces Francis I. to continue American exploration and introduces Cartier to him, i., p. 36, 111; commissions Cartier, i., p. 36.

CHACTCHIOUMAS, (Red Crabs) Louisiana tribe, vi., p. 39, n.

CHAGOUAMIGON, or ST. MICHAEL'S ISLAND, in Lake Superior, iii., p. 49; situation, ib., n.; Hurons at, ii., p. 271, n.; F. Mesnard, as Charlevoix supposes, invited there by Hurons, iii., p. 49; Allouez at, iii., p. 101; concourse of Indians at that island, what F. Allouez does there, ib.; F. Nicolas at, 119; le Sueur sent to found establishment at, iv., p. 242.

CHAGRES RIVER discovered, i., p. 29.

CHAILLONS, J. B. DE SAINT OURS DES, commands a party against English, v., p. 204; commands a company in de Ramezay's expedition, 219; detached on a scout, 220.

CHAISE, MR. DE LA, Commissary sent to Louisiana, vi., p. 69, n.

CHAISE F. FRANCIS DE LA, confessor to the King, liquor question referred to, his opinion, iii., p. 196.

CHALEURS BAY, discovered and named by Cartier, i., p. 37, 112, n.; called Baye des Espagnols, 113.

CHALLUS, NICHOLAS, notice of Florida tract by, in Benzoni's Novæ Novi Orbis, i., p. 70.

CHAMAT, or CHAMOT, French officer killed by Mohawks, iii., p. 87.

CHAMBAUTS, SIEUR DES, King's attorney at Montreal, commands Montreal militia on Frontenac's expedition, v., p. 13.

CHAMBLY, CAPT. JAMES DE, of the Carignan Salieres regiment, builds Fort Chambly, iii., p. 83; commands rear of Tracy's army, 90; grant to 112, n.; commandant in Acadia, 187; besieged and wounded by Dutch at Pentagoët, 188· his men surrender, ib.; re-appointed Governor, 210; Governor of Grenada, 211.

CHAMBLY, SIEUR HERTEL DE, killed on Haverhill expedition, v., p. 207.

CHAMBLY, Fort St. Louis, or Chambly, built at, iii., p. 83; advantage of, ib.; Courcelle at, 89; du Plessis besieged by Mohawks and Mohegans, at, 298; result of Dutch Mohawk irruption at, iv. p. 19; English Mohegan ravages near, 193, n.; de Valrenes sent to relieve, p. 203; fortified against Iroquois, 236; Desbergeres in command, ib., n.; de Vaudreuil's army camps at, v., p. 220; called Fort Ponchartrain, ib. n; Vaudreuil encamps at, 146.

CHAMBLY RAPIDS, Champlain at, ii., p. 12;

CHAMPFLOURS, MR. DE, Governor of Three Rivers, obtains Iroquois prisoners, ii., p. 175; they propose peace to, ib., informs de Montmagny ib.; at public audience of Iroquois deputies, 178.

CHAMPIGNY, NOROY, JOHN BOCHART, SEIGNEUR DE, Intendant of New France, sketch of, ii., p. 282, n.; related to Lauson, ib.; precedes Denonville, 276, 282; seizes Iroquois, 282, n.; evacuates and destroys Catarocouy, iv., p. 32; opinion as to, 34–5; starts for Quebec to meet Phips, 153; concurs with Frontenac as to du Tast, 201; on liquor question, 232; opposes restoration of Fort Frontenac, 265; letter to Ponchartrain, 266; on Placentia, 274; goes to Montreal on Iroquois expedition, v., p. 12; opinion as to advanced posts, 65; consequences of following his advice, 67; aspires to be Governor-General, 96; sends Vincelotte to France, ib., n.; at last assembly for general peace, v., p. 149; smokes the calumet, 152; returns to France, 156; succeeded by Beauharnois, 156, n., 282, n.

CHAMPIGNY, MADAME DE, wife of preceding, at obsequies of The Rat, v., p. 147.

CHAMPLAIN, SAMUEL DE, navy captain, born at Brouage, ii., p. 88, n.; fought for Henry IV. during civil war, ib.; mistake of as to Cartier, ib.; his voyage to Mexico, i., p. 246, n.; his works, i., p. 75–76;

CHAMPLAIN, (*continued.*)
recent editions, 246, n., vi. p. 124; his first voyage to Canada, i., p. 49; 247; opinion as to limits of Acadia, 248; takes possession of Cape Mallebarre, and Cape Cod for French King, i., p. 49, 253; continues discoveries, 257; trades in St. Lawrence, 259; founds city of Quebec, i., p. 50, 260; justifies Jesuits in the De Guercheville affair, 263; tries to bring that lady into relations with de Monts, 274, 285; returns to Quebec, its condition, ii., p. 7; why he marches against the Iroquois, p. 8; with his allies, p. 12; first expedition against them, p. 12; discovers a lake to which he gives his name, i., p. 51, ii., p. 15; success of his expedition, p. 16–7; wounded, p. 21; returns to France, 19; back at Quebec, 20; second Iroquois expedition, 21; wounded, 21; takes a Huron to France and leaves a French boy with Hurons, p. 23; marries Helen Boullé, p. 23, n., 88, n.; induces the Count de Soissons to obtain Viceroyalty, p. 24; his lieuteuant, ib.; confirmed in office by the Prince de Condé; back in Canada, ib.; deceived by Vignau, ascends the Ottawa, ib.; returns to France and forms an association for trade, p. 25; takes Recollects to Canada, ib.; goes up to Huron country, p. 27; his route, ib., n.; Iroquois expedition, wounded and forced to retreat, 25–8; winters among Hurons for want of a guide, p. 29; goes to France, baffles Indian conspiracy against the French, p. 30; exacts reparation, p. 31; courage in upholding colony through all adversities, 32; brings his family to Quebec, ib.; his firmness, letters of Louis XIII. to, 34; sends Recollects to Hurons on ascertaining their evil designs, 34; builds fort at Quebec of stone, 35; takes his family back to France, 35; condition of Quebec on his return, 38; enter the Society of New France, 43; summoned by English to surrender Quebec, his reply, 44; extremity to which he is reduced, 46; surrenders, on what conditions, 48; advice to settlers, 50; descends to Tadoussac, 51; endeavors to regain an apostate and traitor, 52; carried to England, 55, n.; held for ransom, ib.; his remarks on companies, 57; induces King to insist on restoration of Canada, 57; Gov. or Lieutenant of Card. Richelieu and Gen. of fleet, 64; sails to it with a squadron, ib.; his views as to the Hurons and their country, ib.; action on refusal of Hurons to take missionaries, 69; why he desired them to go, ib.; death and eulogium, 88; place of burial, 283; portrait, 88, n.

CHAMPLAIN, parish in Canada, iron mines in, iii., p. 98; a son of la Touche, seigneur de, killed at Quebec, iv. p. 177.

CHAMPMÊLIN, COUNT DE, Commodore, arrives at Dauphin island, vi., p. 55; prepares to besiege Pensacola, ib.; enters the Bay, 57; captures Pensacola, the Spanish ships, &c., 58; does not retaliate for Spanish cruelty, 59; demolishes part of Fort Pensacola, 60; distributes royal presents to Indians, 62; delays his departure, ib.; sails, 63; testimony in Council to Mr. St. Denys, 65.

CHAOUACHAS, Louysiana Indians, sing calumet to l'Epinai, vi., p. 39; destroyed by negroes at Perrier's orders, vi., p. 90.

CHAOUANONS, or SHAWNEES, Indians near Iroquois, nearly destroyed by them, iii., p. 174. See SHAWNEES.

CHAPEAU ROUGE, Post on Newfoundland, origin of name, iii., p. 142.

CHAPTER of Quebec, creation of, iii., p. 26; revenues, ib.; who constitute the, ib.; who nominate to the benefices, ib.

CHARITY, or CHRISTIAN ISLAND, formerly St. Joseph's, ii., p. 226, n.

CHARLEMAGNE, REV. MR., imprisoned and banished, v., p. 299.

CHARLES IX., King of France, approves French settlement in Florida, i., p. 133; and sending only Huguenots, 135; gives Coligni three ships, p. 148; gives fifty thousand crowns to de Laudonniere, 149; sends a large convoy, receives the Chevalier de Gourgues ill on his return from Florida, p. 237.

CHARLES II., King of England, seizes New Netherland, ii., p. 11; grants it to Duke of York, ib.; disavows seizure of Fort Bourbon, iii., p. 269.

CHARLES V. grants Venezuela to the Velsers, i., p. 35.

CHARLESBOURG ROYAL, fort built in 1541 by Cartier at Cap Rouge river, i., p. 130, n.; rebuilt in 1542, by Roberval, and called France Roi, ib.

CHARLESFORT, Ribault's fortress on the Chenonceau or Archer's Creek, near Beaufort, i., p. 42, 137, n.; abandoned, 146; not restored by Laudonniere, ib.

CHARLESTON, or CHARLES ESTON, on Hudson Bay, i., p. 54, iii., p. 272, n, 293; French captured near, retake English ship, 293.

CHARLESTON, S. C., Port Royal near, i., p. 42.

CHARNISÉ, CHARLES DE MENOU, SEIGNEUR D'AULNAY DE, notice of, iii., p. 131-2, n.; commands under his kinsman, Com. Isaac de Razilly, 128; acts for Capt. Claude de Razilly, 129, n.; abandons la Heve, ib.; acquires de Razilly's rights; attacks fort on St. John's during la Tour's absence, 130; disgraceful conduct of, ib., 131; Governor of Acadia in 1647, p. 129; had fort on Penobscot, 130; has Capuchins, ib.; death of, 131, n.; le Borgne, by decree of Parliament of Paris, succeeds to, 131-2; la Tour marries widow of, ib.; his son Joseph seeks confirmation of father's patent, 132, n.

CHARON, FRANCIS, founds General Hospital at Montreal, iv., p. 234, n.

CHARTRES, FATHER LEONARD DE, Vice Prefect of the Capuchin mission, taken at Port Royal, iii., p. 134, n.

CHASSAIGNE, JOHN BOUILLET, SIEUR DE LA, notice of, iv., p. 142, n.; commandant at La Chine reports fleet of canoes, 143; at battle of La Prairie, 205; on de Ramezay's expedition, v., p. 218.

CHASSE, F. PETER DE LA, Jesuit, brings Abénaquis to aid Quebec, v., p. 240; urges French government to settle Abénaquis boundary, 271, n.; wishes to attend a conference between English and Abénaquis, 272; writes to Governor of New England, in the name of the latter, ib.; reply of Sulpitian Superior, to his request for prayers for F. Rasles, 281; report to Vaudreuil, on Abénaquis, 302; notice of letter of, i., p. 89.

CHASTE, EYMARD DE, Knight of Malta, Governor of Dieppe, acquires Chauvin's rights, i., p. 246; enlists Champlain, ib.; death, 247.

CHASTELAIN, FATHER PETER, Jesuit, goes to Hurons, ii., p. 94, n.; visits Byssirinins, 95.

CHASY, MR. DE, nephew of de Tracy, killed by Iroquois, iii., p. 87; murderer said to have been strangled by Tracy's order, for boasting of it, 88; doubts as to this, 88, n. This officer called Chasi, Chasy, Chazy and Chusy.

CHATEAUFORT, MARK ANTHONY BRAS DE FER DE, administers government after Champlain's death, ii., p. 91, n.

CHATEAUGUAY, Seigneury of, iv., p. 260.

CHATEAGUÉ, I. LOUIS LE MOYNE DE, sketch of, killed at siege of Fort Nelson, iv., p. 260.

CHATEAUGUE, II. ANTHONY LE MOYNE DE, brother of preceding, iv., p. 260, n.; sent by Bienville, to St. Joseph's Bay, vi., p. 42; refers Matamoros to Bienville, ib., n.; abandons it, why? ib.; commands Indians at siege of Pensacola, 44; takes possession of the fort, 45; compelled to surrender, 49; Spanish commander threatens not to spare, unless de Serigny surrenders, 51; harshness of Governor of Havana, to, 59; returns to Louysiana as King's Lieutenant, and resumes command at Maubile, 65; removed from office, 75, n.

CHATEAUMORAND, MR, DE, navy captain said by Charlevoix to have sailed with d'Iberville, to discover mouth of Mississippi, v., p. 117; met him in West Indies, ib., n.; sends de Graff to sound entrance to Pensacola Bay, 119; returns to France when d'Iberville reports discovery of mouth of Mississippi, 118, n., 120, n.

CHATELAIN, see CHASTELAIN.

CHATS, LES, Iroquois, defeated at, iv., p. 139.

CHATTE, Commander de, see CHASTE.

CHAUCHETIERE, F. CLAUDE, Jesuit, writes life of Catharine Tegahkouita, iv., p. 283.

CHAUDIERE, Abénaqui mission on the, iv., p. 133, 233; see SAINT FRANCIS.

CHAUDIERE FALLS, on the Ottawa, Senecas hunting at, iv., p. 217; St. Michel to be escorted to, 218.

CHAUDIERE NOIRE, Iroquois Chief, see BLACK KETTLE.

CHAUMONOT, F. PETER JOSEPH MARY, Jesuit, sketch of, ii., p, 262, n.; preaches to Neuter Nation, 152; founds Huron colony on Isle Orleans, 262; sent to Onondaga, well received, 262; speech at a council there, 277; what he found at the Senecas, resumes care of Hurons at Quebec and Beauport, ii., p. 262, n.; iii., p. 12; founds Huron mission of Loretto, ib.; his writings, ib.; interpreter, iii., p. 151.

CHAUMONT, CHEVALIER ALEX. DE, on de Tracy's Mohawk campaign, iii., p. 90.

CHAUSSEGROS DE LERY, fortifies Quebec, v., p. 307, n.

CHAUVIGNERIE, LOUIS MARAY, SIEUR DE LA, sent to Onondaga, v., p. 138, n.; with Oneidas, 139; finds them indisposed to peace, ib.; sent to Iroquois, 236; takes up hatchet in Governor-General's name at a council of several Indian tribes, 239; at Niagara, 236, n.

CHAUVIN, navy captain, succeeds to La Roche's commission and rights, i., p. 245; his errors, ib.; leaves men at Tadoussac, 246.; death, ib.; vi., p. 123.

CHAVEZ, NUSLO DE, Spaniard, founds Santa Cruz de La Sierra, i., p. 41.

CHAVIN, PETER, left by Champlain, in command at Quebec, ii., p, 19, n., 20.

CHAZEL, CHEVALIER DE, Intendant of New France, lost on the Chameau, v., p. 309.

CHEBUCTO, see CHEDABOUCTOU.

CHEDABOUCTOU, port in Acadia, now Manchester; Denys and la Giraudiere at, iii., p. 136; pillaged by English, iv., p. 15; rendezvous for vessels in New York expedition, iv., p. 27; ordered to be evacuated, 159; taken by English, 160–1; what defeats projected settlement at, v., p. 255.

CHEDOTEL, Marquis de la Roche's pilot, i., p. 243; Henry IV. orders him to bring off Frenchmen left on Sable Island, by de la Roche, 245.

CHEFDEVILLE, Sulpitian, relative of la Sale, accompanies him, iv., p. 62, 72; saved at wreck of frigate, 86; left in Fort St. Louys, Texas, and apparently killed, 89.

CHEGOUTIMI, F. Albanel embarks at, iii., p. 233.

CHENONCEAU RIVER, Charles Fort on, i., p. 137.

CHEPAR, CHEPART or CHOPART, MR. DE, commandant at Natchez, quarrels with Indians, vi., p. 81; blind confidence of, ib.; killed, 82.

CHEROKEES, French killed by, v., p. 307, n.

CHESAPEAKE BAY, explored by Smith, i., p. 50.

CHESNAYE, SIEUR DE, distinguished at capture of St. John, v., p. 213.

CHESNAYE, LA, iv., p. 50; attacked by Black Kettle, 220.

CHESNE, DAVID DU, one of Hundred Associates, ii., p. 39.

CHESNE, LE BERT DU, see BERT DU CHESNE, LE.

CHESNEAU, JAMES DU, Intendant of New France, succeeds Talon, iii., p. 67; brings order making Intendant first President, iii., p. 67; grants Sault St. Louis to Iroquois Christians, iii., p. 191; quarrels with Frontenac, iii., p. 189, 193; King's letter, 193; Colbert censures his conduct in regard to Liquor question, 193; recalled, 215; where wrong in his quarrel with Frontenac, 215; advice of, to Frontenac, 220.

CHETIMACHAS, Louysiana Indians on banks of Micissipi near New Orleans, vi., p. 41.

CHEVALIER, SIEUR DE, Officer of Naxoat garrison, attacked by English, escapes to woods, killed in ambush, v., pp. 29–30.

CHEVALIER, SERGEANT, left by English in command of Port Royal, iv., p. 159.

CHEVRIER, PETER, Baron of Fancamp, sends out settlers for Montreal, ii., p. 130.

CHIAPAS discovered by Ordas, i., p. 36.

CHICACHAS, see CHICKASAWS.

CHICAGOU, called by Charlevoix, Miami village, what befel Nicholas Perrot at, iii., p. 166; Charlevoix makes Marquette and Joliet separate at, iii., p. 181; Marquette winters at, ib.; La Sale at, 213, n.

CHICAGOU, Illinois chief, in France, vi., p. 76, n.

CHICHIKATALO, Miami chief, speaks at General Congress, v., p. 143.

CHICASAWS, Louysiana Indians, instigated by English against French, v., p. 124; sing calumet to l'Epinai, vi., p. 39, n.; ask peace, 70; alliance with Foxes, v., p. 309; English urge to war to obtain prisoners, vi., p. 24; war with French, 70; plot destruction of all Louysiana, p. 77; Natchez report as coming to

their aid, 99; feeling as to, 101; try to draw allies into a conspiracy, 102 ; Chief at Maubile, 103; complains that all northern tribes pursue his tribe, ib.; Natché chief and men among, 115; surprise Tonicas, 116; make war on us, 118; excite Negro insurrection, 119; gain a part of Choctaws who turn on them, ib.; urge our allies to declare against us, ib.; our losses in war with, 121.

Chicora, discovered by Aylion, i., p. 32.

Chicot River, rendezvous of N. Y. and Indian forces, v., p. 217.

Chine, la, See La Chine.

Chingouessi, chief of the Ottawas-Sinagos, speaks at General Congress, v., p. 143, n.

Chinoshahgeh, or Gannogarae, Seneca town destroyed by Denonville, iii., p. 289, n.

Chipacafi, chief of the Caoitas, vi., p. 105.

Chippewas, (the Saulteux or Ojibway) visited by Jesuits, ii., p. 137; defeat Mohawks and Oneidas, iii., p. 64; driven to Lake Huron by Sioux, iii., p. 196; le Sueur to form alliance between Sioux and, iv., p. 242.

Choctaws, Louysiana Indians, receive presents from Queen of England, v., p. 211; plunder and massacre English storekeepers, vi., p. 24; sing calumet to l'Epinai, 39, n.; English try to win, 68; fidelity and disinterestedness, ib.; eastern part join the plot for exterminating French, 79; deputies to Perrier, 80; their perfidious and selfish policy, ib.; Perrier summons two Choctaw chiefs, 89; what he learns from a Choctaw, 90; small tribes warn Perrier to distrust, 89; Natchez chant calumet to, but they prepare for war, 90; English send goods to, 91; le Sueur sounds them, 93; leads 700 against Natchez, 94; attack and defeat them, 96; why they did not close the war at once, ib.; ill humor, insolence and cupidity, 97; suspected of wishing to betray French at siege of Natchez fort, 99; a Choctaw addresses Natchez, 99; reproached, ib.; Natchez gives up our prisoners to Choctaws, from whom we have to redeem them, 100; reception by Natchez after French massacre, 101; profane Church vessels, ib.; bad character and insolence, ib.; have to be humored, ib.; English urge them to attack us, 102; give them presents, ib.; Perrier calls a Council of, at Maubile, 103; result, 104; jealousy of Eastern and Western bands, 104; Perrier wishes to dispense with them in war, ib.; a part gained by Chickasaws, but turn on them, 119.

Cholenec, F. Peter le, Jesuit, notice of letters of, i., p. 88 ; life of Catharine Tegahkouita, iv., p. 283.

Chouard, Medard, Sieur des Groseilliers. See Groseilliers.

Chouard, Medard II, son of last, treats with English, in regard to Hudson Bay, iii., p. 237 ; sails from the Bay in English ship, iv., p. 39.

Chouchouacha, animal worshipped by Bayagoulas, v., p. 122.

Chouguen, or Techoueguen, river of Onondagas, peculiarities of, v., p. 15; Iroquois wish Frontenac to meet them at, iii., p. 218, 219, n. ; French scouts at iv., p. 269 ; Frontenac at, v., p. 14 ; English build fort at mouth of, v., p. 112, 266, 308, n.; see Oswego River.

Chouontouarouon, probably Chonontouaronon or Sonontouaronon, the Senecas, ii., p. 28.

Christiana Sea, i., p. 53 ; iii., p. 230.

Christina, founded, i., p. 55.

Chubb, or Chubd, commander of Fort Pemkuit, v., p. 25 ; treachery of, v., p. 23 ; reply to summons, 25 ; capitulates, ib.

Church, Major Benjamin ; menaces Villebon, on the St. John's, iv., 227 ; at Fort Pemquid, 228 ; violence at Baubassin, v., p. 28 ; superseded by Col. Hawthorn, 30, n. ; attacks Port Royal, v., p. 170, n.

Church,—v., p. 28.

Cibola, discovered by Mark de Niza, i., p. 38 ; Cornero (Coronado,) sent to, 39.

Cibou Isles, v., p. 285.

Cinaloa, discovered by Guzman, i., p. 36.

Cintra, Gonzalo de, killed at Angra, i., p. 16.

Citry de la Guette, notice of his translation of the Relation of the Gentleman of Elvas, i., p. 83.

Claese, Lawrence, N. Y. interpreter at Onondaga, v., p. 138, n.

Clamcoets, Indians of St. Bernard's bay, Texas, called by Spaniards Caranca-

CLAMCOETS, *(continued.)* guaces, iv., p. 75, n.; manners &c., 75; carry off some French, 69; plunder la Sale's wrecked storeship, 70; kill two French, 71; prowl around French, 73; steal tools of workmen, 73; French make enemies of, 75; character of their country, 76; massacre several French, 84; take Fort St. Louis and massacre almost all the French, 112; Spaniards carry of French captives from, 114; disappear between 1840, and 1851, 75, n.

CLARENTIN, SIMON, member of the Company of a Hundred, ii., p. 169.

CLARK, LIEUT. THADDEUS, falls at Kaskebé (Falmouth), iv., p. 134.

CLASBY (CLEASBY) Captain of the Sapphire (Zephyr), fires his ship, v., p. 36, n.; taken by de Brouillan after a sharp action, 37.

CLAYTON'S regiment, loss of, in Walker's shipwreck, v., p. 247, n.

CLEMENTS, Captain, sent out by Coxe, v., p. 124, n.

CLÉRAMBAUT, M., Genealogist of the King's Orders, aids Charlevoix, i., p. 95.

CLERCQ, LE, one of la Sale's men, disappears, iv., p. 88.

CLERCQ, F. CHRISTIAN LE, Recollect, works of, i., p. 85–6; error as to Gaspesians, ii., p. 120.

CLERCQ, F. MAXIME LE, Recollect, sketch of, iv., p. 63, n.; accompanies la Sale, iv., p. 62, 73, n.; left in Fort St. Louis, massacred there, 89.

CLERMONT, ALEXANDER SAMUEL, CHEVALIER DE, Captain, rescues children from Iroquois, iv., p. 141–2; reports Iroquois force on Lake Champlain, 145; killed at siege of Quebec, 177.

CLIGNANCOURT, RENÉ D'AMOUR, SIEUR DE, relieves Fort Naxoat, v., p. 31; sent by settlers to Vaudreuil after reduction of Port Royal, 235.

CLOSSE, RAPHAEL LAMBERT, Major of Montreal, sketch of, iii., p. 46, n.; marries Elizabeth Moyen, ib.; exploits, ii., p. 251, n.; iii.; p. 46; death of, 46–7, n.; St. Lambert Street named after ib.

COAHUILA, Mexican town, St. Denys sent to, v., p. 21.

COAL MINES, Nova Scotia, i., p. 250; Isle Royale, v., p. 283.

COCHEM discovered, i., p. 21.

COCHEM ISDAND, fort Santiago erected on, i., p. 25.

COCKIN'S STRAITS, i., p. 51.

COCOS ISLANDS, i., p. 31.

CODERE, DU, Commandant at Yazoos, killed at Natchez, while trying to save Father du Poisson, vi., p. 82.

CODOGDACHOS, Texas tribe, iv., p. 80, n.

COLA, post in Lapland, i., p. 48.

COLAPISSAS, Louysiana Indians (Aquelonpissas, men who hear and see) kill many Natchitoches and carry off women, vi., p. 19; sing calumet to l'Epinai, 39, n.; forty warriors join Perrier's force against Natchez, 107.

COLBERT, JOHN BAPTIST, Minister of State, recalls de Mésy, iii., p. 75; influence of 79, 80, n.; Memoirs of Talon to, 84; views as to French settlements, 92; prejudiced against Jesuits for not frenchifying Indians, changes his views and feelings towards them, 97; orders to de Courcelles in regard to de Bouteroue, 121; sends an agent to Acadia to report on the province, 139; accepts Talon's offer to go, 187; answer to Temple's proposals, ib.; instructions to du Chesneau on the liquor question, 195; adopts his advice, ib.; death, 200; succeeded by his son de Seignelay, ib.; why he ignored English operations in Hudson's Bay, 231.

COLBERT or Mississippi River, iii., p. 213, n.; iv., p. 68, n.

COLDEN, CADWALLADER, error as to Schuyler's expedition, iv., p. 208, n.

COLIGNI, GASPAR, ADMIRAL DE, projects Hugenot colony in Brazil, its result, i., p. 132; turns his views to Florida, 42, 133; sends a new convoy, 135; new expedition, 148; prejudiced against de Laudonniere, 180; recalls him to France, 181; instructions to Ribaut in regard to Menendez, 192–3; hatred against, prevents Court from avenging massacre of French in Florida, 223.

COLIN, companion of the Chevalier d'Aux, burned iv., p. 141, n.

COLLEGE OF QUEBEC, founded by René Rohaut, ii., p. 87.

COLLET CAPTAIN, repulses Wheeler at Martinique, iv., p. 244, n.

COLLIER, MR., partner of de Monts, ii., p. 20.

COLOMBET, LIEUTENANT DE, killed in action with Iroquois, iv., p. 142.
COLOMBIERE, REV. J., Great Archdeacon, V. Gen., &c., preaches at service after deliverance of Quebec, iv., p. 190, n.; cured by intercession of Catharine Tegahkouita, iv., p. 295.
COLON, DIEGO, Jamaica and Porto Rico, settled under orders of, i., p. 27.
COLORADO RIVER, explored by Kino, i., p. 62.
COLORADO RIVER, Texas, La Sale probably reached, iv., p. 88, n.
COLUMBUS, CHRISTOPHER, discoveries of, i., pp. 19–24; fabulous story as to, 23.
COLUMBUS, LOUIS, grandson of Christopher, made Duke of Veraguas, i., p. 25.
COMANCHES, called Padoucas by French, v., p. 184, n.
COMMERCE, liberty of, iii., p. 99; permitted to gentlemen, iv., p. 16; decline of trade in furs, v., p. 265; revolution in commerce of Louysiana, vi., p. 32; Perrier's views on, p. 105
COMPANIES, French, for trade and colonization, viz.:
COMPAGNIE DES CENT ASSOCIÉS. See Company of the Hundred Associates.
COMPAGNIE DES INDES. See India Company.
COMPAGNIE DES INDES OCCIDENTALES. See West India Company.
COMPAGNIE DE M. DE MONTS. See De Monts.
COMPAGNIE DU NORD. See Northern Company.
COMPAGNIE D'OCCIDENT, See Western Company.
COMPAGNIE DES PECHES SEDENTAIRES. See Sedentary Fishery Company.
COMPANIES, Champlain's opinion of, ii., p. 57; Raudot's, v., p. 292.
COMPANISE, Ottawa chief, attacks Iroquois, v., p. 163; Tonti and Vincennes attack him and release prisoners, v., p. 169.
COMPANY OF THE HUNDRED ASSOCIATES, called Company of New France. Plan, privileges, concession from Louis, XIII., ii., p. 39; Champlain's remarks on, 57, resumes possession of Canada, and sends a fleet, ii., p. 63; why it declines to permit Recollects to return, ii., p. 65, iii., p. 147; neglects Canada, ii., p 104; juridically justifies Jesuits against calumnies, 168; continues to neglect Canada, 237; surrenders it to the King, iii., p. 66; conditions on which he gave up fur trade to settlers, iv., p. 79.
COMPANY'S LAND, i., p. 56.
CONCEPTION, Huron town, defeat of braves of, ii., p. 220, n.
CONCEPTION BAY, Newfoundland, named by Cortereal, i., p. 23; Guy forms settlement at, iii., p. 140.
CONCEPTION ISLAND, discovered by John de Nova, i., p. 24.
CONCESSIONS, arrival of the first in Louysiana, Errors in regard to, vi., p. 40; several Concessionaries serve at the siege of Pensacola, 44; some Concessions at the Natchitoches, 64.
CONDÉ, Henry de Bourbon II., Prince of, Viceroy of New France, ii., p. 24; appoints Champlain lieutenant, ib.; does little for the colony, p. 31; Marshal Themines acts during his imprisonment, ib.; sells his office to his brother-in-law, the Duke de Montmorenci, p. 32.
CONESTOGAS. See ANDASTES.
CONGÉS, what they were, their utility, v., p. 66; orders not carried out, 77.
CONGO discovered, i., p. 18.
CONGREGATION SISTERS, see Sisters of the Congregation.
CONIL, EDWARD, Portuguese, discovers Straits of Sunda, i., p. 35.
CONNECTICUT, means Long river, ii., p. 156, n.; called River of the Sokokis, ib.; joins New York in expedition against Montreal, iv., p. 145, n.; sends Fitch and Johnson's companies, 146, n.; Fitz-John Winthrop of Connecticut commands, ib.
CONSTANTIN, F. NICHOLAS B., Recollect, at settlement of Detroit, v., p. 154; seized by Ottawas, delivered and killed, 186.
CONTI, Prince of, favors la Sale, and gives him the Chevalier de Tonti, iii., p. 200.
CONTRECŒUR, ANTHONY PECODY, SIEUR DE. grant to, iii., p. 112.
CONTREVILLE takes possession of Louisbourg, v., p. 296.
COPPER MINES in Acadia, i., pp. 250, 254; on Blue Earth river, v., p. 134, vi., p. 12.
CORDE, SIMON DE, exploration of, i., p. 48.
CORDOVA, FRANCIS FERNANDEZ, i., p. 30.
CORIANA, canton of Venezuela, i., p. 38.
CORLAR, Indian name for Governor of New York, ii., p. 124, iii., p. 251, n.

CORLAR, 'French and Indian name of Schenectady, its origin, ii., p. 11, iii., p. 88, n.; destruction, iv., p. 123.

CORNEILLE, THOMAS, errors in Geographical Dictionary of, i., p. 68.

CORNEJO, DON FRANCISCO, Commander of the Barlovento Squadron, ordered to Pensacola, vi., p. 47; countermanded, ib.; fresh orders to sail, 49; ready with a fleet to sail from Vera Cruz to reduce Louysiana, 62.

CORNELISZNAY, CORNELIUS, Dutch Discoveries of, i., 46.

CORNERO, or CORNEDO, (CORONADO,) Francis Vasquez, sent to Cibola and Quivira, i., p. 38.

CORQUIZANO, MARTIN YÑIGUEZ DE, reduces Yucatan, i., p. 35.

CORROIS, Louysiana Indians, intermingled with Yazoos, vi., p. 85; unite to massacre French, ib.; defeated and nearly destroyed by Akansas, 102; the rest in a fort with Natchez, 115; join Chickasaws to aid the Natchez, 116.

CORTEREAL, GASPAR DE, a Portuguese gentleman, discoveries of in Northern America, i., p. 23, 105; fate of, 23; names Conception Bay, i., p. 23.

CORTEREAL, MICHAEL, brother of preceding, i., p. 32.

CORTEZ, HERNAN DE, conquers Mexico, i., p. 31; sends out explorers, 32; puts an end to Mexican Empire, 33; discoveries of officers of, ib.; discovers California, 37; sends Tello to complete explorations, 38.

CORVO, one of the Azores, i., p. 16; statue found on, 17; meridian fixed at, ib.

COSA, JOHN DE LA, discoveries of, i., p. 22.

COSSET, CAPTAIN, commands Ribaut's four ships, his manœuvres when attacked by Spaniards, i., p. 190; informs Ribaut, 192.

COSTEBELLE, SIEUR PASTOUR DE, reinforces Placentia, iv., p. 164; settlers refuse to obey, 165; reports English terms, 224; governor of Placentia, approves Saint Ovide's design to besiege St. John, v., p. 212; St. Ovide informs him of the success of his enterprise, 214; censures St. Ovide and orders him to return to Placentia, 215; project of, to expel English from Newfoundland, but does not receive promised aid, 231; attempt on Carbonniere, ib.; notifies Vaudreuil, 238; English attack Placentia, what saves it? 253; refuses an officer to attack Port Royal, 256, governor of Isle Royale or Cape Breton, 296; urges Acadians to remove there, ib., n.; succeeded by St. Ovide, ib.

COTE, SIEUR DE LA, King's Scrivener in Acadia, supports the Chevalier de Villebon in defence of Naxoat, v., p. 31; dismounts an English gun, 32.

COTE DE LAUSON, Militia of, iv., p. 167.

COTTON, F. PETER, Jesuit Confessor to Henry IV.; exertions to send missionaries to Acadia, i., p. 260; F. d'Orleans censures him for allowing Mme. de Guercherville to do so much, 263; Champlain defends, ib.; but blames him for preventing her joining Mr. de Monts, ib.

COUDRE, iv., p. 123; Charlevoix's name for JOHN SANDERS GLEN, which see.

COUILLARD family advised to remain at Quebec, ii., p. 51.

COULONGES, SIEUR DE, sent to Akansas, vi., p. 107; wounded by Natchez, 108; taken and burned by Chickasaws, 122, n.

COUNCIL OF QUEBEC, letter of to Commissioners of New England, ii., p. 214; reorganized, iii., 67, 74, n.

COURCELAS, MR. DE, a Louysiana officer burnt by Chickasaws, vi., p. 122, n.

COURCELLES, DANIEL DE REMI, SEIGNEUR DE, Governor General of New France, instructions of, iii., p. 81; regulates tithes, iii., p. 24, n.; Mohawk expedition, iii., p. 88; Charlevoix's account corrected, pp. 88–9, n.; commands van against Mohawks, 90; prejudiced against the missionaries, 97; obtains a Jesuit for the Senecas, 116; good qualities and defects. Colbert's letter to, 121; his military activity, 123; his expedition against the Iroquois, its objects and results, 124; health affected, asks recall, ib.; what defeats his projected road between Quebec and Acadia, 139; punishes French assassins of Iroquois chief, and reduces all the Indians to peace, 151; sends belts to Oneidas and Senecas, ib., n.; sponsor for Garaconthié, 153; deprived of aid from France; maintains French authority by the ascendency he had acquired, 161; haughty tone to Senecas, ib.; winks at their misconduct, ib.; projects fort at Catarocouy, 175; induces his successor to fa-

vor it, 176 ; returns to France ; character of, ib.

Coureurs de Bois, see Bushlopers. Orders as to iii., p. 194.

Cournoyer, Madame de, cured by F. Druillettes, ii., p. 247.

Courtemanche, Sieur Tilly de Repentigny, a Canadian gentleman, proprictor of Fort Pontchartrain, iii., 145 ; Portneuf's lieutenant in Casco Bay expedition, iv., p. 133 ; distinguished at capture of fort, ib. ; why sent to the Ottawas by Frontenac, 192 ; sent to notify Michilimakinac Indians of Freneh success against English, and to Miamis, iv., p. 200 ; commands a party against Mohawks, 233 ; at Michilimakinac, 242 ; defeats Iroquois on the St. Joseph's, 270 ; why sent to Northern and Western tribes, 111 ; on St, Joseph's 141 ; visits all the nations to obtain delegates, ib. ; sent to Boston to exchange prisoners, 176 ; stories of an Esquimaux girl, held by, i., p. 125.

Coussinoc, now Augusta, Me., ii., p.214, n.

Couture, William, companion of F. Jogues, ii., p. 141 ; might have escaped, but surrenders, ib. ; cruel treatment and piety of, 142 ; saved by an Iroquois chief, 147 ; and brought back to colony, 180 ; acts as interpreter, 181 ; brings Mohawk chiefs, iii., p. 88, n. ; descendants of, ii., p. 141, n.

Couture, met by Cavelier and his party at Akansas ; what took him there, iv., p. 108 ; induces the Akansas to relieve Cavelier and give him guides, escorts them to the Kappas, 109.

"Covering Body," explained, iii., p. 257.

Covillam, Peter de, travels of, i., p. 19.

Cow Bay, Cape Breton, v., p. 284.

Coxe, Daniel, attempts to settle Louisiana, v., p. 124, n., 126 ; Huguenots with, 127, n.

Cozumel, i., p. 30.

Cramoisy, Sebastian, king's printer, works on Canada printed by, i., p. 77, 81; member of company of One Hundred, ii., p. 44, n.

Crees, see Cristinaux, Kilistinons.

Creoles of Louysiana, gallant conduct at siege of Natchez, Perrier's opinion of, vi., p. 102.

Cresnay, Crenet, or Creant, Baron de, said to have been commandant at Natchez, vi., p. 100, n. ; said to have been commandant of Louysiana troops ; accompanies Perrier, p. 108 ; Natchez surrender to, 116-7.

Creux, Father Francis du, account of his Historia Canadensis, i., p. 81.

Crevier, (?Joseph,) Seigneur of Saint François, attends his uncle Hertel on the Salmon Falls expedition; iv., p. 130 ; killed 132 ; taken and tortured by Iroquois, 240, n.

Crisasi, see Crisafy.

Crisafy, Chevalier Thomas de, iv., p. 195 ; gallant conduct at St. Sulpice, iv., p. 194 ; ordered to Cataracouy, 251 ; sets out, 265 ; success 268 ; dies of chagrin, iv., p. 196, n. ; v., p. 11. See vol. vi., p. 127.

Crisafy, Anthony, Marquis de, iv., p. 195 ; Governor of Three Rivers, 196 ; repulses Iroquois, 216 ; seasonably reinforced at Sault St. Louis, 232 ; in charge of a fort during Frontenac's expedition, v., p. 15; death of, iv., p. 196, n. ; see vol. vi., p. 127.

Cristinaux, see Kilistinons, Crees.

Croix, La, mutineer at Caroline, i., p. 166; executed, 170.

Cromwell, Oliver, grants Acadia to Temple, Crown and la Tour, iii., p. 132, n.

Crown Point, Champlain's battle with the Iroquois, near, ii., p. 16; Ramezai defeats a party near, v., p. 219; English propose to occupy, 220.

Crown, William, Cromwell grants Acadia to Temple, la Tour and, iii., p. 137, n.

Crozat, Mr. J., obtains from French King monopoly of Louysiania trade and extensive grants, vi., p. 17; takes la Motte Cadillac in as a partner, 18; what defeated his monopoly, 36; complaints by and against him, 37; resigns grant to King, 37.

Crucifixion of a Christian child by Mohawks, ii., p. 198.

Cuba discovered, i., p. 19.

Cucagua, Garcilasso's name for Micissipi, i., p. 40; iii., p. 214, n. ; v., p. 120, n. vi., p. 11.

Cubagua, discovered, i., p. 21.

Cumana, discovered, i., p. 21; French pri soners sent to, vi., p. 46.

Culuacan, i., p. 38.

CUSSI, MR. DE, Governor of St. Domingo (or of Tortugas) visits la Sale at Petit Goave, iv., p. 65 ; kindness to la Sale, 66–7.

DABLON, SIMON, one of the first members of the company of a Hundred Associates, ii., p. 39.

DABLON, F. CLAUDE, Jesuit, sketch of, ii., p. 262, n. ; sent to Onondaga, 262 ; why he goes to Quebec, 266 ; returns, 267 ; expedition up the Saguenay, iii., p. 39 ; founds mission of Sault St. Mary's, p. 119 ; visits Mascoutin country with F. Allouez, and overturns an idol, 182 ; not diverted from visiting Outagamis, or Foxes, 183 ; recalled to Quebec, 185 ; Superior from 1670 to 1688, ii., p. 262, n. ; his writings, ib.

DACAN, SIEUR, sent with F. Hennepin, to explore upper Mississippi, i., p. 57, 83 ; iii., p. 206 ; detained for a time prisoner among Sioux, 207 ; name misprinted for Dacau, iii., p. 206, n.

DACARETTE, young colonist at Placentia, takes command of French, captures English frigate and eludes two hostile vessels, v., p. 232.

DACASHATA, Seneca chief, v., p. 18, n.

DACOTAS, called Nadwechiwek by Algonquins, and Sioux by French, iii., p. 31, n. ; their tribes, ib.

DAILLON, F. JOSEPH DE LA ROCHE, (or D'ALLION,) Recollect, at Quebec, ii., p. 36 ; starts for Hurons, but forced to return, 37 ; preaches to Neuter Nation, ib., n. ; 152.

DAIMANVILLE, or DÁMANVILLE, or DAINMAVILLE, REV. MR. on la Sale's expedition, iv., p. 62; narrative of, 71, n.; see MAJULLE.

DALE, SIR THOMAS, treats members of Guercheville's colony as pirates, i., p. 281, n.

DALMAS, F. ANTHONY, Jesuit, killed at Hudson Bay, iv., p. 243.

DAMISOKANTIK, Abenaqui mission at., v., p. 167, n.

DAMOUR, Canadian gentleman, iv., p. 158.

DAMVILLE, FRANCIS CHRISTOPHER DE LÉVIS, DUKE DE, Viceroy, 1644–60, iii., p. 80, n.

DANES, discoveries of, i., p. 53, 57.

DANIEL F. ANTHONY, Jesuit, native of Dieppe, ii., p. 213 ; at Cape Breton, ib., n. ; suffers much from Hurons, ii., p. 76 ; takes Huron boys to college at Quebec, p. 92 ; how he reaches it, ib. ; killed by Iroquois, giving his life for his flock, 210–213 ; sketch of, 213, n.

DANISH RIVER, Hudson Bay, i., p. 56.

DANISH SHIP takes northern pigmies to Denmark, i., p. 127.

DARAN, FATHER ADRIAN, Jesuit, sent to Hurons, ii., p. 210 ; returns to Europe, 250, n.

DARDENNES, Canadian scout, reports to Champmêlin the condition of Pensacola, vi., p. 56.

DAUPHIN ISLAND, (Madagascar,) i., p. 56.

DAUPHIN ISLAND, first called Massacre Island, v., p. 120 ; storehouses, &c., built here by d'Iberville, vi., p. 14 ; fort on, ib. ; headquarters of colony, ib. ; plundered by English pirates, 16 ; port of, closes while Mr. de l'Epinai is fortifying, vi., p. 14, 39 ; Spaniards attack it ineffectually for several days, p. 49–53.

DAUPHIN, PORT, or ST. ANNE, on Isle Royale, v., p. 285 ; description of, ib. ; why Louisbourg preferred, 296.

DAUVERSIERE, JEROME LE ROYER DE LA, projects settlement of Montreal; ii., p. 129.

DAVAULT, hunter for Fort St. Louis, discovers plot against Joutel, iv., p. 74.

DAVID, Emperor of Abyssinia, i., p. 29.

DAVILA, GIL GONZALES, discovers Nicoya, i., p. 33.

DAVILA, PEDRARIAS DE, settles Santa Maria and Cartagena, i., p. 29 ; sends Espinoza to found Panama, i., p. 31.

DAVION, REV. ANTHONY, missionary to the Tonicas, v., p. 128, n. ; his labors, ib.; saves a Natché Indian, advice to French, vi., p. 28.

DAVIS, JOHN, Englishman, discoveries of, i., p. 45.

DAVIS, CAPT. SYLVANUS, succeeds Capt. Willard in command of Fort Loyal, Casco Bay; forced to surrender to Portneuf, iv., p. 136, n. ; account of, ib.; taken to Quebec, 136 ; his declaration, 134, n. ; exchanged, 187, n.

DAVIS STRAITS, discovered, i., p. 45, 46.

DAVITY, the "Monde" of, i., p. 67.

DAVOST, F. AMBROSE, Jesuit, sufferings, of among Hurons, ii., p.76; dies at sea, 170.

DEBRÉ, see BRAY, DE.

DEERFIELD, attacked by Hertel de Rouville, v., p. 161; Rev. John Williams taken there, ib., n.; again attacked, 216, n.

DELAUNAY, JOHN, of Rouen, receives Cavelier at the Arkansas, iv., p. 108.

DELIETTO, SIEUR, commandant at the Illinois, related to Tonti, v., p. 131; induces head chief of Natchez to make reparation to Bienville, vi., p. 72; death of, ib.

DELISLE, commandant at Pensacola, vi., p. 60, n.; see LILLE.

DELISLE, commandant at Fort Bourbon, v., p. 304, n.

DELLIUS, REV. GODFREY, Dutch minister, notice of, v., p. 83, n.; sent to Frontenac by Bellomont, v., p. 80; pretensions of, 91; begins a Mohawk mission, 106; driven from Albany, 107.

DENIS, JOHN, of Honfleur, publishes map of Newfoundland, &c., in 1506, i., p. 26.

DENIS, ST. PIERRE, taken, iv., p. 30, n.

DENONVILLE, JAMES RENÉ DE BRISAY, Marquis de, Governor General of Canada, sketch of, iii.,; p. 258, n.; arrives at Quebec and goes up to Cataracouy, 258-9; his opinion of the state of the colony, 261; projects fort at Niagara, 262; letter to from Governor of New York, 263; reply, ib.; prepares to reduce Senecas, 268; letter to de Seignelay, ib.; gives Northern Company an officer and soldiers to expel English from Hudson Bay, 270; declares war, 274; representation to King, 275; said to have arrested Iroquois chiefs whom he had invited to a conference at Catarocony, 276; doubts as to this, 276, n.; invites Green Bay Indians to join him, 279; plan of expedition; not deceived by Governor of New York, 280; harmony with Intendant, 282; at Catarocony, 283; correspondence with Governor of New York, 284; punishes a deserter who guided English to Michilimakinac, ib.; builds Fort Sables; attacked by Senecas near Boughton Hill, 286-7, n.; place discussed, 289, n.; ravages the canton, 290; builds a fort at Niagara, and garrisons it, ib.; labors to divide the cantons, 292; information from the Baron de St. Castin, 294; report to the King on trade, fisheries, Acadia and Newfoundland; New Seneca expedition prevented, 295; embarrassed by royal orders, 296; reflections, 296; Governor of New York demands an explanation, 300; F. Vaillant sent, his instructions, 300; sends convoy to Catarocuoy, 302; efforts to gain Onondaga, 302; gives audience to a deputy, 304; insolence of the Indians, ib.; conditions proposed by him, 305; abandons Fort Niagara, 306; asks de Seignelay to send Iroquois at Marseilles back by young de Serigny, 306; makes a truce with Iroquois, ib.; letter to from Governor of New York, ib.; marches against an Iroquois party, 307; report to de Seignelay on F. de Lamberville and the Iroquois and Abénaqui missions, 307-8; why anxious in regard to the colony, 309; remarks on bushlopers and the Iroquois war, 310; exaggerates somewhat, 311; lacks vigor, ib.; anxious to make peace, iv., p. 11; discontent of our allies, 12; recall proposed, iv., p. 21; trouble in Montreal Island, ravaged by Iroquois, 29; reasons for evacuating and demolishing Fort Catarocouy, 32–3; appointed Sub-Governor of the Princes of France, 33; memoir to de Seignelay on affairs of New France, 44; advises laying waste all New York up to Albany, 46; opinion of King and ministry on his memoir, 46; object in Seneca war, 49; associated with Fenelon, iii., p. 258, n.; death of, ib.

DENYS, JOHN, of Honfleur, makes earliest map of the St. Lawrence, i., p. 106, 26.

DENYS DE FRONSAC, NICHOLAS, Proprietor and King's Governor of part of Acadia, iii., p. 128, 129, n.; work of, i., p. 81; limits he assigns to colony, 248; account of its fertility, at Cape Breton with colonists, 132; troubles with le Borgne, 132; restored to his rights, 133; reply to summons to surrender Chedabouctou, 136; India Company deceived, but restores his rights, 137; ruined by fire, ib.; eulogium of, ib.; cited by Bp. St. Valier, ii., p. 121.

DENYS DE ST. SIMON, nephew of preceding, iii., p. 231. See ST. SIMON.

DENYS DE BONAVENTURE, see BONAVENTURE.

DENYS DE LA RONDE, see RONDE.

DENYS, Captain of Tadoussac, iii., p. 233.

DENYS, commandant of Fort at Kaskebé (Casco Bay), iv., p. 136. See DAVIS, SYLVANUS.

DEQUEN, REV. JOHN, Jesuit Superior, iv., p. 306; sketch of, ii., p. 272; sends missionaries to Ottawas, ib.; contest with de Queylus, iii., p. 21; death of, ii., p. 272, n.; iii., p. 27, n.

DESAVENTURADAS, Spanish name of Juan Fernandez island, i., p. 43.

DESCAYRAC, CAPTAIN PETER, see ESCAIRAC D'.

DESIDERI, FATHER HIPPOLYTE, Florentine Jesuit, enters Thibet, i., p. 62.

DESLOGES, one of La Sale's volunteers, killed by Indians, iv., p. 71.

DESNOS, MR., navy captain, brings reinforcements to Canada, with orders to remain, iii., p. 255.

DESNOYERS, MADAME, prisoner among Natchez, sent to Loubois with proposals, detained, vi., p. 98.

DESPENSENS, SIEUR, acting as major in St. Ovide's St. John expedition, distinguished in capture of the fort, v., p. 213; sent to France by St. Ovide to report success, 214.

DETROIT, strait between Lake Erie and Lake Huron, Du Luht and Tonti assemble Indians at, iii., p. 279–80; De Callieres founds settlement of, v., p. 136; discussion with Teganissorens as to, ib.; la Motte Cadillac founds Fort Pontchartrain and Detroit, 154, fired by Indians, 164; Ottawas dislike, 165; objections to, ib.; disapproved by Vaudreuil, ib.; Indian troubles at, 184–190; menaced by Foxes, 257; they are besieged, 259.

DEYUDEHAAKDOH, or TOTIAKTO, Seneca town destroyed by Denonville, iii., p. 289, n.

DIAZ, BARTHOLOMEW and PETER, discover the Cape of Good Hope, i., p. 19.

DIEPPE trades with Guinea, i., p. 13; Aubert, pilot of, 106; Verrazano writes from, 108; Ribaut, native of, 135; sails from, 180; Ursuline and Hospital nuns from, ii., p. 110; de Chatte, Governor of, i., p. 246.

DIGG'S LAND, discovered by Button, i., p. 51.

DIMMOCK, CAPT. at Port Royal, v., p. 198, n.

DINONDADIES, English form for Tionontatez, the Petuns, ii., p. 228. See TIONNONTATEZ.

DIOURSE, Capt. of the Philippe, vi., p. 51, n.

DIRON, see ARTAGUETTE, D'.

DIONAKARONDÉ, Indian name of Chev. d'Aux, iv., p. 221, n.

DISCOURSE of a Great Sea Captain, praised by Ramusio, i., p. 132.

DIXON, JOHN, carried to Virginia, i., p. 281, n.

DOGFISH, i., p. 268; vi., p.

DOLPHIN RIVER, discovered by Ribaut, i., p. 135; Laudonniere at, 149; called St. Augustine by Menendez, 188.

DOLLARD, ADAM, Sieur des Ormeaux, heroic fight at Longsault, iii., p. 33, n.

DOLLIER DE CASSON, FRANCIS of Saint Sulpice, account of, sent to Nipissing, iii., p. 122, n.; goes to Seneca country, ib.; sails through Lake Erie and St. Clair, ib.; map of Lake Erie, ib.; History of Montreal by, vi., p. 126.

DOLU, MR., Grand Audiencier of France, acts for Viceroy de Montmorenci, ii., p. 32.

DOMAGAYA, Indian taken to France by Cartier and brought back, i., p. 117; 118, n.

DOMERGUE, SIEUR, killed in ambush with his detachment, iv., pp. 205-6.

DOMINICA, de Gourgues at, i., p. 226.

DONGAN, COL. THOMAS, Governor of New York, sketch of, iii., p. 217, n.; seizes St. Castin's wine, 211, n.; efforts to gain fur trade through Iroquois, 217, 234; orders sent to, 226; requested to join de la Barre in Seneca war or stand neutral, 248; result, ib.; pretensions to Iroquois country in letter to Denonville, 263; instigates them to attack us, and endeavors to reduce Sault St. Louis and Mountain Iroquois, 265; sends English to Michilimakinac to trade, 266; brings over English Jesuits, ib., n.; intrigues to excite Iroquois against us, 267; favors surprise of Fort Nelson, 269; further intrigues, 274; fails to delude Denonville, ib.; prevents Seneca attack on Illinois, 280; routes Iroquois, 281; correspondence with Denonville, 283–4; second English convoy to Michilimakinac and its fate, 284; intrigues with Iroquois, promises English Jesuits to

Christian Iroquois, 291 ; threatens Denonville with open hostility, 291 ; in spite of orders from London instigates Iroquois to war, 298 ; afraid of reprisals, 299 ; sends Magregorie to ask explanation of belt presented to Iroquois by F. de Lamberville, 300 ; does not permit F. Vaillant to come through Mohawks, 303 ; urges Iroquois to hostilities while restoring prisoners to us, and notifying Denonville of the orders of both Kings for neutrality, 281, 301, 307 ; succeeded as Governor of New York by Sir Edmond Andros, 308.

DONGÉ F. PETER, Jesuit, brought over by d'Iberville, v., p. 127 ; ordered to return from Louysiana, ib.; death of, 130.

DONNACONA, Indian chief of Stadaconé, i., p. 117, n.; visits Cartier, i., p. 117 ; endeavors to prevent his going to Hochelaga, ib.; taken to France by Cartier, 122, n.; relates almost incredible things to that navigator, 124 ; lived four or five years in France, 122, n.

DOUAY, F. ANASTASIUS, Recollect, sketch of, iv., p. 63, n.; accompanies La Sale in search of the Micissipi, iv., 63 ; present at his death, 96 ; proceeds to Illinois, 107 ; with d'Iberville at the mouth, v., p. 120.

DOUBLET, Ile St. Jean granted to, v., p. 300.

DOUBLET, CAP, i., p. 61.

DOUCETTE, English Governor of Nova Scotia, demands absolute oath of Acadians, v., p. 296, n.

DOUTRELEAU, F. STEPHEN, Jesuit, wounded by Yazoos while saying mass ; his wonderful escape, vi., p. 86 ; taken to New Orleans, 88 ; joins army as chaplain, 89.

DOVER, N. H., capture of, iv., p. 41, n.

DOVERSIERE, ROYER DE LA. See DAUVERSIERE.

DOYEN, ANDREW, settler at Placentia, kills a corporal and two soldiers, iv., p. 165.

DRAKE, SIR FRANCIS, Sarmiento sent against, i., p. 45.

DRIEUILLETTES (DREUILLETTES), F. GABRIEL, Jesuit, first Abénaqui missionary, ii., p. 201 ; sent to Boston to negotiate neutrality between French and English colonies, 214 ; result, ib.; sent back with Godfrey, ib.; commission and papers, 214–7 ; result, 217–8, n.; labors in Northern Canada, 243 ; iii., p. 20 ; obtains information as to Hudson Bay and Wisconsin, iii., p. 20 ; miracles ascribed to, ii., p. 247 ; friendship sought by English, ib.; goes to the Ottawa country, 272 ; said to have returned to the Abénaquis, 275 ; goes North to found a Kilistinon mission, iii., p. 39 ; in the West, 196, n.; death, ii., p. 248, n.

DROUET DE RICHARDVILLE, only prisoner spared by Chickasaws, vi., p. 121, n.; his narrative cited, 121–2, n.

DUBOS, JOSEPH, Canadian partisan, mortally wounded by Indians near Kinderhook, v., p. 49 ; dies at Albany, ib.

DUCASSE, Captain in the French navy, Governor of St. Domingo, v., p. 118 ; Iberville meets, ib. ; outmanœuvres Admiral Graydon, v., p. 162.

DUCHESNEAU, JAMES, Intendant, iii., p. 67, 191 ; see CHESNEAU.

DUCLOS, MR., Commissaire Ordonnateur of Louysiana, vi., p. 17 ; judicial powers vested in Governor and, 18 ; memoir on Louysiana, 35 ; succeeded by Hubert, 38 ; acts well at Cap François, 35 ; Intendant of Leeward Isles, ib.

DUCLOS, Clerk of Perrot, iv., p. 158.

DUCLOS, Captain of a coaster, plundered by deserters, vi., p. 69.

DUCLOS, French officer, distinguished at siege of Quebec, iv., p. 181.

DUDLEY, JOSEPH, Governor General of New England, ii., p. 214 ; meets Eastern Indians, v., p. 160 ; prevents attack on Port Royal, 171 ; negotiates an exchange of prisoners with Vaudreuil, really to reconnoitre Quebec, p. 175 ; his son at Quebec measures fortifications, 176 ; not sincere in proposing neutrality, v., p. 180, 191 ; plans expulsion of French from Acadia, 191 ; correspondence as to siege of Port Royal, 195 ; offers to go in person, his son sent, 196 ; Queen notifies him of her determination to reduce Acadia, 201 , recalls an expedition of 500 men, 208 ; cannot induce the Abénaquis to remain neutral, 225 ; learns Subercase's project, 226 ; refuses to exchange prisoners, v., p. 234, 237.

DUGUÉ, SIDRAC, commands corps in de la Barre's army, iii., p. 249.

DUGUÉ, brother of Boisbriant, v., p. 58;

Dugué, (*continued.*)
commands Profond, v., p. 56. See Gué.

Duhaut, Sieur one of La Sale's associates, lost, but regains Fort St. Louys, iv., p. 83; conspires, p. 87; accompanies La Sale on his last excursion, 89; assassinates him, 93; seizes the command and divides La Sale's property with Lachevêque, 97; gives Cavelier half of the goods, 103; killed by Hiens, 103.

Duhaut, Dominic, younger brother of preceding, iv., p. 83; at St. Louis, ib.; accompanies La Sale on one of his excursions, 87; fate unknown, 88; La Sale accused of having killed him with his own hands, 95.

Duke of York's Island, i., p. 58.

Dumas, F. John, Jesuit, arrives, vi., p. 76, n.

Dumesnil, La Sale's servant, devoured by an alligator, iv., p. 88.

Dumont, Elambart, companion of F. Vaillant, iii., p. 301, n.

Dumont, Mr., author of Memoires de la Louisiane, wife of, taken at Natchez, vi., p. 83.

Duperon, F. Francis, Jesuit, returns to Europe, ii., p. 250, n.

Dupont, Gravé, i., p. 281 n.; ii., p. 8, n; see Pontgravé.

Dupuy, Claude Thomas, Intendant, v., p. 309.

Dupuys, Zachary, French officer, commandant of fort at Quebec, ii., p. 267, n.; leads a French colony to Onondaga, 267; his reception, 276; measures adopted by, on hearing of a plot to massacre French, iii., p. 15; his escape, 17.

Dupuys, Paul, Lieutenant Particulier at Quebec, Aide Major at the siege, sounds the tocsin, iv., p. 182. See Puys.

Dupuys, Lieutenant, son of the preceding, defends Fort Chambly under de Valrenes, iv., p. 203; gallant conduct on a retreat, v., p. 205; sent to New York, v., p. 222; to Boston, 234; Vaudreuil's high opinion of, ib.

Durand, Rev. Justinian, kept two years in prison at Boston, v., p. 299, n.

Durantaye, Oliver Morel de la, sketch of, iv., p. 53, n; 138, n.; Gentleman of the Comté Nantois, Captain in the Carignan Salieres regiment, iii., p. 112; iv., p. 53; commandant at Michilimakinac, endeavors to relieve Fort St. Louis, Illinois, 244; ordered to assemble Indians and march to Niagara, 245, 280; finds no French there, difficulty in appeasing Indians, 247; pursues English traders who had reached Michilimakinac in his absence, 265; gains esteem and confidence of the Indians, 280; ordered to conduct them to Niagara, 281; captures sixty English on the way to Michilimakinac, 284; in the van, 286, n.; at Niagara and at Fort des Sables, 287; deceived by the Rat, he shoots an Iroquois, iv., p. 14; skill in retaining our allies, 53-4; why recalled from Michilimakinac, 137; defeats an Iroquois party back of Boucherville, 269; commands a battalion in Frontenac's expedition, v., p. 13; councillor in the Superior Council of Quebec, iv., p. 138, n.

Durham, N. H., formerly Oyster river, destroyed by Villieu, iv., p. 256, n.

Dutch, discoveries of, i., pp. 46, 52; take Amboyna from Portuguese, 50; settle New Netherland, 51; ii., p. 9; build Manhatte and Fort Orange, p. 10; first treaty with Mohawks, p. 75; supply Iroquois with fire-arms, ii., p. 139; de Montmagny complains of, p. 140; he prevents Indian hostilities against, ib.; intervene in behalf of Jogues, 148; offer to deliver him, 157; save him, 158; never declared against French, ii., p. 11; taunt Christian Indians, iii., p. 154; threaten French missionaries, 192; deprived of New Netherland by English, ii., p. 11; yield it in exchange for Surinam, ib.; take Pentagoët, iii., pp. 188, 194.

Dutch East India Company, formed, i., p. 49; Hudson in employ of, ii., p. 9.

Dyagodiyu, Denonville's battle field, iii., p. 287, n.

Dyudoosot or Gannounata, Seneca town, destroyed by Denonville, iii., p. 289, n.

Eagle, The, chief of the Sault St. Louis Iroquois, v., p. 151.

Eams, Captain, of the Sorlings, defeated by Bonaventure, iv., p. 274, n.

Earl Bristol's Island, i., p. 54.

Earl Danby's Island, i., p. 54.

Earthquakes in Canada, predicted, iii., p. 57; account of, 57–61.

Eau, Chevalier Pierre d,' Sieur de Jol-

LIET, (wrote d'Aux, iv., p. 52, 141, n.,) reduced captain, sent to Onondaga as envoy, iv., p. 52; companions burned, 141, n.; escapes from New York and recaptured, 221; sent to Boston, 141–190; escapes from Boston, 141, 219: reaches Quebec, 141; called also Do, iv., p. 52; Indian name, Dionakaronde; see vi., p. 127.

ECHON, Indian name of F. Brebeuf, ii., p. 221, n.

EDEL'S LAND, New Holland, i., p. 53.

EDGAR, THOMAS, discovers and names Edgar's Isle, i., p. 52.

EDZERIMET, EDZIRMET or EGEREMET, Canibas chief, treats with English, iv., p. 255; mentioned, v., p. 26.

EFFIAT, ANTHONY COIFFIER RUZÉ, MARSHAL D', Superintendent of Finances, one of the Hundred Associates, ii., p. 43.

EHWAE, Huron town, destroyed by Iroquois, ii., p. 153, n.

EKARENNIONDI, Petun town, called St. Mathias, ii., p. 228, n.

ELIOT, REV. JOHN, entertains Father Druillettes, ii., p. 214, n.; writes to Canada in favor of Indians, 256, n.

ELIZABETH, Queen of England, invites de Gourgues to enter her service, i., p. 237; discoveries under direction of, i., p. 44–5; Virginia named in honor of, 45.

ELOAOUESSEN, chief of the Nansoakouetons, speaks at General Congress, v., p. 143.

ELVAS, a gentleman of, writes an account of Soto's expedition, i., p. 134 n.

ENARHONON. a Huron tribe, ii., p. 72, n.

ENCISO, BACHELOR, founds San Sebastian, i., p. 27.

ENDICOT, GOV. JOHN, of Massachusetts, d'Aulnay concludes treaty with, ii.,, p. 131, n.

ENGLISH, relieve French in Florida, i., p. 158; attempt to settle among Canibas, 273; pretext of for expelling French from St. Savior's and Acadia, 279; wrest New Netherlands from the Dutch, ii., p. 10; iii., p. 71; hostilities against the French during siege of Rochelle, 44; capture de Roquemont's fleet, 45; conquer Canada, 48; why Acadia so easily restored by, 59; continue to trade with Canada Indians in violation of treaty of St. Germain, 63; unpopular with natives, 66; propose alliance between New France and the English colonies not to be affected by European wars, 213; what defeated the project, 217; seek friendship of F. Dreuillettes, 247; attack Cape Breton, iii., p. 93; usurpations in Acadia, 125; repulsed from Cape Sable, 127; seize Acadia and neighboring provinces, 135; break their word with le Borgne, ib.; take Port de la Héve, ib.; hold conquest till treaty of Breda, ib.; pleading as to Newfoundland, 140; settle on Kennebec, receive de Lusson, 170; recalled to New England, 170; seize Acadia in time of peace, 188; excite Iroquois against us, 209; build Fort Pemkuit, 210; try to involve Abénaquis and Iroquois, ib.; seize Acadia and its dependencies for the fifth time, 211; no right to Hudson Bay, 230; led there by French deserters and build forts, 231; French and English on the bay, 234; deserters give them Fort Bourbon, 237; use our deserters to excite Iroquois against us, then sell them in Jamaica, 242; twenty-six English killed by Senecas, 248; promise to aid Iroquois in new war, 250; seek Western trade, 262; instigate attack on Ottawas, 264; try to seduce Iroquois Christians, 265; received by our allies at Michilimakinac, 266; seize fort on St. Teresa river, Hudson Bay, 269; expelled, 270; advantage over us in trade, 273; treaty of neutrality with, ib.; excite Iroquois, 281-291; defeated on Lake Huron, 284; repulsed at Fort St. Anne, Hudson Bay, 293; prisoners capture ship from, ib.; summons St. Castin to surrender Pentagoêt, 294; foment war between Iroquois and us for the sake of trade, 298; efforts to debauch Abenaquis, iii., 308; iv., p. 19; plunder Pentagoët, p. 15; memoir on, 20; negotiations with, 22; war with, 23; projects against, 24; complicity of in massacre of Lachine, 31 n.; Iberville defeats in Hudson Bay, 37; expelled from Pemquid and other forts by Abénaquis, 40; frontiers ravaged by, 44; incompatibility of French and, 44; promise Iroquois to expel French, ib.; hate the Jesuits, ib.; statement of prisoner to Spaniards, 113, n.; defeated at Schenectady, 123; their loss, 126; their

ENGLISH, (*continued.*)
provinces defeated at Casco, 133 ; Chev. d'Aux delivered to, 141 ; menace Canada by way of Lake George, 143; its failure, 144, n.; surprise some French, 149; send fleet against French possessions, 152 ; take Acadia, 154 ; violate capitulation, 157 ; pursue Perrot, 158 ; disgraceful conduct, iv., p. 157, n.; 161, n.; and at Isle Percée, iv., p. 161 ; repulsed at Chedabouctou, 160 ; take Placentia, 165 ; before Quebec, 169 ; defeated at Beauport, 177 ; ships cannonade Quebec, but driven off, 178 ; troops repulsed, 179 ; third defeat with great loss, 181 ; decamp, leaving artillery, 183; their loss, 186 ; the English-Iroquois-Mohegan force against Montreal breaks up, 184 : accused of attempting to poison French, 185 ; accused of cowardice by Iroquois, 186 ; defeated by Canibas, 188 ; bad faith of, ib.; menace Montreal, 191 ; surprise French, 191–3 ; surprise French at La Prairie, but are finally defeated, 204 ; their loss, 206; fleet sent to St. Lawrence to check, 222; besiege Placentia but are defeated, 223; ravages of, 226 ; preparations, 226 ; attack Martinique, 241 ; treat with Miamis, 242 ; repulsed at Martinique, 244 ; how they won Iroquois to their side, 247 ; Abénaquis continue to harass, 255 ; build a fort at Onondaga, ib.; territory ravaged by Abénaquis, 256 ; Port Nelson captured from and named Fort Bourbon, 261 ; treachery toward Abénaquis, 273 ; do not defend fort at Onondaga, v., p. 17 ; conduct in regard to Oneidas, 19 ; defend Pemquid badly, 25 ; maltreat Villieu and people of Beaubassin, 28 ; besiege but fail to take Naxoat, 30 ; their Newfoundland colonies, 33 ; St. John their headquarters, 35 ; defeated, 36 ; surrender Fort St. John, 44 ; their errors, 47 ; compensate Onondagas, 51 ; take Fort Bourbon, 52 ; violate capitulation, 53 ; Iberville recovers it after taking two ships, 54–9 ; resolve to expel French from Newfoundland ; fortify St. John, 73 ; peace with, 80 ; correspondence with, 85 ; badly handled by our allies, 87 ; pretensions of, 91 ; rebuild Pemaquid and try to secure Kennebec, 92 ; claim compensation for Hudson Bay, 93 ; allowed to return to Newfoundland, ib.; Abénaquis terms with, 97 ; Iroquois policy, 100 ; envoy of at Onondaga, 104 ; Tegannisorens' reply to, 106 ; begin Mohawk mission, 106 ; wish to fill Iroquois country with forts, 112 ; trade with Chickasaw and instigate murder of priest, 124 ; send Barr with French refugees to Mississippi, 124–6 ; Spain wishes to keep them from the Mississippi, 128 ; Iroquois cantons oppose their occupying Detroit, 137 ; traverse our peace with Iroquois, 138 ; failure at Placentia, 156 ; urge Iroquois to expel missionaries, 157 ; Callieres thwarts, 158 ; expeditions against them in New England and Newfoundland, 160–9 ; retire from before Placentia, 162 ; Montigni attacks, 167 ; raise siege of Port Royal, 171 ; losses in Newfoundland, 172 ; capture a royal vessel, 174 ; twice repulsed at Port Royal, 192 ; fisheries, 202 ; defeated at Hewreuil (Haverhill), 205 ; expedition recalled, 208 ; themselves to blame for our Indian incursions, 210 ; their treatment of prisoners, ib.; try to debauch our Louisiana Indians, 211 ; with Iroquois attack Canada, 216 ; build forts between New York and Lake Champlain, 218, 219 ; failure of Chambly expedition, 220 ; preparations, 237 ; defeated near Port Royal, 238, 255 ; our allies trade with, 240 ; quarrel with Iroquois, 247; fate of Walker's Quebec fleet, ib.; failure of designs against Montreal and Quebec, 252; what saved them in Acadia, 253 ; Foxes form alliance with and attempt to deliver up Detroit, 257 ; contemptuous language of a Pottawatami chief concerning, 260 ; monopolize fur trade, 265 ; care as to Iroquois, 266 ; pretensions over Abenaquis, 267 ; treachery, 272 ; carry off Baron St. Castin, 274 ; set a price on Rale's head, 275 ; attack Narantsoak, ib.; war with Abénaquis, 277 ; attack Narantsoak and kill Father Rale, 278; their indignities, 279 ; continue Abénaqui war, 281 ; prudent management of colonies, 287 ; the military force of the colonies, 301 ; try to win Abenaquis, 302 ; Placentia and Port Nelson ceded, 303 ; cruelty, ravage Dauphin Island, vi., p. 16 ; send out Indian war parties,

24 ; officer arrested and sent to Mobile, ib.; he is killed by the Tomés, ib.; their storehouse at the Choctaws pillaged and people murdered, ib., Indian conspiracy against ib.; ransomed by Bienville, ib.; see importance of Louisiana, 36 ; attack French ships and excuse themselves, 45 ; soldiers desert to, 67 ; Indian plan of introducing, after slaughter of French, 84 ; Choctaws refuse to receive their goods without consulting Perrier, 91 ; Natchez report English aid, 99 ; supposed to intend joining Chickasaws against us, 101 ; urge Choctaws to declare against us ; 102 ; the head chief of the Caouitas complain of, 105 ; manage all Chickasaw movements, 120.

English Turn, on the Mississippi ; Barr induced to turn back at, v., p. 124, n.

Enjalran, Father John, note on, iii., p. 288, n.; warns La Durantaye of approach of Seneca-English party, iii., p. 184 ; wounded in Seneca battle, 288; services of, in West, ib.; sent to Western tribes, v., p. 111; returns, 139; his difficulties, 141; strange application of Hurons to, 147; rescues Iroquois prisoners, 142; interpeter at Congress, v., p. 150.

Entouohonorons, enemies of Hurons, ii., p. 28, n.; attacked by Hurons and Champlain, ib ; repulse their assailants from their palisade town, ib.; supposed to be Senecas, ib.; more probably the Wenro, p. 28, n.; p. 84, n.; Lake Ontario called Lake of, ib.

Epicerinyen, see Nipissings.

Epinay, Mr. de l', conducts troops to Newfoundland, v., p. 172; reaches Louysiana, vi., p. 31; as Governor, vi., p. 38; fortifies Dauphin island, 39; begins New Orleans and appoints a Governor, 40; passes liquor law, 41, n.; turns over government to Bienville, ib.

Eries, Canadian tribe, formerly called Cat Nation, called Riqueronon (Rigneronon) by Iroquois, ii., 266, n.; oil springs near territory of, 190, n.; Kentaienton, a town of, 266,n.; destroyed by Iroquois, 266, n.

Erigoanna, Texas tribe atwar with Bracamos, iv., p. 90, n.

Erigouechkak, Indians visited by Father Buteux, ii., p. 246, n.

Erlach, Mr. d', Swiss gentleman, Ensign in Florida, explores country, i., p. 150; ordered to lead back his prisoners to their cacique, 162; accompanies Outinaa, cacique in war, kills Potanou, 164; recalled to Caroline, 165; his general's confidence in, ib.; valor of, on an important occasion, 177.

Escairac, Pierre d', (properly Descayrac) mortally wounded in action at la Prairie de la Magdeleine, died a few days after, iv., p. 205.

Escovar, Peter de, discoveries of i., p. 18.

Esgly, Mr. d', burnt by Chicasaws, vi., p. 122, n.

Esopus, Arasapha probably, iii., p. 72.

Espejo, Anthony de, Spaniard, explores New Mexico, i., p. 44.

Espinay, Couillard de l', Seneschal de Lauson killed in attempting to relieve, iii., p. 35.

Espinoza, Diego de, founds Panama, i., p. 31.

Espinoza, Gonzalo Gomez de, succeeds Magellan and first circumnavigates globe, i., p. 32.

Esquibel, John de, settles Jamaica, i., p. 27.

Esquimaux, Indians of Labrador and Hudson Bay, i., p. 125; stories of pygmies and monsters, i., p. 125; drink salt water, 126; mode of sailing, 127; wars of Acadians on, iii., p. 30; conversion of some, iii., p. 30; adventures of a woman, ib.; in Newfoundland, 144; fables as to that island, ib.; mode of travelling on ice, iii., p. 229.

Estampe, Mr. d', Gentleman of Comminge, reconnoitres San Matheo, i., p. 228.

Estenduere, Admiral de l', v., p. 245. n.

Estotiland, fabulous country, stories as to, i., pp. 18, 20, 44.

Estrade, Godfrey, Count d', Viceroy of New France, 1662–1686, iii., p. 80, n.

Estrées et de Tourpes, John Count d', Viceroy, 1686–1707, iii., p. 80, n.; v., p. 188, n.

Estrées, Mary Victor, Count d', Viceroy, 1707–1737, iii., p. 80, n.; v., p. 188, n.

Etechemins, Indians, formerly occupied all from Port Royal to Kennebec, i., p. 276; afterwards called Malecites, 277; Biard's estimates of their numbers, 267, n.; Province of the Etechemins, formerly called Norumbegua, its limits, i., p. 249.

ETIENNE, of Geneva, mutinies against Laudonniere i., p. 166; punished, 170.

ETRÉES, MARSHAL D', opposes Huguenots settling in Louisiana, v., p. 127.

ETRÉES, COUNT D', retakes Cayenne, i., p. 54.

EU, Biard retires to Jesuit College at, i., p. 262.

EURE, a Texas river so named, iv., p. 90,n.

FABER, CAPT. FRANÇOIS LEFEBVRE, SIEUR DU PLESSYS, sent in pursuit of Iroquois, iv., p. 220.

FAIRPORT or BLACKPORT, Newfoundland, ii., p. 59.

FALAISE, SIEUR DE, see GANNES.

FALMOUTH, Jogues at, ii., p. 160, n.

FALSE BEACH BAY, Cape Breton, v., p. 284.

FAMINE, LA, Bay on Lake Ontario, Frontenac advised not to meet Iroquois at, iii., p. 219, n.; de la Barre at, 253; origin of name, ib.; called Kaihohage by Colden, 254, n.; now Salmon river, ib.; The Rat said by Charlevoix to have ambushed at, iv., p. 12.

FARIA Y SOUSA, ANTHONY DE, Portuguese, discoveries of, i., p. 39.

FARINE, CHIEF DE LA, see FLOUR CHIEF.

FAYAL, one of the Azores, i., p. 16; Biard at, 284.

FEASTS where all must be eaten, iii., p. 16.

FELIX, Recollect Father, in Acadia, see CAPPE. •

FENELON, ABBÉ FRANÇOIS DE SALIGNAC, notice of, iii., p. 110, n., 190, n.; half-brother of Archbp. of Cambray, ib, n.; missionary to Iroquois on Lake Ontario, p. 109; imprisoned by Frontenac, p. 189.

FENELON, FRANÇOIS DE SALIGNAC, Archbishop of Cambray, half-brother of preceding, iii., p. 110, n.; Denonville connected with in charge of princes of the blood, 258, n.

FENWICK, BISHOP BENEDICT, erects monument to Rale, v., p. 281, n.

FERDERMAN or VREDEMAN, NICHOLAS, German, discoveries of, i., p. 38.

FERRO, one of the Canaries, i., p. 14; French adopt as meridian, 17.

FERRYLAND, Newfoundland, settled by Lord Baltimore, iii., p. 140, n.; occupied by Kirke, vi., p. 126; Cleasby retires to, v., p. 36; taken by de Brouillan, 37, 39; by Amariton, 161; by Subercase, 174.

FERTÉ, LIEUT. LA, takes Governor of New Savannah, iv., p. 37.

FERTÉ, ABBÉ DE LA MAGDELAINE, see MAGDELAINE.

FEUQUIERES, ISAAC DE PAS, MARQUIS DE, Viceroy, 1660–2, iii., p. 80, n.

FIRST MASS in Canada, ii., p. 25, n., first marriage, p. 30.

FITCH, CAPTAIN, commands Connecticut company in Montreal expedition, iv., p. 146, n.; Winthrop turns over command to, 147, n.

FLAT RAPID, Iroquois defeated at, iv., p. 212.

FLECHE, REV. JESSÉ, baptism by, i., p. 262, n.

FLEMISH BASTARD, son of Mohawk woman by a Dutchman; attacks Father le Moyne on his way, after concluding peace at Onondaga, 258; he attacks the Ottawas and Hurons, his lame apology for the attack on Father Garreau, 274; met by de Sorel, heading a Mohawk party, and pretends he is on his way to treat of peace with de Tracy, iii., p. 87; taken to Quebec, ib.; a prisoner, 88; set at liberty, 93; called by English, Smit's Jan, vi., p. 125.

FLETCHER, BENJAMIN, Governor of New York, v., p. 19, n.

FLEURIAU, CHARLES, one of the Hundred Associates, ii., p. 169.

FLORES, one of the Azores, i., p. 16.

FLORIDA, Floridians, discovery, i., p. 28; extent assigned by Spaniards, i., p. 133; described, 137; sources of wealth, 137; character of Floridians, 138; animals, 140; trees, 140; chief bears name of tribe, 157; strange customs, 158; mode of making war, 160; ideas of thunder, 163; most to be feared when friendly, 172; refuse to give food to starving French, 176; relent on seeing them relieved, 178; French settle in, i., p. 42; English, i., p. 45; Spaniards, i., p. 184; conditions imposed on Menendez, 183.

FLOUR CHIEF, (Chef de la Farine,) Natché, originator of massacre, vi., p. 111; not noble, 113; surrenders, 111; escapes, 112; treacherously kills Tonica chief, 116; defeated and killed by St. Denys at Natchitoches, 118.

FOND DU LAC, du Luht at, iii., p. 245, n.

FONTAINE, ABEL MARION DE (?dit) LA, leads

Senecas and English to Michilimakinac, taken by Durantaye and shot, iii., p. 284–6; execution of, condemned by La Hontan, 286.

FONTAINE, SIEUR, informs Loubois of St. Denys' victory over Natchez, vi., p. 118.

FONTARABIE, companion of F. Buteux, killed with him, ii., p. 249, n.

FONTENU, MR. DE, sent as commissary to Acadia. Transfers establishment at Naxoat to Port Royal, v., p. 113.

FORBES, CAPTAIN, Engineer of Annapolis, killed, v., p. 238.

FOREST, FRANCIS DAUPIN, SIEUR DE LA, v., p. 131; Major of Catarocouy, goes to France with La Sale; commended, iii., p. 215; brings Iroquois deputies to Montreal, 221; declines to be commandant at Catarocouy, and goes to meet La Sale, 259; bears Gov. Gen.'s order to Mr. de la Durantaye, 284–5; conditions on which King allows him to retain Fort St. Louis, Illinois, 276; his wise conduct in Illinois, v., p. 131; succeeded by Buisson, p. 257.

FORÊT, MR. DE LA, Commandant at Fort Nelson, iv., p. 262; forced to surrender Fort Bourbon to the English v., p. 53.

FORILLON, English post on Newfoundland. See FERRYLAND. Corruption of Farallones.

FORILLON, LE, remarkable rock on the coast of Cape Breton, v., p. 284.

FRANCE, NEW, see CANADA.

FORT ALIBAMON, vi., p. 26.

FORT BILOXI OR MAUREPAS, built by Iberville, v., p. 123.

FORT DE LA BOULAYE, on the Mississippi, v., p. 125, n.

FORT BOURBON, Hudson Bay, so named by d'Iberville, iv., p. 261; la Forêt, Governor of, 262; captured by English, v., p. 52; Serigny fails to reach, ib.; surrenders, 53; recaptured by Iberville, 58; Jérémie's sufferings at, 304; surrendered, 305.

FORT CAROLINE, see CAROLINE.

FORT CATAROCOUY, see FORT FRONTENAC.

FORT CHAMBLY, see CHAMBLY.

FORT CHARTRES, St. Ange, Commandant at, vi., p. 71.

FORT CHATEAUGUÉ, Des Marais, commandant of, killed by Iroquois, iv., p. 150.

FORT CREVECOUR, La Sale's fort in Illinois, iii., p. 206; Charlevoix makes Hennepin return to, ib.; revolt at, 208; Iroquois invest, 211; abandoned by Tonty, ib.; La Sale at, 213.

FORT FRONTENAC, see CATAROCOUY.

FORT GEMESIE, GEMISICK OR JEMSET, on St. John's river, opposite Gagetown, N. B., built by Grandfontaine, iv., p. 159; restored to France, iii., p. 138; de Marson taken at, 188; taken by English, 211; Villebon retires to, iv., p. 159; abandoned, v., p. 24; replaced by Naxoat, ib.; half as far up as Naxoat, 30. See FORT ST. JOHN.

FORT LOYAL at Falmouth, Casco Bay, now Portland, taken by Portneuf, iv., p. 133.

FORT OF THE MIAMIS, built by La Sale, iii., p. 203; La Sale reaches, 215, n.

FORT MICHILIMAKINAC restored, iv., p. 265. See MICHILIMAKINAC.

FORT DE LA MINE, Guinea, i., p. 13.

FORT MISSISSIPPI, at Poverty Point, v., p. 125, n.

FORT MONSIPI OR MONSOUSIPIOU, taken by French, iii., pp. 270–1.

FORT LA MOTTE on Lake Champlain, Western Iroquois to meet at, iv., p. 146, n. See FORT ST. ANNE.

FORT NAXOAT replaces Fort Jemset, v., p. 24; Iberville lands supplies at, ib., attacked by New England forces, 30; siege raised, 33; Iberville fails to relieve, 54; Nesmond ordered to relieve, 72; Villebon dies at, 113; garrison transferred to Port Royal, 113–4.

FORT NELSON, expedition against, iv., p. 251, 259; described, 260; capitulates, 261; called by French Fort Bourbon.

FORT ORANGE founded, i., p. 50; ii., p. 10; F. Jogues at, ii., pp. 156, 187; Poncet coldly received at, 253; Le Moyne at, iii., p. 16; taken by English and called Albany, ii., p. 11.

FORT ORLEANS on the Missouri, v., p. 184.

FORT PEMAQUID OR PEMQUID OR PEMKUIT, built by Andros, iii., p. 210; site, ib., n.; account of, iv., p. 40, n.; taken by Canibas, 40, 43; rebuilt in 1692, p. 227, n.; failure of Villebon's attempt on, 228; English base hopes on, 255; Indian treaty at, ib.; Bomazeen and other Abénaquis seized at, 273; v., p. 23.

FORT PENTAGOET, built by la Tour, iii., p.

FORT PENTAGOET, (*continued.*) 129; held by Commander de Razilly, ib.; taken by English, 135; by Dutch, 188, 294. See PENTAGOET.

FORT PONTCHARTRAIN, Labrador, iii., p. 145.

FORT PONTCHARTRAIN, Detroit, founded by La Motte Cadillac, v., p. 154, n.

FORT PONTCHARTRAIN DE CHAMBLY, v., p. 220, n. See CHAMBLY.

FORT PRUDHOMME, temporary work of La Sale, iii., p. 214, n.; La Sale sick at, 215, n.

FORT QUITCHITCHOUAN or QUICHYCHOUAN, taken by French, iii., p. 271, n.; called St. Anne, 274; English repulsed at, ib.; French prisoners capture English ship near, iii., 293; Iberville at, iv., p. 37; taken by English, iv., p. 243; reinforced by English, 261.

FORT LA REINE, on the Assiniboin, v., p. 311.

FORT RICHELIEU, on Sorel river, begun by Montmagny, ii., p. 133; Iroquois repulsed at, ib.; Father de Noue dies in trying to reach, 183; Jogues at, 187; Fort Sorel built on site of, iii., p. 82.

FORT ROLAND, Lieut. Robeyre ordered to occupy and hold, iv., p. 30; taken by Iroquois, ib.

FORT RUPERT, built by English on the Nemiscau, iii., p. 231; taken by Maricourt, 271.

FORT ST. ANNE or LA MOTTE, on an island in Lake Champlain, first white post in Vermont, iii., p. 90, n.; de Tracy at, ib.; missionaries detained at, 109, n.; Western Iroquois to meet at, iv., p. 146, n.

FORT ST. ANNE, Hudson Bay, see FORT QUITCHITCHOUAN.

FORT SAN CARLOS, at Pensacola, v., p. 118, n.; vi., p. 43; Spaniards at, alarmed 53; surrenders, 58; demolished, 60.

FORT ST. GEORGE, Africa, i., p. 18.

FORT ST. JOHN, near Biloxi, vi., p. 19, n.

FORT ST. JOHN or on the St. John, founded by la Tour, iii., p. 128; confirmed to him, 129, n.; reduced by d'Aulnay, 130–1; recovered by la Tour, p. 132; menaced by la Borgne and taken by English, 133–4; Joybert de Marson in command of, p. 186; taken by English, 211.

FORT SAN JUAN BAUTISTA, at Presidio del Norte, vi., p. 20.

FORT ST. LOUIS, at Cape Sable, defended by la Tour against his father, iii., p. 125-6.

FORT ST. LOUIS or CHAMBLY, see CHAMBLY.

FORT ST. LOUIS, at Placentia, iii., p. 141; iv., pp. 225–6; v., p. 161, n.

FORT ST. LOUIS, Illinois, traced by La Sale, iii., p. 208; begun by Tonty, ib.; at Starved Rock, ib., n.; v., p., 132; near Utica, v., p. 132, n.; La Sale reoccupies, iii., p. 213; leaves, 215, n.; seized by de la Barre, 243; de Baugy repulses Iroquois attack on, 244; Cavelier's party at 110; to be only Western post. iv., p. 276.

FORT ST. LOUIS, Hudson Bay, iv., p. 137.

FORT ST. LOUIS, La Sale's Texas fort. See ST. LOUIS.

FORT ST. PIERRE, in Cape Breton, erected by St. Denys, iii., p. 133; taken by la Giraudiere and exchanged for Chedabouctou, 137.

FORT ST. TERESA, why so called, iii., p. 82· de Courcelle at, 89, n.

FORT SIGUENZA on Santa Rosa island, vi., p. 43, n.; abandoned by French and reoccupied by Spaniards, 48, 53.

FORT SOREL, built, iii., p. 82; repaired by, Chev. ST. Jean, iv., p. 236, n.

FORT TOULOUSE among the Alibamons, vi., p. 25, n.; revolt at, 67, n.

FORT WILLIAM, one of the defences of St. John, Newfoundland, taken by storm, v., p. 213.

FORT WILLIAM HENRY, see FORT PEMAQUID.

FORTUNATE ISLANDS, i., p. 17.

FOUCAULT, REV. NICHOLAS, Canadian missionary killed on Mississippi, v., p. 124.

FOURCHE, LA, French surprised at, by Capt. John Schuyler, iv., p. 149; by Peter Schuyler, 204. See SOUCHE.

FOURNEAUX, DES, mutineer against Laudonniere, i., p. 166; punished, 170.

FOX, LUKE, called Luxfox in Charlevoix, said to have taken possession of Hudson Bay, no English title thereby, iii., p. 230.

FOX RIVER, Allouez ascends, iii., p. 120, n.; Marquette on, 179.

FOXES or OUTAGAMIS, Indian tribe, Father Allouez visits, iii., 105, 120, n., 185; their country, 182; fail to meet St. Lusson,

168, n.; idol of, 182; indisposed towards French, 183; said to have joined Durantaye, 246; propose moving to Iroquois country, iv., p. 266; rescue Perrot from Miamis, v., p. 65; several at Montreal, at war with Iroquois, 67; by war render Illinois warlike, 130; promise to send delegates to General Congress, 141; solicit a Jesuit missionary, 144; quarrel with Ojibways, 144; dress and speech of their deputy at the Congress, 151; their character, 257; settle near Detroit in order to deliver it to English, ib.; besieged by combined force, 259; vigorous defence, ib.; peace refused, 260; escape, but nearly all massacred at Presque Isle, 264; ravages of, 305; Louvigny's expedition against, ib.; invested at Butte des Morts, 306; terms made, hostages given, some die of small pox, ib.; bad faith to Vaudreuil, 309; renew hostilities, ib.; alliance with Sioux and Chickasaws, ib.; drive Illinois from their river, v., p, 309; vi., p. 71; besiege them at the Rock and Pimiteoui, 71; repulsed with loss, ib.

France, New, see Canada.

France Prime, Roberval's name for the St. Lawrence, i., p. 130.

France Roi, Roberval's name for Fort Charlesbourg Royal, i., p. 130, n.

Francheville, Rev. Peter de Repentigny de, repulses Phips at River Ouelle, iv., p. 169.

Francis I., of France, sends out Verrazzano to make discoveries in America, i., p. 33, 107; he sends Jacques Cartier with the same design, 36, 111; discoveries reported to, 113; commission and powers given to Roberval, 129; after Roberval's death takes no interest in Canada, 132.

Franciscans, twelve accompany Menendez, i., p. 186; carry information to Viceroy of Mexico, vi., p. 47. See Capucin, Recollect.

François, Brother Luke le, Recollect Painter, arrives, iii., p. 149, n.

Freeman, Rev. Bernardus, missionary to Mohawks, v., p. 107, n.

'remin, F. James, Jesuit, sketch of, ii., p. 268, n.; iii., p. 109, n.; missionary on Cape Breton, iii., p. 30, 109, n.; sent to Onondaga, ii., p. 267; returns to Mohawks after war, iii., p. 109; iv., p. 284; goes from Mohawks to Senecas, p. 116; conducts Christian Iroquois at La Prairie, 191.

Fremeuse, English post in Newfoundland, taken by de Brouillan, v., p. 37; English come up with French at, p. 162.

French, first to trade with N. America, i., p. 104; easily induced to return to Europe, 146; extremity of those who evacuted Florida, 147; misled by reports of mines in Florida, 151; piracy of a party, 168; suffer from famine, 175; why disgusted with Florida, 178; a Frenchman guides Spaniards to attack Ft. Caroline, 200; fate of prisoners, 206; evacuate Florida, 235; continue fisheries, 241; early attempts to settle, 241; misconduct of, to Acadian Indians, 267; adventure of some after capture of St. Savior's, 281; a Frenchman accuses Jesuits, 283; errors of, in Acadia, 285; settle Canada i., p. 260; in Canada Indians plot against, ii., p. 30; murdered byIndians, 38; edifying conduct of first, 99; care taken in selecting, ib.; Iroquois artifice to prevent French aiding Hurons, 123; Iroquois say that compared to French other whites cannot speak, 264; settle in Onondaga, 267; a Frenchman adopted by Onondagas, saves colony by a stratagem, iii., p. 16; kind treatment and piety of French prisoners in that canton, who write to Maissonneuve, 36; a French martyr to conjugal chastity, 52; exemplary conduct of French in Tracy's expedition against Mohawks, 94; though always victorious in Newfoundland, have to cede their posts to English, 146, Indians robbed and murdered by, 149, punished, 150, losses in Hudson Bay through two deserters, 237, English use French deserters to win Iroquois and then sell them in Jamaica, 242, French deserters guide English to western posts of Canada, 262, welcomed by English governor, 268, a Frenchman guiding English to Michilimakinac is put to death, 284; Baron la Hontan condemns it, 286; some of two French sailors in Hudson Bay, 293; French soldiers fight badly in the Seneca war, 289; despised by Denonville, ib.; French Canadians do wonders, ib.; why several French abandon fur trade, iv., p. 16; surprised at Lachine, 29; English and Iroquois project to expel French from Canada, 31; Ottawa, in-

FRENCH, (*continued.*)
vectives against, 56; contempt with which Indians come to regard them, 57; surprised by Iroquois, 149; exploit of three Frenchmen in Hudson Bay, 243; a Frenchman in a paroxysm of frenzy kills surgeon of Fort St. Anne, and then kills Father Dalmas, 243; state of French in Newfoundland, v., p. 34; errors of in their colonies, 47; two Frenchwomen, captives at Mohawk, brought back to Quebec, 50; French plundered by Sioux, 64; English resolve to expel from Newfoundland, 71; French captives among Iroquois refuse to return, 105; a French soldier killed by Ottawas, 186; treatment of English prisoners by French in Canada, 210, 234; English in Carolina endeavor to seduce Louysiana Indians and depreciate French, 211; condition of at Port Royal when taken by English, 231; three Frenchmen sent by Vaudreuil arrested at Albany, 237; liberty given by English to Acadian French in order to retain them, 296; a new English governor disturbs them, 297; French treacherously murdered by Indians in Hudson Bay, 304; French in Louysiana despised by Indians, vi., p. 35; many French go to Spaniards, 48; at Pensacola refuse to fight against Spaniards, 49; several taken in arms against their King put to death, 51; massacre of by Natchez, 81; Yazoos, 86; two French killed near Mobile by Tioux, 95; two burned by Natchez, 96.

FRENCH BAY, (BAIE FRANÇOISE), see BAY OF FUNDY.

FRENCH BAY, limits of, province of, i., p. 249.

FRENCH CAPE, probably Matanzas inlet, i., p. 135; inconvenient, 152.

FRENCH REFUGEES, see HUGUENOTS.

FRESNIERE, ZACHARY HERTEL, SIEUR DE LA, eldest son of Francis Hertel, iv., p. 132; wounded, ib.; praised, ib.; taken by Iroquois with his brother, 219, 240; delivered and return to Quebec, when supposed dead, 252.

FRIESELAND, i., p. 20.

FRITZ, SAMUEL, German Jesuit, discovers source of Amazon, i., p. 55.

FROBISHER, SIR MARTIN, discovers Frobisher's Strait, i., p. 43; West England, 44; voyages of, 90.

FROBISHER'S STRAIT, i., p. 43.

FRONSAC, MR. DENYS DE, cited by Bp. de St. Valier, ii., p. 120; see DENYS.

FRONSAC PASSAGE, v., p. 282–3.

FRONTENAC, LOUIS DE BUADE, COUNT DE FRONTENAC ET DU PALUAU, Governor General of New France, sketch of, iii., p. 177, n.; succeeds de Courcelles, 176; builds Fort at Catarocouy, ib.; it and Lake Ontario bear his name, ib.; his character, ib.; his prejuidices and violence involve the Colony in trouble, 90; will not allow missionaries at Sault St. Louis to remove their missions, 191; his exaggerated report to Colbert on the Iroquois, 192; claims presidency of Superior Council, 193; quarrel with the Intendant, ib.; regrets not putting him in prison, ib.; reproached by the King, 194; orders to, as to bushlopers, 194; advises La Sale to go to France, 199; writes to the King in his favor, 200; the King and ministry condemn his conduct, 215; successor appointed, 216; exertions to prevent ill results of the murder of Annanhac, 219; his reply to an insolent proposal of the Iroquois, 219; refuses to go to Catarocouy to meet envoys as he had promised, 220; why he declines to act on Intendant's suggestion, ib.; prepares for war, ib.; the Iroquois send a delegation to amuse him, 221; deputation of Indians from Michilimakinac, 221; his remarks to them, ib.; returns to France, ib.; what induces the King to send him over again as Governor General, iv., p. 22; change in his conduct, ib.; his surety, ib.; his orders as to the New York project, 24; why he arrived too late, 27; his instructions left for de la Caffinière, 27; tidings he receives at Ile Percée, 28; at Quebec, 29; ascends to Montreal, 31; distress on that island, ib.; why he condemns Denonville's order to destroy Fort Catarcouy, 33; eagerness to prevent it, ib.; hears of its evacuation, 34; hopes to regain Iroquois, 47; sends back four of their chiefs brought over from France, 48; receives a satisfactory letter from Father Carheil, labors to restore reputation of French among Indians, 54–7; his plan for restoring Colony, iv., p. 121; promises a speedy change in affairs to Hurons and Ottawas, ib.; sends out three parties against the English, 122;

how he arranges an accident by which two of our parties attacked each other, 128 ; care in selecting men for these expeditions, 130 ; convoy and presents to Michilimakinac, 137; recall of de la Durantaye, ib.; precautions against attack, 141 ; prepares for an approaching Iroquois force, 144 ; persuades Ottawas and other Northern Indians to make no peace or truce with the Iroquois, 144 ; means of gaining them, ib.; at Prairie de la Magdeleine to protect Montreal, 146 ; reviews army, ib.; holds Indian council, ib.; dissolves it and dismisses allies in good spirits, 148 ; experiences a reverse from over confidence in scouts, 149 ; upbraids Oureouharé with the reverses sustained from Iroquois, 151 ; chief's reply made him, ib.; regrets his ill humor, 152 ; tidings of an English fleet, ib.; why unexpected, ib.; puts Quebec in a state of defence, 152 ; arrives and adds new works, 167 ; forecast, orders timely and well executed, 168 ; English admiral's summons, 171 ; his reply, his plan of defending Quebec, 173; orders a retreat after first action, 177 ; advances at the head of his troops on St. Charles' river, 180 ; enemy retire, 182 ; praises those engaged and gives Sieur Carré cannon abandoned by English, 184 ; exchanges prisoners with English admiral, 187 ; memoir on cod fisheries, 192 ; groundless suspicions of Sault St. Louis Indians and their missionary, 197 , his letter to minister, 192, 197 ; persuades allies to continue war against Iroquois, 200 ; why he agrees that du Tast need not go to Hudson Bay, 201 ; reply to proposals of Governor of New England, 211 ; his proposals to the minister and the reply, 212.; proposes expedition against Mohawks, 213 ; courteous reception of Nelson, sent prisoner to Quebec, 214 ; detains the Soleil d'Afrique several months, 215 ; sends expedition against Iroquois, 217 ; at Montreal dispatches St. Michel to Michilimakinac, followed by de St. Pierre, 218 ; leads 300 militia to Montreal, 221; Ottawas refuse to join in an expedition against the Iroquois, ib.; returns to Quebec, ib.; sends word to Court of Phib's preparations, p. 222 ; sends d'Iberville and de Bonaventure to reduce Fort Pemkuit, 227 ; failure, 228 ; flourishing condition of colony due to his great talents, 229; complaints against him, 229 ; difficulty on account of Nelson, 231 ; expedition against Mohawks, 233 ; fortifies Quebec, 236 ; uneasy about Michilimakinac, 237; sends d'Argentuil there, 237 ; reply to peace proposals of Tareha, an Oneida chief, 238 ; judgment on a letter from Father Milet, 239 ; tidings of great English preparations and Iroquois doings, 239 ; sends the Chevalier de Vaudreuil against Iroquois, who menace Montreal, 240 ; goes up there to meet deputies of Northern and Western tribes, 242 ; conference, ib.; steps to secure upper tribes, ib.; tidings from Hudson Bay and Acadia, 243 ; Tareha comes with very insulting proposals, 244 ; his reception of that Indian, 245; an Oneida woman comes expressly to see him from the high opinion she had conceived of him, ib.; why he did not break off all negotiations with the Iroquois, 250; warned of their design, 250 ; why he listens to their ambassadors, ib.; cordiality to chief of embassy, ib.; gives him a present for himself and Garakonthié, ib.; advantage gained by this embassy, 251 ; receives deputies of the upper nations, 252 ; his course to prevent their breaking with us, ib.; ineffectual efforts to restore Catarocouy, 251 ; warned not to depend on peace with the Iroquois, 252 ; gives audience to new deputies in presence of delegates of our allies, ib.; his attitude there, ib.; receives Oneida delegates sternly, 254; why he negotiates again with the Iroquois, 262; opinion of his conduct in Canada ; letter of Pontchartrain to, 263 ; restores Catarocuoy against general opinion of the colony, 265 ; his motives as given to the minister, 267 ; proposals to minister, ib.; forms a camp on Isle Perrot, 269 ; dexterity at an audience where delegates of our allies speak ill, 272 ; his protection desired by a Siou for his nation, ib.; his report to Pontchartrain on English designs, 274 ; he decides to march against the Iroquois, v., p. 9; measures adopted, 10 ; approves de Callieres' opinion as to the expedition, 11 ; his orders, ib.; at Montreal, 12 ; at La Chine, ib.; disposition of his army, 13 ; encamps on Isle

FRONTENAC, (*continued.*)
Perrot, ib.; order of march, 14; a Frenchman comes from Oneida with proposals of peace from that canton: his reply, 17; he sends the Chev. de Vaudreuil to that canton, his orders, 18; his reception of the envoys brought by Vaudreuil, 19; deliberation as to his course and opinions as to that adopted, 20; he thinks he has driven the Iroquois to accept peace on his conditions, 22; expeditions against them; at Quebec, 23; orders from home, ib.; an unsuccessful expedition against the Iroquois, 48; his reply to de Callieres in regard to the Oneidas, v., p. 50; his reception of those Indians, ib.; haughty conduct of Mohawks, 51; his reply, ib.; why he detains them during the winter, ib.; prevents Christian Iroquois leaving the colony, ib.; mysterious orders from Court, 52; difficulty in regard to Iroquois and his course; new troubles, 65; how he extricates himself, 66; critical position, ib.; eludes royal orders as to congés, 67; audience to Upper Tribes, 69; learns meaning of orders, 70; opinion as to the project, ib.; King doubts his ability to head New England expedition, 71; his rank in case he went, and his substitute, ib.; why he did not use all the troops he had to humble the Iroquois, 76; new orders as to Bushlopers, 77; Pontchartrain's orders, ib.; his course, 78; the new Governor General of New England restores French prisoners and sets up his claims over the Iroquois, 81; his conclusions from the reported conference of the Gov. Gen. of New England with the Iroquois and his course, 84; his reception of the Iroquois who came to settle at Sault St. Louys and Montreal, 85; he receives a second letter from Bellomont, ib.; his reply, 88; makes no reply as to missionaries, 90; his death, good and bad qualities, 93; the Iroquois come to deplore his death, 94; esteem entertained for him by the Rat, the Huron chief; his burial, 93; funeral oration, 94, n.; removal of remains vi., p. 127.

FRONTENAC, MADAME DE, iii., p. 177, n.

FRYE, REV. JONATHAN, of Lovewell's party, scalps Indians, v., p. 279, n.

FUERTE VENTURA, one of Canaries, i., p. 14.

FUR TRADE, first grasped at by Dongan, iv., p. 17, n; English drive French from, 16.

GABATTO, GABOT or CABOT, JOHN, a Venetian and his three sons explore Newfoundland and a part of the continent of North America for the King of England, but do not land, i., p. 20, 105.

GABOTO or GABOT, SEBASTIAN, enters Rio de Solis, or La Plata, i., p. 34; note as to voyages of, 105.

GABORI BAY, on Isle Royale or Cape Breton, description of, v., p. 284.

GACHIE, Gascon gentleman lost on de Gourgues' Florida expedition, i., p. 236.

GAENSERA, GANNAGARO or GAZEROARE, Seneca town taken possession of by Denonville, iii., p. 289, n.; identified by Mr. Marshal with Gaosaehgasah, ib.

GAGNIEGATON, iii., p. 301, n., an Iroquois ambassador, insolent proposals of to Denonville, is sent back by Frontenac, iv., p. 48; again at Montreal boldly expresses himself to de Callieres, 50; Frontenac refuses to give him an audience, ib.; Oureouharé treats with him, by the sanction of Gov. Gen., 51.

GAGNIEGUÉHAGA, or KAJINJAHAGA, Mohawk name for themselves, ii., p. 146, n.

GAHAYANDUK, Seneca town destroyed by Denonville, iii., p. 289, n.

GAHRONHO, Sillery Algonquin chief defeats Iroquois, iii., p. 64.

GALETTE, LA., iii., p. 225–252.

GALINIER, (GALINÉE,) RENÉ DE BRÉHANT DE, Sulpitian, arrives, iii., p. 23; accompanies Dollier de Casson, 122, n.

GALLEGO, HERNAN de, pilot, i., p. 43.

GALVE, Bay of Santa Maria de, (Pensacola Bay) vi., p. 43.

GALVES, GASPAR DE SANDOVAL, SILVA Y MENDOZA, COUNT OF, Viceroy of Mexico, sends Alonzo de Leon to Espiritu Santo bay, iv., p. 113, n., vi., p. 43.

GAMA, VASCO DE, discoveries of, i., p. 20.

GAMART OF ROUEN, pilot of John Denys, i., p. 106, n.; vi., p. 43.

GAMBIA RIVER, i., p. 16.

GAMBIE, PETER, French soldier, discoveries of in Florida, robbed and murdered by Indians, i., p. 171.

GANABARA, Indian name for Rio Janeiro, i., p. 42.

GANDAGAN, Seneca town, iii., p. 12.

GANDAHOUAGUÉ, Mohawk town, position of, ii., p. 146, n.; vi., p. 125; Father Jogues killed there, ii., p. 146, n.; Catherine Tegahkouita born there, iv., p. 284 ; visited by Bruyas, iii., p. 109, n.; mission established there by F. Lamberville, iv., p. 285 ; F. Pierron labors at aided by Garakonthié, iii., p. 157 ; various forms of the name, ii., p. 146, n.

GANDASETEIAGON, Iroquois town on Quinte Bay, also Gandatsetiagon, iii., p. 110, n.

GANERASKÉ, Cayuga town on Quinte Bay, iii., p. 110, n.

GANEYOUSSÉ, Iroquois seized at, iii., p. 276, n.

GANNEAKTENA, CATHARINE, foundress of La Prairie, an Erie, ii., p. 266, n, iii., p. 191.

GANNENTAHA, Lake in Onondaga canton, salt springs on, ii., p. 189.

GANNES, LOUIS DE, SIEUR DE FALAISE, arrives at Naxoat from Quebec, v., p. 32 ; distinguished at defence of Naxoat, p. 31–2, at Port Royal, 227, n.; account of defence of, ib.

GANNEYOUSSES, Belmont's term for Sault St. Louis Iroquois, iv., p. 193, n.

GANNIAGWARI, Great She Bear, name of Mohawks as a tribe, ii., p. 145.

GANNOGARAE, see CHINOSHAHGEH.

GANNOUNATA, see DYUDOOSOT.

GARAKONTHIÉ, DANIEL, Onondaga chief, meets Father le Moyne, iii., p. 41 ; his character, love for French, services he renders them. Refined policy and wide caution of this chief, 42 ; spokesman of delegation sent to Governor General, 44; prudence as to events on voyage, ib.; reception at Montreal and Quebec, ib.; succeeds in liberating all the French prisoners, 52; renewed labors for peace and to deliver prisoners, 70; meets de Tracy at Quebec, 85 ; his reception, 86 ; bewails death of Father le Moyne, 85 ; apostrophé of, ib., n.; retains F. Garnier at Onondaga and builds him a cabin and a chapel, 109 ; brings two missionaries from Quebec, ib.; reproaches Ottawas for their shameful treatment of missionaries; baptized by bishop, the Gov. Gen. and Intendant's daughter being sponsors, iii., p. 152; aids F. Pierron at Gandaouagué, p. 157 ; unsuccessful attempt to make the Oneidas more docile to missionary, 158 ; death of, iii., p. 196, n.; his grandson taken, v., p. 11, n.

GARAKONTHIÉ, II.,—brother of preceding, deputed to treat of peace, iii., p. 254 ; speaks well, ib.; moderation of the Onondagas to Lamberville ascribed to him, 278 ; prevents violent measures in his canton, 292 ; Frontenac depends much on him, iv., p. 52; continues to serve the French ; zeal for religion ; why he remained in his canton, 246 ; send belts to Frontenac, 250 ; receives presents from him, ib.; his death, v., p. 155 ; his nephew offers to succeed him as correspondent of the French and is accepted, ib.

GARANGOUAS, MARGARET, Iroquois woman, courage and martyrdom, iv., p. 301.

GARCIA, FATHER GREGORIO, Spanish Dominican, his Origen de los Indios noticed, i., p. 92.

GARDEUR DE REPENTIGNY, MARY M. LE, marries John P. Godefroy, ii., p. 216, n.

GARDEUR, SIEUR DE TILLY LE, commands Indians in Frontenac's Iroquois expedition, v., p. 12; confusion as to, p. 12, n.; see BEAUVAIS, RENÉ LE GARDEUR DE.

GARIOYE, Iroquois of Sault St. Louis, his son an envoy, iv., p. 249, n.

GARISTATSI and GANNAGENROGEN, Mohawk deserters, inform Senecas of Denonville's plans, iii., p. 286, n.

GARGOT, SIEUR, Louis XIV. grants Placentia with title of Governor to, obstacles in taking possession, iii., p. 146.

GARISTARSIA, (Iron) Iroquois defeated and killed by Sillery Algonquins, iii., p. 64.

GARNIER, FATHER CHARLES, Jesuit, sketch of, ii., p. 230 ; Huron name Ouracha, 231, n.; visits several Indian tribes, ii., p. 94 ; nobly sacrifices his life for his flock and is killed by Iroquois, 229.

GARNIER, FATHER JULIAN, Jesuit, notice of iii., p. 109, n.; missionary to the Iroquois, iii., p. 109 ; La Sale prejudiced against, iii., p. 203, n.; retained at Onondaga by Garakonthié, who builds him a cabin and chapel, ib.; sent to Senecas in 1702, v., p. 155, n.

GARREAU, FATHER LEONARD, Jesuit, baffles plot at St. Matthew's, ii., p. 232 ; starts

GARREAU, F. LEONARD, (*continued.*) with Ottawas for their country, 272 ; is mortally wounded by Mohawks, 274: dies at Montreal, 275 ; sketch of, ib.

GAS, DU, Courcelles, lieutenant, iii., p. 89, n.

GASPESIANS, Canada Indians, same as Acadians, or Micmacs, ii., p. 119 ; origin of name, ii., p. 119 ; le Clercq's theory as to, ii., p. 120 ; wandering life prevents their conversion, ib.; why called Porte Croix, ib.; at Miscou, ii., p. 119.

GASPESIE, limits of province of, i., p. 249 ; called also Bay of St. Lawrence, ib.

GATES, SIR THOMAS, Governor of Virginia, i., p. 281, n.

GATINEAU, SIEUR, nephew of Hertel, on Hertel's expedition, iv., p. 130 ; sent to report success to Frontenac, 132.

GAUDAIS, MR., commissioned commissary in Canada, iii., p. 65 ; receives oath of allegiance of the colony and takes possession in the King's name, 66 ; returns to France, 69–70.

GAULIN, REV. MICHAEL A., Indian missionary in Acadia, asks for an officer to attack Port Royal, v., p. 256 ; urged to press Acadians to remove, p. 296 ; imprisoned, 297, n.; submits to English rule, 299, n.

GAULS, William Postel believes America visited by, for codfishery, i., p. 104.

GAYEN, one of La Sale's party wounded, iv., p. 71, n.

GEMESIE, see FORT GEMESIE.

GEMMERAYE, (Christopher Dufrost de Lajemmerais) Lieut., a Breton gentleman, attacked while escorting a convoy to Michilimakinac, iv., p. 139 ; defeated while escorting an Indian convoy, 219 ; menaced by Iroquois while commandant at Catarocouy, v., p. 79 ; consults Frontenac as to attacking them, ib.; the general's reply, ib.; father of Mme d'Youville, foundress of the Sœurs Grises, iv., p. 139, n.

GENDRE, MR. LE, of Rouen, partner of de Monts, ii., p. 20.

GENS DE FOURCHE, Illinois tribe, dance calumet to l'Epinai, vi., p. 39.

GEORGIA, NEW, settled by Ogelthorpe, i., p. 64.

GERRISH, SUSAN, exchanged, iv., p. 187, n.

GERVAIS, Brother Recollect, with le Caron, ii., p 45, n.

GESSE, CAPT. DE LA, son of de Ramezay, lost on the Chameau, v., p. 309.

GEUDREVILLE, errors in Atlas of, i., p. 68 ; dressed up La Hontan, p. 87.

GHILLAM or GILLAM, ZACHARY, discovers Rupert's River, Hudson Bay, i., p. 57 ; iii., pp. 231, 236, n.

GIBSON, SIR JOHN, commands force brought over to St. John by Neville, v., p. 73, n.

GIFFORD, MARY LOUISA, marries de Lauson Charny, ii., p. 279, n.

GIGUIERE, (Giguère) a Canadian, reconnoiters Schenectady, iv., p. 123.

GIJON, part of Menendez's fleet sails from, i., p. 186.

GILBERT, SIR HUMPHREY, called by Charlevoix, Gilbert Humphrey, i., p. 45, and Humbert Humphrey, iii., p. 140 ; takes possession of Newfoundland in name of Queen Elizabeth, i., p. 45 ; wrecked on Isle Sable, i., p. 48, while trying to get cattle, i., p. 245, n.; said to have lived there two years, i., p. 48, iii., p. 140.

GILL, CAPT., at Bonavista, v., p. 169.

GIRARD, F. FRANCIS, Recollect, taken by English, ii., p. 46, n.

GIRAUDIERE, SIEUR DE LA, obtains by stratagem from West India Company a grant infringing Denys' patent, iii., p. 136 ; attacks him at Chedabouctou, ib.; submits to judgment of the company annulling his grant, ib.

GLEN, JOHN SANDERS, Major of Schenectady, taken, iv., p. 123 ; called Coudre by Charlevoix, ib.

GOA taken by Albuquerque, i., p. 27.

GOAT ISLAND, i., p. 254.

GODEFROY, LIEUT. JOHN PAUL, Councillor of New France, sent to Boston as plenipotentiary to conclude a treaty of neutrality, ii., p. 215 ; iii., p. 67 ; notice of, 216, n.; result of his mission, 217–8, n.; is Charlevoix in error as to? 247, n.; vi., p. 125.

GODEFROY DE LINCTOT, JOHN, of Three Rivers, Major of Three Rivers, ii., p. 247 ; see vi., p. 125.

GODET, (Godé,) NICHOLAS, killed by Oneidas, iii., p. 14, n.

GODS, (Godet,) an Englishman through whom Preston, English Ambassador in France treats with Radisson, iii., p. 237.

GOJAM, KINGDOM OF, i., p. 52 ; Gold coast discoveries on, i., p. 18.

GOLLEVILLE, MR. DE, sent by de l'Epinay to Vera Cruz to trade ; his success, vi., p. 38.

GOMEZ, FERDINAND, discoveries of, i., p. 18.

GONANNHATENHA, FRANCES, an Iroquois, sent to the stake by her own sister, out of hatred to Christianity, iv., p. 299.

GONNEVILLE, BINET PAULMIER DE, discovers Southern continent, i., p. 25.

GONZALEZ, ANDREW, his convoy captured by French, vi., p. 59.

GONZALEZ, ANTHONY, discoverer, i., p. 15.

GORDON, CAPT. GEO., of the Leostaffe, v., p. 227, n.

GORGADES OF PLINY, i., p. 17.

GOSNOLD, Voyage of, i., p. 90.

GOUENTAGRANDI, SUSANNA, see SUSANNA.

GOUPIL, B. RENÉ, Jesuit novice, taken with Father Jogues, his sufferings, ii., p. 142 ; death, 148 ; life written by F. Jogues, 142, n.

GOURGUES, CHEVALIER DOMINIC DE, early adventures, i., p. 224; never in the Pacific, 224 ; resolves to avenge French slaughtered in Florida by Spaniards, 223; preparations, 225 ; in America, 226 ; unfolds his project to his men, ib. ; Florida Indians favorable, 227; reconnoitres San Matheo, 228 ; takes a fort by storm and puts garrison to the sword ; takes a second fort and marches on San Matheo, 231 ; captures it, booty, rewards the Indians, treatment of Spaniards, 232–4 ; reflections, 235 ; razes forts, ib. ; regret of Indians on his departure, 236 ; at Rochelle, ib. ; nearly taken by Spaniards, 236 ; ill-received at court, 237 ; refuses to enter service of Queen Elizabeth, ib. ; recovers King's favor, ib.; dies on his way to take command of fleet of Don Antonio, soidisant King of Portugal, ib. ; silence of Spanish archives as to capture of San Matheo, 238, n. ; difficulties in story of, vi., p. 123.

GOUROU, ii., p. 90.

GOUSY, CAPT. DE, left in command of fort at St. Joseph's Bay, vi., p. 42, n.

GOUTTINS, SIEUR DES, commissaire ordonnateur in Acadia, iv., p. 156 ; taken prisoner by English, 157; Villebon takes him to Port Royal, 215 ; at Fort Jemset ; upright conduct, it saves him on another occasion, 216.

GOYELLE, or GOVION, JOHN, a Breton gentleman on Cartier's second voyage, i., p. 118.

GOYOGOUIN, see CAYUGAS, ii., p. 190.

GOYON or GOUYON, captain of the Mars, vi., p. 55, n. ; sound Pensacola bay, 56.

GRACIOSA, discovered by Mendaña, i., p. 47.

GRAFF, LIEUT. LAWRENCE DE, sent by de Châteaumorand to sound port of Pensacola, v., p. 119, a flibustier, known as Lorencillo, ib., n.

GRAIS, CAPT. LOUIS JOSEPH LE GOUES, CHEVALIER DE, commands battalion in Frontenac's Iroquois expedition, v., p. 13.

GRANCHES, MARY KATHERINE DES, wife of Cartier, i., p. 131.

GRANDFONTAINE, HUBERT D' ANDIGNY, CHEVALIER DE, French plenipotentiary at Boston, signs agreement as to restitution of places seized by English, iii., p. 138 ; appoints Joliet, iii., p. 179, n. ; as Governor of Acadia, resides at Pentagoët, 186 ; relieved by de Chambly, 187; appoints St. Castin his lieutenant, 211.

GRANDE GUEULE, or BIG THROAT, French nickname of Oureouati, transformed by La Hontan into the pretended Indian name Grangula, and by Colden into Garangula, iii., p. 254, n. ; at Quebec, p. 86, n. ; meets de la Barre, 254 ; at Montreal, 303 ; Charlevoix calls him Haaskouaun, and makes him a Seneca, 303–4.

GRANDPRÉ, LAMBERT BOUCHER, SIEUR DE, Major of Three Rivers, commands his militia in Frontenac's expedition, v., p. 13.

GRANDVILLE, PETER BEQUART, SIEUR DE, ensign in the regt. Carignan Salieres, iv., p. 170, n. ; lieutenant, ib. ; commands militia in Denonville's campaign, iii., p. 283, n. ; sent by Provôt to watch Phips, 153 ; captured, 170 ; exchanged, 187, n. ; commands Beauport militia in Frontenac's expedition, v., p. 13.

GRANGE, CAPT. LA, French officer, opposes Ribault's plan of attacking Spanish fleet, i., p. 193 ; reluctantly embarks, ib. ; drowned in wreck of fleet, vi., p. 123.

GRANGE, SIEUR DE LA, a partisan, exploit in Newfoundland, takes an English frigate, v., p. 169; captured on his way to France in his prize ; commissioned in the Royal navy, 170.

GRANGER, a brave colonist at Port Royal, v., p. 199.

GRAVE, or GREVE, gravel beach for drying cod, iii., 141–2.

GRAVE, SIEUR DE, commandant at Yazoos, Chickasaws solicit peace from, vi., p. 70.

GRAVERAN, BR. COSMAS, Recollect, iii., p. 148, n.

GRAVIER, REV. JAMES, Jesuit, establishes flourishing Illinois mission, v., p. 132; among Peorias, 133, n.; prevents Kaskaskias from descending Mississippi, v., p. 153, n.

GRAYDON, English Vice Admiral, sails with a squadron to besiege Placentia, v., p. 162; misses Ducasse's squadron, 163; malcontent; oppressive acts of; dares not attack Placentia, ib.

GREASON, ROBERT, killed, iv., p. 134, n.

GREAT BURIN BAY, N. F., rendezvous of Nesmond and des Ursins, v., p. 71.

GREAT MOHAWK, THE, sketch of, sent to Mohawk, iii., p. 292; initiates Mohawk emigration, p. 191, n.; conversion of, 196, n.; at the capture of Schenectady, iv., p. 123; killed by Abénaquis, 128; eulogy, 129;

GREEN BAY, called BAY DES PUANTS, visited by Allouez, iii., p. 120; Marquette starts from, 179; Tonti and F. Membré at Jesuit mission, 212; La Sale represented as being at, 215–223.

GREENLAND, first voyages to, i., p. 13.

GREEN RIVER, now BLUE EARTH, copper mine on.

GRENVILLE, RICHARD, settles in Florida, i., p. 45.

GRESLON, FATHER ADRIAN, Jesuit, sent to Hurons, ii., p. 210, n.; at St. Mathews, 232; returns to Europe, 250, n.; meets Huron woman in China, 232, n.

GRIEU, CAPT., THE CHEV. DE, of the Maréchal de Villars, vi., p. 44, n.; takes Spanish prisoners to Havana, 45; his vessel seized, 46.

GRIFFIN, THE, vessel built by la Sale on Lake Erie, iii., p. 202; Indian idea of its fate, 204; opinions as to the place of its construction, iii., p. 202, n.

GRIJALVA, JOHN DE, discoveries of, i., p. 30.

GRILLET, French Jesuit, explores Cayenne, i., p. 57.

GRIMEAU, Canadian, pilots French ships into Pensacola harbor, vi., p. 57, n. ennobled, ib.

GROLLET, Rochelle sailor, or Provençal, deserts la Sale, meets Joutel among the Cenis, iv., p. 100; information as to Micissipi, 101; taken by Spaniards among the Cenis, 113; sent to Spain, then to Mexico, then to mines of New Mexico, 113, n., 114.

GROS, SIEUR LE, storekeeper at St. Louis settlement, iv., p. 73; conspiracy against, ib.; death, 75, n., 83.

GROSEILLIERS, MEDARD CHOUART DES, French Canadian, notice of, iii., p. 230–1, n.; penetrates to Sioux, and brings down furs, iii., p. 48, n.; takes English to Hudson Bay; 230; pardoned by King, sets out to expel English, 233; discovers Bourbon and St. Teresa rivers, i., p. 59, iii., p. 234; builds a fort, 234; ill-received at Quebec and in France, 236; goes over to English, 236; his first wife a daughter of Abraham Martin, 230, n.; second wife Teresa, sister of Radisson, 234; his son, Medard Chouart, faithful to French, 237.

GROTIUS, HUGO, notice of works on Origin of Indians, i., p. 78–79.

GROTON, capture of, ii., p. 257; attacked by Taxous, iv., p. 257, n.

GROUTANT, Frenchman in Florida, brings proposals from a chief to de Laudonniere, i., p. 173.

GUAÇO, DON GREGORIO, Commandant at Havana, sends a fleet against Carolina, vi., p. 45; seizes two French ships, 46; sends fleet to retake Pensacola, ib.; report to Viceroy of Mexico, ib.; replaces deserters, 47.

GUADALAJARA, founded by Oñate, i., p. 36.

GUAHAN, i., p. 59, 63.

GUANAHANI, i., p. 19.

GUAST, PIERRE DE, see MONTS DE.

GUÉ, SIDRAC DU, SIEUR DE BOIS-BRIANT, with de la Barre, iii., p. 250; with Denonville, 287, n.

GUERCHEVILLE, ANTOINETTE DE PONS MARCHIONESS DE, wife of Duke de Rochefoucauld Liancourt, zeal and liberality for Acadian mission, i., p. 262; purchases de Monts' rights, 263; obtains royal patent, ib., n.; collects at Court to buy off Huguenot partners of de Poutrincourt,

who refuse Jesuits passage, signs a treaty with Biencourt in favor of the Fathers, 263; Champlain's apology for this step, ib.; projects new settlement, 274; its situation, 277; its destruction, 279; error, 285-6; sends la Saussaye to England to obtain indemnity for destruction of St. Sauveur, 285; ship restored to, 285, n.

GUENIN, F. HILARION, Recollect, iii., p. 148-9, n.

GUENOT, Director at Natchez, killed, vi., p. 72, n.

GUERIN, JOHN, Father Mesnard's servant, attends him on a dangerous excursion, seeks lost missionary, iii., p. 49; baptizes many Ottawa children, 51; tragical death while at prayer, ib.

GUERRA, CHRISTOPHER, discovers Ayola, i., p. 22.

GUERRERO, DON FRANCISCO, Cornejo ordered to join squadron of, vi., p. 49.

GUIANA, Sir Walter Raleigh's expedition to, i., p. 47.

GUIGNAS, REV. IGNATIUS, Jesuit, visits Sioux, iii., p. 32, n.; iv., p. 273, n.

GUILBAUT, or GUILBAULT, partner of le Borgne, builds fort at la Héve, attacked by English, capitulates, iii., p. 135.

GUILLORÉ, kills F. Dalmas, iv., p. 243.

GUILLORY Isle near Dauphin Island, Spanish descent on, repulsed by Trudeau, vi., p. 52.

GUINEA, Dieppe trade with, i., p. 13.

GUIPSON, COLONEL, arrives at St. John with 1000 Irish, v., p. 73; see GIBSON.

GUY, (called by Charlevoix GUYAS,) JOHN of Bristol, settles at Conception Bay, Newfoundland, iii., p. 140.

GUYENNE, F. ALEXIS DE, Jesuit, arrives, vi., p. 76, n.

GUZMAN, , Governor of Pensacola, welcomes an English officer, vi., p. 24.

GUZMAN, NUÑO DE, Spaniard, discovers Cinaloa, i., p. 36.

HAASKOUAUN, Seneca chief sent to Denonville, treatment of officer from Catarocouy, iii., p. 300; haughty proposals, 304. See GRANDE GUEULE, OUREOUATI.

HAIVE, see HEVE.

HALIMACANI, Indian name of the Somme, i., p. 229; see 163, n.

HAMEL, ENSIGN DU, iv., p. 64; his party surprised, 71, n.

HAOUATCHOUATH, chief of St. Francis Abénaquis, vi., p. 151.

HARATSIONS, Onondaga chief, v., p. 101.

HARLAY DE CHANVALLON, FRANCIS DE, Archbishop of Paris, his decision on liquor question, iii., p. 196.

HARMON, CAPT., plunders Norridgewalk, and carries off Rale's dictionary and strong box, v., p. 276; on Rale's death, 280, n.

HASSAKY, chief of the Ottawas, Kiskakons, v., p. 143, n.

HATFIELD, ravaged, i., p. 87.

HAVERHILL, (Hevvreuil,) taken by Perriere and Rouville, v., p. 206.

HAVRE DE L'ANGLOIS, LOUYSBOURG, v., p. 284.

HAVRE DE GRACE, Ribault puts in at, i., p. 181; De Monts fits out at, 247-251; Champlain at, 247, n.

HAWES, discoveries of, i., p. 58; v., p. 151.

HAWKES, ADMIRAL, v., p. 245.

HAWKINS, JOHN, English commander, relieves French in Florida, i., p. 177; censures their neglect of agriculture, 178, n.

HAWKINS, SIR RICHARD, discovers Southern lands, i., p. 46, 61.

HAWTHORN, COL., supersedes Church, v., p. 30, n.

HAYTI, discovered, i., p. 19.

HEATH, CAPT., destroys Indian town. v., p. 277, n.

HEBAHAMOS, Texas Indian, see BRACAMOS.

HEBERT, ANNE, first woman married in Canada, ii., p. 30.

HEBERT, LOUIS, settled at Port Royal, ii., p. 51; builds first house at Quebec, 34, n.; house guarded, 50.

HEHONGUERONON, Huron name of the Kichesipirini, ii., p. 164, n.

HELIOT, REV. JOHN, ii., p. 256, n.; see ELIOT.

HENNEPIN, FATHER LOUIS, Recollect, sketch of, iii., p. 201, embarks for Canada with la Sale, ib.; discovers the Upper Mississippi up to St. Anthony of Padua's Falls, which he discovers, i., p. 58, 83, iii., p. 206; prisoner among the Sioux, 207; rescued by du Luht, iv., p. 31, n.; pretended voyage down to the mouth, iii., p. 207, n.; his account of la Sale's death, iv., p. 93; d'Iberville exposes false statements of, 121; his books lead to Dutch and English attempts to settle

HENNEPIN, F. LOUIS, (*continued.*) Louisiana, v., p. 126; his works, i., p. 83-4, iii., p. 201, n.; v., p. 121-6.

HENRIQUEZ, GARCIAS, discovers May Islands, i., p. 34.

HENRY III., of Castile, i., p. 14.

HENRY III., of France grants the Marquis de la Roche the same commission as Roberval had of Francis I., i., p. 241.

HENRY IV., of France confirms grant to de la Roche, i., p. 241; sends for French left on Isle Sable, 245; gives them presents, ib.; orders Poutrincourt to take Jesuits to Acadia, 260; disobeyed and censures Poutrincourt, 261; his death, 262.

HENRY VII., of England, sends John Gabot and his sons to explore, i., p. 20.

HENRY, Infante of Portugal, Count of Viseu, occupies Canaries, i., p. 15; builds fort at Arguyn, 16; Cape Verde islands discovered in name of, 17.

HERBAUT, MR. D', Commissioner, fixes Canada boundary at St. George river, v., p. 93.

HERE, CHEV. D', lieutenant on ship in which la Sale sails, iv., p. 63.

HEREDIA, DON PEDRO DE, Spaniard builds Carthagena, i., p. 36.

HERITZOON, Martin of Vries, discoveries, i., p. 55.

HERMAPHRODITES in Florida, i., p. 138.

HERMIT, L', see L'HERMITE.

HEROIC ACTION of a Christian family, iv., p. 304.

HERRERA, ANTONIO DE, account of his Historia General, i., p. 73.

HERRERA, PETER VALDEZ, plants Spanish flag on Caroline, i., p. 203.

HERTEL, FRANCIS, SIEUR DE CHAMBLY, sketch of, iii., p. 43, n., iv., p. 130; captured in his youth by Iroquois, and maltreated, iii., p. 43; expedition against Salmon Falls, iv., p. 130; commended to court by Frontenac, 130; joins de Portneuf's party, 132; distinguished at capture of Kaskebé (Casco) 137; also at siege of Quebec, 177; ennobled by King, 177; one son sent on scout, kills five English, 202; five sons sent to the Abénaquis, surprise and kill several English, v., p. 161; one arrested at Albany set at liberty, 246; alive in 1721, iii., p. 44.

HERTEL DE ROUVILLE, see ROUVILLE.

HERTEL DE COURNOYER, see COURNOYER.

HERTEL DE LA FRESNIERE, see FRESNIERE.

HERVAUX, Chevalier relieves Placentia, iv. p. 164.

HERVEAU, FATHER CÆSAREUS, Recollect, shipwrecked with Talon on his way tc Canada, iii., p. 148.

HESPERIDES, what islands were they, i., p. 17.

HEVE, or HAIVE, LA, position of, iii., p. 135, n.; iv., p. 18; fertility, i., p. 250; Mme. de Guercheville's arms set up at, 275; Saussaye should have occupied, 286; in grant to Claude de Razilly, ii., p. 64; iii., p. 129, n.; Commander de Razilly settles families at, ib.; dies, p. 128, n.; d'Aubray abandons, 129; inhabitants transferred to Port Royal, 130; burnt by le Borgne, 133; Guilbault and the younger le Borgne at, 135; taken by English, ib.; advantages of, iv., p. 18; Subercase projects settlement at, v., p. 225; Iberville unable to embark Indians at, v., p. 27.

HEVVREUIL, see HAVERHILL.

HIENS, Dutch freebooter, joins la Sale at Petit Goave, iv., p. 89; reviled by Moranget resolves on vengeance, 91; sent to Cenis for provisions, 98; kills Duhaut, as he tells Joutel to avenge la Sale, 103; wishes to kill Larchevêque, but Joutel reconciles them, 104; goes to war with the Cenis, ib.; refuses to go to the Illinois, 106; seizes most of la Sale's property, but gives some to Joutel and Cavelier, 107; obliges the latter to give him a document exonerating him from any part in la Sale's death, ib.

HIENS RIVER, Texas, iv., p. 90, n.

HILA, (GILA,) RIVER, explored by F. Kino, i., p. 62.

HILICOPILE, Florida chief, guides Gourgues, i., p. 229.

HILL, BRIG. JOHN, commands English forces to besiege Quebec, v., p. 248; regiments under him, ib., n.; his manifesto, ib.; loss of fleet bearing him, 147, 252.

HILTON, COL., on Port Royal expedition, v., p. 191, n.

HOANDORAN, murderer of Rev. Mr. Lemaitre, converted, iii., p. 44.

HOCHELAGA, Indian town in Canada, i., p. 119; where Montreal now stands, its

form and position, i., 119, n.; Cartier's reception there, i., p. 37, 119; name discussed, 119, n.; people of, 120; language, 119, n.; disappears before Champlain's visit, 246.

HODENOSAUNEE, Seneca name for Iroquois, ii., p. 189.

HOLY CROSS, or Brazil, i., p. 22.

HONAREENHAX, LOUIS, kills F. Chabanel, ii. p. 231, n.

HONDURAS, discovered by Columbus, i., p. 24.

HONFLEUR, i., pp. 259, 275; ii., pp. 20, 30.

HONTAN, ET HERLECHE, ARMAND LOUIS DE DELONDARCE DE LA HONTAN, BARON DE LA, notice of, iii., p. 286; vi., p. 126; censures Denonville, ib,; seconded Captain, his voyages, i., p. 86; sent from Quebec to Placentia, iv., p. 223; detached with sixty men to check English, ib.; sent to English admiral, 224; reports to de Brouillan, ib.; silence of French documents as to, iii., p. 286, n.; vi., p. 126.

HOONHOUENTSIONTAOUET, STEPHEN, death of, iv., p. 303.

HOPEHOOD, Abénaqui chief, iv., p. 128, n.; 132, n.

HOPE ISLAND, discovered, i., p. 51.

HORSES, first in Canada, iii., p. 82.

HORNN, GEORGE, notice of work on Origin of Americans, i., p. 80; identifies Iroquois and Yrcans, ii., p. 189, n.

HOSPITAL BROTHERS, founded by Francis Charon, iv., p. 234, n.; encourage manufactures, v., p. 182, n.

HOSPITAL NUNS, to be established in Canada, ii., p. 100; notice of those of Dieppe, iii., p. 113, n.; arrival at Quebec of three from Dieppe, ii., p. 102; Charlevoix makes them take charge of hospital at Sylleri, 103, 185; their sufferings, 104; erection of hospital at Montreal, iii., p. 27; those of Quebec have to leave monastery as too exposed to Iroquois attacks, iii., p. 33–4; account of Mother Catherine of St. Augustine, hospital nun, iii., p. 112; take charge of General Hospital, iv., p. 17, n.; during siege of Quebec, p. 178, n.

HOSTA, CAPT. D', defeats an Iroquois attack on his Michilimakinac convoy, iv., p. 138; sends a prisoner to Frontenac, 140; killed at La Prairie, 141, n., 205.

HOTEL DIEU, Quebec, ii., p. 185, n.

HOTEL DIEU, Montreal, iii., p. 27, burned, v., p. 308, n.

HOTINONCHIENDI, Huron, and HOTINONSIONNI, Mohawk name for Iroquois, ii., p. 189, n.

HOUEL, LOUIS, one of the earliest members of the Company of One Hundred, ii., p. 39.

HUBERT, MR., succeeds Duclos as Commissaire Ordonnateur in Louysiana, vi., p. 38.

HUDSON BAY, Anschild enters in 1591, i., p. 46; visited by Hudson, 51; names given by James, 54; discoveries in, 57; Druillettes obtains information as to, iii., p. 20; some Algonquins take refuge on, iii., p. 30; Indians of, propose league with French against Iroquois, ib.; description of Hudson Bay and Strait, iii., p. 226; Hudson never took possession of, i., p. 51; iii., p. 230; affairs at, 269; capture of three English forts at, 270–1; conference with French plenipotentiaries in England as to, defeated, iv., p. 23; William and Mary proclaimed there by London Company, iv., p. 37; possession taken of for France, 259; King orders expulsion of English from, 275; importance of fur trade, v., p. 59; English acquire possession of by treaty of Utrecht, ib.; left to France by that of Ryswick, v., p. 93; 80, n.; several French killed there by Indians, 304.

HUDSON, HENRY, after an ineffectual attempt to discover a northern passage to China, ii., p. 9, lands on Cape Cod, p. 10, discovers Manhatte river, i., p. 50, 82; ii., p. 10; said to have sold Manhatte to the Dutch, ii., p. 10; iii., p. 72; never took possession of Hudson Bay, i., p. 51; iii., p. 230; notice of his Detectio Freti, i., p. 82.

HUDSON STRAIT, iii., p. 226; v., p. 54–5.

HUET or HURÉ, REV. MR., Chaplain of Apalaches, vi., p. 15, n.

HUGUENOTS attempt to settle Florida; destroyed by Menendez, i., p. 201; with Capt. Barr on the Mississippi, v., p. 127, n.; offer to settle in Louisiana, 127; offer refused, ib.

HUITZ, RAPHAEL, English sailor, Spanish expedition on report of, iv., p. 113, n.

HUMFREY, SIR GILBERT, i., p. 45, and

HUMFREY, SIR HUMBERT, iii., p. 140, Charlevoix's erroneous names for Sir Humphrey Gilbert.

HURIER, one of la Sale's companions, disappears, iv., p. 88.

HURONS, Indian tribe in Canada; called Attigouatan, or Attignaouantan, ii., p. 27, n.; towns of, p. 27, n., 28, n.; prepare to march against Iroquois, ii., p. 8; set out with Champlain, 12; victory of, 17; induce him to go on a new expedition, i., p. 51; ii., p. 25; their route, p. 28, n.; reach and attack Entouohonorons, p. 28; fight badly, 28; compelled to retreat, 29; refuse Champlain a guide to Quebec, 29; Champlain endeavors to win them, 30; plot against French, 34; character, 70; come down in numbers to meet Champlain, 68; refuse to take two missionaries to their country, 69; their origin, different names, origin of term Huron, 71; families into which divided, 72; extent and description of their country, 73; easy and important for French to have made a solid settlement there, 74; they ill-treat missionaries, 76; obstacles to their conversion, 115; take umbrage at every thing, 82; begin to lay aside prejudice for Christianity, why? 85; comparison of Huron and Algonquin tribes, 118; cannot be induced to send children to Quebec to be educated, 92; strangely deceived by Iroquois, 93; haughtiness before English take Quebec, 94; what rendered them more docile to instructions of missionaries, 96; gain some advantages over the Iroquois, 105; position of the Huron mission, 110; some Hurons allow Father Lalemant to be ill-treated, 112; charity to Wenroh tribe ruined by Iroquois, 121; a Huron sacrifices himself to draw Iroquois into an ambuscade, 122; they do not profit by their victories, 123; according to ancient tradition expelled former inhabitants of Montreal, 127; consequence of their remissness in war, ib.; conversions among, 134; great Huron convoy under Ahasistari taken by Iroquois, 138; divine justice on a Huron village, 153; exploit of a young Christian Huron, 154; a Huron escapes from the Mohawk and brings tidings of F. Jogues to Quebec, 154; deplorable condition of the Huron nation, 162; fervor of the Christians, 163; animated with the apostolic spirit, ib.; some go to the Neuter Nation to announce Christ, ib.; extremity to which mission is reduced, 170; reply of two Hurons to de Montmagny on his asking for two Iroquois prisoners, ii., p. 176; St. Joseph's attacked by Iroquois, 193; exploit of three Hurons, ib.; Huron Idolaters prejudice Mohawks against missionaries, 195; defeat Iroquois, 209; Andastes offer to aid Hurons, who do not accept it, 209; hunters of St. Ignatius surprised by Iroquois, 210; apathy, ib.; St. Joseph's or Teananstayae destroyed by Iroquois and all the people butchered, 210–1; they defeat the Iroquois and their bravest fall into an ambuscade, 220; an apostate Huron advises executioners of Fathers Brebeuf and Lalemant to baptize them with boiling water, 223; the Hurons disperse, 226; retire to St. Joseph's Island, 226; constancy and fervor in their misfortunes, 227; (see Tionontates, incorrectly styled in Charlevoix's Index, "the true Hurons. Some Hurons conspire against the missionaries; the result, 231; visible protection of heaven on a Huron man and woman, 232; new misfortunes of the Hurons, 233; many go down to Quebec, 234; Hurons under Atironta surprised by a handful of Iroquois, 235; a great many Hurons come down to Quebec, their reception 235; what became of most of the others, 236; the inhabitants of St. Michael's and another Huron town give themselves to the Iroquois and are well received, ii., p. 236, iii., p. 12; others, rashly taking the field against the Mohawks, are betrayed by one of their braves and defeated, ii., p. 238; piety of those who remain at Quebec, 240; Huron Christians defeat a Mohawk party, 252; 257, n.; fervor of Christian Huron captives among the Iroquois, 257; piety of those on Isle Orleans, 259; some Hurons oppose the establishment of Christianity at Onondaga, 265; many Hurons carried off from Isle Orleans by the Mohawks, 268; dispersion of a great number of others, 271;

Hurons, (*continued.*)
persion of a great number of others, 271; others offer to give themselves up to the Mohawks, and repent, 278; their embarrassment, 279; the Bear tribe joins the Mohawks, 280; they are summoned by the Onondagas to keep a similar promise, their reply, 281; fervor of the Huron captives in the Seneca canton, and the effects it produces, iii., p. 12; those who give themselves up to the Onondagas treated as prisoners of war, 13; a young Huron woman a martyr of conjugal chastity, ib.; some Tionontates insult the Sioux and many are slain, 32; some Hurons retired inland invite Father Mesnard to visit them, iii., p. 49; abandon him on the way, p. 50; F. Allouez visits them, 103; fruit of his labors, 104; ward off small pox better than other Indians do, 154; Father Chaumonot assembles many at Notre Dame de Foye and Lorette, 154; The Tionontates Hurons remove to Michilimakinac, 170; Michilimakinac Hurons send delegates to Montreal, 221; attacked by Iroquois, 241; join Durantaye, 246; with de la Barre, 249; attacked by Iroquois at Saguinam, 264; favor English trade, 265; they are with difficulty prevented from treating with the Senecas, 281; the Hurons in the Seneca campaign, 281, 283, n.; those of Michilimakinac treat with Iroquois, 296; oppose the peace between the French and Iroquois, iv., p. 12; steps taken by the Rat to defeat it, 12; instigate Ottawas to make peace with the Senecas, but do not appear themselves, iv., p. 55; why they deferred declaring openly, 56; the Ottawa invectives against the French attributed to, 57; they serve under de Longueuil, 167; they protest their devotion to the French; harass Iroquois, iv., p. 200; the Lorette Hurons commanded at La Prairie by Ouraouharé, iv., p. 203; they march against the Mohawks, 233; speech of a Huron at a public audience, 242; the Michilimakinac Hurons treat with the Iroquois, 270; and conclude peace, 277; put Iroquois on their guard, 278; several taken by the Iroquois, ib.; suspected of preventing Ottawas from joining Frontenac's expedition, 279; the Lorette Hurons join it, v., p. 12; conference at Montreal between Hurons and Frontenac, 69; several led by Baron settle near Albany, 67; Hurons with La Motte Cadillac at Montreal, ib.; defeat Iroquois parties, 68, 78; at Montreal treaty, 111; their totem, ib.; about to attack Iroquois, 141; at the obsequies of the Rat and receive compliments, v., p. 147–8; promise Joncaire to remain always faithful, ib.; decimated by contagious disease, ib.; a Huron chief at the General Congress, the only one who did not ask suppression of the liquor trade, 153; the Hurons who had removed from Michilimakinac to Detroit show inclination for English, 163; the Commandant at Detroit urges them to take field against the Sioux, 184; they fire on the Ottawas, 186; with Miamis plot massacre of French, 202; Lorette Hurons on a war party against English, return, why? 205; Detroit Hurons induce our other Indian allies to declare war in defence of the colony, v., p. 240; march to aid of French at Detroit, 258; urge the allies not to lose time, ib.; distinguished more than others in this expedition and sustain heaviest loss, 264; join in letter to Governor of Mass., 273, n.

Iberville, Pierre le Moyne, Sieur d', Canadian gentleman, sketch of, iii., p. 270, n.; volunteer in Hudson Bay expedition, takes an English ship by boarding, 270; with his brother St. Helene takes Fort Quitchitchouen, 271; in Hudson Bay, 293; repulses English who besiege him there, and captures their vessel, iv., p. 37–8; takes two English ships in Hudson Bay, 38; stormy weather prevents his taking a third, 39; volunteer in Schenectady expedition, 122; induces Sanders Glen to surrender, 125; selected with du Tast for an expedition to Hudson Bay, 201; at Quebec with two ships from Hudson Bay loaded with furs, iv., p. 213; goes to France, ib.; at Quebec, too late for Port Nelson expedition, 227; fails to take Fort Pemkuit, 228; sent again to attack Port Nelson, 259; his success there, 260; sails to Rochelle, 262; ordered to attack Fort Pemkuit, 275; and proceed to Placentia, ib.; intelligence on reaching Acadia, v., p. 24; captures the Newport, ib.; besieges

IBERVILLE, (*continued.*)
and takes Pemkuit, 25; avoids an English squadron and reaches Placentia, 27; proposes to drive English out of Newfoundland, 35; what prevented his junction with de Brouillan, ib., de Brouillan opposes attack on Carbonniere island, 37; devotion of Canadians to, 38; his difficulties with de Brouillan, 37–9; his moderation, ib.; his report to Pontchartrain, 40; sends de Bonaventure to France, 40; the consequence, ib.; fresh trouble with de Brouillan, ib.; marches on St. John, 41; routs an English party, ib.; his other exploits, 42; de Brouillan's want of courtesy to, 45; his moderation, ib.; fresh trouble, 46; conquests in Newfoundland, ib.; why he did not completely reduce that island, 48; instructions from the Court, ib.; sets out for Hudson Bay, 48, 53; danger at its entrance, 55; while separated from his other ships attacks three English vessels, takes one and sinks another, ib.; wrecked, 57; his ships come up, ib.; he takes Fort Bourbon, ib.; returns to France, 59; suggests to Pontchartrain the idea of discovering the mouth of the Micissipi, and erecting a fort there, 117; sets out, ib.; confers with Ducasse, Governor of St. Domingo, 118; off Pensacola, ib.; discoveries, 119; finds mouth of Micissipi, i., p. 62; v., p. 120; ascends the river, detects errors in Tonti and Hennepin, 120; visits the Bayagoulas and their temple, 121; how convinced that he is on the Micissipi, 122; well received by Oumas, ib.; finds a letter of Tonti, 123; builds a fort, 123; returns to France, ib.; back in Louysiana, 124; tidings of the English, ib.; Tonti disavows the relation published in his name, 125; places fort on Mississippi badly, ib.; projects a city among the Natchez, 128; makes Biloxi the headquarters of Louysiana, ib.; instructions of the ministry in regard to trade, 129; not his fault that bisons were not raised, ib.; sends Le Sueur to explore more thoroughly the copper mines on Green River, vi., p. 12; arrives in 1701, vi., p. 14, n.; settlement on Maubile river, 14; erects storehouses and barracks on Massacre Island, which he calls Dauphin Island, ib.; projected city Rosalie among the Natchez, vi., p. 31.

IDOL on Fox river thrown down by missionaries, iii., p. 182.

IHONATIRIA, (see ST. JOSEPH), Huron town, ii., p. 77, 210, n.; called by Charlevoix Ihouhatiri.

ILE, see ISLE.

ILLINOIS, Indians, introduction of Christianity to, iii., p. 105; names, ib.; reception of Marquette and Joliet, iii., p. 180–1; v., p. 131; Iroquois begin to harass, iii., p. 181; why la Sale depended on them, v., p. 131; gained by Tonti, iii., p. 205; their attachment to us cooled by Iroquois, 205; less friendly to la Sale, ib.; some join him, 206; Tonti mediates between them and Iroquois, 209; Senecas refuse to include them in the peace, 254; the Iroquois continue to make war on them, 259; Tonti able to bring only 80 to the Seneca war, 280; good and bad qualities; attack Iroquois, v., p. 102; Jesuits establish a flourishing mission among, v., p. 130; attachment and fidelity to the French, ib.; what sustained it, 131; more warlike, 130; Fathers Marquette and Allouez attempt to establish a mission among, 131–2; success of Father Gravier, 132; fervor of this mission, ib.; all Christians, 133; de Courtemanche prevents their warring on Iroquois, 142; make them promise to send deputies to the General Congress for peace, ib.; their deputies die on the way, and confide their interests to Onanguicé, 152; de Callieres' injunctions to them through Onanguicé in regard to plundered Frenchmen, ib.; English endeavor to trade with; march to defend Detroit against Foxes, 258; remark of one of their chiefs to Fox's deputy, 261; their country detached from New France and connected with Louysiana, vi p. 37; besieged at the Rock and at Pimiteouy by the Foxes they retire to the Micissipi, v., p. 309; vi., p. 71; Chicachas conceal from them their design of destroying Louysiana French, 79; their fidelity and attachment certain, 94; Chickasaws fail to draw them into plot against French, and their reply, 102; further fruitless solicitations of the Chickasaws, 119. See KASKASKIAS, METCHIGAMEAS, TAMAROIS.

ILLINOIS RIVER, Marquette finds Kaskaskias on iii., p. 181, n.; La Sale descends, 213 ; called Seignelay by Membré, ib., n.

INDIANE, harbor on Cape Breton, its situation, v., p. 285.

INDIAN CHRISTIANS, Details on the Life and Death of some, iv., pp. 283, &c.

INDIAN JUGGLERS, or medicine men, ii., p. 13 ; called by Champlain Ostemoy and Pilotois, p. 13 ; in Florida Ionas, i., p. 139, 143, 144, 175.

INDIANS, Works on origin of, noticed, i., pp. 78–79, 80, 92 ; on manners and customs of, 91, 94; first Canadian taken to France, 106 ; treatment of Verrazani's sailor, 109; early stories as to, 124; some taken by Cartier, 122 ; Florida Indians welcome French, 136 ; account of, 138, &c.; strange customs, 158; war customs, 160; war among Florida tribes, 173; make a league with de Gourgues, 228; Indians of Acadia, 264, &c.; extravagant customs of the Malecites, 278 ; mode of treating to avoid being despised, ii., p. 27 ; conspiracy against French detected, 30; French murdered by, ib.; conduct on capture of Quebec, 66; what set them against English, ib.; dissimulation of, 78; character, 86 ; seminary for sons of, 91 ; nothing should be too easily given, 98; obstacles to missions among, 115; traditions, 127; speeches, 136 ; missionaries to, 167 ; often spread false accounts, 255 ; adoption among, iii., p. 16 ; feast where all must be eaten, ib.; chiefs oppose liquor, 54–5 ; Jesuits decline to undertake to frenchify, 97; notices of various attempts, ib., n; Allouez preaches to several tribes with little fruit, 101, &c.; resent punishment of any of their people, 218 ; who makes reparation for murder, ib.; Denonville opposes frenchifying, 259 ; precautions necessary before baptizing, iv., p. 286; easily ascribe bad motives, 287; young do not address old by proper name, ib.; human respect, ib.; French proximity dangerous to, 198; mode of defying, v., p. 15; delighted to hear others speak their language, 203 ; cruelty, 272 ; Indians, at Hudson Bay massacre several French men, 304 ; sieze powder and reduce French to distress, 305 ; several tribes settle near Maubile, vi., p. 14; their continual wars retard progress of Louysiana, 35; despise French, ib.; welcome l'Epinai, 39 ; at siege of Pensacola 44; earnest for French, 50, &c.; around Fort Pensacola, 58; chant calumet to de Champmêlin, 62 ; Bienville restores Magdalen river Indians treachously carried off, 66; English attempts to debauch, 68 ; many tribes make war on French, 71; missionaries to Louysiana Indians, 76 ; religion the only means of uniting them to us, 79; almost all tribes on Mississippi drawn into plot by Chicasaws, 89; services rendered to Perrier by allied, 107; refuse to pursue Natchez, 114.

INFANTE JOHN, discovers Cape of Good Hope, i., p. 19.

INGOLDSBY, MAJ. RICHARD, Lt. Gov. of New York, appoints Nicholson to command Canada expedition, v., p. 217, n.

INTENDANT, First in Canada, functions of, iii., p. 67. See ROBERT, BOUTEROUE, TALON, DUCHESNEAU, DE MEULLES, CHAMPIGNY, BEAUHARNOIS, BEGON, CHAZEL.

IONAS, Florida medicine men, honors paid to, i., p. 139; given to magic, ib.; feared, 103; pretend to hold communication with the gods, ib.; prophetic statement of one, 175.

IOWAS, Indians of the Dakota family, iii., p. 31, n.

IPIGUIT RIVER, Acadia, English ravages there, v., p. 171; probably Cobequid Bay, 172, n.

IRONDEQUOIT BAY, Denonville erects fort at, iii., p. 285; called Riviere des Sables, ib.; various forms of Indian name, ib., n.

IROQUET, ii., p. 9, n.; name of an Indian tribe believed to be ancient inhabitants of Montreal Island and which no longer appears, ii., p. 128; Algonquins, ib., n.; the Onontchataronon of the Hurons, ib.

IROQUOIS, Indian Confederation in Canada, ii., p. 188 ; allied to Hurons and Andastouez, 72 ; origin of the name, 189 ; their own name and its meaning, 72, 189, n.; country said to have been occupied by, 13; extent of territory, divided into Mohawks, Oneïdas, Onondagas, Cayugas and Senecas, (see those names), ii., pp. 189–90, n.; Champlain joins their enemies against, 12; what sustained them, ib.; cause of their ascendency, 13 ; defeated

IROQUOIS, (*continued.*)
on Lake Champlain by the allies, 17; Entouohonorons, supposed to be Iroquois attacked by allies repel them, 28; invade Canada in three corps but repulsed, 32; take a Recollect prisoner, 33; French lose opportunity of winning or reducing them, 75; divide and ruin Hurons, 94; emboldened by weakness of Cananda, ib.; insult Governor General at Three Rivers, 95; renew war, 105; first Christian, ib.; an Iroquois Augustinian, ib.; scatter a whole nation, 121; defeated, 128; endeavor to detach French from Hurons, 123; insult Governor, 125; their relation to Montreal examined, 128; defeat a Huron party and capture Father Jogues, 139; repulsed at Fort Richelieu, 143; destroy Huron town Ehwae, 153; inclined to peace, 174–8; Montmagny gives them public audience, 179; renew hostilities, 188; difference between Upper and Lower Iroquois, 188; origin of the name Iroquois, 189; extent of country, 188; plants, 190–1; animals, 192; attack Hurons again, 193; after great carnage destroy St. Joseph's and kill Father Daniel, 211; destroy two other Huron towns and burn Fathers de Brebeuf and Lallemant, 218; meet with a check but soon avenge it, 220; raise siege of St. Mary's in a panic, 221; destroy St. John's and kill Father Garnier, 229; pursue Hurons on their retreat and slaughter many, 233; depopulate a vast territory by the terror of their name, 234; one of their parties approach Three Rivers and kill the Governor who sallies out, 245; what augments their forces, ib.; fill north with fire and sword, ib.; why the Upper Iroquois wish to make peace with the French, 260; courage and virtue of a Christian Iroquois woman and child, 265; the Iroquois reduce the Colony to great straits, iii., p. 33; dear bought victory at Long Sault, ib.; their design, 33; the Upper Iroquois repulse Andastes and make incursions into Virginia, whence they penetrate to the sea and the Spanish parts, iii., p. 45; some Iroquois defeated in the Colony during the earthquakes, 64; other defeats, ib., n.; alarmed, p. 65; why they remain in arms during peace, 70; neglect to avail ourselves of humiliation of Iroquois to establish Christianity among them, 93; obstacles to their conversion, 110; importance of having missionaries among them, 116; try to get Ottawas to bring them furs to sell to the English, 123; an Iroquois chief murdered and robbed by French, the consequence, iii., p. 149; Garakonthié restores peace with Ottawas, 152; Upper Iroquois roughly handled by Andastes become more docile to the missionaries, 158; Christians resolve to emigrate, 163; destroy almost utterly the Andastes and Shawnees, iii., p. 174; approve design of erecting a fort at Catarocouy, not perceiving that it is intended to hold them in check, 175; Dutch excite them to renew war against us, and they are so inclined, 192; defeat Illinois, origin of war, 205; Tonti mediates, 209; English seek to harass us through them, ib.; force Tonti to abandon the Illinois river, 211; menace the colony, 217; why they defer war, ib.; wish to oblige Frontenac to come to them, 220; five Iroquois deputies at Montreal, 221; bad faith, ib.; English and Dutch excite them to war against us, 222; means of subduing them, 225; treat with de la Barre in bad faith, 241; insolent reply to that general, 242; why more advantageous for them to trade with Dutch and English than with French, ib.; fear French more than they wish to show, ib.; send an embassy to de la Barre to blind him, 243; march on Fort St. Louis, Illinois and plunder French traders on the way, 244; repulsed, ib.; Iroquois of Sault St. Louis in de la Barre's army, 249; his opinion of this nation, ib.; irruption into Saguinam, 264; Governor of New York excites them against us, and tries to allure Iroquois Christians within his jurisdiction, 265; attack Miamis and Illinois, 269; principal Iroquois chiefs arrested by stratagem at Catarocouy, to be sent to the galleys, 276; Iroquois of Sault and Mountian with Denonville, 283, n.; thirty Iroquois attack a convoy, and behead two Frenchmen, 302; Father de Lambervile induces them to hold back a war party formed against our settlements, and to send deputies to the Governor General,

303; deputies escorted to Lake St. Francis by more than a thousand braves, ib.; alarm a French officer, ib.; scatter through the colony and fill it with terror, 304; besiege Catarocouy, burning hay and killing cattle, 305· attack a bark on Lake Ontario, ib.; their commander raises siege of Catarocouy, 305; conditions on which Denonville grants peace, ib.; writes to the Court to obtain good treatment and restoration of those in the galleys, 306; they give hostages, 306; again in arms in the colony, 307; Denonville marches against them, and takes several, ib.; Iroquois Christians send out parties against heathen Iroquois, iv., p. 12; Iroquois deputies surprised and defeated by a Huron chief, who puts one to death, 14; Andros prevents their sending deputies to Denonville, 14; ravages, 16; fur trade with English, 16; fall on a section of Montreal Island; they take and burn many, iv., p. 29; ravage much of the island and take a fort, 30; one of their detachments defeated, 31; their project to expel the French from Canada, 32; necessity of maintaining missionaries among them, 44; put a great war party in the field, 50; often change wives, 297; Iroquois at Sault St. Louis and the Mountain on the Schenectady expedition, iv., p. 123; refuse to attack Albany, ib.; their position at this time, ib., n.; Iroquois attack a Michilimakinac convoy and are defeated, 138–9; arrest an envoy from the Governor General and send him to Manhatte, 141; burn two of his companions and commit several hostilities, 141; raid on Point au Tremble, 142; kill two French officers, 142, with English and Mohegans prepare to attack Montreal, 145, n.; quarrel with English and withdraw, 146, n.; on Phipps' expedition, 185, n.; why they accuse the English of cowardice, 186; their policy in regard to English and French, 186; success of Iroquois war parties, iv., p. 191; a war party posted on the Ottawa, 193; Vaudreuil when about to march learns that they have retired, 199; invade the colony and are pursued by Oureouharé, 212; continue hostilities and are at last beaten, 216; eight hundred Iroquois invade colony in vain, 232; a large force menaces Montreal but retires, 240–1; adhere to their policy in regard to French and English, 248; Governor General warned to distrust, 249; send deputies to Frontenac, ib.; attempt to debauch our allies, 251; continue hollow negotiations, 252; able to raise 3000 men, 255; King advises driving them to extremity, 263; renew hostilities 264; insolent propositions to Frontenac, ib.; fail to seduce our allies, 266; invade the colony and are twice checked, 269; defeated by our allies who had begun to negotiate with them, 276; opinions as to the mode of destroying them, v., p. 9; prisoners taken from, how treated, 11· surprise some Frenchmen, ib.; defy Frontenac, 15; great distress in their country, 22; Frontenac sends several parties against them, ib.; haughtier than ever, 48; several fruitless parties against them, 49; renew hostilities v., p. 52; but thwarted by de Callieres, ib.; continue to delude French, 63; invade colony, 64; a party of, beaten by the Rat, v., p. 68 what prevented Frontenac's using all his forces to humble them, 76; disposed to peace, 84; convened by Bellomont of, 83 Conference, 84; Frontenac sees the relation of the English and Iroquois, 85 they refuse to include our allies in the peace, ib.; Bellomont wrong in saying they complained of missionaries, 91; assert independence, 93; not mentioned in regulating limits, 93; deplore death of Frontenac, 94; seem inclined to renew war, 94; proposals to de Callieres, and his reply, 95; they ask for Fathers Bruyas, and Lamberville and for Maricourt, ib.; compliment de Callieres on his appointment and seem to delay peace only out of respect for English, 99; fail to keep their word with de Callieres at instigation of Bellomont, ib.; Callieres shows his object, 100; send to apologize, ib.; two cantons avowed by two others send delegates, 101; complain of Ottawas, 102; reply of de Callieres to their demands, 102; new English efforts to prevent their making peace with French, 104; reflection on the reception of their deputies at Montreal 109; de Callieres gives them audience in presence of the deputies of our allies, 109; they sign a provisional treaty,

Iroquois, (*continued.*)
110; Bellomont provokes them by attempts to intimidate, 112; attacked while hunting by Ottawas, 100; complain to de Callieres, 135; his reply, 136; their opinion of settlement at Detroit, ib.; they prevent English settling there, 137; de Callieres' reply to their envoys on the point, ib.; frivolous excuses for not restoring prisoners, 145; Iroquois of Sault St. Louis and the Mountain condole with Hurons on the Rat's death, 147; Iroquois Christians at the General Congress, 151; what passed between de Callieres and the deputies of the cantons after the treaty of peace, 153; ask and obtain Jesuits, 155; whom the English ask them to dismiss, 157; our allies treat with English, through, ib.; de Callieres endeavors to thwart these intrigues, 158; Vaudreuil urges them to neutrality between us and English, 160; some attacked by Ottawas near Catarocouy, 163; Schuyler's efforts to seduce Iroquois Christians, 164; some consent and are put to shame by Abénaquis, ib.; hostility of Miamis to, 163, 165; ineffectual Congress of Cantons at Albany, 166; Pontchartrain against openly allowing their mediation with English, ib.; satisfied for Ottawa outrages, 179; Ottawas make reparation 182; Vaudreuil prevents their attacking them, ib.; La Motte Cadillac invites them in force to Detroit, 188; they act well, and New York is spared on their account, 190; Iroquois plot with Miamis to massacre Detroit French, 202; neutrality of, 203; Vaudreuil deceived by an Iroquois, 215; Four cantons declare against us, 216; preparations, 217; fifteen hundred men sent against them, 218; they defeat English campaign against us, 221; send deputies to Vaudreuil, 222; English Governor uses every means to induce them to take up arms again, 225; Vaudreuil promises them satisfaction for an insult of our allies and appeases them, ib.; strongly urged to declare against us, 235; Vaudreuil sends them three officers, who bring delegates to Montreal, 236; their interview with Vaudreuil, 239; quarrel with English, 247; six hundred join Nicholson to attack district of Montreal, but abandon him, 252; natural antipathy between these two nations, ib.; why they will always be enemies of the French, 253; reconciled to English, ib.; Vaudreuil gains them by his affability, 256; Foxes form alliance with English through Iroquois, 257; Louis XIV. cedes to Queen Anne his rights over the Cantons, who protest that they are free, 266; English treat with them cautiously, ib.; they renew their alliance with Vaudreuil, 300; alliance with the Foxes, but do not seem to aid them, 305; send belt to Louis XV., v., p. 307.

Iroquois of La Prairie, origin of mission, iii., p. 164, 191; remove to Sault St. Louis and styled Iroquois of the Sault, 191.

Iroquois of the Mountain, see Mountain.

Iroquois of the Sault, on Denonville's expedition, iii., p. 283, n.; some Iroquois of Sault St. Louis killed by Dutch Mohawk party, iv., p. 191; treat with Mohawks, 196; corrupted at Montreal, 198; commanded by Paul at La Prairie, 203; Iroquois attempt to surprise, 216; some captured, ib.; defeat Mohawks on Lake Champlain, 216–7; involve Manteht's party in difficulty, 235; called Karigouistes, 249; attempt to surprise Sault St. Louis, repulsed by Marquis of Crisafi, iv., p. 216; Iroquois of Sault and Mountain under Vaudreuil surprise Black Kettle, 220; on Frontenac's expedition, v., p. 12; bring report of council held by Bellomont, 83; Schuyler tampers with, 166, 204; on Ramzai's expedition, 219; at Montreal, 240; address Gov. of Mass., 273, n., see Ganeyousses, Karigouistes.

Isabel in St. Domingo, first city in New World, i., p. 20.

Isla Santa, Columbus' first name for the continent of America, i., p. 21.

Isle, Charles le Gardeur de Tilly, Sieur de l', iv., p. 143.

Isle des Allumettes, ii., p. 166, n.

Isle aux Chevres, the Annibal repulsed at, v., p. 201, n.

Isle aux Coudres discovered by Cartier, i., p. 116; increased and formed by earthquake, iii., p. 64; Phips at, iv., p. 153.

Isle de France, settlers from desired, iii., p. 81.

Isle of May, i., p. 17

Isle Menane, Lapis lazuli at, i., p. 250.

Isle aux Œufs, Sir Hovenden Walker wrecked at, v., p. 248, 252.

Isle Orleans, called Bacchus Island by Cartier, i., p. 116; Hurons on, ii., p. 258; their piety, 259; Hurons carried off from, 278, etc.; Phips at, iv., p. 166; militia of, 167; d'Orvilliers thrown into, 186.

Isle des Oyseaux, situation and discovery, i., p. 113.

Isle Percée, plundered and church profaned by English, iv., p. 161; Frontenac hears ill tidings at, iv., p. 28; Recollects at, iv., p. 28, 161.

Isle Perrot, Frontenac forms a camp on, iv., p. 269.

Isle à la Pierre, iii., p. 46, n.

Isle à Pierre à Fusil, Cape Breton, v., p. 285.

Isle Platte, near Cape Breton, called also Isle à Pierres à Fusil, v., p. 285.

Isle Royale, (formerly and subsequently Cape Breton Island, which see).

Isles of the States, i., p. 56.

Isle St. Jean, now Prince Edward's Island, v., p. 299; granted to St. Pierre, ib.; to Doublet, 300; projected settlement on, ib.

Isles St. Pierre, their situation, iii., p. 142; now only remaining French possessions, ib., n.

Isle Surgere, or Ship Island, convenient harbor at, vi., p. 15.

Isle Toulouse, or Balize, Perrier de Salverte at, vi., p. 106.

Italians, first discoveries of New World due to, i., p. 107; adventures of an Italian companion of la Sale, iv., p. 112. See Crisafy, Tonti, Bressani.

Itasca Lake, absurdity of this name of Schoolcraft's, iii., p. 207.

Ites, Capt., ship of, taken by de Brouillan, report as to St. John, v., p. 35.

Jacatra, ancient city in Java, i., p. 53.

Jackman, Charles, English, discoveries of, i., p. 44.

Jacques Cartier's Fort, i., p. 117, n.

Jacques Cartier's River, not the St. Croix of Cartier, i., p. 116, n.

Jallot, Medard, St. Denys' valet, left at Caouis, vi., p. 21; acquires repute as a surgeon, 22.

Jamaica, discovered by Columbus and called Santiago, i., p. 20; settled, 27; Spanish Governor of, captured by Huguenots from Fort Caroline, 168; but see Barcia, ib., n.

Jamay, Father Denis, Commissary of the Recollects, arrives in Canada, ii., p. 25, n.

James I. of England grants to Earl of Stirling all the territory wrested from French, i., p. 249.

James, Capt., discoveries of, in Hudson Bay, i., p. 54.

James River, Va., i., p. 50.

Jamestown, Va., founded, i., p. 50; Biard taken to, i., p. 281.

Jane Thomas of St. Agnes of Vannes, hospital nun, arrives, iii., p. 114.

Japan discovered, i., p. 39; the Zipangu of Marco Polo, 40.

Jardin, Capt. du, refuses to receive Jesuits as passengers, i., p. 262, n.

Jemme, English sailor, see Hiens.

Jemset, Jembac, Jemsac, see Fort Gemesic.

Jérémie, Sieur ——, memoir on Hudson Bay, i., p. 90; notice of, v., p. 59; personally known by Charlevoix, ib.; repulses English at Fort Bourbon, 53; sent out in 1708, 304; sufferings, ib.; ordered to deliver fort to English, 305.

Jesuits, Relations of, i., p. 77; ii., p. 93, n.; iii., p. 189, n.; Menendez agrees to take, i., p. 183; takes eight to Florida, 186; Henry IV. wishes some sent to Acadia, i., p. 260; passage refused, 261; justified by Champlain as to the treaty made by Madame de Guercheville in their favor, 263; what neutralized their labors, 275; go to St. Savior's, 275; after its capture, 281; noble conduct of, at the Azores and in England, 284; other Jesuits sent to Canada, ii., p. 35; badly received at Quebec, 36; received in their house by Recollects, ib.; suffer from Calvinists at Quebec, ib.; a French refugee persuades English that they are very rich, ib.; why they alone returned to Canada after its restoration, 65; character of the Jesuits in Canada, 77; why they desire to establish Huron mission, 74; the

JESUITS, (*continued.*)
Dutch speak ill of them to the Hurons, 83; their charity and disinterestedness dispel prejudice of Indians, 85; effect produced in France by their letters, 93; their views in introducing Ursulines and Hospital Nuns in Canada, 100; sufferings in the missions, 113; their occupations, ib.; reflections on their conduct, 114; their exercises and flying missions, 166; Canada Company justifies them against the charge of trading, 168; calumniated in France, 169; some Hurons conspire against them, 231; their intrepidity baffles them, and many conspirators are converted, 232; several obliged to return to France, 237, 250; resign Canadian parishes to Bishop of Petræa, iii., p. 22; de Mési's complaints to the Council against them, and the Council's opinion, 75; the Court wishes to compel them to frenchify the Indians, 96; Colbert lays aside his prejudice against, on this point, ib.; Iroquois said by Bellomont to complain of, &c., v., p. 86; Bellomont threatens to hang any found in the Iroquois cantons, 112; why they abandon Louisiana, 129; the cantons ask for Jesuits and receive them well, 153; a Jesuit accompanies La Motte Cadillac to Detroit, 154; they establish several missions among the Louisiana Indians, vi., p. 76. See MISSIONARIES.

JEUNE, FATHER PAUL LE, Jesuit, sketch of, iii., p. 21, n.; arrives at Quebec, ii., p. 65; selected by Commander de Sylleri to establish Indian town, 98; nominated by Queen Mother for the bishopric of Canada, iii., p. 21; works of, i., p. 77, iii., p. 22, n.

JOGUES, FATHER ISAAC, Jesuit, sketch of, ii., p. 197; visits the Chippewas, 137; recalled, ib.; taken by Iroquois rather than desert his neophytes, 140; cruelly treated on Lake Champlain, 143; converts many, 148; writes to Montmagny on Hurons and Iroquois, 154; learns that death is decided on, 156; accompanies Indians to fish, ib.; returns to the village, 157; reply to a Dutch officer who offers to save him, 158; his escape, ib.; in France, 160; Queen Mother sends for him, 161; the Pope permits him to say mass with mutilated hands, ib.; his character, ib.; visits Mohawks twice, 186; is abandoned by his guides on his third visit, 194; has a presentiment of his death, 195; seized and put to death, 196; conduct of his murderer, 197; his Iroquois name, ib.; effect produced on a Norman gentleman by the pèrusal of his life and sufferings, iii., p. 113; Smith loses his Journal, 186, n.

JOHANNIS, French officer distinguished at St. John, v., p. 213.

JOHN, FRANCIS, Frenchman, guide to Menendez, i., p. 196, n.

JOHNSON, CAPT., commands Connecticut company under Fitz John Winthrop, i., p. 146, n.

JOLIET, SIEUR LOUIS, sketch of, iii., p. 179; discovers the Micissipi with F. Marquette, i., p. 57; iii., p. 179; returns to Quebec, iii., p. 199, n.; consulted by La Salle; 122, n, 198, n.; rewarded with Anticosti island, 179, n.; his wife taken by English but exchanged, iv., p. 153, 187.

JOLIET, ZACHARY, brother of preceding, bears Durantaye's letter to Frontenac, iv., p. 54.

JOLIET, MLLE., (CLARE F. BISSOT,) wife of Louis, taken, iv., p. 153; exchanged, 187.

JONCAIRE, SIEUR THOMAS DE, French officer, Iroquois deputies ask that he return with them, v., p. 102; Governor consents, ib.; negotiates with Senecas, his influence with them, 105; sent to Onondaga, 138; to Seneca, 139; returns to the Iroquois, successful negotiations, 140: Iroquois tell de Callieres that Joncaire did not press the point of restoring prisoners, 145; he admits it, 145; heads the Iroquois of Sault St. Louis to compliment Hurons, 147; also those of the Mountain, 148; accompanies deputies to the General Congress on their return to bring back prisoners, 153; recovers only a few, 154; accompanies Seneca deputies to their canton and brings thence a head chief, 159; returns with him, 160; notifies Governor Gen. of Schuyler's intrigues, 164; Senecas send him to Governor of Canada to complain of Ottawa aggressions, 165; sent back with promises of prompt satisfaction, 165-6; his prudence, 203; commands rear guard in

Ramezai's expedition, 219; well received by Senecas and brings delegates to Montreal, 236; negotiates successfully with Senecas, 239, 256; at Niagara, 308, n.

JONCHERE, (JONQUIERE) MR. DE LA, cannot obtain permission to sell cargo at Vera Cruz, vi., p. 18.

JONQUIERE, JAMES PETER DE TAFANELL, MARQUIS DE LA, Governor of Canada, vi., p. 18, n.

JORDIS, SIEUR DES, Commandant at Catarocouy, induces some Ottawas to accompany French against Iroquois, v., p. 12; on Ramezai's expedition, 219.

JOSEPH, Iroquois captive, and first baptized, ii., p. 107.

JOSEPH, a Christian, gives notice of attack on Detroit, v., p. 257.

JOURDAN, river in Carolina, discovery of, i., p. 134; sought in vain by Ribaut. 136.

JOUTEL, SIEUR, Notice of his "Journal Historique du dernier voyage," i., p. 87–8; accompanies la Sale on his last voyage, iv., p. 63; la Sale appoints him to complete Fort St. Louis, 72; he puts in irons some who conspired to kill him and delivers them to la Sale with proofs of their plot, 74; receives orders to join la Sale, 74; left at Fort St. Louis as commandant, 83; believes he can suspend orders on one occasion, ib.; hears bad news of la Sale, ib.; uneasiness on seeing many of his people die or desert, 87; mutiny against him, ib.; makes sure of Duhaut, 87; la Sale gives him care of camp, 92; his orders, ib.; information given him by Larchevêque after la Sale's death, and his reply, 97; sent to the Cenis for provisions, 98; what occurred on the way, ib.; his reception by the Indians, 99; sends his comrades back to camp and remains with Cenis, 100; adventures of two French deserters, who come to see him, ib.; he warns Larchevêque of Hiens' design to kill him, and reconciles them, 104; starts for Illinois, 107; at Akansas, 108; in the Illinois, 110; obliged to winter there and goes to France, 111.

JOUVENCY, F. JOSEPH, Jesuit, His Historia Societatis Jesu, noticed, i., p. 87.

JOYBERT, SIEUR DE SOULANGES ET DE MARSON, PIERRE, Fort Gemisick and Port Royal surrender to, iii., p. 138, n. See MARSON.

JUAN FERNANDEZ, Islands of, discovered, i., p. 43; names of, ib.

JUCHEREAU DE ST. DENYS, NICHOLAS, wounded at siege of Quebec, iv., p. 177; ennobled, ib., n.; notice of, ib.

JUCHEREAU SIEUR, attempts a settlement on the Wabash but abandons it, v., p. 133–4.

JUCHEREAU DE ST. DENYS, see ST. DENYS.

JUMEAU, FATHER EMMANUEL, Recollect, at Isle Percée, iv., p. 161.

JUSTICE, how administered in Canada before appointment of Intendant and Superior Councils, iii., p. 66; how subsequently, 68; subaltern judges, 69; salaries, ib.

KADESQUIT, probably Bangor, i., p. 275, n.

KAIHOHAGUÉ, Colden's name for La Famine, iii., p. 254, n.

KAINE'S REGIMENT, loss of, in Walker's shipwreck, v., p. 247, n.

KAKIOUKIOUAY, Indian name of Bourbon river or Port Nelson, iii., p. 234, n.

KAMALASTIGOUIA, or FOND DU LAC, iii., p. 245.

KAMTSCHATKA, i., p. 60.

KANEEDA, near Onondaga, v., p. 138, n.

KAPPAS, Louysiana tribe that have disappeared, iv., p. 109, n.; Charlevoix mistaken, the Quapaws still subsist, ib, n.

KARESIS or KAREZI, Indians near Sioux, iii., p. 106.

KARIGOUISTES, Colden's name for Sault St. Louis Iroquois, iv., p. 249. See GANNEYOUSSES, IROQUOIS OF THE SAULT.

KASKASKIAS, Illinois tribe found by Marquette, iii., p. 181; called Kuilka in Thevenot, ib.; visited by Marquette, v., p. 131; Courtemanche prevents their attacking Canses, 142; remove with Chief Roensa to the Mississippi, 152, n.; at New Orleans bewail missionaries killed by the Natchez and Yazoos, vi., p. 102; marks of fidelity and religion, ib.

KASKEBÉ, (Charlevoix's form for Casco Bay) fort in New England taken by de Portneuf, iv., p. 133; English too late to save, 136; it was Falmouth, now Portland, Maine, 133, n.

KIENOUCHES, Ottawa tribe, iii., p. 218, n.

KENNEBEC, called in Charlevoix Kinibequi, Quinibequi, (i., p. 49;) explored, i., p.

KENNEBEC, (*continued.*)
49; De Monts explores to, 253; Capuchin hospice on, ii., p. 202; Druillettes labors among Indians on, ib., p. 214; under jurisdiction of Plymouth, ib., n.; English on warned off by St. Lusson, iii., p. 170; Charlevoix supposes they removed, ib.; Portneuf at, iv., p. 133; the English think of settling on this river, v., 92; Villebon claims it as boundary of New France, ib., n.; English by surprise settle on this river, 270; result, ib.

KENTAIENTON, an Erie town, ii., p. 266, n.

KENTE, Cayuga town on Quinte Bay, iii., p. 109; Indians seized at, 276, n.

KERTK, (KIRKE,) SIR DAVID, notice of, vi., p. 124; French refugee in English service summons Quebec, ii., p. 44; captures a French fleet, 45; haste to capture Quebec before announcement of peace, 52, 54; at Quebec, ib.; his opinion of Canada, ib.; harshness to Champlain 50, 55, n.; duped by his own bad faith, 54; for various forms of name see ii., p. 44, n.; aids Shirley to reduce Acadia, 59, n.; obtains grant of Newfoundland, vi., p. 124; succeeds Ld. Baltimore at Ferryland, ib.; La Tour applies to, iii., p. 131, n.; Radisson marries daughter of, 232, n.; receives him on return from Hudson Bay, ib.

KERTK, (KIRKE,) LOUIS, brother of preceding, notice of, vi., p. 124; takes Quebec, ii., p. 48; acts well, 50; induces many settlers to remain, ib.; changes somewhat, 53.

KERTK, (KIRKE,) THOMAS, brother of preceding, notice of, vi., p. 124; at Quebec, ii., p. 48; nearly captured on his return to Tadoussac by Emeric de Caen, 51; ignoble conduct, ib.; killed, vi., p. 124.

KEWEENAW, BAY, iii., p. 50.

KICAPOUS, (KIKAPOOS,) Indian tribe not summoned by de St. Lusson, iii., p. 168; kill Father de la Ribourde, 212; promise to send delegates to Montreal, v., p. 142; join Foxes against Detroit 257.

KICHESIPIRINI or HEHONQUERONON, Indians at Ile des Allumettes on the Ottawa, conversion of chief, ii., p. 164; ratify peace with Iroquois, p. 182.

KICHICHOUANE, iii., p. 271. See FORT QUITCHITCHOUEN.

KIEFT, WILLIAM, Gov. of New Netherland, aids F. Jogues and F. Bressani, 161, 174, n.; announces death of Jogues to Montmagny, 195.

KIGGINS, Captain of the Arundel, called Sikik by Charlevoix, v., p. 30; attacks Fort Naxoat, ib.

KILISTINON, KIRISTINONS, CRISTINAUX or CRIQUES, (CREES,) Indian tribe of the Algonquin race, their religion, character, inroads, iii., p. 107; Dablon and Druillettes set out to found mission among, 39; divisions of, 107, n.

KIMPECH, town of, i., p. 30.

KINDERHOOK, French party defeated near, v., p. 49.

KINNIBEKI. See KENNEBEC.

KINO, FATHER EUSEBIUS FRANCIS, German Jesuit, explores Hila and Colorada, i., p. 62.

KIOTSAETON, Mohawk wounded trying to save F. Jogues, ii., p. 151, n.

KIRIVIDI, English post in Newfoundland, English captured at, v., p. 45.

KIRKE, SIR DAVID. See KERTK.

KIRONOMES, Texas tribe, iv., p. 88, n.

KISKAKONS, an Ottawa tribe, their difficulty on account of murder of Annanhac, a Seneca chief, iii., p. 218; allowed to build forts, 220; send deputies to Montreal, 221; refuse reparation, ib.; Onaské chief of, iv., p. 277.

KOLLY, MESSRS., father and son, among the first victims of Natchez massacre, vi., p. 81.

KOLNA, IVAN W', or JOHN OF KOLNO, Polish navigator, i., p. 105. See JOHN SCALVE.

KONDIARONK, Huron chief, known among French by name of The Rat, which see, iv., p. 12.

KOROA, La Sale at, iii., p. 215, n.

KOUACHOUC, or SAINTES HUILES RIVER, Hudson Bay, iv., p. 37, n.

KEYN, the GREAT MOHAWK, iii., p. 191, n.; 196, n.; 292, n.; death, iv., p. 128-9.

KUIT, Mascoutin chief, v., p. 263, n.

KWAPAHAG, Abénaquis of, join in letter to Governor of Massachusetts, v., p. 273.

LABADIE, JAN, endeavors to ransom Father Jogues, ii., p. 148, n.; announces his death, 195, n.

LABRADOR, or LABORADOR, discovered, i., pp. 18, 20, 105; Fort Pontchartrain,

iii., p. 145 ; noticed, 226 ; Bourdon coasts along, 230.

Labrador in Cape Breton, (Bras d'or,) v., p. 282, 285.

Ladak, i., p. 62.

Lachau, or Lachere, a French soldier unjustly punished by Captain Albert, devoured by his comrades, i., p. 147-8.

Lachine, origin of name, iii., p. 122, n.; massacre by Iroquois at, iv., p. 29 ; English complicity in massacre, p. 31, n.; Iroquois ravages at, 191, n.; Remi curé at, p. 296.

Ladrone Islands discovered by Magellan, i., p. 32 ; called by him Archipelago of St. Lazarus, and now Marian Islands, ib.; occupied by Spaniards, 59 ; converted, ib.; names of, ib.

Laet, John, de. Account of his Novus Orbis, i., p. 77 ; of his Notæ ad Dissertationem Hugonis Grotii, 79 ; of his Responsio, ib.; criticised by Poisson, ib.; Champlain controverts his remarks on Jesuits, 264 ; see 280.

Lafitau, Father Joseph Francis, French Jesuit, notice of his "Mœurs des Sauvages," i., p. 91 ; discovers ginseng, v., p. 307, n.

Lagaspi, Miguel Lopez de, Spaniard, settles Philippines, i., p. 40 ; builds Cebu, 42 ; takes possession of Ladrones, 59.

Laguide, Madeleine de, niece of Talon, wife of Gov. Perrot, iii., p. 123.

Lake Alimipegon, or Alimibegong, empties into Lake Superior ; F. Allouez visits Christian Indians there, iii., p. 107.

Lake of the Assiniboils, erroneous statement as to, iii., p. 207, n.; James' Bay reached by way of, 230, n.

Lake Champlain, discovered and named by Champlain, i., p. 51 ; ii., p. 15, 18, n.; errors as to, i., p. 70 ; Mohawk name of, ii., p. 18, n.; Fort St. Anne, erected on island in, iii., p. 90, vi., p. 126; fatal encounter near, iv., p. 128 ; Mohawks defeated on, iv., p. 217 ; English repulsed on, v., p. 219.

Lake of the Conibas, above New Mexico, discovered, i., p. 51.

Lake Entouohonorons, Ontario so called, ii., p. 28.

Lake Erie, first crossed by Dollier de Casson, iii., p. 122, n.

Lake Gannentaha, or Onondaga, ii., p. 189, n., 276 ; salt springs near, ib.; Frontenac at, v., p. 15 ; Bruyas at, 103.

Lake George, Florida, probably visited by d'Ottigny, i., p. 173, n.

Lake George, called by French Lake St. Sacrement, ii., p. 15, p. 186 ; error as to, i., p. 70 ; English at, v., p. 220.

Lake Huron, currents of, iii., p. 171.

Lake Kisikami, ii., p. 246, n.

Lake Laurichoca, source of Amazon, i., p. 55.

Lake Michigan, iii., p. 120 ; various forms and meaning of name, ib., n.; F. Marquette on, 171.

Lake of the Mistassins, extent of, meaning of name, iii., p. 232.

Lake Nemiscau, English ascend to, i., p. 56 ; F. Albanel at, iii., p. 232.

Lake Nikisipique, (Winnipeseogee) rendezvous, v., p. 204, n.

Lake Nipissing, Champlain goes to Hurons by way of, ii., p. 27, n.; Algonquins at, 29.

Lake Onondaga, ii., p. 189.

Lake Ontario, called Lake of the Entouohonorons, iii., p. 176, n.

Lake Pontchartrain, Perrier sends to Choctaws on, vi., p. 89.

Lake St. Clare visited by Dollier de Casson, ii., p. 122, n.

Lake St. Francis, 1,200 Iroquois at, iii., p. 304 ; cannon concealed at, iv., p. 34 ; Iroquois at, 232.

Lake St. John, Dablon and Druillettes at, iii., p. 39 ; description of, ib.; Albanel winters at, iii., p. 231.

Lake St. Pierre, or St. Peters, situation and extent, Cartier at, i., p. 118 ; Jogues taken near, 140 ; Bressani also, 171, n ; limit of Montreal jurisdiction, iii., p. 256.

Lake St. Sacrement, now Lake George, discovered and named by F. Jogues, ii., p. 15, 186, n.; he makes canoes at 187, n.; Denonville pursues Mohawks and Mohegans to, iii., p. 307 ; La Plaque discovers Anglo-Indian force on, iv., p. 143 ; error as to corrected, i., p. 70.

Lake St. Thomas, Attikamegues near, ii., p. 118.

Lake Simcoe, ii., p. 28, n.

Lake Superior, remarks on its currents iii., p. 171.

LAKE OF THE TWO MOUNTAINS, its situation and extent, iii., p. 273 ; Father Garreau killed near, ib.; Indian mission removed to, v., p. 308, n.

LAKE WARE, i., p. 172, n.

LALANDE, JOHN, young Frenchman of Dieppe, killed with Father Jogues, ii., p. 191-6.

LALANDE, ELIZABETH, taken by English, v., p. 153 ; suggests to Phipps an exchange of prisoners, is sent to Frontenac, who consents to it, 187. See vi., p. 128.

LALEMANT, proper form of name of three missionaries, Charles, Gabriel and Jerome, given by Charlevoix as LALLEMANT, which see.

LALIBERTÉ, of Three Rivers, martyr of conjugal chastity, iii., p. 52.

LALLEMANT, FATHER CHARLES, at Pentagoët with la Saussaye, ii., p. 35 ; at Quebec, ib.; twice wrecked, 46 ; letter of, in Mercure, i., p. 76 ; induces de Lauson to cede Montreal to Associates, ii., p. 130.

LALLEMANT, F. GABRIEL, nephew of preceding, goes to Hurons, ii., p. 210, n,; refuses to fly from St. Louis on approach of Iroquois, 219 ; taken, ib.; burnt, 222-5 ; body carried to St. Mary's, 221, n.; thence to Quebec, ib.; sketch of, 225, n.; Indian name, ib.

LALLEMANT, FATHER JEROME, Jesuit, sketch of, ii., 267, n.; uncle of preceding, strange adventure of, at Ile des Allumettes, ii., p. 166 ; goes to France to solicit aid from Canada Co. but is not heard, 237 ; succeeded as Superior by le Mercier, 267, n.; brought back by Bp. of Petræa, iii., p. 22 ; sends missionaries to various places, 29 ; result of interceding for a squaw's pardon with d'Avaugour, 53 ; warned of earthquake, 58.

LAMBERVILLE, FATHER JAMES DE, Jesuit, joins de la Barre from Onondaga, iii., p. 250; Governor of New York asks Iroquois to surrender, 265 ; leaves Onondaga for Quebec, 268 ; founds a Mohawk mission, iv., p. 285 ; first conversation with Catharine Tegahkouita and its result, ib.; he baptizes her, 236 ; defends her when calumniated, 287 ; sent to Onondaga, v., p. 155, n.; dies at Sault St. Louis, iv., p. 286.

LAMBERVILLE, FATHER JOHN DE, Jesuit, elder brother of preceding, missionary at Onondaga, reports to Frontenac, iii., p. 218 ; induces Iroquois to treat at Catarocouy, 220 ; informs Gov. of New York of what passed between his envoy and the Onondagas, 253 ; reports to Mr. de la Barre the disposition of the Senecas, 250, 256 ; detects intrigues of Governor of New York, and goes to Quebec to notify Denonville ; he is sent back to Onondaga and negotiates successfully, 267 ; reports at Quebec, 268 ; orders he receives, ib.; Governor's uneasiness as to, 277 ; used to draw several chiefs to Catarocouy, without being aware of the design, 278 ; generosity of the Onondagas on this occasion, 278 ; interview between him and Onondagas who had taken some prisoners near Catarocouy, 299; Denonville urges him to try to detach Onondagas from other cantons, 302 ; his success, 303 ; Denonville bears testimony in his letters to the Minister to Lamberville's services for the colony, 307; Indians beg de Callieres to recall him from France, v., p. 94.

LAMETS, SIEUR, de la Saussaye's pilot, escapes into the woods after capture of St. Savior's, i., p. 280 ; re-embarks, 281 ; called le Bailleur by Biard, 280, n.

LANCASTER, attacked by Abenakis, v., p. 78, n.; 167, n.

LAND OF CONCORD, New Holland, i., p. 52.

LANDE, LA, see LALANDE.

LANZAROTA, one of the Canaries, i., p. 14.

LANZAROTE, discovers the Senegal, i., p. 16.

LAPIS LAZULI, rock of, on coast of Acadia, i., p. 250.

LA PRAIRIE DE LA MAGDELEINE, granted to James de la Ferté, Abbé de la Magdeleine, and by him to Jesuits, iii., p. 164; Iroquois Christians settle there, ib.; why unable to remain, 191 ; remove to Portage river, iv., p. 123; Frontenac, assembles troops at, 146 ; Indian council at, ib.; Iroquois ravages near, 193; action at, with Peter Schuyler's party, 202.

LARCHEVÊQUE, of a good family at Bayonne, iv., p. 94, n.; accompanies la Sale on his last voyage, 89 ; approves plan of assassinating Moranget, 91 ; a partner of la Sale, 94 ; he and Duhaut divide his

effects, 97; nearly killed by Hiens, but saved by Joutel, 104; why he did not follow Cavelier to Illinois, 107; captured by the Spaniards, 113; sent to Spain, then to Mexico, and then to New Mexico to work in the mines, 113, n., 114; called d'Yvetot in some accounts, p. 94.

LASSA, capital of Thibet, i., pp. 62–3.

LATTAIGNANT, GABRIEL, one of the Hundred Associates, ii., p. 39.

LAUDONNIERE, (LANDONNIERE, LAUDOUINIÈRE,) RENÉ DE `GOULAINE DE, French gentleman, sent to Florida with three ships, i., p. 148; present to, from Charles IX., p. 149; what befell him in Dolphin and May Rivers, ib.; explores, 151; deluded by mine-hunting, ib.; repents, ib.; deliberates as to a site, 152; does not restore Charlefort, ib.; builds Caroline on the May, (St. John's,) ib.; refuses to accompany Saturiova to war, 159; wrests prisoners from him, 161; turns a storm to account, 163; mutiny, 165; apparently suppressed, 166; breaks out afresh, 167; their violence, ib.; punishment of those who returned to Caroline, 170; reconciles Saturiova and his enemies, 172; precautions for provisions and defence, 173; proposed conquest of Apalache Mountains, 173; aids Outina, 174; out of provisions, 175; an unjust war, 176; relieved by English when about to sail back to France, 177; what prevents his departure, 179; hears of complaints made against him to the Court, 180; wishes to return to France, 181; Ribaut leaves him in command of Caroline, and against his advice goes to attack the Spanish squadron with all the colony forces, 193; difficult position, 200; attack, 201; valor and escape, 202; saves part of his people, 204; their extremity, ib.; young Ribaut treats him ill, 205; long sick in England, 206; reception in France, ib.; account of his Histoire Notable, i., p. 71.

LAUSON, JOHN DE, member of the Hundred Associates, ii., p. 130, 244, n.; cedes Montreal to Associates, ii., p. 130; appointed Governor-General of New France, 244; prior services, ib.; condition of the Colony, 245; defeats Mohawks, 252; delivers F. Poncet from the hands of the Iroquois, 255; grants lands at Onondaga to Jesuits, 264; blamed for suffering Hurons to be carried off from Isle Orleans, 269; why he put up with a Mohawk insult, ib.; returns to France, 279; Intendant Champigny related to, iii., p. 282, n.

LAUSON-CHARNY, CHARLES DE, Acting Governor-General of New France, ii., p. 279, n.; submits to Mohawk insolence, 278–9; reply to Onondagas, 281; returns to France, 279, n.; iii., p. 14; ordained priest, ii., p, 279, n.; returns with Bp. Laval, ib.

LAUSON, JOHN DE, Seneschal of New France, brother of preceding, killed by Iroquois, ii., p. 279, n.; iii., p. 35, 66.

LAUSON, SIEUR DE, commands an English prize, v., p, 27; Micmacs with, ib.

LAVAL, FATHER, ANTHONY, Jesuit, Royal Professor of Hydrography at Toulon, arrives in Louysiana, vi., p. 64; unable to make observation at mouth of Micissipi, ib.; praised by Count de Toulouse, ib.

LAVAL-MONTMORENCY, FRANCIS XAVIER DE, sketch of, iii., p. 20; known as Abbé de Montigny, ib.; appointed Bishop of Petræa and Vicar Apostolic of New France, ib.; arrives, iii., p. 20; opposes liquor trade, p. 55; complains to the King, 56; Mesy quarrels with, 73; made bishop of Quebec, 122; obtains revenues of Abbey of Maubec, ib.; goes to France, 123; resigns, death of, v., p. 210, n.

LAVARE, castle of, intended for De la Warre, iii., p. 72;

LAVERDIERE AND CASGRAIN, Abbés, discover Champlain's tomb, ii., p. 283; edit Champlain, vi., p. 123; edit Jesuit Journal, 129.

LAW, JOHN, forms Western company, vi., p. 37; sends out colonists, 68, n.

LAYE, SIEUR DE, commands colonists in attack on Natchez, vi., p. 100; fails to blockade fort, 109.

LAZOU, CAPT., vessel of, seized by mutineers, vi., p. 67, n.

LEAKE, SIR JOHN, English naval commander, ravages Newfoundland, v., p. 162, n.

LEGAUFFRE, REV. MR., proposed for Bishop of Montreal, ii., p. 183, iii., p. 20, n.

LEIGHTON, JOHN, High Sheriff of York, ordered to apprehend Father Rale, v., p. 271, n.

LEISLER, JACOB, Governor of New York, agrees with New England to invade Montreal, iv., p. 145, n.; seizes pork for men, 146, n.; accepts Winthrop as commander, 146, n.; arrests Winthrop, 147, n.; releases him, ib.

LEMAITRE, see MAITRE.

LENGLET DU FRESNOY, errors of, i., p. 69; works noticed, 69, 93, 94.

LEOGANE, St. Domingo, v., p. 118.

LEON, ALONZO DE, reaches site of La Salle's fort, iv., p. 113, n.

LEON, JOHN PONCE DE, conquers Porto Rico, i., p. 27; discovers and names Florida, 28, 134; Bay of, 171.

LEPINAI, see L'EPINAI.

LEROLES, LOUIS DE CANCHY, SIEUR DE, cousin of de Tracy taken by Iroquois, iii., p. 87; see NOIROLLE.

LERY, BARON DE LERY ET DE ST. JUST, VISCOUNT DE GRIEU, attempts to settle Sable Island, i., p. 107, n., 243; doubts as to, vi., p. 123.

LESCALETTE, or LESQUELET, SIEUR DE, French officer sent to Pensacola by Chateaumorand, v., p. 118.

LESCARBOT, MARK, advocate in the Parliament of Paris, i., p. 257; his works, i., p. 75, 257; remarks on Verazani's discoveries, 109; he imagines a lake in Florida, 173; accompanies Poutrincourt to Acadia and renders great service to the settlement of Port Royal, 257; his eulogy on Mamberton, 270; he reproaches Champlain, ii., p. 90.

LETTRES EDIFIANTES noticed, i., p. 88–9.

LEVERETT, CAPT. JOHN, with Sedgwick reduces Port Royal, iii., p. 134.

LEVERETT, MR., of Council of Massachusetts, at Port Royal, v., p. 196, n.

LEVINGSTON, see LIVINGSTON.

LEWIN'S LAND discovered, i., p. 53.

LEWIS ISLAND, pretended discovery of, i., p. 63.

L'HERMITE, MR., Major of Placentia, drives English out of two redoubts at Bay of Bulls, (Baboul) v., p. 36; Acadians ask him as a leader to retake Port Royal, v., p. 256; why Governor of Placentia refused to send him, ib.; sent to obtain permission for Acadians to remove, 296, n.

LIEGE, BARON DE MEAN, DEAN OF, v., p. 174.

LIEGOIS, BROTHER JOHN, Jesuit lay brother, killed by Mohawk, ii., p. 260; notice of, ib., n.

LIGNERY (? CONSTANT LE MARCHANT) DE, commands a company on Ramezay's expedition, v., p. 219.

LILLE, MR. DE, first lieutenant of the Count de Champmêlin, summons Governor of Pensacola, vi., p. 58; apparently left in command, 60, n.

LIMA, or VILLA DE LOS REYES, founded by Pizarro, i., p. 37.

LIMITS of New France and New England, v., p. 92.

LIMOGES, FATHER JOSEPH DE, Jesuit, notice of, vi., p. 76, n.; goes from Canada to Louysiana, v., p. 129; founds Baiagoula mission, vi., p. 76, n.; ordered to leave it, v., p. 129; returns to France, vi., p. 76, n.

LIMOILOU, residence of Cartier, i., p. 131.

LIMOSNY, ANTHONY DE, Gentleman of Saintonge, lost on de Gourgues' expedition, i., p. 236.

LINARES, F. DE ALENCASTRE, NOROÑA Y SILVA, Duke de, Viceroy of Mexico, vi., p. 21, n.

LINCTOT, SIEUR GODEFROY DE, Canadian gentleman, distinguished in Newfoundland, v., p. 174; negotiates with Foxes, 308.

LINSCHOOTEN, JOHN HUYGHENS VAN, i., p. 46.

LIONNE, FATHER MARTIN DE, Jesuit, called by Charlevoix Martin Lionnes, missions of on Gulf of St. Laurence, ii., p. 119, iii., p. 30, n.

LIOTOT, La Sale's surgeon on his last voyage, iv., p. 89; resolves to punish Moranget for violent language, 91; sent to Cenis for provisions, 98; killed by a sailor, 103.

LIQUOR TRADE IN CANADA, troubles as to, iii., p. 53; discussions as to in Canada and France, 195; forbidden in Indian villages, 196; disorders caused by in Acadia, 308; Brisacier's letter on, iv., p. 230; Ottawa deputies at General Congress ask suppression of, v., p. 153; evil effects on domiciliated Iroquois, 204.

LIRIA-BARWICH, succeed to duchy of Veraguas, i., p. 25.

LISBON, English fleet intended to reduce Canada, sent to, v., p. 222.

LISLE, CHEVALIER DE, commandant at Three Rivers, ii., p. 91; praised, ib.; succeeded by Champflours, 123.

LITTLE CAPE BRETON, v., p. 284.

LIVERPOOL, modern name of Port Rossignol, i., p. 251.

LIVINGSTON, PHILIP, notice of, v., p. 175; sent to Quebec, ib.; nephew of Col. Vetch, ib.; sent to Vaudreuil by Nicholson, 233; entertained at Penobscot by Baron St. Castin, who subsequently saves his life, ib., n.

LO, CHEVALIER DE, naval ensign, killed at siege of St. John, Newf., v., p. 173.

LOCHON, sent to work Marameg mines, vi., p. 18, n.

LOIRE DES URSINS, MESS. DE LA, brothers, one sent to Natchez, vi., p. 24; escape from Natchez, 26; start from Maubile with Bienville, to punish them, 28; the elder perishes in the massacre after a gallant defence, 82.

LONDON HUDSON BAY COMPANY claims all Hudson Bay as English, and orders William and Mary to be proclaimed, iv., p. 37.

LONGPRÉ, JAMES SIMON, SIEUR DE, father of Mother Catharine of St. Augustine refuses to allow her to go to Canada, iii., p. 112; what induces him to yield, 113.

LONG SAULT, or LONG RAPIDS, on the Ottawa, Dollard's famous fight at, iii, p. 33; Iroquois posted at, iv., p. 199; Black Kettle defeated at, 220.

LONGUEIL, CHARLES LE MOYNE, BARON DE, notice of, v., p. 256, 310, n.; commands militia in Denonville's campaign, iii., p. 283, n.; with Indians reconnoitres English fleet, iv., p. 167; drives English boats back to ships, 175; exploit of, 179; wounded, 180; negotiations at Onondaga, v., p. 166; again there, 236, 9; King's Lieutenant at Montreal, 236; left there in command during expected siege of Quebec, 246; again negotiating at Onondaga, 256; administered colony after Vaudreuil's death, 310, n.; why not made Governor, ib.

LONGUEIL, MR. DE, killed at Cap St. Antoine, v., p. 307, n.

LONGUEVILLE, CHEVALIER DE LA, brings Indians for siege of Pensacola to Rio Perdido, vi., p. 56.

LORD WESTON'S ISLAND, i., p. 54.

LORETTE, Huron Indian mission three leagues from Quebec founded by F. Chaumonot, iii., p. 154, and n.; Mohawks emigrate to, 163; Hurons of with de la Barre, 249; at La Prairie, iv., p. 203; with Manteht, 233; on Frontenac's expedition, v., p. 12; prisoners given to, 11.

LOTBINIERE, MARY FRANCES CHARTIER DE, widow of Pierre de Joybert de Soulanges et de Marson, iii., p. 187, n.

LOUBOIS, CHEVALIER DE, Major of New Orleans, commander in the Natchez war, vi., p. 94; joins army at Tonica Bay, 95; fate of his envoys sent to propose peace, 96; Natchez terms, 95; inactivity blamed, 94, n.; at Natchez, 97; fruitless attempt at parley, ib.; attacks forts, 98; delays, ib.; seeks only to rescue captives, 99; Natchez elude him, 100; marches to deliver St. Denys at Natchitoches, but hears of enemy's repulse, 118.

LOUIS XII. of France, Canada not first discovered in his reign, i., p. 107.

LOUIS XIII. of France grants privileges to company of New France, ii., p. 39; demands restitution of Canada from England, 58.

LOUIS XIV. of France, ordinance and regulations as to Canadian parishes, iii., p. 24; writes to de la Barre, 25; acts in favor of clergy of New France, 26; sends aid to Canada, and a commissary to take possession of Placentia, 53; prohibits liquor trade with Indians, 55; sends more aid to Canada, and resumes the Colony into his own hands, 65; includes it in grant to West India Co., 79; petitioned for colonists from certain provinces, 80; orders investigation, and if necessary, trial of de Mésy, 81; sends settlers, and the Carignan-Salieres regiment to Canada, 81; grants freedom of trade, 99; grants Placentia with the title of Governor to Sieur Gargot, 146; sends Poype as governor and commissary there, ib.; instructions to that officer, 147; letters to Governor-General and Intendant in re-

LOUIS XIV., (*continued.*) gard to their disputes and the Superior Council, 196; his measures as to the Indian liquor trade, ib.; instructions to de la Barre and de Meules, 216; dispatch to de la Barre, 226; sends aid to Canada, 226, 255; his orders to de la Barre, 255; complains in vain of English invasion of Port Nelson, 270; Denonville's representation to on the proposed arrangement between the crowns in regard to Hudson Bay, 273; orders in consequence, ib.; orders as to Iroquois taken in war, 275; explains his orders as to distant posts, 296; approves projected conquest of New York, iv., p. 21; reappoints Frontenac, 22; his instructions, ib.; directs him to favor Northern Company, 23; recommendations as to Acadia and New York, ib.; well concerted measures for taking New York, 24; approves Denonville's memoir, but not the New York expedition, 36; advice as to maintaining war, 46; strikes a medal to commemorate defence of Quebec, 190; assumes defensive in Canada, 212; praises the Abenaquis and writes Frontenac in their favor, 214; his measures to prevent English reaching Quebec, and to expel them from Newfoundland, 222; wishes Frontenac to drive Iroquois to the wall, 263; orders in regard to Fort Pemkuit, Hudson Bay and Newfoundland, 275; suppresses most of the remote posts, 276; again orders attack on Fort Pemkuit, v., p. 24; orders to Frontenac, 52; instructions to d'Iberville, 54; not indemnified for Canadian expenses by the capture of Fort Bourbon, 59; prohibits French going to upper country, 65; opinions as to this order and its modification, 66; instructions to Nesmond for New England expedition, 71; ordinance against voyageurs, 77; forbids officers on frontier posts to trade, ib.; orders to de Callieres in regard to Fort Catarocouy, 97; sends him orders through Governor of New England to arrest hostilities, 98; sends de Fontenu to visit Acadia, 113; declines to allow Huguenots in Carolina to settle in Louisiana, 127; measures to establish religion in that province, 129; orders Canadians to be sent to Placentia to attack English, 172; permits manufactures in Canada under conditions, 181; why he cedes to Queen Anne, Acadia, Newfoundland and Hudson Bay, 266; his annual outlay for Canada, 288; grants Crozat monopoly of Louisiana, and extensive concessions, vi., p. 7; instructions to La Motte Cadillac as to the formation of a Louysiana Council, ib.; death of, v., p. 307, n.

LOUIS XV., accession of, v., p. 307, n.; does not receive well a wampum belt, ib.

LOUISBOURG, formerly HAVRE à L'ANGLOIS, v., p. 284; taken possession of, 296; city founded, ib.; its position, ib.; religious concerns, ib.; Costebelle governor of, ib.

LOUISE, Algonquin woman, her fervor and virtues, iv., p. 307.

LOUISIANA, LOUYSIANA, name given by la Sale to part of the Micissipi Valley, iv., p. 58; its limits, ib.; English efforts to excite Indians against us, v., p. 211; various opinions as to, vi., p. 11; slow growth of, ib.; in 1700, ib.; when it took the form of a colony, 15; condition when Crozat took it and when he gave it up, 32; its commercial availability, 33; Crozat's ideas, 36; Chickasaw design to destroy, p. 79; coin struck for at Rochelle, 77, 122.

LOUVIGNY, LOUIS DE LA PORTE, SIEUR DE, notice of, iv., p. 137, 252, n.; seconded captain, ib.; commandant at Mackinac, pp. 137, 218, 237, 242; fears a rupture, 250; brings down convoy, 252; succeeded by la Motte Cadillac, p. 264; winter expedition against Iroquois, v., p. 10; to command expedition against Mohawks, 76; sent to Ottawas to compel reparation to Iroquois, 179; restores missionaries to Michilimakinac, 183; restores fort Michilimakinac, 265; conducts Fox War, 305–9; Governor-elect of Three Rivers, lost on the Chameau, 309; iv., p. 137.

LOUYSIANE, RELATION DE LA, noticed, i., p. 90.

LOVELACE, LORD, to command Vetch's Canada expedition, v., p. 217, n.; but dies, ib.

LOYSA, GARCIAS DE, discoveries, of, i., p. 34.

LOYSEL, JOHN B., account of, i., p. 63.

LUBER, wife of President, daughter of Perrot, v., p. 163, n.

LUGO, FERNANDO DE, Spaniard, explores Magdalena River, i., p. 38.

LUHT, see LUTH.

LUNA, DON TRISTAN DE, calls Pensacola St. Mary's Bay, vi., p. 43.

LUQUES, SIEUR DE, one of Tracy's officers, drowned in Lake Champlain, iii., p. 93, n.

LUSIGNAN, PAUL LOUIS DASMARD, CHEVALIER DE, reduced captain, killed by Iroquois ambuscade, iv., p. 220.

LUSIGNY, MR., an officer in Count de Frontenac's guards, iv., p. 30, n.

LUSSER, CAPTAIN DE, Swiss, sent to ascertain condition of Choctaws, vi., p. 90; ordered to march part of fusileers to Red River, 108; repulses a Natchez sortie, 109.

LUTH, (properly LUHT,) DANIEL GREYSOLON DU, French officer, notice of, iv., p. 30, n.; rescues Hennepin, 31, n.; shoots two Indians, assassins of Frenchmen, iii., p. 217; result, 218; ordered to assemble Western tribes, 245; to intrench at mouth of Detroit River, 279; in Denonville's van, 286, n.; defeats Iroquois at Lake of Two Mountains, iv., p. 30–1; miraculously cured by invoking Catherine Tehgahkwita, 295.

LUXFOX; iii., p. 230. See FOX, LUKE.

LYS, SIEUR DE, Engineer at Carolina, i., p. 193.

MACARDI. See MACCARTNEY.

MACASSAR discovered, i., pp. 28, 34.

MACCARTNEY, GEN., what prevented his being sent to Acadia, v., p. 191, n.; a creature of Marlborough's, to command Canada expedition, 217.

MACÉ, SISTER, arrives, iii., p. 27, n.

MACÉ, MR., imprisoned by Chepar, vi., p. 81, n.; wife killed by Natchez, 82, n.

MACHIM discovered, i., p. 28.

MACHIN, an Englishman, discoverer of Madeira, i., p. 15.

MADAGASCAR, called St. Lawrence, i., p. 26; occupied by French, 56.

MADAME or MAUREPAS ISLANDS, v., p. 284.

MADEIRA discovered, i., p. 15; origin of name, ib.; La Salle at, iv., p. 64.

MADOCKAWANDO, Abénaquis chief treats with English, iv., p. 255; Baron de St. Castin marries Matilda, daughter of, v., p. 274, n.

MAGDELEINE, JAMES DE LA FERTÉ, ABBE DE LA, King's almoner, &c., one of the Hundred Associates, ii., p. 43; justifies the Jesuits, 169; La Prairie granted to, iv., p. 163; given by, to Jesuits, ib.

MAGDELEINE, LA PRAIRIE DE. See LA PRAIRIE.

MAGDALENE, RIVER, Louysiana, operations at, vi., p. 66.

MAGDALEN ISLANDS, granted to St. Pierre, v., p. 300.

MAGDALEN, Huron town, defeat of braves of, ii., p. 220, n.

MAGDALENA RIVER, New Granada, discovered, i., p. 38.

MAGELLAN or MAGHAILHANS, FERDINAND DE, discovers Straits, &c., i., p. 31; discovers Ladrone or Mariane Islands, 32, killed, ib.

MAGELLAN'S STRAITS, i., 46.

MAGNON, COMMODORE DE, to accompany de Nesmond in his New England expedition, v., p. 71.

MAGREGORIE, COL. PATRICK, sketch of, iii., p. 285, n.; leads a party to Michilimakinac, 284; captured by la Durantaye, ib.; sent by Dongan to Denonville, 300.

MAHEOUALA, Tangibao town, iii., p. 214, n.

M'AHIGAN ATICQ, Indian chief kills two Frenchmen, ii., p. 45, n.

MAHINGANS or LOUPS, See MOHEGANS.

MAHU, JAMES, exploration of, i., p. 48.

MAILLARD, CAPT., French, rescues Laudonniere in his ship Levrier, i., p. 204–5, n.

MAILLÉ-BRÉZÉ, DUKE DE, acts as Viceroy, iii., p. 80.

MAILLET, Sister, of the Hôtel Dieu, arrives, iii., p. 27.

MAIRE, REV. MR. LA, arrives in Louysiana, vi., p. 16, n.

MAIRE, JAMES or JACOB LE, Dutch, discoveries of, i., p. 52; discovers Cape Horn, ib.; loses a day in circumnavigating, ib.;

MAIRE'S STRAITS, LE, i., p. 46.

MAISONNEUVE, PAUL DE CHOMEDEY, SIEUR DE, gentleman of Champagne, takes possession of Montreal as governor in the name of a Society, ii., pp. 126, 130; zeal for conversion of Indians, 163; godfather of Tesswehat, 166; goes to France and brings out settlers, 250; brings over Margaret Bourgeoys, ii., p. 250; iii., p. 27; Onondagas treat with, ii., 252; Cayuga information to, ib.; continues to gov-

MAISONNEUVE, (*continued.*) ern after cession of island to Seminary of St. Sulpice, iii., p. 27; his reply to proposition of Onondagas and Cayugas, 37; information sent to, by French captives at Onondaga, removed by de Mesy, 74; removed from office by de Tracy and sent back to France, 83; resigns, 123; dies, 83, n. See vi., p. 126.

MAISONNEUVE, Champlain goes to St. Malo, in ship of, ii., p. 25.

MAITRE, REV. JAMES LE, priest of Montreal, killed by Iroquois, iii., p. 35; sketch of, ib., n.

MAIZERETS, REV. LOUIS ANGO DE, arrives, iii., p. 22, n.

MAJULLE, REV. MR., called also Daimanville, Sulpitian, embarks with la Sale, iv., p. 62; but returns, 71.

MALBOUCHIA, MALBANTIA, a supposed Indian name of Micissipi, v., p. 120; observations on, ib., n.

MALDIVES, discovered by Almeyda, i., p. 26.

MALDONADO, DON DIEGO DE, re-discovers Pensacola Bay, vi., p. 43; calls it Port of Anchusi, ib.

MALEBARRE, CAPE, i., p. 253, 257. See CAPE MALLEBARRE.

MALECITES, Acadian Indians near Pentagöet, also called Etechemins, i., p. 276; part of Abenaquis tribes, ii., p. 201; Governor of New England frightens them into a treaty, iv., p. 255; their missionary and Villieu attend them on expedition against the Oyster River, 256; again intimidated and reassured, 257; chiefs at Quebec protest fidelity, 258; at siege of Pemkuit, v., p. 25; left in distress by French they depend on English, 194.

MALHERBE, FRANCIS, carries bodies of Brebeuf and Lalemant to St. Mary's. ii., p. 221, n.

MALIGNE RIVER in Texas, encountered by la Sale, iv., p. 84, n., 90, n.

MALLEBARRE, now Nauset harbor, i., p. 253.

MALOMINES, (MENOMONEES,) Indian tribe on Lake Michigan, called also by French Folles Avoines, v., p. 142; the modern Menomonees, meet de Lusson, iii., p. 168; promise to send deputies to Montreal, v., p. 142; march to the relief of Detroit, 259.

MALOT, BROTHER LOUIS, Jesuit, lay brother lost in a shipwreck, ii., p. 46.

MAMBERTOU, HENRY, Acadian Chief, said by Lescarbot to have been over a hundred when he saw him, i., p. 269; friend of missionaries, and teaches them language, 270; baptized Henry in honor of Henry IV., ib.; what led to his conversion, 271; death and burial, 270, 272.

MAMBERTOU, LOUIS, son of preceding, strange proposal of, to a missionary, i., p. 273.

MAMBRÉ, or MEMBRÉ, F. ZENOBIUS, a Recollect with La Salle, iii., p. 203; v., p. 132; aids Tonti to reconcile Illinois and Iroquois, 209; returns to France, 222; de la Barre warns minister against, ib.; accompanies la Sale on last expedition, iv., p. 62; on an excursion, 73, n.; left in Fort St. Louis, and apparently massacred there, 89.

MANHATTE, (MANHATTAN,) bay and river discovered by Henry Hudson, i., p. 50; city founded there by Dutch, ib., ii., p. 10; called New Amsterdam, 11; pretended submission of, to Argal, i., p. 283, n.; Jogues at, ii., p. 160; called New York after capture by English, ib.; condition of in 1688, iv., p. 20; Caffiniere to attack, 24–5; to be ravaged, v., p. 71; see NEW YORK.

MANILLA founded, i., p. 43.

MANITOUCHAGAN, Ottawa orator speaks at La Prairie, iv., p. 147.

MANITOULINE ISLAND, in Lake Huron, why Hurons would not retire to, ii., p. 226; some encamp on, 236; Ottawas retire to, 270; St. Lusson winters on, iii., p. 166.

MANNEVAL, see MENNEVAL.

MANSE, MLLE (JANE,) sent out by Society, sketch of, iii., p. 189; in charge of women, ii., p. 126, 130; receives Hospital Nuns and takes charge of their business, 130; death of, iii., p. 189.

MANTEHT, NICHOLAS D'AILLEBOUST, SIEUR DE, son of d'Ailleboust des Musseaux, sketch of, iv., p. 31, 122; defeats an Iroquois party in the Lake of the Two Mountains, 30–1; lieutenant on Schenectady expedition, 122; cannot persuade

Indians to attack Orange, (Albany,) ib.; his conduct on the expedition, 124; heavy loss on home march, 126; commands Three Rivers men in great war party against Mohawks, 233; sent to Michilimakinac, 242; repulsed and killed in assault on Fort St. Anne, Hudson Bay, iv., p. 31, n.; v., p. 224.

MAQUA, Algonquin name for Mohawk tribe, ii., p. 145, n.

MARACAIBO, Gulf of, i., p. 21.

MARAIS, (MARETS,) JOHN LE METTEYER, SIEUR DES, reduced captain, and his valet killed by Iroquois, p. 150.

MARAMEG, mines on, vi., p. 18, n.

MARAÑAON, MARANHAM, MARÑAON or MARAÑON, discovery of, i., p. 22, 39.

MARCH, COLONEL, at Port Royal, v., p. 191, n.; forced to raise siege of Port Royal, v., p. 194; halts for orders, indignation against, complain of disobedience of officers, 195; reinforced and made governor of Acadia, 196; turns over command to Wainwright, ib., n.; sent to build Fort at Saco, 200 n.

MARCHAND, CAPT., commandant of Fort Toulouse, killed by his men, vi., p. 68, n.

MAREMEGS, iii., p. 119, n.

MAREST, FATHER JOSEPH, Jesuit, urged to return to Michilimakinac, v., p. 182; visits Sioux, iii., p. 32.

MAREST, FATHER GABRIEL, Jesuit, notice of letters of, i., p. 88; among Illinois, v., p. 133.

MAREUIL, F. PETER DE, Jesuit, missionary at Onondaga, notifies Vaudreuil that English urge Iroquois to war, v., p. 215; ordered to leave mission, 216; house and church burned, 223; a prisoner at Albany, ib.; exchanged for Lieut. Staats, 221; sees hollowness of Anglo-Iroquois alliance, ib.; reports heavy losses of English, 222; dies in France, 215, n.

MARGARITA ISLAND, i., p. 21.

MARGONET or MARGONNE, CLAUDE, one of the Hundred Associates, ii., p. 169; vi., p. 124.

MARGUERIE, FRANCIS, prisoner among Iroquois sent to Governor of Three Rivers with proposals; his advice, ii., p. 123; uncle of Frs. Hertel, iii., p. 43, n.

MARIANE or LADRONE ISLANDS, discovered by Magellan, i., p. 32; occupied by Spaniards, 59; named in honor of Queen Mariana of Austria, ib.

MARICOURT, PAUL LE MOYNE, SIEUR DE, sketch of, iii., p. 270, n.; volunteer at Hudson Bay, 270; sent by Iberville to harass English, iv., p. 38; commandant of French posts there, 39; brings down and secures Phips' flag, 174, n.; compels English boats to return to ships, 175; commands Indian corps in Frontenac's expedition, v., p. 12; appointed to a winter campaign, 20; Iroquois ask to treat with him, 94; presents Iroquois deputies, 101; starts for General Council at Onondaga, 103; his speech, 104; secret of his popularity with the Onondagas, 105; sent to Onondaga, 138, n.; at Montreal with deputies, 141; at Onondaga, 140; takes Jesuits there, 155; his death, 166.

MARIE, MR., d'Aulnay's envoy at Boston, iii., p. 131, n.

MARIEGALANTE, planters carried off from, iv., p. 162.

MARIET, REV. MR., Sulpitian, iii., p. 110.

MARIGNY, PRESIDENT DE, de Gourgues retires to house of at Rouen, during his disgrace, i., p. 237.

MARIGNY, SIEUR DE, left as lieutenant at Port Nelson, iv., p. 262; goes to St. Domingo, ib., n.

MARIN, or MORIN, French officer killed by Mohawks, iii., p. 87.

MARINE, Archives in the Depôt de la, consulted by Charlevoix, i., p. 96.

MARK, COLONEL, Charlevoix's form for March, Col., which see.

MARLE, SIEUR DE, on la Sale's last expedition, 89; forced to give the finishing stroke to Moranget, 90, n.; drowned on his way to the Illinois, 108.

MAROT, CAPTAIN, relieves la Tour at Cape Sable, iii., p. 127.

MARQUESAS or MENDOZA ISLANDS, discovered, i., p. 47.

MARQUET, (MORGUET, MORQUET,) F. DENYS, Recollect, embarks with La Sale, but falls sick and lands, iv., p. 63.

MARQUETTE, FATHER JAMES, Jesuit, sketch of, iii., p. 179; called Peter by Charlevoix, i., p. 57; goes west, iii., p. 120, n.; at Sault St. Mary's, 119; conducts Hurons to Michilimakinac, 171; observations on country, ib.; on currents, 172;

MARQUETTE, (*continued.*)
with Joliet discovers the Micissipi, i., p. 57, iii., p. 179 ; winters at Chicago, iii., p. 179, n.; founds mission at Kaskaskia, ib.; death, ib., 182, n.; Charlevoix's errors as to return, death, &c., 181–2, 185–6; notice of Journal, i., p. 83; iii., p. 180.

MARQUEZ, PEDRO MENENDEZ, nephew of the Adelantado, i., p. 184; appointed Admiral and sent on to the Canaries, ib.

MARSOLET, NICHOLAS, French Calvinist, deserts to English at Quebec, ii., p. 50.

MARSON, PIERRE DE JOYBERT, SIEUR DE SOULANGES ET DE, notice of, iii., p. 186, n.; Port Royal surrenders to, 138, n.; commands Fort Gemesie on St. John's, 186, 188 ; taken by English, 188 ; his daughter marries Vaudreuil, 187, n.; Mme. de Marson obtains Vaudreuil's appointment as Governor General, v., p. 159.

MARTIGNY, JOHN BAPTIST LE MOYNE, SIEUR DE, cousin of Iberville, v., p. 55 ; reconnoitres Fort Bourbon, ib.; placed in command by d'Iberville, 58.

MARTIN, COMMODORE GEO., at Port Royal, v., p. 227, n.

MARTIN VAES' ISLAND, i., p. 52.

MARTIN, ABRAHAM, who gave name to Plains of Abraham, ii., p. 51; des Groseilliers son-in-law of, iii., p. 230, n.

MARTIN, DOM CLAUDE, Benedictine, notice of his Vie de la Ven. M. Marie de l'Incarnation, i., p. 82; iii., p. 189, n.; letter to, from his mother, iv., p. 305.

MARTINE, FRANCISCO, rescues French prisoners, iv., p. 114, n.

MARTINEZ, ANTONIO JOSEPH, vi., p. 59.

MARTINIERE, BRUZEN LA, Belgian, works of, noticed, i., p. 68, 93.

MARTINIQUE attacked by Sir Francis Wheeler, iv., p. 241.

MARTYRS, THE, discovered, i., p. 29.

MARY DE MEDICIS, Queen Regent of France, liberality of, to Acadian missionaries, i., p. 262; her orders as to their passage disobeyed, ib.

MARY OF THE INCARNATION, her life, i., p. 82 ; sketch of, iii., p. 189 ; Ursuline of Tours, selected to found a convent in Canada, arrives at Quebec, ii. , p. 101 ; her letters, i., p. 83 ; ii., p. 258 ; remains in convent almost alone, iii., p. 34, n.; earthquake of 1663 revealed to, what happened to her on that occasion, iii., p. 58; her account of the fervor of the Christian Indians, iv., p. 305.

MARY OF ST. JOSEPH, Ursuline, sets out for Quebec, ii., p. 101 ; eulogium on, ib.

MARYLAND, settled, i., p. 54 ; Seneca massacres in, iii., p. 248.

MASCARENHAS, PEDRO, Portuguese, discovers Bantam, i., p. 35.

MASCOUCHE RIVER, Indians murdered near, iii., p. 150, n.

MASCOUTINS, MASKOUTINS, ASSISTAERONON OR FIRE NATION, meaning of name, iii., p. 183 and n.; Allouez among, 120, n.; at war with Sioux, 166, n.; at de Lusson's formal act of possession, 168 ; their country, 183 ; visited by Fathers Allouez and Dablon, 182 ; reception of the missionaries, ib.; Senecas complain of, p. 257 ; think of settling near the Iroquois, iv., p. 266 ; some settle on the Wabash, v., p. 133 ; averse to the gospel, and are scattered by disease, ib.; de Courtemanche induces them to disarm, p. 142 ; in Fox plot to give Detroit to the English, 257 ; attacked and many killed by our allies, ib.

MASSACHUSETTS agrees to furnish men for expedition against Quebec, iv., p. 145, n.; retains them after attack on Casco, ib.; did not recover for years from Phips' defeat, p. 189, n.; compelled to issue paper money, ib., n.

MASSACRE ISLAND, why so called, situation, discovery, afterwards Dauphin Island, v., p. 120 ; storehouses, &c., erected on, vi., p. 14 ; port closed, ib., n.

MASSÉ, FATHER ENEMOND, Jesuit, chosen for Acadia, i., p. 260; not well received, 270 ; Membertou dies with, 271; strange proposal made to, 273 ; returns to St. Malo, France, 281, n.; at Quebec, ii., p. 35 ; returns again after restoration of Canada to France, 64 ; his death, 183 ; a monument recently erected over his grave at Sillery.

MASSIOT, MR., of Rochelle, owner of one of La Sale's ships, iv., p. 62.

MATAGORDA BAY, supposed by some to have been occupied by La Sale, iv., p. 68, n., 82, n.

MATAMOROS, DON JUAN PEDRO DE, notice of vi., p. 44, n.; Governor of Pensacola,

remonstrates against occupation of St. Joseph's Bay, 42, n.; calls on Governor of St. Joseph's for aid, 44; surrenders to de Serigny, 45; embarks for Havana, ib.; restored to command of Pensacola, 49; hearing of approach of a French squadron, wishes to burn his fort and retire to Santa Rosa Island, 54; summoned to surrender, 58; forced by officers to do so, ib.; taken to France, 44, n.

MATAN, Magellan killed at, i., p. 32.

MATANE RIVER, Canada, situation and advantages of, iv., p. 17; v., p. 74; Riverin's establishment at, ib.; English fleet seen at, 246.

MATANZAS INLET, massacre of French probably at, i., p. 214.

MATAOUANDO, (MADOCKAWANDO,) Malecite chief, negotiates with Governor of New England, iv., p. 255; Villieu and Thury induce him to desist, 256; distinguished on Villieu's expedition against the English, ib.; St. Castin marries daughter of, 211.

MATHIEU, (MATTHEW,) CAPTAIN, English hostage during negotiations at Port Royal, v., p. 230.

MATSUMAY, visited by Father de Angelis, i., p. 53; opinions as to, 60.

MATTHEWS, CAPTAIN, of the Chester, v., p. 227, n.

MAUBEC, an Abbey in France, conferred on the Bishopric and Chapter of Quebec, iii., p. 122.

MAUBILE, the Mauvilla of Garcilasso, river in Louysiana, situation, v., p. 119; battle fought here between Spaniards and Indians, ib., n.; to be taken possession of, though not essential, 127; settlement on, vi., p. 14; Indians settle there, 15; fort built by Vigne Voisin, 15, n.; soil poor, 16; Spaniards enter and capture convoy on, 50; but are defeated, ib.; Chateaugué resumes command at, 65; d'Artaguette commandant at, 80; projected massacre of French at, 80, 91; French killed near, 89–90; Perrier convenes Choctaws at, 103.

MAUFILS, PETER, student at Quebec, mortally wounded at siege, iv., p. 182.

MAUGRAS, SIEUR, joins Hertel with five Algonquins and returns, iv., p. 132.

MAURE or MAUZE, M., member of the Council, ii., p. 216.

MAUREPAS, MR. DE, Perrier de Salverte's letter to, vi., p. 106.

MAURICE OF NASSAU, Prince, sends out exploring expedition, i., p. 46.

MAURICE ISLAND, i., p. 47.

MAURICE VON NASSAU'S LAND, i., p. 52.

MAY RIVER, now St. John's, Florida, by whom so named, i., p. 42, 136; Ribaut takes possession, and plants French arms, ib.; Laudonniere well received, i., p. 42, 149; kind of worship paid by Indians to French arms, 149; beauty of country, 150; Laudonniere builds Fort Caroline there, i., p. 42; Ribaut tries to reach, p. 209; de Gourgues at, 227.

MAYA, DIEGO DE, a Spanish captain, opposes attack on Fort Caroline, i., p. 197; sinks a French vessel, 203.

MEAUPOU, CHEVALIER DE, commanding the Seine, attacked by Virginia fleet, in spite of bravery forced to surrender, v., p. 174.

MECHASSIPI, see MICISSIPI.

MECHIN, CAPTAIN, commanding the Count de Toulouse, vi., p. 44; takes Governor of Pensacola and his officers to Havana, 45; his vessel seized there, 46.

MECHOACAN, discovered by Parillas, i., p. 33.

MEDICINE MEN, on St. Lawrence, ii., p. 13; among Hurons, p. 79; see AUTMOINS, IONAS, OSTEMOY, PILOTOIS.

MEDOKTECK, Abénaquis of, join in letter to Governor of Mass., v., p. 273, n.

MEDRANO, JUAN VELEZ DE, Spanish captain, distinguished at capture of Fort Caroline, i., p. 208; at Cañaveral, p. 222.

MEESUCONTEE, v., p. 167, n.

MEGAPOLENSIS, REV. DR. JOHANNES, Dutch minister at New Amsterdam, F. Jogues writes to, ii., p. 187; Le Moyne announces discovery of salt springs to, iii., p. 15, n.

MELIAPOR, Vasco de Gama at, i., 24; body of St. Thomas found at, 33.

MELINDA discovered, i., p. 20.

MEMBRE, see MAMBRÉ.

MENADOU or PANADOU BAY, Cape Breton, v., p. 284.

MENANE ISLAND, near Acadia, what recommends it, i., p. 250.

MENDAÑA, ALVARO DE, Spaniard, discovers Solomon's Islands, i., p. 43; Marquesas Islands, 47.

MENDEZ, DON FRANCISCO, Spanish captain sent to Viceroy of New Spain, vi., p. 49.

MENDIETA, DON ANTONIO, Spanish captain, reconnoitres Dauphin Island, vi., p. 50.

MENDOZA, DON ANTONIO DE, Spaniard, sends out explorers, i., p. 39.

MENDOZA, PETER DE, founds Buenos Ayres, i., p. 37.

MENENDEZ, BARTHOLOMEW, (brother of following,) appointed commandant of St. Augustine, i., p. 197.

MENENDEZ DE AVILES, DON PEDRO, Captain-General and Adelantado of Florida, motive of his voyage, i., p. 182; contract with Philip II., 183; preparations, 184; delays, 185; fleet scattered, 186; at Porto Rico, hears of Ribaut's loss of time, 187; in Florida, 187; enters Dolphin River, and calls it St. Augustine, 188; resolves to attack French vessels, 189; the result, 191; sails back to St. Augustine River, 192; takes possession and selects ground to build a fort, 194; nearly captured by French, 195; saved by a tempest, ib.; piety and courage, ib.; proposes to attack Caroline, 196; council of war after some discussion agrees, 197; near Caroline he hesitates and consults officers, 199; their advice, ib.; takes Caroline, 200; fails to capture vessels in river, 203; changes name of Caroline to San Matheo, and builds a church, 207; received in triumph at St. Augustine, 208; loses his fleet, 209; puts Ribaut and all his French except Catholics to death, 206, 209, 220; what was thought of this execution at St. Augustine, 221; goes in pursuit of French intrenched at Cañaveral, near Bahama Channel, ib.; the result, 222.

MENENDEZ MARQUEZ, PEDRO, son of Alvar Sanchez de Aviles, and nephew of the two preceding, admiral of the Florida fleet, sails for the Canaries, i., p. 184; royal treasurer in Florida, 186.

MENESEZ, EDWARD DE, transports relics of St. Thomas to Goa, i., p. 33.

MENNEVAL, ROBINEAU DE, son of Baron de Bekancourt, Governor of Acadia, iv., p. 23; Caffiniere to explain his plan of campaign to, 27; attacked by English, 154; sends to make terms, as he is unable to make a defence, 155; surrenders, 156; declared a prisoner and sent to England, 158, 190.

MENOIL, MR., member of the Council of New France, ii., p. 216, n.

MENOMONEES, see MALOMINES.

MERAS, DOCTOR SOLIS DE LAS, brother-in-law of Menendez, writes an account, i., p. 72, 214.

MERCED, RELIGIOUS OF LA, with Menendez, i., p. 186.

MERCIER, FATHER FRANCIS LE, Jesuit, Superior-General of the missions of New France, leads missionaries to Onondaga, ii., p. 267; sketch of, ib., n.

MERCŒUR, DUKE DE, said to have imprisoned de la Roche, i., p. 244; question examined, ib., note.

MERCURE FRANÇOIS, Canada matter in the, i., p. 76.

MERMET, FATHER JOHN, Jesuit, endeavors to convert Mascoutins, his charity, fails of success, v., p. 133.

MERVEILLEUX, SIEUR LE, Swiss captain, sent to French settlements to organize defences, vi., p. 89; intrenches at Tonica Bay, 95.

MESMES, ENSIGN DE, with de Gourgues, i., p. 232.

MESNARD, (MÉNARD,) FATHER RENÉ, Jesuit, missionary to the Iroquois, selected for Onondaga, ii., p. 262, n.; sent, 267; founds Cayuga mission, 277; success in Cayuga and Oneida, iii., p. 12; sufferings on his way to the Ottawas, 47; Bishop Laval's words to, 48; lost in the woods, 50; veneration entertained for him by French and Indians, ib.; sort of worship paid by Sioux to his breviary and cassock, ib.; place of his death, ib., n.

MESNIL (-HEURRY,) CAPTAIN JAMES DU, SIEUR DE ST. MARC, commands a battallion of regulars in Frontenac's expedition, v., p. 13

MÉSY, AUGUSTINE DE SAFFRAY-, major of the Citadel of Caon, appointed Governor-General of New France, iii., p. 65; at Quebec, ib.; reply to Cayuga proposals of peace, 71; quarrels with bishop and Superior Council, 73; violence, 74; accusations against, ib.; defence, ib.; recalled, 75; King orders his trial, 81; he dies in ignorance of these steps, 76,

84 ; appoints de la Potherie to act after his death, 76.

Métaberoutine, Indian name of Three Rivers, vi., p. 124.

Metawando, see Matawando.

Meules, Chevalier de, Intendant of New France, iii., p. 216 ; instructions, ib. ; at Quebec, 222 ; complains of de la Barre's slowness, 253 ; builds Intendant's palace and church of Our Lady of Victory, 260 ; visits Acadia, its condition, 261 ; removed, 284, n. ; returns to France, his report on Acadia, 295.

Mexico, Cortez effects conquest of, i., p. 32–3.

Mexplex, Sieur, sent by de Loubois to reconnoitre Natchez, and make proposals of peace, vi., p. 95 ; the Indians kill three of his men and take him with two others, ib. ; burned, 96.

May Islands, i., p. 34.

Miamis, Canada tribe, situation of this nation, visited by Allouez, iii., p. 120, n. ; how Tetinchoua received Perrot, 166 ; not then at Chicago, ib., n. ; Father Marquette supposed by Charlevoix to have settled at Chicagou among the, 181 ; join Mascoutins, 184 ; mission among those on St. Joseph's River, 203 ; deputies of, at Montreal, 221 ; Iroquois war parties against, 241 ; attack Senecas, 257 ; rescue survivors of Niagara garrison, 291, n. ; Frontenac's measures to prevent their treating with English, iv., p. 242 ; Iroquois wish to force them to declare against us, 269 ; de Courtemanche by their aid defeats Iroquois, 270 ; defeat by Sioux and again in endeavoring to retrieve it, v. p. 64 ; reprisals on Frenchmen going to Sioux, ib. ; threaten to burn Perrot, 65 ; warned by the Rat, 66 ; Iroquois complain of hostilities of, 102 ; de Callieres represents it as a reprisal, ib. ; a whole village carried off by Sioux, 111 ; de Courtemanche finds them about to attack Iroquois, v., p. 141 ; they wish to renew the war, 163 ; hostilities against Iroquois, 165 ; kill some Ottawas, 183 ; troubles in consequence at Detroit, 185 ; resentment at la Motte Cadillac for not giving them the head of an Ottawa chief as he promised, 190 ; clamorous for justice on Ottawas, missionary removed, they kill some Frenchmen, and plot death of all at Detroit, 202 ; Cadillac's dishonorable treaty with, 203 ; do not keep it, ib. ; said to have been defeated by Cadillac, ib. ; resolve to go to St. Joseph's, 307, n. ; refuse to join Chickasaws in war against us, vi., p. 119.

Michabou, the Great Hare, legend as to, iii., p. 105.

Michel, James, French Calvinist, officer on English fleet conquering Quebec, ii., p. 52 ; enables Kerck to capture de Roquemont's squadron, 53 ; quarrels with English, ib. ; his fury, death and funeral, 54.

Michigan, Lake, observations on currents of, iii., p. 171.

Michilimakinac, description and disadvantages of, iii., p. 170 ; Ottawas said to have retired to, iii., p. 270 ; Tionontatez do, 271, n. ; Marquette leads latter thither, iii., p. 170 ; position of his mission at, ib. ; Tonti and La Sale at, 213, n., 214 ; Seneca chief killed at, 218 ; Durantaye in command at, 245 ; English at, 284 ; English on way to, captured by Durantaye, ib. ; Courtemanche and Repentigny sent to, iv., p. 200 ; St. Michel sent to, 218 ; Iroquois prisoners brought to, 269 ; Argenteuil brings French from, v., p. 22 ; King wishes to suppress, 65 ; necessity of preserving, ib. ; English claim, 91 ; Courtemanche's operations at, 142 ; Cadillac having drawn Indians from, missionaries abandon and burn house at, 182 ; Father Marest returns to, with Louvigny, ib. ; Ottawas from Detroit return to, 187 ; Indians from, at Quebec, 237 ; why Vaudreuil restores fort at, 265.

Micissipi or Mechassipi, (Mississippi, Great River, iii., p. 178;) De Soto dies on, i., p. 40 ; Alvarado descends to mouth of, ib. ; Marquette and Joliet discover, iii., p. 179 ; Hennepin and Dacan ascend to St. Anthony's Falls, 206 ; la Salle descends to Gulf and takes possession, 213 ; difficulty of ascending, 215 ; La Salle passes mouth of, iv., p. 68 ; requests Beaujeu to examine on his way back, ib., n. ; Iberville enters, v., p. 120 ; English enter, 123 ; bar at mouth vi., p. 40 ; names of, i., p. 40 ; iii., pp. 178–9, n. ; v., p. 120, n. See Cucagua Malbantia, Malbouchia, Palizada.

MICMACS, Acadian Indians, same as Acadians, Souriquois, Gaspesians, i., p. 264; included among Abénaqui nations, ib.; at war with Esquimaux, 265; chiefs called Sagamos, ib.; manners of, 265–6; Biard's estimate of, 267, n.; decrease of, ib.; missions to, iii., p. 30; attack Oyster River with Villieu, iv., p. 256; aid d'Iberville to capture an English ship, v., p. 24; with Bonaventure, besiege Pemkuit, 25; wish to board an English fleet, 27; d'Iberville does not take them to Newfoundland, ib.; three refuse to leave him, 28; Subercase reports their great destitution, p. 194; join in letter to Governor of Mass., p. 273, n.

MIKINAC, an Algonquin, marches against English, iv., p. 278.

MILET, FATHER PETER, Jesuit, notice of, iii., p. 109, n.; sent to Iroquois, ib.; leaves Oneida and joins de la Barre, 250, n.; why summoned to Catarocouy, 268; unconsciously used to entrap Iroquois, 277; captured by Oneidas, p. 277; iv., p. 50; his sufferings, p. 238; adopted by a woman who saves his life, 245; false statements of his deliverance, 50, n.; writes to Frontenac, 238; at Quebec after five years' slavery, 254; Oneidas ask his return, v., p. 50; his attachment for them, ib.; account of his captivity, iv., p. 50, &c.

MINDANAO, discovered by Corquizano, i., p. 35.

MINE, CAPTAIN DE LA, joins Vaudreuil, his valor against Iroquois, iv., p. 194.

MINES, LES, district in Acadia, i., p. 252, n.; menaced by English, v., p. 171; seasonably relieved, ib.

MINES, of copper in Acadia, i., p. 250; on Green River, vi., p. 12; of coal in Acadia, i., p. 250; of silver, said to have been discovered in Illinois, vi., p. 25; of iron in various places, iii., p. 99.

MINET, SIEUR, engineer, abandons la Sale and returns to France, iv., p. 71.

MINISTERS, Dutch, seek to prejudice Christian Iroquois against Jesuits, reply of Indians, iii., p. 154.

MINISTERS, English, despised by Iroquois, v., p. 91; one attempts to pervert Abénaquis, 268; controversy with Father Rasle, ib.; he withdraws, 269. See BAXTER, REV. JOSEPH.

MINQUAS, same as Andastes, Susquehannas, Conestogas, ii., p. 72, n.

MIQUELON, iii., p. 142, n.

MIRABICHI, god of waters, according to some Indian tribes, iii., p. 103. See MISSIBIZI.

MIRAGOINE, establishment of, plundered by Spaniards, vi., p. 50, n.

MIRE BAY, in Cape Breton, v., p. 284.

MISCOU ISLAND, in the Gulf of St. Lawrence, position and trade, ii., p. 119; death and labors of Father Tursis at, ib.; granted to Count de St. Pierre, v., p. 299.

MISCOUNAGUACHIT, a place in Northern Canada to which Indians invite a Jesuit, iii., p. 234.

MISKOUASOUATH, Fox chief, his attire at the General Congress, v., p. 151.

MISSIBIZI, Ottawa deity, called by Perrot "The Great Tiger," iii., p. 103.

MISSION OF THE ANNUNCIATION OF OUR LADY, iii., p. 154, n.

MISSIONARIES, character of the Canadian, ii., pp. 66–8; overscrupulous as to baptism, 85; general view of, 77–86; sufferings of the, p. 113; occupations, ib.; life, 114; manner of instruction, ib.; obstacles, 115; objections answered, 116; several killed, 196, 210, 219, 229, 248, 275; iii., p. 50; difference observed by Iroquois between them and Dutch clergy, 154; complain of liquor trade, 195; Court prejudiced against them, ib.; it is undeceived, 195–6; their services to Canada, 281; Dénonville deems them necessary among the Indians, 308; abandon Indians of Pentagoët on account of disorders caused by liquor, ib.; Dénonville's testimony to de Seignelay in favor of, iv., p. 44; English regard them as their most dangerous enemies, ib.; succeed in preventing Ottawa negotiations with Iroquois, 54; Frontenac's unfounded suspicions against those of Sault St. Louis, 197; why they ceased agitating the liquor question, 230; false accusations of Bellomont, v., p. 90; in Louysiana 129; one killed at the Tonicas, 124; abandon Michilimakinac, 182; retain Iroquois in neu-

trality, 203; Vaudreuil urges those in Acadia to retain Indians in our alliance, 235; Vaudreuil and missionaries of domiciliated Indians baffle English intrigues, 240; they keep the Abénaquis from an English alliance, 303.

MISSIONS, general view of missions of New France, ii., p. 110, &c., 209; scandals in, caused by liquor, iii., p. 54; we neglect to profit by humiliation of Iroquois to plant missions, 94; several are abandoned, 95; among the Iroquois, 108, 116; among the Algonquins, 119.

MISSISSIPPI, see MICISSIPI.

MISSOURI, a great river emptying into the Micissipi, iii., p. 180.

MISSOURITES, a Louysiana tribe of the Dacota family, iii., p. 31; some come to relief of Detroit against Foxes, v., p. 258; some go to France, vi., p. 76, n.

MISTASSINS, Indians of Northern Canada, visited by Father Albanel, iii., p. 231.

MISTASSINS LAKE, extent of, iii., p. 232.

MITCHIGAMIAS, Illinois, send to New Orleans to mourn for missionaries killed by Natchez and Yazoos, vi., p. 102; marks of attachment to French and to religion, ib.

MITIWEMEG, Algonquin chief, abandons Dollard, iii., p. 33.

MOBILIANS, dance calumet to l'Epinai, vi., p. 39.

MOHAWKS, Iroquois canton, name of tribe and people, ii., p. 145; towns of, 146, n.; defeat Hurons under Ahasistari, ii., p. 138; conversions effected by Father Jogues, 150; capture Father Bressani, 171; the only one openly opposed to French and Christianity, 182; receive presents but do not surrender Father Jogues, 156; ratify peace and throw suspicion on other cantons, 182; description of their canton, 189, n.; why they put Father Jogues to death, 196; hostilities and cruelties, 198; with Senecas attack St. Ignatius, 210; renew war with Hurons, 210; defeat an Algonquin-Huron party, ii., p. 245–6; one party defeated, 252; another ravages around Quebec and takes Father Poncet, 253; make peace, 256; attack Father le Moyne and kill one of his guides, 258; kill a Jesuit lay brother, 260; forced to make peace, 261; wish to prevent French settlement at Onondaga, 268; carry off many Hurons from Isle Orleans and insult Governor-General, ib.; carry off more Hurons, 280; haughty address to Governor-General, 278; endeavor to surprise Three Rivers, some punished, they retire, iii., p. 19; violate the peace and ill-treat prisoners, 43; at war with Abénaquis, Mohegans and French, 45; defeated by Chippeways, 64; kill three French officers, 87; brutality of a chief, 88; de Tracy executes him, ib.; Courcelle and Tracy's expedition against them and its result, 89, &c.; all their towns destroyed, 91; ask peace and a missionary, and obtain them, 108; progress of the Faith in, 116; courage of Christian women in defending their faith, 155; Mohawk chief insults missionary, 155; repairs his fault, 156; resolution adopted by canton in regard to religion, 157; cause of Mohawk migration to Canada, 196; make peace with Mohegans, 196, n.; account of two Mohawk women, 163; The Great Mohawk sent by Denonville to sound this canton, 293; he stops a war-party and converts four Mohawks, ib.; through his nephew negotiates with Oneidas and Onondagas, 294; Mohawks besiege Chambly, ravage the country and are repulsed, 298; enter colony, pursued by Dénonville and some taken, 307; Mohegans draw them into a war-party against us, iv., p. 50; with Mohegans pursue French, 126, n.; Mohawks and Dutch at Chambly, 145; an expedition against Montreal, 145, n.; attacked by smallpox, 184; forces, 185; surprise Sault St. Louis Iroquois, 191, treacherous parleys, ib.; a Mohawk-Cayuga party escapes from Bienville, 196; Mohawks and English defeated at La Prairie, 203; French expedition against, 213; raids, 216; defeated by Sault St. Louis Iroquois, 216-7; French and Indians ravage Mohawk canton, 233; two Mohawks at Montreal, ill received, 249; proposed expedition against, v., p. 10; march to aid Oneidas, but return, 19; Mohawk deserter from the Mountain burned, ib.; Frontenac orders expedition against, v., p. 48; Mohawk and Mohegan party defeat French, 49; Mohawks prevent Oneidas settling

MOHAWKS, (*continued.*)
in the colony, 50; send back two prisoners to Frontenac with an insolent message, 50; Frontenac proposes expedition against, 76; Mohawks at Sault St. Louis, 85; declare to Bellomont that no one has any right over their country, &c., 83; propose to detain Iroquois of Sault St. Louis till their prisoners are restored, but he disapproves, 84; Frontenac orders Mohawks to be well received at the Sault, 85; invites them to Montreal, ib.; other cantons treat of peace without the Mohawks, 101; Dellius' mission among Mohawks, 106, 107, n.; Mohawks promise to send deputies to Congress at Montreal, but do not, 111; totem, 111; deputies arrive late, apologize and sign the treaty, 154; the Governor of Albany wishes them to send back Mohegans who had removed to their canton, 164; he builds a fort in their canton, 209; they side against us from necessity, 221; promise Vaudreuil never to declare against us, 223; fears that they cannot keep their word, 223–4.

MOHAWK, THE GREAT, converted, iii., p. 191, n.; 196, n. See KRYN.

MOHAWK RIVER, ii., p. 189, n.

MOHEGANS, (LOUPS,) murdered by French, iii., p. 149; conversion of woman attacked by, 163; make peace with Mohawks, 196, n.; aid Senecas, 257; with Mohawks attack Fort Chambly, 298; pursued by Denonville, 307; form party against us, iv., p. 50; pursue French, 126, n.; in Montreal expedition, 1690, 145, n.; attacked by smallpox, 184; operations against French, 188; at La Prairie, 202; win over Miamis, 242; ordered to attack Mohawks, v., p. 108; Courtemanche finds some on the St. Joseph's, 141; remove from near Albany to Mohawks, 164; Malecites and Canibas trade with English through, 194.

MOINGWENA, Illinois town and tribe, iii., p. 180, n.; v., p. 131, n.

MOLUCCAS, discovered, i., p. 28; names of, ib.

MOMBAZA, discovered, i., p. 20.

MONA, cacique of, supplies de Gourgues, i., p. 226.

MONCARVILLE, SIEUR DE, at siege of Quebec, iv., p. 180, n.

MONCLOVA, MELCHIOR PORTOCARRERO LASO DE LA VEGA, CONDE DE LA, Viceroy of Mexico, 1686–8, sends to break up La Sale's settlement, iv., p. 113, n.

MONGOULACHAS, Louisiana tribe, v., p. 121, 123, n. See QUINIPISSAS.

MONHEGAN, Canibas wish to attack, iv., p. 43.

MONSEIGNAT, CHARLES DE, Secretary of Frontenac, iv., p. 121, n., &c.

MONSIPI, FORT, on Hudson Bay, taken from English, iii., p. 270.

MONSONI RIVER, iii., p. 270.

MONSONIS meets St. Lusson, iii., p. 168; English fort among, 231.

MONSTERS, in Canada according to early accounts, i., p. 124, etc.

MONTAGUE, LA, settler at New York, writes to La Potherie, iii., p. 19.

MONTAGNEZ, or LOWER ALGONQUINS, situation of, ii., p. 8, and note, prayers in language of, 9, n.; origin of name, ib.; induce Champlain to join them on an expedition against Iroquois, pp. 8, 12–17, 21; one causes panic, 19; reception at their village, ib.; join him at Quebec and accompany him to Sorel, 21; some received at Sillery, 98; attend Tadoussac mission, 118, 243; attend a public audience given to Iroquois, 178; attacked by Sokokis, 185; almost destroyed by small pox, iii., p. 153, n.; join in letter to governor of Massachuetts, v., p. 273, n.

MONTAGNY, French officer, probably same as Morin, iii., p. 87.

MONTAIGU, LORD, induces English court to restore Canada to France, ii., p. 58.

MONTCLERIE, LIEUT. DE LA, ambuscaded by Iroquois, gallantly fights his way through, iv., p. 220–1.

MONTEJO, FRANCISCO DE, reduces Yucatan, i., p. 35.

MONTESSON ISLAND, Abénaquis on, v., p. 167.

MONTEZUMA, emperor of Mexico, submits, i., p. 32.

MONTIGNY, SIEUR LA MARQUE DE, notice of, v., p. 46; volunteer on Schenectady expedition, iv., p. 122; wounded there, 125; at siege of Pemkuit, v., p. 25; highly distinguished in Newfoundland,

p. 42, 44; sent to aid Abénaquis, 167; attacks Lancaster in New England, ib, n.; in Newfoundland, 172; valor and success, 174; commands van in Ramezai's expedition, 218; sent out to reconnoitre enemy, 220.

MONTIGNY, REV. FRANCIS JOLLIET, of the Seminary of Quebec, conducts several missionaries to Louysiana, v., p. 129; labors among Taensas, 130, n.; soon retired, ib., iv.

MONT LOUIS, situation and description, iv., p. 18; advantages for sedentary fishery, p. 18; attempt to establish one, p. 17; failure of a new attempt, v., p. 74–5.

MONTLUC, MARSHAL DE, King's lieutenant in Guienne, commissions de Gourges, i., p. 225; after his return advises him to go to Court, p. 237.

MÔNTMAGNY, CHARLES HUAULT DE, Knight of Malta, Governor General of New France, ii., p. 91; unable to carry out Champlain's views, 92; unable to punish Iroquois insult, 95; his reception of the Ursulines and Hospital Nuns, 102; sends deputies to treat with Iroquois, 124; they carry off his allies during negotiation, 125; his Iroquois name, Ononthio, applied to all French governors, 124; puts the Montreal Society in possession of that island, 126; builds a fort at the mouth of the Sorel river, 133; complains in vain to Governor of New Netherland about arms furnished to Iroquois by Dutch, 138; prevents war parties against Dutch, ib., n.; repulses an Iroquois party at Fort Richelieu, 143; his exertions to deliver Father Jogues, 155; his embarrassment, 174; interview with Hurons as to Iroquois, prisoners, 175; gives Father Brebeuf an escort to return to Hurons, 177; gives a public audience to the Iroquois deputies to conclude peace, 178; reluctantly permits Father Jogues to go, 187; information of missionary sent to, 195; why recalled, 203; proposed by Court as a model for Colonial governors, 204; said to have died at St. Kitts, ib., n.

MONTMORENCI, MARSHAL DUKE DE, Viceroy of New France, ii., p. 32; makes Champlain his lieutenant, ib.; confides Canadian affairs to Dolu, 32; sells his right to the Duke de Ventadour, 35; executed, 32, n.

MONTMORENCY COMPANY, formed in 1622, ii., p. 33; associates, ib., n.

MONTORGUEIL, SIEUR DE, lieutenant in Villebon's company ordered to evacuate Chedabouctou, iv., p. 159–60; orders came too late, ib.; attacked, vigorous defence and honorable capitulation, 160–1.

MONTORTIER, MR. DE, Navy captain, brings reinforcements to Canada, and is ordered to stay there, iii., p. 255.

MONTOUR, English acquire influence through, v., p. 204, n.

MONTREAL, mountain at, called Mont Royal by Cartier, whence name extended to Island, i., p. 37, 120; Indian town Hochelaga found by Cartier, where Montreal now stands, 117; modern Iroquois names of, 118, n., 119, n.; old Algonquin name, 128, n.; Champlain at, ii., pp. 23, 24, 25; grant of isle to a company which takes possession, 130; notice of Motifs de la Société de Montreal, i., p. 82; object of society, ii., p. 125; tradition as to first inhabitants, 127; note as to settlement of, 129; bishop proposed for, 183; especially consecrated to Mary, 251; progress of, 250; Iroquois defeated by settlers of, 251, n.; Iroquois cause great alarms at, iii., p. 18; ceded to Seminary of St. Sulpice, who take possession, 23; Iroquois defeat and kill Town Major, 46; change in the judiciary of the island, 69; fervor and piety of the people how maintained, 96; limits of government of Montreal, 256; Perrot governor of, ib.; Iroquois ravages on the island, iv., p. 28, (See La Chine;) sends out Schenectady expedition, 122–6; English expedition against, in 1690, 145, n.; militia of, during siege of Quebec, 176; Manteht's expedition starts from, 232; fortifications at, 236; great convoy at, 241; Frontenac's conference with Ottawas at, 242, he assembles army at, v., p. 12; treaty at, 111; destructive fire at, p. 308, n.; Governors and commandants of, iii., p. 123; vi., p. 126. See MAISONNEUVE, PERROT.

MONTREAL COMPANY, de Lauson grants island to, ii., p. 130; New France Company confirms grant to, ib.

MONT ROYAL, name given by Cartier, i., p. 37.

MONTS, PETER DE GUAST, SIEUR DE, Governor of Pons, gentleman-in-ordinary of the chamber, obtains from Henry IV. letters patent as Vice Admiral and Lieutenant-Gen. in Canada, with monopoly of trade and freedom of religion for himself, i., p. 247 ; what he undertakes, 248; his character, first outfit, goes to Acadia, i., p. 49, 251 ; settlement on St. Croix Island, i., p. 49, 252 ; explores coast, i., p. 49 ; names Baie Françoise, 252, n.; seeks another spot for colony and decides on Port Royal, 253 ; cedes Port Royal to Poutrincourt, 255 ; loses monopoly, 258 ; makes new arrangement with Poutrincourt, ib.; commission cancelled, ib.; not repaid for his advances, ib.; his mistakes, ib.; recovers somewhat, 259 ; new error, ib.; forms a new company and sends ships to Canada, ib.; loses all hope of retrieving his fortunes, ii., p. 23 ; Champlain's advice to, ib.; offers to establish a colony for Mme. de Guercheville, 275.

MONTS' COMPANY, DE, does nothing for the colonization of Canada, i., p. 260.

MONTS, MR. DE, sent as Commissary to Canada, iii., p. 53 ; takes possession of Placentia for the King, ib.

MOODY, WILLIAM, v., p. 219, n.

MOOR, REV. THOROUGHGOOD, missionary to Mohawks, v., p. 107, n.

MORANGET, MR. DE, la Sale's nephew, with him on last expedition, iv., p. 62; wounded by Indians, 71 ; left in first fort, 73 ; sent in search of frigate, 84 ; on last march, 89 ; reviles some of the party, who assassinate him, 91.

MORBIHAN COMPANY, project of, ii., p. 38, n.

MORGUES, JAMES LE MOYNE, SIEUR DE, accompanies Laudonniere to Florida, i., p. 149 ; his account does not always agree with that commander's, 149, 153 ; escapes with him after capture of Caroline, 202 ; his "Brevis Narratio" noticed, 72 ; published by de Bry, 149, n.

MORIENNE BAY, Cape Breton, now Casco Bay, v., p. 284.

MOSCOSO, LOUIS DE, leads remnants of Soto's forces back to Mexico, i., p. 135 ; vi., p. 11.

MOTA, ANTONIO, in Japan, i., p. 39.

MOTHE, CAPTAIN PETER DE ST. PAUL, SIEUR DE LA, builds Fort St. Anne, iii., p. 90 ; vi., p. 126 ; acts as commandant at Montreal in absence of Maisonneuve, 1669–70, vi., p. 126.

MOTIN, DAME JANE, widow of La Tour, iii., p. 132, n.

MOTTE CADILLAC, see CADILLAC.

MOTTE EGRON, MR. DE LA, commands the Northern Company's ship Hardi, v., p. 52 ; wrecked and drowned, 53.

MOTTE, MR. DE LUSSIERE, SEIGNEUR DE LA LUSSAUDIERE, CHEVALIER DE LA, reduced captain, appointed to defend colony from Sorel River to Quebec, iv., p. 142 ; repulses Iroquois, 150 ; surprised and slain, 151.

MOTTE, LE VILIN, SIEUR DE LA, la Saussaye's lieutenant at Mount Desert, accompanies Father Biart to Indians, i., p. 277 ; defends ship against English, 279; surrenders for want of cannon, 280; goes to Virginia, 281.

MOUCOUACADI, Acadian port, whalers taken in, i., p. 251.

MOULTON, CAPTAIN, commands at Rale s death, v., p. 280.

MOUNTAIN, IROQUOIS OF THE, Sulpitian mission, founded by de Belmont, iii., p. 117, n.; attacked, iv., p. 193, n.; removed to Sault au Recollet and Lake of the Two Mountains, iii., p. 117; v., p. 166; Indians of, retire to Montreal, 198; Onondagas send belt to, iv., p. 198; they prove their fidelity, 199 ; at battle of la Prairie, 203 ; at Black Kettle's defeat, 220 ; Oureouharé at, 246 ; on Frontenac's expedition, v., p. 12; Totathiron, great chief, killed, 49; Schuyler tampers with, 166, 204 ; in the expedition against Mohawks, 233 ; two of this village desert to Senecas, v., p. 15–16; escape of two women and a child of this village, 17 ; chief of, killed in an attack on a French party by mistake, 49; offer to attack Iroquois, 57 ; troubles caused by liquor, 204; on the march against English withdraw, 205 ; discovered to have promised Schuyler not to fight English, 208; Vaudreuil treats them with great contempt, ib.; they repair their fault, 209 ; zeal for defence of the colony, p. 240; In-

dians of, address Governor of Mass., p. 273, n.

MOUNT DESERT ISLAND, near mouth of Penobscot, Father Biard begins settlement of St. Sauveur on, i., p. 271; frequented by English fishermen, 279 ; settlement on, destroyed by Argal, ib.; Iberville at, v., p. 27 ; Vincellotte at, 51.

MOUY CHARLES DE, (SIEUR DE LA MAILLERAYE,) Vice-Admiral of France, induces Francis I. to send Cartier to America, i., p. 114.

MOXOS, visited by Father Baraza, i., p. 57.

MOYEN, JOHN B., SIEUR DES GRANGES, killed by Iroquois, iii., p. 46, n.; his daughter Elizabeth marries Lambert Closse, ib.

MOYNE, CHARLES LE, brings in chiefs, iii., p. 86, n.; commands Montreal troops in Tracy's expedition, 90, n.; sent to Senecas, 242 ; asked by cantons to negotiate peace, 250; well received, 252 ; two of his sons report to de la Barre, ib.

MOYNE, FRANCIS LE, see BIENVILLE.

MOYNE, JAMES LE, see ST. HELENE.

MOYNE, JOSEPH LE, see SERIGNY.

MOYNE, LOUIS LE, see CHATEAUGUÉ.

MOYNE, PAUL LE, see MARICOURT.

MOYNE, PETER LE, see IBERVILLE.

MOYNE, LE, FATHER SIMON, Jesuit, sketch of, iii., p. 86, n.; sent to Onondaga to ratify peace, ii., p. 257 ; reception, ib.; baptizes some Iroquois, ib.; discovers salt springs at Onondaga, 257, n.; attacked on his return, 258 ; goes to the Mohawks, 261; dangers, ib.; replies to Mohawks in name of Governor General, 280 ; accompanies Hurons to the Mohawk, 281 ; retires to Fort Orange and Manhattan, gives information of the salt springs and negotiates commercial treaty, iii., p. 15 ; brought back to Quebec, 19; goes the fifth time to negotiate with the Iroquois, 38; runs great risks, 41, reception at Onondaga, ib.; speech at a Council of three cantons, 42; his position at Onondaga, 51 ; brings back French prisoners, 52 ; death, 87 ; Garakonthié comes to Quebec to mourn for, 85 ; Garakonthié's apostrophe to, 86, n.

MOZAMBIQUE, discovered, i., p. 20.

MUANBISSEK, Abénaquis of, join in letter to Gov. of Mass., v., p. 273, n.

MULLENS, MAJOR, at Port Royal, v., p. 228, n.

MUNIER, or MEUSNIER, PETER, witness or accomplice in la Sale's death, iv., p. 94; remains among Cenis, 107; taken by Spaniards, 113.

MUNK, JOHN, a Dane, discovers Christiana Sea and New Denmark, i., p. 53.

MURAT, LIEUTENANT, repulses Iroquois, surprised and disappears, iv., p. 151.

MUSQUAKIES, proper name of Foxes, iii., p. 105, n.

MUSSEAUX, CHARLES J. D'AILLEBOUST DES, commandant at Montreal, sends out Lambert Closse, ii., p. 251, n.; Manteht, a son of, iv., p. 31, 122, n.

MUYS, NICHOLAS DANEAUX, SEIGNEUR DE, notice of, vi., p. 17, n.; sent with Valrenes to defend Chambly, iv., p. 203 ; commands battalion in Frontenac's expedition, v., p. 13 ; sent with Canadians and regulars to Placentia, p. 22; Brouillan's envoy to Iberville, 39; Brouillan proposes him for commander, 40 ; ordered to burn houses near Fort St. John, 44 ; suggested as governor of St. John, 45 ; appointed governor of Louysiana, but dies on the way, v., p. 46, n.; vi., p. 17.

NACOGDOCHES, Texas tribe, iv., p. 80, n.; mission among, vi., p. 24, n.

NAANSI, Texas tribe, iv., p. 108, n.

NABIRI, Texas tribe, iv., p. 108, n.

NAGCODOCHES, Texas tribe, iv., p. 80, n.

NAHOUDIKHÉ, Texas tribe, iv., p. 108, n.

NANFAN, Lt. Gov. of N. Y., succeeds Bellomont, v., p. 138, n.; sends Bleecker and Schuyler to Onondaga, ib.; at Conference in Albany obtains deed of most of Canada, 140, n.

NARAKAMIGOU, Abénaquis of, join in letter to governor of Massachusetts, v., p. 273, n.

NARANTSOAK, see NORRIDGEWALK.

NARVAEZ, PAMPHILO DE, discovers country of Apalaches, i., p. 35; discoverer of Pensacola, vi., p. 43 ; perishes miserably in Florida without making a single settlement, i., p. 134.

NASSAU STRAIT, discovered, i., p. 47.

NASSITOCHES, sing calumet to l'Epinai, vi., p. 39.

NASSOHOS, Texas tribe, iv., p. 108, n.

NASSONIS, or ASSONIS, described by Charlevoix under the name of Ayennis, iv., p.

NASSONIS, (*continued.*) 80; branch of the Texas Indians, ib., n.; Joutel's party reach, 108, n.

NATCHEZ, Indian tribe of Louisiana, La Salle plants cross at, iii., p. 214, n.; Iberville at, v., p. 124, n.; la Motte Cadillac puts up storehouses at, vi., p. 24; English excite against French, ib.; Cadillac refuses their calumet, 25, n.; kill four Frenchmen and attempt to kill Mess. la Loire, 26; rob and kill a Frenchman, 28; expedition against, ib.; Bienville's message to Great Chief, and his reply, 29; terms of peace, 30; sing calumet to l'Epinai, 39; Capt. Blondel sent to, 40; renew hostilities, 72; many declare against us, ib.; Delietto induces Great Chief to give up to Bienville head of Old Hair, &c., 72; no missionaries among, 76; massacre French colony among them, 81; war against, 89; what hastened the massacre 91; Choctaws held back by French from destroying Natchez, le Sueur leads 700 Choctaws against, 94; burn two Frenchmen, 96; attempt to reduce Tonicas, 95; insolent proposal to de Loubois, ib.; defeated by Choctaws at Bayou St. Catherine, 96, n.; saved by, negroes, 96; desperate defence against French, 97; threaten to murder all their prisoners, if they do not raise siege, 99; delude and outwit French, 100; profane sacred vessels and church vestments taken at massacre, 101; interrupt commerce by their ravages, 103; preparations to attack in their stronghold, 109; defence of forts, ib.; head chief and two others come to French camp, detained, 111; one escapes, ib.; others surrender, 112; escape of most of, 114; Head Chief and others sold as slaves in St. Domingo, 114, n., 115; treachery toward Tonicas, 116-7; besiege St. Denys at Natchitoches, 117; defeated, 118.

NATCHITOCHES, Indians on Red River, some settle among Colapissas, vi., p. 19; Bienville and St. Denys form alliance with, ib.; attacked by Colapissas while retiring, 19; rest join St. Denys at old settlement, ib.; fort on their island, 20; sing calumet to l'Epinai, 39; grants near them, 64; St. Denys sent back to, 65; some seen among Natchez at time of massacre, 91; St. Denys answers for fidelity, ib.; abandon their village to superior force of Natchez, 118; pursue them after their defeat, ib.

NATCHITOS, Texas tribe, iv., p. 108, n.

NATCHOOS, Texas tribe, iv., p. 108, n.

NATION DE BŒUF, (Sioux Sédentaires,) iii., p. 50, n.

NATION DES MONTS PELEZ, iii., p. 40, n.

NATISCOTEC, Indian name of Anticosti, i., p. 37, 115, n.; meaning of, 115, n.

NAVEDACHES, Texas tribe, iv., p. 80, n.

NAXOAT, see FORT NAXOAT.

NAZONES, Texas tribe, mission among, iv., p. 24, n.

NEGABAMAT, NOEL, a Montagnez chief, first to settle at Sillery, ii., p. 98, n.; ratifies peace, p. 181.

NEGROES, Natchez secure some before killing French, vi., p. 82; those captured well treated, 84; they massacre thirty Chaouachas, 90; one hundred and fifty captured from Natchez by Choctaws, 96; others save Natchez from utter ruin, 96; fifteen negroes fight well against Natchez, 100; on Perrier's expedition, ib.; Natchez surrender those in their hands, 110; discovery of negro plot in New Orleans instigated by Chicasaws, 119.

NEHETHOWUCK, true name of Crees, iii., p. 107, n.

NEKOUBA RIVER, Druillettes and Dablon at, iii., p. 39; fair at source of, 40.

NELSON, Hudson's pilot, i., p. 51; his pretended taking possession of Hudson Bay gives English no right, i., p. 51; iii., p. 230; discovers and names Nelson or Bourbon river, iii., p. 230, n.

NELSON, WILLIAM, nephew of Sir Thomas Temple, iii., p. 187, n.; notice of, iv., p. 231, n.; a prisoner, iv., p. 213; at Quebec, 214; well received by Frontenac, ib.; induces two French soldiers to desert and so defeats Pemkuit expedition, 229; sends to Governor of New England a statement of position of Quebec, 236.

NELSON RIVER, called by French Bourbon river, iii., p. 235.

NEMISCAU RIVER, iii., p. 231, 271.

NENASKOUMAT, one of the first settlers, at Sillery, ii., p. 98, n.

NEPTUNE, THE, first ship to enter the Micissipi, vi., p. 40.

NESCAMBIOUIT, Abénaqui chief received by

Louis XIV. at Versailles, v., p. 42; greatly distinguished in Newfoundland, 42-4; accompanies de Montigny on an expedition against English, 174; distinguished, ib., display of valor, wears sword given by Louis XIV., wounded, 207; Penhallow's account of, ib., n.

NESMOND, MARQUIS DE, commands naval expedition against New England, v., p. 70; its failure, ib.

NEUTRAL ISLAND, the St. Croix of de Monts, i., p. 252.

NEUTRAL NATION, or ATTIWANDARONK, ii., p. 73 ; origin of French name, 151 ; position, ib, n.; character, 152; solicit missionaries, ib.; visited by F. de la Roche Daillon, 37, n., 152 ; by Brebeuf and Chaumonot, 152; little fruit of mission, 153; Hurons announce gospel to, 163 ; destroyed by Iroquois, 271, n.; remnant join Hurons on Lake Superior, ib.; towns of, ib.; form part of Senecas, ib.

NEUVILLETTE, DANIEL ROBINEAU, SIEUR DE, youngest son of the Baron of Bekancourt, v., p. 30; and brother of Chev. de Villebon, p. 30; informs him that an English fleet menaces Naxoat, ib.; pursues English, p. 33; sent against English corsairs and killed, p. 157, n.

NEVADO, a pretended river near Labrador discovered by Cortereal, i., p. 106.

NEW ALBION, discovered by Drake, i., p. 44.

NEW ALEXANDRIA, Earl of Stirling calls part of his grant, i., p. 250.

NEW AMSTERDAM or MANHATTE, taken by English and called New York, iii., p. 72. See MANHATTE, NEW YORK.

NEW ANDALUSIA, limits of, i., p, 27.

NEW BISCAY, i., p. 41.

NEW DENMARK, i., p. 53.

NEW ENGLAND, proposes alliance and neutrality, ii., p. 213 ; letter to Commissioners of, p. 214; earthquake in, iii., p. 62.

NEWFOUNDLAND, Conception Bay in, discovered and named, i., p. 23 ; Basques, Bretons and Normans take fish on Great Bank, p. 25, 106 ; John Denis of Honfleur publishes map of, in 1506, i., p. 26; Humphrey Gilbert takes possesion of, i., p. 45 ; iii., p. 104 ; White's tract on, i., p. 89; Memoire touchant Terre Neuve, p. 89; visited by Cabot, p. 20, 105 ; Cortereal, p. 23, 105 ; Humphrey (Gilbert,) i., p. 45; iii., p. 140; names in, given by Stirling, ii., p. 59; Guy settles at Conception Bay, iii., p. 140; de Monts takes possession of Placentia in, p. 53 ; Lord Baltimore settles at Ferryland, p. 140, n.; Sir David Kirke settles there, p. 131; vi., p. 126 ; French settle at Placentia, iii., p. 141: described, p. 140; climate, p. 143; natives, 144; English, though constantly defeated in, retain, 146 ; neglected by French Court, ib.; governor sent over, ib.; orders not obeyed, ib.; fort built at Placentia, 141 ; Frontenac delayed at Great Bank of, iv., p. 27; du Palais fails to relieve, 222; English attack, 223 ; position of English and French in, in 1696, v., p. 33 ; d'Iberville proposes to expel English, 35 ; de Brouillan's expedition against English in, 36 ; what prevented Iberville from totally expelling English from, 48; English project for expelling French, 71; what de Nesmond was to do in, 71-3 ; English forces sent to, 73; English re-occupy, 93; successful French expedition, 172; St. Ovide's plan for expelling English, 212; capture of St. John, 213; French expedition in, 231; given up to England by the treaty of Utrecht, 266.

NEW FRANCE, name first applied on Ulpius' globe, 1542, ii., p. 20, n.; used by Cartier, ib.; name ascribed by Biard to Verrazani, ib.; Charlevoix attributed it to a much later date, p. 20 ; Protestants excluded from, 65 ; judicious choice of settlers, ib.; missionaries of, pp. 66-8 ; fur trade, iv., p. 16 ; boundary fixed at St. George's river, v., p. 93.

NEW GALICIA, i., p. 41.

NEW GUINEA, discovered, i., p. 35, 50.

NEW HOLLAND, discovered, i., p. 47, 53.

NEWICHAWANNICK, Indian name of Salmon Falls, iv., p. 131, n.

NEW ISLANDS, discovered, i., p. 61.

NEW JERSEY, founded by Swedes, ii., p.11; occupied by English, ib.

NEW LONDON or FORT ST. GEORGE, i., p. 136; vi., p. 46.

NEW MEXICO, discovered and named, i., p. 44.

NEW NETHERLAND, i., p. 50 ; name when given, ii., p. 10; iii., p. 72 ; described by F. Jogues, ii., p. 160; earthquake in, iii., p. 62 ; taken by English and called by

NEW NETHERLAND, (*continued.*) them NEW YORK, ii., p. 11 ; iii., p. 172 ; Surinam given to Dutch for, v., p. 91.

NEW ORLEANS, founded, vi., p. 40; laid out by la Tour, ib., n.; headquarters removed to, p. 67; Charlevoix's account of, at his visit, ib., n.; ravaged by hurricane, 69 ; Perrier's precautions as to, 94; negro plot at, 119.

NEW PLYMOUTH, in New England, founded, i., p. 53.

NEW SEGOVIA, i., p. 41.

NEW SOUTH WALES, Hudson Bay, i., p. 54.

NEW SPAIN, discovered, i., p. 31 ; conquered, ib.

NEW SWEDEN, settled, i., p. 55 ; ii., p. 11 ; conquered by Dutch, i., p. 56; supposed by Charlevoix to be the present New Jersey, ii., p. 11.

NEW WALES, i., p. 51.

NEW WEST FRISELAND, discovered, i., p. 47.

NEW YORK, formerly Nieuw Netherland, wrested from Dutch by English, iii., p. 72; granted by Charles II. to Duke of York, ib.; Dongan Governor of, p. 217 ; Andros Governor of, 308 ; trade with, profitable to Iroquois, iv., p. 16 ; de Callieres' project for conquest of, 20 ; plan after conquest of, 25 ; failure of enterprise, 26 ; new project, 35 ; Denonville's advice to lay waste up to Albany, 45–6 ; civil war in, p. 248 ; Fletcher Governor of, v., p. 19, n.; conquest of, easier than of New England, p. 70 ; Nesmond to attack, after taking Boston, ib.; Bellomont governor of, v., p. 80 ; why Vaudreuil did not attack, 179 ; panic at, p. 200, n.; troops assembled in to attack Chambly, 215 ; Mareuil at N. Y. City, p. 216 ; loss of colony by Vetch's expedition, p. 220, n.

NEZ PERCÉS, Algonquin tribe, iii., p. 119 ; same as AMIKOUEK or BEAVER Indains, 120, n.

NIAGARA, river between Lake Erie and Lake Ontario, la Sale plans fort at, and leaves Tonti there with 30 men, iii., p. 202 ; failure of Indians to meet de la Barre at, 247 ; fort at, projected, 263 ; built, garrisoned, abandoned after great mortality, 290–1 ; besieged, 299 ; reinforcement sent to, 302; Denonville makes its abandonment a favor to Iroquois, 306; our allies complain of, iv., p. 53 ; Joncaire at, v., p. 308, n.; Senecas permit us to restore fort at, 266, 308, n.

NICARAGUA, conquered, i., p. 33.

NICOLAS, FATHER LOUIS, Jesuit, account of, iii., p. 108, n.; accompanies Allouez to the Ottawas, 108 ; brings Indians to Quebec and returns to Chagoimegon with them, 119.

NICOLAS ISLAND, v., p. 277, n.

NICOLET, JOHN, sent to the Iroquois as deputy of Governor General, ii., p. 124 ; how received, ib.; explorations in the west, 137, n.

NICHOLSON, FRANCIS, Lt. Gov. of New York, New England and Virginia, Gov. of Maryland and Virginia, v., p. 227, n.; appointed by Ingoldsby commander in chief of English forces against Canada, p. 217, n.; at Boston, 225; besieges Port Royal, 227 ; Subercase capitulates to, 230; regrets giving him favorable terms, 231 ; sends capitulation to Vaudreuil, 233 ; pretensions to rest of Acadia, 233 ; threats, ib.; proposes exchange of prisoners, 234 ; Vaudreuil's reply, ib.; refuses to exchange, 237 ; marches to attack Montreal, 245 ; falls back, 246 ; prepares for next year, 247; six hundred Iroquois join him to attack Montreal, 252.

NICOYA, discovered by Gil Davila, i., p. 33.

NICUESSA, DIEGO, discoveries and settlements, i., p. 27; fights Indians, 36.

NIGAMON, an Indian hostage, ii., p. 31.

NIKA, Indian hunter with la Sale, iv., p. 89; murdered, 91.

NILE, source of, discovered by Father Paez or Pais, i., p. 52.

NIÑO, PERO ALONZO, discovers Ayola, i., p. 22.

NIPISSINGS, real Algonquins, called also Nipissiriniens, ii., p. 72; meaning of name, p. 95, n.; Bysirinien, p. 95; Huron name, ib., n.; Allouez visits them on Lake Alimpegon, to which they had retired, iii., p. 107; nearly destroyed, 236, n.; Dollier de Casson visits, iii., p. 122, n.; protest fidelity to Frontenac, iv., p. 272 ; on his Iroquois expedition, v., p. 13; on Ramezay's, 219; zeal for defence of colony, 240, n.

NISIBOUROUNIK, a division of the Kilistinons or Crees, iii., p. 107, n.

NITARIKYK, chief of the Nipissings, iii., p. 122, n.

NIZA, (i.e., Nice in Savoy) Friar Mark of, Italian, called Spanish Franciscan by Charlevoix, discovers Cibola, i., p. 38.

NOENSA, see ROENSA.

NOIROLLES, see LEROLLES.

NOLLI, ANTHONY, discovers Cape Verde islands, i., p. 17.

NOMBRE DE DIOS, i., p. 36.

NORIMBEGA, what it was, i., p. 249, 253; river of, said by Charlevoix to be the Pentagoët, i., p. 275, n.; but according, to Jean Alphonse the Bay of Fundy, vi., p. 124.

NORIS, ADMIRAL, at St. John with 23 ships, v., p. 73.

NORMANS, when they began to to take cod on Newfoundland and the neighboring shores, i., p. 25, 106; desired as colonists, iii., p. 81.

NORO, or the Porcupine, Fox chief, v., p. 144.

NORRIDGEWALK, NARANTSOAK, Abénaqui town, Druillettes at, ii., p. 214, n.; Rale missionary at, v., p. 268; New England expedition against, 271; letter of Indians of to Governor of Massachusetts, 273, n.; Rale's church at, ib.; plundered by English, 275; English fail to carry off Rale from, 276; rendezvous of Indians, 277; surprised by New Englanders who kill Rale, 278; Father de Syressme at, 281, n.

NORTHERN COMPANY, formed at Quebec, iii., p. 233; send Radisson and Groseilliers to Hudson Bay, ib.; censure them, 236; their loss, 237; offer to aid Niagara, 261, n.; undertake to recover Hudson Bay, 270; send Motte Egron, iv., p. 53; at expense of Du Tast's fleet, 200.

NOTRE DAME DES ANGES, first Jesuit chapel at Quebec, position of, i., p. 117, n.

NOTRE DAME DE FOYE, Huron mission near Quebec, iii., p. 154, n.

NOUE, FATHER ANNE DE, Jesuit, son of the Lord of Prieres, and page at Court, ii., p. 184, n.; early labors in Canada, 37; returns after country restored to France, 65; what delayed his going to Huron country, 69; death and eulogy, 183.

NOUE, LIEUT. DE LA, sent against Mohawks, iv., p. 233; takes a fort, 234; wounded, 235; death of, 234, n.

NOUVEL, FATHER HENRY, Jesuit, missionary in the West, iii., p. 196, n.

NOVA, JOHN DE, discoveries of, i., p. 24.

NOVA SCOTIA, limits of, i., p. 249. See ACADIA.

NOVA ZEMBLA, discovered by Barrow, i., p. 42.

NOYAN, CAPT. PETER J. PAYEN, SIEUR DE, and his brother, an ensign, nephews of Bienville, cashiered, and sent to France, vi., p. 75, n.

NOYANT, MR. DE, commanding the Aigle, vi., p. 16.

NOYROT, FATHER PHILIBERT, Jesuit, Superior of missions of New France, ii., p. 37; lost on a ship he had chartered to relieve Quebec, p. 46.

NUT TREES on St. John's river, i., p. 255.

NUYTS' LAND, discovered, i., p. 54.

NUYTS, PETER DE, discoveries of, i., p. 54.

OCHASTEGUINS, Champlain's name for Hurons and Iroquois, ii., p. 69.

OCHOA, DON MARTIN DE, Spanish captain, leads the van of Menendez' force, i., p. 198; reconnoitres the fort and takes a prisoner, 201.

OFFAGOULAS, Louysiana Indians, intermingled with Yazoos, vi., p. 85; refuse to join them in the plot, 86; retire to Tonicas, 86; fidelity, 86, 95.

OGLETHORPE, GEN. JAMES E., founds Georgia, i., p. 64; ransoms Drouet de Richarville, vi., p. 121, n.

OHARITA, or St. John the Evangelist, Tionnontate or Petun town destroyed by Iroquois, ii., p. 229.

OIL SPRINGS, discovered, ii., p. 151, n.

OIOGUÉ, Mohawk name for Hudson, ii., p. 146, n., 187, n.

OJEDA, ALPHONSO DE, Vesputius accompanies, i., p. 21; discoveries and settlements by, 27; battle with Indians, 36.

OJIBWAYS, ii., p. 137, n.

OLABALKEBICHE, Natché chief, vi., p. 114, n. See STUNG SERPENT.

OLBEAU, FATHER JOHN, Recollect, at Quebec, ii., p. 25; only priest in colony, 30.

OLD HAIR, Natché chief of Apple village, his head given up to Bienville, vi., p. 72.

OLEANÇON, SIEUR DE, at siege of Quebec, iv., p. 180.

OLIER, REV. JOHN JAMES, sketch of, ii., p. 129; founder of Seminary of St. Sulpice and of Montreal, ib.

OLOCOTORA, (OLOTOCARA, OLOTORACA,) nephew of Saturioua reconnoitres San Matheo, i., p. 228; exploit of, 230; brings in a prisoner, 232; imagines hè is to fall in the attack, ib.; his request to de Gourgues, 233; regrets Chevalier's departure, 236.

ONANGUICÉ, Pottawatami chief, complains to Frontenac, v., p. 69; his speech at the Peace Council, 143; introduces Sac deputy to de Callieres, 144; his attire at the General Congress, 151; speaks in name of Illinois, 152; de Callieres' message to them, ib.

ONASKÉ, Ottawa chief, his services to commandant at Michilimakinac, iv., p. 277; marches against Iroquois, 278.

OÑATE, CHRISTOPHER DE, founds Guadalajara or Xalisco, i., p. 36.

OÑATE, JOHN DE, conquers New Mexico and founds San Juan, i., p. 48; discovers Rio del Norte and Lake de los Conibas, 51.

ONATHAKA, or OATHKAQUA, chief on east coast of Florida, Laudonniere ransoms two Spaniards from, i., p. 171.

ONDAKOUT, JOACHIM, Huron, adventures of, ii., p. 269, 276.

ONDATAUAUAT, ONDATAOUATOUAT, Ottawas, ii., p. 270, n.

ONDESSON, ONDESSONE, ONDESSONK, name of a Huron chief, ii., p. 109; Huron name of Tesswehat or le Borgne de l'Isle, 164, n.; of Father Jogues, 251; of Father le Moyne, ib.

ONEIDAS, ONNEYOUTH, one of five Iroquois cantons, situation and description of ii., p. 190; defeat Algonquins and Hurons, 245; Oneidas ask peace, 252; several embrace Christianity, iii., p. 12; they kill three Frenchmen, 14; d'Aillebout retaliates, ib.; Garakonthié turns back an Oneida war party, 44; repulsed by Chippeways, 64; ask peace of de Tracy, 87; why he did not treat them as he did the Mohawks, 93; ask de Courcelles for a missionary and peace, 108; indocile, 117; some murdered by French, 150, n.; Bruyas effects little among, 158; de la Barre sends a belt to ask their neutrality, 249; offer their mediation, 250; Father Milet falls into their hands, 277; his sufferings, ib.; a woman saves his life, ib.; subsequent notice of her, iv., p. 244–5; a Mohawk Christian negotiates successfully for French, with Oneidas, iii., p. 292: deputies at Montreal ask peace, 305; Oneida and Mohegan war party against French, iv., p. 50; expedition against Montreal, p. 145, n.; surprised at St. Sulpice, 194; Beaucourt sent against, 213, n.; attack French and allies, 234; defeated but harass our men on their retreat, 235; proposals to Frontenac, 238; attack Mantcht, 245; again ask peace, v., p. 17; Frontenac's conditions, 18; Vaudreuil ravages this canton and brings several chiefs and French prisoners, ib.; several Oneidas settle in Canada, p. 50; why all do not, ib.; an Oneida chief at Montreal, 63; Frontenac's reply, 64; why this canton sends no deputies to de Callieres, 102; but sends to Gov. of New England, ib.; an Oneida put in prison by Governor of New England, 108; totem, 111; sends no deputies to Montreal, 111; seem ill-disposed to peace and give no prisoners, 139.

ONEUGIOURÉ, Mohawk town, ii., p. 146, n., 187, n.

ONHOUENTSIOUANN, Iroquois deputy at Montreal, v., p. 94, n.

ONKWE HONWE, name used by Hurons and Iroquois, ii., p. 72, n.

ONNEIOUT. See ONEIDA, ii., p. 190.

ONNONOUAGAREN, Mohawk chief, iv., p. 193, n.

ONNONTAGUÉ, ii., p. 190. See ONONDAGA.

ONOHARE, JOSEPH, Algonquin, burnt by Iroquois, ii., p. 238.

ONONDAGA, TOWN, Jesuits received at, ii., p. 275.

ONONDAGAS, chief of the five Iroquois cantons, ii., p. 189; situation, description, peculiarities, ib.; they treat of peace with French, 251; Father le Moyne sent to, 257; receive two Jesuits sent by Gov. General, 262; projected French colony at Onondaga, 267; carried out, 276; treat French well, ib.; summon Hurons of Isle Orleans to join them, 281; reply of Governor General to Onondagas, ib.; refuse to take Jesuits with the Hurons, iii., p. 13; treat Hurons as prisoners, p. 13; conspire against French who escape from canton, 14–8; treat prisoners well, 36; Christian church in this canton, ib.,

ask peace, ib.; pre-eminence of this canton, ib.; 200 Onondagas attack Montreal island, and kill the town major, 46; envoys attacked by Algonquins, 70; invite French to restore settlement, offer to send daughters to Ursulines at Quebec as hostages, 65; ask peace of de Tracy, 85; attack Western Indians, 241; act in bad faith with de la Barre, ib.; he sends them a belt to obtain their neutrality, 249; reply to a deputy from Governor of New York, 251; de la Barre's confidence in, 252; urge Father Lamberville to report to Governor of New York what passed between his deputy and the Onondagas, 253; guarantee peace, ib.; their envoy speaks well, 254; Father Lamberville negotiates successfully with this canton, 267; noble and generous conduct of the sachems after the seizure of the principal Iroquois chiefs at Catarocouy, 278; a Mohawk negotiates for the French, 292; Onondagas capture Frenchmen near Catarocouy, 299; Father de Lamberville treats with them successfully, 299; labors to win them over, 300; they send deputies with a force, ib.; prisoners collected by, iv., p. 49; Frontenac will treat only with this canton, 52; Father de Carheil's estimate of these Indians, 55; they intrigue to draw away the Christian Iroquois but fail, 198; send belt to bewail death of St. Helene 199; try to tamper with Iroquois of the Mountain, ib.; abortive expedition against, 213, n.; Black Kettle's party at Chaudiere Falls, 217; English fort at Onondaga, 240, 255; send envoys, 249; war parties sent against French, 269; Stephen Tegannanokoa tortured at, 298; Francis Gonannhatenha put to death by, 299; Mary Garangouas, 301; Onondaga informed by a deserter of Frontenac's approach, v., p. 15; they burn their great village at the approach of the French army, 16; also their fort, ib.; their error in doing so, 17; country ravaged, 18; heroic death of an old man of this canton, ib.; they prevent the Oneidas removing to Canada, 50; English compensate further losses and aid them to rebuild, 57; pretend to accompany Oneidas to Canada to settle, 63; defeated by Hurons and Algonquins, 78-9; Frontenac's reply to English governor's complaints on this, 90, two delegates of this canton at Montreal, 101; what passed between them and the Gov. Gen., ib.; French deputies at a General Council at Onondaga, 103; totem of, 111; Vaudreuil sends deputies to Onondaga, 138; Onondagas send embassy to Ottawas, 157; seem ill-disposed, 159; Vaudreuil secures canton by Longueil's diplomacy, 166; treaty concluded at Onondaga to make war on French, 216; speech of an orator at a great council at Onondaga on the balance of power, 221; deputies of the canton and Vaudreuil, 222; Baron Longueuil at Onondaga, leads deputies to Montreal, 236; how Vaudreuil treats with these deputies, 239.

ONOHARE, see ONAHARE.

ONONTHIO, Iroquois word, meaning Great Mountain, given as the translation of Montmagny, and applied to all subsequent Governors-General of New France, iii., p. 124.

ONTAOUONOUÉS, (ONKWE-HONWÉ,) name of Hurons, its meaning, ii., p. 72.

ONTARIO, meaning of, ii., p. 84, n.

OQUELOUSSAS, (BLACK WATER,) Louysiana tribe, vi., p. 39, n.

ORANGE, see FORT ORANGE, ALBANY.

ORANGER, D', Florida mutineer, turns pirate and takes several Spanish prizes, i., p. 168; takes Governor of Jamaica, ib.; is duped and taken, 169.

ORDAZ, DIEGO DE, officer of Cortez, i., p. 31, 32; discovers Chiapa, 36; ascends Orinoco, ib.

ORELLANA, FRANCIS, Spaniard, discovers Amazon, i., p. 39.

ORINOCO RIVER, discovered by Columbus, i., p. 21.

ORLEANS, FATHER PETER J. D', Jesuit, blames Father Coton for Madame de Guercheville's treaty in their favor, though Champlain justifies her, i. p. 263.

ORLEANS, DUKE OF, refuses to allow Huguenots to settle in Louysiana, v., p. 127.

ORRY, M., on La Salle's expedition, killed by Indians, iv., p. 71.

ORVILLE, MR. D', appointed lieutenant by de Monts, i., p. 253, n.

ORVILLIERS, CAPTAIN CLAUDE D', commandant at Catarocouy, iii., p. 249, 259; succeeded by du Tast, ib.; reconnoitres enemy, ib.; commands one of the corps in Dénonville's Seneca War, 283; throws up and holds Fort des Sables, 285; proposes conference with Onondagas, 299; sends Perelle with Onondaga envoys, 300; throws himself into Isle Orleans after retreat of English fleet, iv., p. 186; defends Chambly, 203; leads a force against Iroquois, but gives up command to Mr. de Beaucourt, 217.

OSAGES, Indian tribe of Dacota family, iii., p. 31; some come to defend Detroit against the Foxes, v., p. 258; some go to France, vi., p. 76, n.

OSKETAEST, report of, v., p. 108.

OSSARAGUÉ, Mohawk fishing station, ii., p. 187, n.

OSSERNENON, or OSSERION, Mohawk town, ii., p. 146, n., 187; probably Gandawagué, ib.

OSSOSSANE, Huron town, ii., p. 210, n.

OSSOTTEOEZ, OTSOTCHOUÉ, Arkansas tribe, iv., p. 108, n.

OSWEGO RIVER, iii., p. 218; see CHOUGUEN.

OTAXESTE, Iroquois envoy, v., p. 94.

OTCHAGRAS, Indian name of Winnebagoes, iii., p. 31; called by French Puants, on Green Bay, ib.; promise to send delegates to General Council at Montreal, v., p. 142.

OTEIONDI, Huron chief, ii., p. 109.

OTIATANHEGUÉ, near Onondaga, iii., p. 41.

OTONABEE RIVER, ii., p. 28, n.

OTOPTATAS, in France, vi., p. 76, n.

OTSINONANNHONT, BARNABY, a Huron, sets out to convert Neuters, ii., p. 163, n.

OTOUACHE, or TOANCHE, Huron town, ii., p. 27, n.

OTTAWA RIVER, called also Great river of the Algonquins, Algonquins on, ii., p. 9, n.; Great river of the Ottawas, 24; Champlain ascends, ib.; Lalemant's adventure on, 111; deserted, 236.

OTTAWAS, or UPPER ALGONQUINS, (OUTAOUAIS, ANDATAHOUAT, ONDATAUAUAT, ONDATAOUATOUAT, ii., p. 270, n.;) supposed by Charlevoix to be on, and levy toll on the Ottawa River, 270; placed by early writers on Manitouline, ib.; adventures of a party coming to Quebec, ib.; their character, 272; few conversions, ib.; missionaries to, attacked by Mohawks, 273; Ottawas abandon missionaries and French, 274; insult Sioux, who drive them out, iii., p. 31; shameful treatment of Father Mesnard, 47; hardened, 48; ask another missionary, 99; one given as ill-treated as others, 100; obstacles to their conversion, ib.; come to Quebec to sell furs, 108; refuse to receive a Jesuit, ib.; seek to renew war with Iroquois, 151; driven to Lake Huron by Sioux, 196, n.; Ottawa-Kiskakons should have made reparation to Senecas, 218; Onondagas, Cayugas and Senecas march against, 241; refuse to join Durantaye, 246; attacked in Saginaw Bay by Iroquois, 264; difficulty in preventing their making peace with Senecas, 281; act badly in engagement with Senecas, 287, n., 288; negotiate with the Senecas, iv., p. 53; invectives against the French, 56; burn an Iroquois, to show that they have no idea of peace with the cantons; bring a great convoy of goods to Montreal with Hurons and other Indians, 142; reply to Iroquois of Sault St. Louis, 147; press Iroquois, 190; keep up harassing Iroquois, 200; some Ottawas killed at La Prairie, 204; 200 at Montreal refuse to march against Iroquois, 221; Iroquois intrigues to detach them from us, 250, 264; protest fidelity, 272; deputies sent to Quebec by Louvigny's influence, are convinced that Iroquois seek only their ruin, 250–1; rude language of deputies to Frontenac, who gains them over, 251; protest fidelity, 272; conclude peace with Iroquois, the motive, 277; send a war-party, defeat Iroquois, 278; act as scouts, v. p. 12; expected in vain at Catarocouy, 14; pretexts to cover up their ill-will, 22; tell Frontenac that he must appease the Miamis, 65; interview of Ottawas with Frontenac, 67; push the Iroquois War vigorously, ib.; Iroquois endeavoring to surprise them defeated by Hurons, 78; young Iroquois braves propose to attack them during the peace negotiations, 79; they strike a blow at the Iroquois, ib.; several Ottawas wait on de Callieres, 100; excuse attack on Iroquois, ib.; reproaches, 101; attack Iroquois hunters, and the reason,

100, 102, 135; totem of, 111; Father Anjelran rescues from their hands two Iroquois prisoners, 142; they ask de Callieres for F. Anjelran and Nicholas Perrot, who are granted to them, and suppression of liquor trade, 153; attack Iroquois near Catarocouy, 163; discontent at settlement of Detroit, the cause, 165; defy commandant at Detroit, routed and obliged to abandon prisoners, 169; refuse satisfaction, 179; Louvigny brings them to their senses, ib.; speech of deputies to Vaudreuil, 180; he reconciles Ottawas and Iroquois, ib.; some Ottawas killed by Miamis, they ask redress from commandant at Detroit in vain, 184; one of the commandants maltreats an Ottawa, 185; his nation takes umbrage at all the others, troubles that ensue, 185; send deputies to Vaudreuil, 188; speech of the chief deputy, ib.; Vaudreuil sends him to la Motte Cadillac, 189; declaration of that commandant, 190; he relents, ib.; Ottawas join de Ramezai's party, 219; an Ottawa chief attacks Mascoutins, v., p. 257.

OTTIGNY, SIEUR DE, Laudonniere's lieutenant in Florida, sent to explore, i., p. 150, 157; kept near him as a trusty man, 166; explorations of, 173; visits a lake, probably Lake George, ib, n.; sent to aid Outina, 174; gains a victory and returns to Caroline, 175; his courage, 177; tragical death, 211.

OUABACHE RIVER, iii., p. 214; the Ohio, ib.

OUABANGUÉ, Chippeway chief, v., p. 144; his attire, 151.

OUABIMANITOU, Mascoutin chief, v., p. 263, n.

OUATCHITAS, RIVER OF THE, see WASHITA.

OUELLE RIVER, Rev. Mr. Francheville repulses Phips at, iv., p. 169, n.

OUENRONRONON, OUENTOUORONON, WEANOHRONON, or WENROHRONON, trade with Dutch, ii., p. 84; perhaps the Antouohonoron of Champlain, ib.; their country, 121, n.; between Neuters and Iroquois, ib.; take refuge among Hurons, ib.

OUFEOGOULAS, (DOG NATION,) vi., p. 39, n.

OUHENSIOUAN, Onondaga chief, v., p. 101, n.

OUILAMEK, Pottawatamie chief, marches against Iroquois, iv., p. 278; speaks well at general peace council, v., p. 143.

OUISCONSING RIVER, by which Marquette and Jolliet enter the Micissipi, i., p. 57; iii., p. 180.

OUMAS, Louysiana tribe, welcome d'Iberville, v., p. 122; sings calumet to l'Epinai, vi., p. 39; F. Limoge among, vi., p. 15, n.

OUMAMIOUEKS, Indians trading at Tadoussac and instructed by missionaries, ii., p. 243; iii., p. 40; lay inland N. W. of Tadoussac, iii., p. 243, n.

OUMASASIKOUEIE, JOSEPH, ii. p. 164, n.

OUREOUHARÉ, Cayuga chief, (for English forms of name see v., p. 152, n.;) one of those sent to the galleys, iv., p. 48; attached to Frontenac, ib.; his advice, ib.; message to cantons, ib.; Head Chief of Iroquois, 49; with Frontenac's knowledge treats with delegates of the cantons, 51; Indian prisoners refused by, 142; reply to Frontenac's reproaches, 151; valor at St. Sulpice, 194; distinguished at La Prairie where he commands Lorette Hurons, 203; exploit of, 212; modesty, 212; refuses chieftaincy of several tribes, 246; retires to the Mountain, ib.; visits his canton in the French interest, 252; brings in 13 French prisoners and deputies of two cantons, ib.; at Quebec, v., p. 79; guarantees his canton, ib.; death, ib.; remark on Our Lord's Passion, 80; why regretted by Frontenac, ib.

OUREOUATÉ, seized by Peré, iii., p. 276, n.

OUREOUATI. See OUTREOUATI.

OURÉOUHATI, iii., p. 44, n.; not the one sent to negotiate between Senecas and French, see p. 254.

OUTAGAMIS, iii., p. 105. See FOXES.

OUTAGOUAINOU, JOHN, defeated by Iroquois, ii., p. 237.

OUTAOUAIS. See OTTAWAS.

OUTCHIBOUS or OUTCHIPOUES, CHIPPEWAYS or SAULTEUX, ii., p. 137, n.; iii., p. 119, n.

OUTINA, a Florida chief, 90 leagues from Caroline, i., p 164; Timagoa subject to, 162; Laudonniere sent to visit him, 164; gains victory with French aid, obtains aid from Laudonniere, 174; intimidated by his Ionas, wishes to retreat, ib.; encouraged by Ottigny and wins a victory, 175; does not pursue fugitives,

OUTINA, (*continued.*)
175 ; seized to extort provision for Carolina, 176 ; the result 176–7 ; defeat of French, ib.

OUTOURÉ, PETER, Huron, providential deliverance, of, ii., p. 232, n.

OUTOUTAGA, real name of John le Blanc or Talon, v., p. 143, n.

OUTREOUHATI, or ORREOUATI, Iroquois chief, confined in irons at Montreal, iii., p. 44; his vengeance, 35, 44; at Montreal as envoy, 303 ; called Grande Gueule by Belmont, ib.

OUTRELEAU, STEPHEN D'. See DOUTRELEAU.

OUYATANONS, now called Weas, a Miami tribe, De Courtemanche prevents their taking up arms against Sioux and Iroquois, v., p. 142 ; they promise to send delegates to Montreal for a general peace, ib.; a Ouyatanon discovers Miami plot to massacre French at Detroit, 239; Vaudreuil delivers some Iroquois prisoners from their hands, 239.

OUYGOUDY RIVER, Indian name of St. John's, i., p. 252.

OVEDEC, original name of the Senegal, i., p. 16.

OYANDER, Iroquois title, iii., p. 163.

OYELAPE, or WHITE EARTH, Natché chief, vi., p. 29.

OYSTER RIVER, now Durham, destroyed by Malecites and Micmacs under Villieu, iv., p. 256.

OZAGE, the Missouri so called, iii., p. 214, n.

PACIFIC OCEAN discovered by Balboa, i., p. 29.

PADOUCAS, French name for Comanches, v., p. 184, n.

PAGET, MR., La Salle insulted by, iv., p. 65.

PAHOUITINGOUACHIRINI, the Chippewas, iii., p. 119, n.

PAILLOUX, MAJOR DE, of the Louysiana troops, sent against Natchez, vi., p. 28 ; builds Fort Rosalie, 30-1 ; made commandant, 31 ; with Bienville lays foundation of New Orleans, 40 ; first governor, ib.; Major-General, 41.

PAINTERS, see PETER LE BER, LUKE LE FRANÇOIS.

PAIS, or PAEZ, FATHER PETER, Portuguese Jesuit, discovers source of Nile, i., p. 52.

PALAIS, CHEVALIER DU, sails with squadron from France, misses English squadron and fails, iv., p. 222.

PALAOS ISLANDS, i., p. 60.

PALAQUECHAUNE, or PALAQUESSON, Texas tribe, iv., p. 90, n.

PALISSADE, appropriate Spanish name for the Micissipi, v., 120.

PALM, FATHER FELIX, Acadian missionary, banished, v., p. 298, n.

PALMER AND WEST, seize wine at Pentagoët, iii., p. 211.

PALONNA, Texas tribe, iv., p. 90, n.

PANADOU or MENADOU BAY, Cape Breton, described, v., p. 284.

PANAMA founded, i., p. 31 ; bishop of, primate of Terrafirma, ib.

PANUCO, PROVINCE OF, i., p. 31.

PANNAWAMSKÉ, examination as to, v., p. 277, n.

PAOUICHTIGOUAN, PAOUITAGOUNG, PAOUITIGOUEIEUHAK, the Saulteurs or Chippeways, ii., p. 137, n.; iii., p. 119, n.

PAOUIRINIOUAGAOU, Indian name of Nelson or Bourbon River, iii., p. 230, n.

PAPILLION, FATHER ROMUALD, Recollect, dies at sea, iii., p. 148, n.

PAPIN, MR., imprisoned by Chépar, vi., p. 81, n.; his wife killed by Natchez, 82, n.

PAPINACHOIS INDIANS, trade at Tadoussac, converted, ii., p. 118, 243 ; iii., p. 40 ; join in letter to Governor of Massachusetts, v., p. 273, n.

PAQUINE, SIEUR, Commissary in Acadia, report of, on Port Royal, iv., p. 18.

PARADIS, MR., French pilot, taken on the Neptune, v., p. 252, n.; Walker disregards advice of, 252.

PARAGUAY RIVER, i., p. 30, 34 ; explored by Ayola, 38.

PARANA RIVER, i., p. 30, 34.

PARAOUSTIS, Florida chiefs, honors paid i., p. 138.

PARAT, SIEUR, Commandant at Placentia, iii., p. 295 ; unable to hold out, iv., p. 164 ; succeeds de la Poype as Governor of Newfoundland, ib.; captured in bed by pirates, complaints of, and against, in France, 164.

PARC, MR. DU, left in command by Champlain in 1610, ii., p. 23, n.

PARHELIONS, at Quebec, iii., p. 56 ; in the West, 173.

PARIA, name of Indians for South America, i., p. 21.

PARISH PRIESTS, regulation as to, iii., p. 22.
PARISHES in Canada, iii., p. 22.
PARISIANS, solicited as settlers, iii., p. 81.
PARMENTIER, JOHN, supposed to be the Great Captain of Ramusio, i., p. 132, n.
PASSADUMKEAG, Indian town destroyed by Westbrooke, v., p. 277, n.
PASCAGOULAS RIVER discovered, v., p. 120; pearls found in, 129, n.
PASQUALIGO, PIETRO, letter of, i., p. 105.
PASSAGE DE FRONSAC, v., p. 282.
PASTON, ROB., Capt. of the Feversham, v., p. 227, n.
PASTOUR DE COSTEBELLE, reinforces Placentia, iv., p. 164; reports to de Brouillan English admiral's terms, 224.
PATENOTES, meaning of term, i., p. 119.
PATENOTES, or Beads of St. Helen, virtues of this plant, i., p. 142; Indian name, ib.
PATIÑO, CAPTAIN ANDRÉ LOPEZ, sent to select a spot on St. Augustine river for a fort, i., p. 194; at capture of Caroline, 201–2; goes with Menendez to attack wrecked French at Cañaveral, 222.
PATISHAL'S boat taken, iv., p. 42–3, n.
PATOULET, JOHN B., Commissary of Marine sent to Acadia, iii., p. 139.
PATT, ARTHUR, discoveries of, i., p. 44.
PATZISIRANDA, APOYOMATSI, ST. HELEN'S BEADS, or PATENOTIES, i., p. 142.
PAUGET, MR., French engineer, builds fort at Balise, vi., p. 70.
PAUL V., POPE, Guy Bentivoglio, Nuncio of, grants faculties to Recollects, ii., p. 25, n.
PAUL, Indian at Sault St. Louis, notice of, iv., p. 207, n.; killed at head of Christian Indians at La Prairie, 203, 207.
PAULMIER, REV. HUGH, arrives, iii., p. 22.
PAWNEES, slavery of, v., p. 224.
PAXTON, CAPTAIN, his ship Newport taken by Iberville, v., p. 24.
PAYON, SIEUR, troops under, sent against Natchez, vi., p. 72.
PAYVA, ALPHONSUS DE, dies near Abyssinia, i., p. 19.
PEARL RIVER, v., p. 127, n.
PEARLS, GULF OF, i., p. 21.
PEARL ISLANDS, i., p. 29.
PEARLS in Louisiana, poor, v., p. 129.
PEARRON, (PIERRON,) F. JOHN, Jesuit, sketch of, iii., p. 155; succeeds Fremin on Mohawk, 116; turns to advantage an insult from a chief, 155; sends a converted squaw to Lorette, 164.
PEGWAKKI, Abénakis of, write to Governor of Massachusetts, v., p. 273, n.
PEKITANONI, name for the Missouri on Marquette's map, iii., p. 180.
PELERIN, REV. MR., arrives, iii., p. 22.
PELTRIE, CHARLES DE GRIVAL, SEIGNEUR DE LA, ii., p. 101, n.
PELTRIE, MAGDALEN DE CHAUVIGNY, DAME DE LA, widow of Charles de Grival, foundress of the Ursulines of Quebec marries Mr. de Bernieres, ii., p. 10; charters a ship at Dieppe, obtains nuns at Tours and Dieppe, ib.; at Quebec, 102; fervor and courage, 103; god-mother, ii., p. 164.
PEMAQUID FORT, see PEMKUIT.
PEMKUIT, FORT, built by English, iii., p. 210; site, ib.; taken by Canibas, iv., p. 40, 43; restored by English, 227; Iberville and Bonaventure fail to take, 228; King orders it to be attacked, 275; why, v., p. 23; captured, 25; described, ib.; English propose to restore, 92; See FORT.
PEMOUSSA, Fox chief, asks du Buisson for peace, v., p. 260; sent to allies, ib.; speech, ib.; returns, 261; saved by du Buisson, 263; given as a hostage, 307; dies of smallpox at Montreal, 307.
PEÑA, CAPT. DON FRANCISCO DE LA, Spaniard forced to enter Pensacola Bay, captured by de Champmêlin, vi., p. 61.
PENANCE, PUBLIC, iv., p. 306.
PENICAUT, Ship Carpenter, author of Relation ou Annales Veritables, i., p. 95; v., p. 118, n.; vi., p. 19; his courses, his knowledge of Indian languages, vi., p. 19; takes some Natchitoches to the Colapissas and induces them to join St. Denys, ib.; saves la Loire at Natchez, 26; imperfect English version of his work, v., p. 118, n.; goes to France on account of eyesight, vi., p. 66, n.
PENN, SIR WILLIAM, i., p. 58.
PENNSYLVANIA founded, i., p. 58.
PENOBSCOT, i., p. 49; Col. Westbrooke destroys town on, v., p. 277, n.
PENSACOLA, Bay and Fort in Florida, discovery, vi., p. 43; names, ib.; settled by Arriola in 1696, v., p. 118; n.; vi., p. 43; Châteaumorand and Iberville not allowed to enter, v., p. 118; Louysiana trade with, vi., p. 33; fort built, 43;

taken by French, 44; governor of Havana prepares to retake, 46; condition, 48; recaptured, 48; works erected, 53; taken from Spaniards by Champmêlin, 58; restored to Spain, 65, n.

PENZOCOLOS, Indians, extinct, v., p. 118, n.

PENTAGOËT RIVER, i., p. 49; bounds Etechemins, p. 249; position, 253; described, 276; Indian name, 275; Armouchiquois formerly between Kinibequi and, 277; taken by Kirk and Stirling, ii., p. 59; restored, ib., n.; Capuchins at, 202; taken by English, iii., p. 135; restored in spite of Sir T. Temple, 139; Grandfontaine at, 186; Chambly at, 187; taken by Dutch, 188; plundered and taken by English, 211; fort demolished by Dutch, 188, 294; restored by St. Castin, 294; English summon him to surrender, ib.; importance, 295; mission at, 308; pillaged, iv., p. 15; exploits of Indians of, 40–3; Indians of, with Villieu, 256; Iberville at, v., p. 25; iv., p. 15; rendezvous of Nesmond and Frontenac, 71; Indians of, address Governor of Massachusetts, 273, n.

PENTHIEVRE, DUKE OF, Charlevoix dedicates his work to, i., p. 1.

PEORIA TRIBE, v., p. 131.

PEOUAREA, Illinois town on the Mississippi, iii., p. 180.

PERCHE, settlers from, solicited, iii., p. 81.

PERÉ, CAPTAIN, i., p. 61.

PERÉ, Mr. Oureouate seized by, iii., p. 276, n.

PERELLE, SIEUR DE LA, French officer, accompanies Iroquois deputies to Montreal, iii., p. 300; alarm of, ib.

PERELLE, SIEUR DE LA, ensign, put under arrest, v., p. 230.

PEREYRA, DIEGO FERNANDEZ, discovers Socotoro, i., p. 25.

PEREZ, ENSIGN FERDINAND, Spanish officer, insolence of, i., p. 199.

PERRAULT, FATHER JULIAN, Jesuit, missionary on Gulf of St. Lawrence, remarks on Gaspesians, ii., p. 119–120.

PERRIER, MR., Commandant General of Louysiana, vi., p. 77; India Co's reply to his call for troops, ib.; on treatment of Indians, 78; treats with Choctaws, 80; on Natchez massacre, 89; destroys Chaouachas, 90; sounds Choctaws, 90; uneasy as to Natchitoches, 91; unable to restore confidence among settlers, 91; resolves to attack Natchez with Western Choctaws, 92; plans, 94; induced to stay at N. Orleans, ib.; sends Chev. de Loubois in his stead, ib.; blamed for Loubois' inactivity, 97; justifies his saving prisoners and negroes, 99; says Natchez reproached Choctaws with being in the plot, ib.; depends on Creoles, 100; warned of English intrigues to rouse Chickasaws against us, 101; asks reinforcements, 102; meets Choctaws at Mobile, 103; declaration of, to a Chickasaw chief, 105; wishes to do without Choctaws, 106; Natchez expedition, 107; joins army, 108; obtains all negroes in hands of Natchez, 110; obliges head chief to come to him, 111; interview, ib.; will not let Le Sueur pursue Natchez, 115; distrusts Canadians, ib.; order to head chief of Tonicas as to Natchez, 116; prepares to pursue Natchez and aid St. Denys, 118; crushes negro plot at N. Orleans, 119, ; expects to be recalled, 120; appointed Governor of Louysiana by King, ib.; returns to France, ib.; succeeded by Bienville, ib.

PERRIER DE SALVERT, MR., brother of preceding, brings him reinforcements from France, vi., p. 106; in Natchez expedition, 107.

PERRIERE, RENÉ BOUCHER DE LA, notice of, v., p. 47, n.; distinguished in Newfoundland, 48; on Indian raid into N. England, 204; abandoned by Christian Iroquois, 205; attacks Haverhill, 205–6; attacks Deerfield, 216, n.; sent to New York, 222, n.

PERROT, FRANCIS MARY, vi., p. 125; Captain in Auvergne regt., iii., p. 123, n.; marries Talon's niece, ib.; appointed Governor of Montreal by Sulpitians, ib.; obtains royal commission, ib.; arrested by Frontenac, 190; quarrels with Sulpitians, transferred to Acadia, 256; succeeded by de Menneval, iv., p. 157; adventures, 158; ill-treated by English, 162; recaptured, 163.

PERROT, NICHOLAS, his work, i., p. 94; sketch of, iii., p. 165, n.; called Metamenens by Indians, ib.; deputed to N. W. Indians, ib.; his adventures and re-

PERROT, (*continued.*) ception by Miamis, 166; engages several tribes in Seneca war, 246; orders to, 280; he appeases discontent at peace, ib.; Denonville's orders to, ib.; sent to Michilimakinac with royal presents, iv., p. 137; in fight with Iroquois, 139; sent to Miamis to break up English trade, 242; nearly burned alive by them, v., p. 65; Foxes say they have no sense since he left, 144; interpreter of remote tribes at General Congress, 150; de Callieres sends him to Ottawas at their request, 153.

PERROT, ISLE, Frontenac's army encamps on, v., p. 13.

PERU, heard of, i., p. 29; Pizarro sails to, 33, 35; Almagro sails to, 34; Atahualpa, King of, put to death, and Inca empire destroyed, 36.

PES, ANDREW DE, sent to break up La Salle's colony, iv., p. 113, n.; explores Pensacola Bay and calls it Galve, vi., p. 43.

PESANT, LE, Ottawa chief, instigator of Detroit troubles, v., p. 185; Vaudreuil insists on his head, 189; reply of Ottawa deputies, 188; Miamis demand his head, 190; pardoned by Cadillac, ib.

PESKADAMIOUKKANTI, (PENTAGOET,) i., p, 275, n.

PESKADOUÉ, (PISCATTOWAY) RIVER, Abnaquis take two forts at Oyster River on iv., p. 256.

PESCADOUET, PESCADOUÉ, now Portsmouth, N. H., party from, attacks Hertel and is repulsed, iv., p. 131–2; Indian from, announces English fleet, 152; Col. March at, v., p. 195.

PESMOKANTI, (PASSAMAQUODDY,) Indians of, address Governor of Massachusetts, v., p. 273, n.

PETIT, REV. LOUIS, captain in the Carignan-Salieres regiment, then priest, sketch of, iv., p. 155; vi., p. 125; sent by Governor of Acadia to Phipps with proposals, 155; taken to Boston, 158; sent back to Port Royal, 190.

PETIT, FATHER MATHURIN LE, Jesuit, Letters of, noticed, i., p. 89; arrives in Louysiana, vi., p. 76, n.

PETIT GOAVE, La Sale puts in at, iv., p. 65.

PETIT HAVRE, French leave prisoners at, v., p. 173.

PETIT NORD, part of Newfoundland, iii p. 142.

PETITE NATION, ii., p. 9, n.

PETITE RACINE, LA, Ottawa chief, envoy to Senecas, dies there, iv., p. 148.

PETTY HARBOR, N. Foundland, v., p. 173.

PETUNS, Indian tribe, allied to Hurons, ii., p. 71, n., 228, n.; see TIONONTATEZ.

PEXOTO, ANTHONY, in Japan, i., p. 39.

PHENOMENA, iii., p. 36, 56, 172, 228.

PHIBS, (PHIPS,) SIR WILLIAM, English admiral, vi., p. 125; iv., p. 155, n.; expedition to co-operate with, 145, n.; summons Menneval to surrender Port Royal, 154; reply of envoy, 155; grants terms, but not in writing, 156; evades capitulation, 157; repulsed at Chedabouctou, 160; grants terms, ib.; outrage at Isle Percée, 161; before Quebec, 169; summons Frontenac, 171; reply, 173; astonished at French defence, 174; ship cut up, 179; sends artillery to troops at Beauport, 175; had reckoned on a diversion, 184; what prevented it, ib.; raises siege, 186; exchanges prisoners, 187; losses and perils of fleet, ib.; his loss, 189, note; in England, solicits new fleet for Quebec, fails, 202; fails to carry off Chevalier Villebon, 226; attempts to assassinate St. Castin, 236; threatens to send cruisers into Gulf of St. Lawrence, and to attack fort on St. John's River, 244; frightens Abenakis into negotiation, 255; mutiny, 257; interview with Abenakis, ib.; recalled, 257; death, 273.

PHILIP II., King of Spain, his object in sending fleet to Florida, i., p. 182; fails to capture Gourgues, 236.

PHILLIPPS, COLONEL RICHARD, Governor of Nova Scotia and Placentia, v., p. 297, n.; called Sir Philip Richard by Charlevoix, p. 297; harasses Acadians, 297; obliged to leave them in peace, 299.

PHILIPPINE ISLANDS, i., p. 39; settlements begun on, 40.

PICARDY, natives of, asked as settlers, iii., p. 81.

PICHON, MR., author of History of Cape Breton, v., p. 282, n.; a traitor, ib.

PICO, one of the Azores, i., p. 16; meridian fixed at, 17.

PICQUEMYANS, i., p. 124.

PIDGEON, CAPTAIN, his party surprised at Bloody Creek, v., p. 238, n., 255, n.

PIERRIA, CAPTAIN ALBERT DE LA, see ALBERT.

PIERRON, FATHER JOHN, Jesuit, iii., p. 109; iv., p. 284; see PEARRON.

PIESKARET, SIMON, Algonquin chief, bravery of, ii., p. 181; ratifies peace, ib.; killed treacherously by Iroquois, 197.

PIJART, FATHER CLAUDE, Jesuit, at Montreal, receives F. Garreau, mortally wounded, ii., p. 275, n.

PIJART, FATHER PETER, Jesuit, returns to Europe, ii., p. 250.

PILLET, CHARLES, killed by Indians, ii., p. 30, n.

PIMITEOUY, ILLINOIS OF, harassed by Foxes, remove to Mississippi, vi., p. 71.

PIÑALOSSA, COUNT DE, ineffectual negotiations with France as to the Santa Barbara mines, iv., p. 116.

PINELO, ANTONIO DE LEON, work of, noticed, i., p. 93.

PINET, FATHER PETER, Jesuit, labors among Illinois, v., p. 133, n.

PINTADOS ISLANDS, Samal, one of the, i., p. 60.

PINTO, FERDINAND MENDEZ, Portuguese, discovers Japan, i., p. 39.

PINZON, VINCENT YAÑEZ, discovers Brazil, i., p. 22, 27; Yucatan, ib., p. 26.

PIRATES, two pirates carry off nine settlers from Mariegalante, and land them at Port Royal, iv., p. 162; seize Villebon's vessels, iv., p. 161; he fails to capture them, 162.

PIZARRO, FRANCISCO, sent to explore, i., p. 32; conquers Peru, 33–36; puts to death King Atahualpa, last of the Incas, 36; founds Lima, 37.

PIZARRO, GONZALES, Spaniard, Governor of Quito, discovers La Canela, i., p. 39.

PLACENTIA, Newfoundland, De Monts takes posession of, iii., p. 53; described, 141; fort built, ib.; Gargot obtains patent and governorship, 146; de la Poype sent to, ib.; importance of, 295; English invade, iv., p. 164; menaced, 165; attacked by English, 223; Pemaquid expedition at, v., p. 23; Frontenac and Champigny's report on, to Pontchartrain, situation in 1695, 35; de Brouillan and Iberville's operations from, 35-48; Serigny at, 48; Nesmond to relieve, 71; English fail to secure, 162; Graydon retires from, 163; English designs on, 215; intend to attack it after Quebec repulse, but fail, 253.

PLAINE, BERNARD D'AMOUR, SIEUR DE, Canadian, brings in prisoners, v., p. 40; distinguished, 47.

PLANTE, SIEUR LERIGÉ DE LA, French officer taken by Iroquois, iv., p. 30; rescued in 1692, 217.

PLANTEROSE, SIEUR, lost in St. Bernard's bay, iv., p. 86.

PLANTS peculiar to Iroquois country, ii., p. 190–1.

PLAQUE, LA, Iroquois chief, iv., p. 143; lieutenant, 144, n.; nephew of the Great Mohawk, ib.; announces Iroquois army, ib.; truth of report, 144; sent out, 237; rescues a French prisoner, ib.; commands Iroquois in Hudson Bay, 262, n.

PLESSIS, SIEUR DU, repulses Mohawks and Mohegans at Fort Chambly, iii., p. 298, n.

PLESSIS, SIEUR DU, distinguished at St. John, v., p. 213.

PLESSYS, BROTHER PACIFICUS DU, Recollect, arrives in Canada, ii., p. 25; great services of, 30; returns to France, 31, n.; burial place, 283.

PESSYS-FABER, FRANCIS LEFEBVRE, SIEUR DU, captain, sent after Black Kettle, iv., p. 220; see PLESSIS.

PLYMOUTH, claims the Kennebec, ii., p. 214, n.; refuses to protect Abénaquis against Iroquois, 217, n.; joins in Montreal expedition, but retains men after attack on Casco, iv., p. 145, n.

POINCI, COMMANDER DE, retains government of West Indies in defiance of King, regulation in consequence, ii., p. 203.

POINT DU GOULET, near Placentia, iv., p. 224.

POINT HURIER, Texas, iv., p. 73, n.

POINT SIGUENZA, on Santa Rosa island, vi., p. 43.

POINT AU TREMBLE, Lt. Colombet killed near, iv., p. 142; Iroquois ravage, 193.

POINTE VERTE, Newfoundland, English burn houses at, iv., p. 226.

POISSON, JOHN B., notice of his Animadversio on Grotius and De Laet, i., p. 79.

POISSON, FATHER PAUL DU, Jesuit, notice of, vi., p. 83, n.; arrives in Louysiana, 76, n.; falls in the Natchez massacre, 83.

POLO, MARCO, mentioned, i., p. 54.

POLYGAMY, in Florida, i., p. 139; Acadia, 265; among Sioux, iii., p. 32; Ottawas, 48.

POMMERAYE, SIEUR DE LA, Breton gentleman with Cartier at Hochelaga, i., p. 118.

POMPIERRE, SIEUR DE, French gentleman, adventures after leaving Caroline, i., p. 213.

PONAMO, (the tom cod,) i., p. 268 vi.; p. 124.

PONCE DE LEON, JOHN, see (LEON,) Bay of, i., p. 171.

PONCET DE LA RIVIERE, FATHER JOSEPH ANTHONY, Jesuit, sketch of, ii., p. 253; induces Chaumonot to come to America, 262, n.; instructs Indians at Montreal, 164; goes to Hurons with F. Bressani, 182; captured by Mohawks, 253; sufferings of, 254; delivered, 255; perilous return, ib.; prayers for, 256; sent to Onondaga but returns, iii., p. 14; returns to France, ii., p. 253, n.; labors in Brittany and Italy, dies at Martinique, ib.

PONS, SIEUR, gentleman of Saintonge, lost in Gourgues' expedition, i., p. 236.

PONTBRIAND, M. DE, Breton gentleman with Cartier at Hochelaga, i., p. 118.

PONTCHARTRAIN, LOUIS PHELYPEAUX, COUNT DE, Chancellor of France, succeeds de Seignelay in Ministry of the Marine, iv., p. 191; Frontenac's Memoir to, 191, 197; reply to Frontenac's proposals, 214; commissions Villebon commandant in Acadia, 214.

PONTCHARTRAIN, JEROME PHELYPEAUX, COUNT DE, son and successor of preceding, explains to Frontenac King's views on Iroquois war, iv., p. 263; report of Frontenac and Champigny on Fort Frontenac, 274; advice to Frontenac as to Iroquois war, 275; Iberville to, v., pp. 40, 43; informs him of English designs, 51; orders from the King, ib.; projects conquest of New England, 70; instructions to Frontenac on congés and Iroquois war, 77; de Callieres' report on temper of Iroquois cantons, 111; Ducasse's report on Iberville, 118; de Callieres to, on Hennepin, 126; instructions to Iberville as to Louysiana trade, 128; instructions to Vaudreuil as to proposed neutrality between French and English, 168 reply to Raudot's plan for relieving Canada, 181; Vaudreuil's report to, on Hudson Bay failure, 224; unable to send Subercase two frigates, 226.

PONTCHARTRAIN, HELEN ROSALIE ANGÉLIQUE DE L'AUBESPINE, COUNTESS DE, a projected city at Natchez to be called Rosalie in honor of, v., p. 31.

PONTGRAVÉ, SIEUR DE, of St. Malo, makes voyages to Tadoussac, i., p. 245; advises Chauvin to solicit de la Roche's commission, ib.; sails to Canada under de Monts, 248; his lieutenant, 253; transfer St. Croix settlement to Port Royal, ib.; disapproves of it, 255; obliged to abandon Port Royal for want of supplies, 256; returns, ib.; praised, 257; sent to trade in St. Lawrence, 259; afraid to treat with Jesuits, 270; his vessels, 281, n.; at Tadoussac, ii., p. 7; Champlain meets, 8, n.; goes to France with Champlain, 19, n.; at Montreal with him, 24, n.; returns to Canada, said by Charlevoix to have gone to France, 25; goes to France for health, 34; in Quebec when summoned by English, 45.

POORPOODUCK, ravaged by Abénaquis, v., p. 161, n.

POPAYAN, discovered, i., p. 38.

POPOCATAPEC, volcano, i., p. 31.

POPULATION of Canada in 1666, iii., p. 111; 1679, 217; in 1714, v., p. 301; n.; of Acadia in 1687, iii., p. 295; of Louisiana in 1704, vi., p. 16.

PORCUPINE INDIANS, trade at Tadoussac, embrace Christianity, ii., p. 118.

PORT DE LA BALEINE, Cape Breton, v., p. 284.

PORT DAUPHIN, Cape Breton, v., pp. 283, 285; called also Port St. Anne, 295; described, ib.; why Louisbourg preferred to, 296.

PORT FORTUNÉ, (Chatham,) i., p. 257.

PORT DE LA HEVE, iii., p. 295; v., p. 27.

PORT DES MINES, Perrot at, iv., p. 158.

PORT AU MOUTON, situation, i., p. 251; called St. Luke's Bay by Stirling, ii., p. 59.

PORT NELSON, origin of name, i., p. 50, 60; iii., p. 234; when given, iii., p. 237; called by French Bourbon river, 234; by Indians Kakioukiouay, ib.; English

prisoners sent to, 272; proposed neutrality of, ib.; Denonville's proposition as to, ib.; taken by English, iv., p. 53; by d'Iberville, 37, 58; Du Tast's fleet intended for, 200; Iberville's project against, 213, 227; described, 259.

PORT NEUF, PETER ROBINEAU DE, son of Baron of Bekancourt, commands Quebec party against Kaskebé, iv., p. 133; called Burneffe in New England accounts, ib., n.; his attack on Casco diverted Massachuetts and Plymouth men from Canadian campaign, 145; sent to Acadia to serve under his brother Villebon, 215; grants lands for an Abénaqui town, v., p. 167, n.

PORT DE PAIX, the St. François captured near, iv., p. 65.

PORT ROSSIGNOL, now Liverpool, N. S., de Monts at, i., p. 251.

PORT ROYAL, (S. C.,) mouth of River St. Croix, name given by Ribaut, i., p. 42, 136; Charlefort built there, p. 136.

PORT ROYAL, Nova Scotia, description, i., p. 253; named by Champlain, 252, n.; De Monts resolves to remove settlement to, 253; neglected, ceded to Poutrincourt, 255; Jesuits at, 263; taken off by Saussaye, 275; destroyed by Argall, 282; taken by Kirk and Stirling, ii., p. 59; restored, 58, n.; elder la Tour retires to, iii., p. 127, n.; his Scotch colonists killed at, 128, n.; granted to Claude de Razilly, 129, n.; administered and then acquired by d'Aulnay, ib.; la Tour and his widow at, 130; le Borgne expelled by English under Sedgwick, 134; restored to French, 138, n.; inhabitants surrender to English, 211; to be fortified, 295; port inconvenient, iv., p. 18; de la Caffiniere unable to provision, 27-8; taken by Phips, 154-8; condition of, when attacked by English, 154; pirates land prisoners from Mariegalante at, 162; their cruelties, ib.; Villebon at, 213; he removes English flag, 215; inhabitants seek English protection, v., p. 92; Naxoat garrison transferred to, but is not put in a state of defence, 113; wretched condition, 114, n.; three English sieges of, 170, 191-4, 224, 226; capture, 230; Vesche commandant, 235; English defeated near, 238, 255; invested by French and Indians, 256; Vesche ill-treats French at, ib.; nearly recaptured, ib.; called Annapolis Royal by English, 267.

PORT ST. ANNE, Denys at, iii., p. 132; described, v., p. 285, 295; see PORT DAUPHIN.

PORT ST. GENEVIEVE, i., p. 115, n.

PORT ST. JOHN, Newfoundland, ii., p. 59.

PORT ST. MARY'S, i., p. 252, n.

PORT ST. NICHOLAS, named by Cartier, i., p. 115; now Pachachibou, ib., n.

PORT ST. NICHOLAS, St. Domingo, de Gourgues at, i., p. 226.

PORT TOULOUSE, Cape Breton, v., p. 282-3; formerly called St. Pierre, 284.

PORTAGE DES CHATS, on the Ottawa, iv., p. 218.

PORTAGE RIVER, Iroquois Christians remove to, iv., p. 123.

PORTE, LOUVIGNY DE LA, see LOUVIGNY.

PORTO BELLO discovered, i., p. 24.

PORTO RICO discovered, i., p. 19; conquered by Ponce de Leon, 27; Menendez at, 187; de Gourgues at, 226.

PORTO SANTO ISLAND discovered, i., p. 14.

PORTSMOUTH, England, Ribaut puts in at, i., p. 181.

PORTSMOUTH, N. H., party from pursues Hertel, iv., p. 131, n.

PORTUGALCOUE, (PORTUGAL COVE,) English post on Newfoundland, English taken at, by Montigny, v., p. 45.

PORTUGUESE expel French from Brazil, i., p. 133.

POSTEL, WILLIAM, his ideas as to early Gaulish voyages to America, i., p. 104.

POTANOU, Florida chief, defeated and killed by Outina by French aid, i., p. 164; successor of same name defeated by French, 174-5.

POTARDIERE, SIEUR DE LA, visits and reports on Canadian iron mines, iii., p. 98.

POTHERIE, JAMES LENEUF DE LA, Governor of Three Rivers, arrests Mohawk spies and saves his place, iii., p. 19; commissioned by de Mésy to act after his death, 76.

POTHERIE, MR. DE BACQUEVILLE DE LA, his Histoire de l'Amérique Septentrionale, noticed, i., p. 90.

POTONCHAN, i., p. 30.

POTOSI, mines of, discovered, i., p. 40.

POTTAWATAMIES, or POUTEOUATAMIS, Canadian Indians, original country, iii., p.

POTTAWATAMIES, (*continued.*)
104, n.; language, ib.; Hurons among, ii., p. 271, n.; 300 at Chagoimegon visited by Allouez, iii., p. 104; strange reception, ib.; docility, ib.; conversion of centenarian and two daughters, 104; his death and funeral, ib.; strange story of Indians, 105; attacked by Senecas, 161; escort Perrot to Chicago, 166; with Miamis, 167; the great Miami chief represents them at de Lusson's taking possession, 168; war vigorously on Iroquois, iv., p. 278, v., p. 67; offer services to colony, with La Motte Cadillac, v., p. 67; complain to de Frontenac, 69; de Courtemanche prevents their marching on Iroquois, 141; promise deputies to Congress, 142; hostility with Mascoutins, 257; fight against Foxes at Detroit, 258; their chief's speech to Foxes, 259.

POULAIN, FATHER WILLIAM, Recollect, arrives in Canada, ii., p. 33, n.; taken by Iroquois about to be burned, 33.

POUTEOUATAMIS. See POTTAWATAMIES.

POUTRINCOURT, JOHN DE BIENCOURT, SIEUR DE, de Mont's lieutenant in Acadia, i., p. 248; relieves Port Royal, 256; supplies and fortifies it, 267; eludes Henry IV.'s order to take over Jesuits, 260; addresses a letter to the Pope, 264; quarrels with Mme. de Guercheville, 274; enters service after English capture Acadia, 282; error at Port Royal, 285; why he abandons it, iii., p. 125; death of, i., 282, n.

POUTRINCOURT, Biencourt, son of preceding also so called, iii., p. 125.

POYPE, MR. DE LA, sent as Commissary to Placentia,, iii., p. 146; and Governor of Newfoundland, iv., p. 164; left destitute, ib.

PRAIRIE, LA. See LAPRAIRIE.

PRAIRIE SQUIRREL, ii., p. 172, n.

PRAIRIES, DES, of St. Malo, aids Champlain seasonably in the battle on the Sorel, ii., p. 22.

PRAIRIES, RIVER DES, situation, ii., p. 37; first Mass said on, 25, n.; Iroquois repulsed near, iv., p. 142; Iroquois ravages on, 193, n.; Oureouharé's exploit at, 212.

PREMONSTRATENSIANS of St. André aux Bois, Acadian mission offered to, v., p. 156, n.

PRESENTS, obligation when received, ii., p. 156.

PRESIDIO DEL NORTE, or SAN JUAN BAUTISTA, Spanish post, situation, vi., p. 20; commandant receives St. Denys, ib.; St. Denys serves him and marries his daughter, 23.

PRESQU'ISLE, near Lake St. Clare, Foxes overthrown at, v., p. 264.

PRESTER JOHN, i., p. 18, 63.

PRESTON, LORD, English ambassador, advises Radisson to go to England, iii., p. 236.

PREVERT, of St. Malo, stories invented by, ii., p. 90.

PRINCE EDWARD'S ISLAND. See ILE ST. JEAN.

PRINCE'S ISLAND, discovered, i., p. 18.

PRINCESS RIVER, Texas, iv., p. 90, n.

PROJECT, of a Series of Histories of the New World, i., p. v.

PROTESTANTS excluded from Canada, ii., p. 67; admitted, iii., p. 81, n.; not allowed to settle in Louysiana.

PROVENÇAL, a, deserts La Sale, found among Cenis, iv., p. 99; Joutel sends him to camp, 100.

PROVOST, or PREVOST, FRANCIS, sketch of, iv., p. 152, n.; Major of Quebec, informs Frontenac of approach of fleet, 152; sends his brother-in-law, de Grandville, on a scout, 153; Frontenac approves his measures for defence of Quebec, 167; announces to Frontena[c] fall of Fort St. Anne, 243. See vi., p. 127.

PRUDHOMME, one of La Salle's men, lost, iii., p. 214, n.

PUANTE RIVER, the Bekancourt, iv., p. 142, n.

PUANTS, name applied to Winnebagoes, and to the Natchez helots, iii., p. 120, n.

PUISEAUX, SIEUR DE MONTRENAULT, receives Maisonneuve at Ste. Foy, ii., p. 130.

PUYS, ZACHARY DU, Commandant of Fort of Quebec, ii., p. 267, n.; leads colony to Onondaga, 267; saves it by a remarkable escape, iii., p. 17; Major of Montreal, 267, n.; commissioned by de Tracy to act in Maisonneuve's absence, iii., p. 123; vi., p. 126.

QUAPPAS, a Dacota tribe, iii., p. 31; the Arkansas of the Algonquins and perhaps the Alligewi, ib.; called Kappas by

QUAPPAS, (*continued.*)
Charlevoix, who supposed them extinct, 109, n.

QUARANTE SOLS, ill-disposed Huron chief, v., p. 145; speaks at general council, ib.; intrigues of, 163; distrusted, ib.

QUARAS, Texas tribe, iv., p. 90, n.

QUEBEC, capital of New France, meaning of name, i., p. 50; situation, founding of, p. 50, 260; condition in 1610–22, ii., p. 7; mentioned, pp. 7, 8, 12, 19, 20, 23, 24, &c.; stone fort at, 35; summoned by English, 44; extremity, 46; taken by English, 48; restored, 63; edifying conduct of people of, 99; reception of Huron exiles at, 235; Mohawk alarm at, 252; blockaded, iii., p. 33; nuns forced to leave convents, ib.; earthquake at, 60–1; tribunals established at, 69; bishopric of, 122; great conflagration at, 222; Church of Our Lady of Victory, and Intendant's palace at, built, 260; Ursuline convent burned, ib.; sends expedition against Casco, iv., p. 13; Bureau of Poor, and General Hospital at, 17; Frontenac sends expedition from, 25; Iberville returns to, after Hudson Bay victory, 39; survivors of La Salle's Texas expedition at, 111; besieged by Phipps, 166; fortified, 168; siege raised, 186; timely arrival of French ships, 189; medal struck for victory at, 190; engraving of medal, ib.; Church of Our Lady of Victory, 190, n.; again menaced, fortified by Frontenac, 236; militia of, v., p. 13; rumor of English preparations against, 52; sloop Mary at, 155, n.; what prevented English fleet reaching, 222; again menaced, 224; Vaudreuil defends, 238; condition of, on hearing of Walker's wreck, 245; zeal and devotedness of people on rumor of new attack, 256; trade at, 265; Louvigny, King's lieutenant at, 306; Vaudreuil dies at, 310.

QUELANHUBECHES, Texas Indians, iv., p. 70.

QUELPAERTS ISLAND, Dutch ship wrecked on, i., p. 48.

QUEN, FATHER JOHN DE. See DEQUEN.

QUENTIN, FATHER JAMES, French Jesuit at St. Sauveur, i., p. 281, n.

QUESADA, FERDINAND PEREZ DE, Spaniard, explores New Granada, i., p. 40.

QUESNE, CAPT. DU, refuses to embark Jesuits, i., p. 262, n.

QUEYLUS, GABRIEL DE THUBIERE DE LEVY, ABBÉ DE LOC DIEU, sent over by Mr. Olier, iii., p. 23, n.; comes as Vicar General of Archbishop of Rouen, 20–3; not recognized, ib.; takes possession of Montreal for Seminary of St. Sulpice, 23; obtains bull erecting Montreal into a parish, ib., n.; arrested and sent back to France, 21, n.

QUEN LE, see DEQUEN.

QUIEUNONTATERONONS, or PETUNS, see TIONONTATERONONS.

QUINETS, Texas Indians, iv., p. 70.

QUINIBEQUI, KENNEBEC, i., pp. 49, 253.

QUINIPISSAS, Louysiana Indians, attack La Sale, iii., pp. 214–5, n.; other names of, v., p. 123; receive Iberville, ib.; see BAIAGOULAS, MONGOULACHAS.

QUINTÉ BAY, situation of, Champlain passes, ii., p. 28, n.; Sulpitian mission at, iii., p. 110; Cayugas at, ib.; Iroquois repulsed at, v., p. 79.

QUIROS, FERDINAND DE, Spaniard, discoveries of, i., p. 49.

QUIROS, TIERRA DE, discovered, i., p. 49.

QUITCHITCHOUAN, FORT, erected, iii., p. 231; see FORT ST. ANNE.

QUITO, i., p. 39.

QUIVIRA, Cornero, (Coronado,) sent to explore, i., p. 39.

QUIXOS, country of, discovered by Gonzales Pizarro, i., p. 39.

RADISSON, PETER ESPRIT DE, Frenchman, discovers Bourbon and St. Teresa rivers, i., p. 57; iii., p. 230; as a deserter, takes English to Hudson Bay, 231; marries Kirke's daughter, 233; undertakes to expel English from Bay, 233; operations there, 233–6; again with English, 236; pensioned by England, 237; puts English in possession, 237, 261.

RAFFEIX, FATHER PETER, Jesuit, chaplain on Tracy's expedition, iii., p. 95, n.

RAGUENEAU, FATHER PAUL, Jesuit, peace envoy to Iroquois, ii., p. 124; brings Hurons to Quebec, 234; Life of Mother Catharine of St. Augustine, by, iii., p 113; censured by Le Clercq, 115, n.

RAIMBAUT, FATHER CHARLES, Jesuit, visits Chippeways, ii., p. 137; recalled to Hurons, ib.; dies, ib., n.; burial-place of 283; properly Raymbault.

RALEIGH, SIR WALTER, send Amidas and Barlow to Virginia, i., p. 45 ; expedition to Guiana, 47.

RAMÉE or BOTOU ISLANDS, known in Cartier's time, v., p. 300 ; granted to Count St. Pierre, ib.

RAMEZAI, CHEV. CLAUDE DE, Governor of Three Rivers, and of Montreal, iv., p. 16 ; Frontenac's orders to, ib.; on his expedition, v., p. 12 ; commands main body, 13 ; uses Abénaquis to prevent Iroquois Christians removing to Albany, 164 ; induces them to return belts, 166 ; not allowed to invade New York, 218 ; marches, ib.; failure, 219 ; defeats a party near Crown Point, ib.; informs Vaudreuil of enemy's design, 220 ; returns to Montreal with militia, 221 ; sent to Montreal, 246 ; administrator in Vaudreuil's absence, 309, n.; death of, 309 ; what became of family, ib.

RAMEZAI, DE LA GESSE. See GESSE.

RAMEZAI, MR. killed near Cap St. Antoine, v., p. 307, n.

RAMON, DON DOMINGO, called by le Pratz, Raimond, and by Charlevoix, Don Pedro de Vilescas, vi., p. 20, n.; his trouble with Asinais in Texas, 23; founds mission, 24 ; suspected by Spanish government, 32 ; killed by Indians, 32, n.

RAMUSIO, JOAN B., work of, i. p. 73 ; remarks on a French author, 74 ; Cartier's voyage in, ib.

RANCOGNE, CHEVALIER DE, his detachment in Newfoundland defeated, v., p. 39.

RAPIDS, on St. John's river, i., p. 254 ; on the Sorel, ii., p. 12 ; F. Viel lost at, 37 ; F. Menard lost near, iii., p. 49 ; on the river of the Onondagas, what befell Frontenac's army at this last, v., p. 15.

RASLES, (RALE,) FATHER SEBASTIAN, Jesuit, notice of, v., p. 281, n.; among the Illinois, 133, n.; Becancourt founded by Abénaquis from a mission of, 167 ; anxious to arrest hostilities, 266 ; attempt of Rev. J. Baxter to pervert flock of, 268 ; their controversies, 269 ; why persecuted by English, 275 ; they wish Abénaquis to surrender or send him away, 275 ; set a price on his head, 275 ; in danger of being carried off, 275 ; church and house pillaged by Harmon, and his dictionary and strong box carried off, p. 276, n.; urged to retire to Quebec, 278 ; his reply, ib.; killed by English, ib.; outrages to his corpse, 279; eulogium on, 280 ; esteemed by flock, ib.; reputation in Canada, 281 ; answer of Superior of Seminary of Montreal, ib.; Letters of, noticed, i., p. 88-9 ; Lives of, v., p. 281 ; estimate of his conduct, v., p. 280 ; monument to, 281, n.

RAT, THE, (GASPAR SOIAGA, or KONDIARONK,) Huron chief, not easily won over by Denonville, iv., p. 12 ; boasts of having killed the peace with the Iroquois, ib.; his perfidious intrigues to involve French and Iroquois in war, 12 ; throws blame on Denonville, 14 ; insolence of Ottawas ascribed to, 57 ; exploit of, v., p. 68; attached to French, ib.; prized by Frontenac ; his speech at a council at Montreal, p. 110 ; compliments de Callieres in the name of western tribes, 141; gives up prisoners and complains of Iroquois, 143 ; falls ill, 145 ; eloquent address, 146 ; death, eulogy, funeral, 147.

RAUDOT, JAMES, Intendant in Canada, v. p. 181 ; prevents litigation, ib.; relieves poor, ib.; encourages manufactures, ib.; summons Western Indians, 236 ; reflections of; memoirs of, 290.

RAUDOT, ANTHONY, son of preceding, Intendant, v., p. 181 ; returns to France, 241, n.; memoirs of, on New France and Cape Breton, 290 ; thinks settlement on latter should be gradual, 294.

RAYE, PETER, a Huguenot, joins English, ii., p. 50.

RAYMBAULT, see RAIMBAUT.

RAZILLY, CAPTAIN CLAUDE DE, brother of commander, La Heve, Port Royal and Sable Island granted to, iii., p. 129, n.; his brother's heir, ib.; d'Aulnay acts for, and then buys out, ib.

RAZILLY, COMMANDER ISAAC DE, kinsman of Cardinal Richelieu, sketch of, iii., p. 128, n.; one of the Hundred Associates, ii., p. 43 ; recalled when about to sail to the relief of Quebec, 52 ; iii., p. 128, n.; vessels under, got ready, ii., p. 58; sails, 64, n.; receives Acadia from English, iii., p. 128 ; act of taking possession in 1630, 139 ; Acadian grant to, ii., p. 63 ; iii., p. 129, n.; settles at la Haive, 64 the St. Croix granted to, 64, n.; efforts to colonize, p. 129, n.; d'Aulnay and la

Razilly, (*continued.*)
Tour command under, 128 ; Acadian affairs after death of, ib.; his rights pass to his brother, Claude, 129, n.; dies at la Heve, ib.

Ré, Francis de, burial place of, ii., p. 283.

Rebou, misprint for Bay of Bulls.

Recalde; Francis, Spanish captain, opposes attack on Caroline, i., p. 197.

Recollects, four go to Canada, ii., p. 25 ; their names, ib., n.; faculties, ib., n.; found Convent of Our Lady of Angels, 32, n.; on Charles river, 34 ; besieged by Iroquois, ib.; induce Ventadour to send Jesuits and lodge them, 35 ; return after restoration opposed by Company of New France, ii., p. 65 ; iii., p. 147 ; Talon obtains their recall and why, iii., p. 147 ; shipwreck of first, 148 ; with la Sale, 201–3 ; missions of, marked on maps, 207 ; Denonville induces to yield chaplaincy of Catarocouy to F. Milet, 268 ; of Isle Percée report to Frontenac, iv., p. 28 ; one at founding of Detroit, v., p. 154 ; house at Detroit burnt, 164, n.; F. Constantin, a Recollect, killed at Detroit, 186 ; sent to Miamis, 202, n.; a missionary in Acadia, 238 ; at Louisbourg, 296, n.

Recueil de Voyages au Nord, Notice of, i., p. 89.

Red River, Soto dies at mouth of, i., p. 40 ; Loubois marches to, vi., p. 118.

Redin, (properly Redding,) Colonel, marines of, in Port Royal expedition, v., p. 227, n.; lands, 228, n.; arranges terms of surrender with Subercase, 230.

Rednap, Colonel, at Port Royal, v., p. 228, n.

Regis, Sieur, officer in the Louysiana troops, sends report from Choctaws to Perrier, vi., pp. 90–1 ; fail to induce them to attack enemy, 119.

Regisseurs, Councillors of State appointed by the King for the rule of Louysiana and the Western Company, vi., p. 69.

Rehoboth, Congress of N. E. Governors at, v., p. 222, n.

Remi, Rev. Mr., parish priest of La Chine, refuses to sanction honors paid to Catharine Tehgahkwita, cured by her intercession, iv., p. 296.

Renards or Outagamis, see Foxes.

Renaud, works lead mines, vi., p. 18, n., 25, n.

Renaudiere, de la, works mines, vi,. p. 18.

Rennes, Father Jogues at, ii., p. 161, n.

Renou, Lieut., brings reinforcements, v., p. 212 ; in assault at St. John, 213.

Renty, Baron de, one of Montreal Company, ii., p. 130.

Repentigni, René le Gardeur de Tilli de, Captain in Carignan-Salieres regiment, pursues Iroquois, iii., p. 82; commands Quebec troops on Tracy's expedition, 90.

Repentigni, Madame de, weaves nettles, white-wood bark, &c., v., p. 181, n.

Repentigni, Alexander le Gardeur de, Sieur de Montesson, volunteers on Schenectady expedition, iv., p. 122 ; at siege of Quebec, 180, n.; sent to Michilimakinac to announce victory, 200 ; killed at Montreal, Sept., 1692, .

Repentigny, or St. Sulpice, action at, iv., p. 194.

Revolt against Laudonniere, i., p. 165.

Rhoade, John, with Dutch, takes Pentagoët, iii., p. 188, n.

Ribaut, James de, son or nephew of following, refuses to surrender, i., p. 203 , misconduct of, 205; reaches Rochelle in the Pearl, 206, n.

Ribaut, John de, sent by Admiral Coligny to settle Florida, i., p. 42, 135; takes possession, explores, thinks he discovers the Jordan, 136 ; takes bays for rivers, ib.; builds Charlesfort, p. 42, 136; names Port Royal, ib.; plants French arms, 137, n.; in France, i., p. 42 ; not in Florida by appointed time, 46 ; at Caroline with large convoy, 179; cause of delay, 181; supports Laudonniere, ib.; restores Caroline, 192 ; his reply to Menendez, 200 ; in spite of council, sails to attack Spaniards, 193 ; driven off by a storm, 195 ; wrecked, 209 ; sends Vasseur to reconnoitre fort, 209; sends Verdier and la Caille to ask terms, 210 ; surrenders and is put to death, 211 ; the indignities said to have been offered his body, 211–2 ; killed probably near Matanzas Inlet, 214, n.; Spanish account of massacre, 214–221.

Ribourde, Father Gabriel de la, Recollect, in Illinois, iii., p. 203, n.; aids

Tonti, 209; lost in woods and killed by Kikapoos, 212, 186; v., p. 132; eulogium on, ib.; place of death, vi., p. 132, n.

Ricard, storekeeper at Natchez, escapes the massacre and reports to Perrier, vi., p. 89, n.

Richard, Philip, see Phillipps, Richard.

Richard, a Frenchman, robbed and murdered by Natchez, vi., p. 28.

Richarville, Drouet de, see Drouet.

Richebourg, Captain de, arrives, vi., p. 25; marches against Natchez, 28; at siege of Pensacola, 43, n.; prisoners sent to Havana in charge of, 45, n.; imprisoned there, 46, n.

Richelet, Mr., translates La Florida del Ynca, i., p. 73.

Richelieu, Cardinal de, establishes Company of New France, ii., p. 39; at its head, 43; controls affairs of Canada as Grand Master, Chief and Superintendent Gen. of the Navigation and Commerce of France, 45; orders Chateauneuf to press restoration of Canada, 58; orders Razilli to get ready to retake it, ib.; his niece founds the Hôtel Dieu, Quebec, p. 100.

Richelieu, or Sorel River, called also River of the Iroquois.

Richelieu, Fort, see Fort Richelieu.

Rigolet, outlet of Onondaga Lake, Onondagas neglect to hold, v., p. 15.

Rio Janeiro, discovered, i., p. 30; called Ganabara by natives, 42.

Rio del Norte, or Colorado, discovered by Oñate, i., p. 51; St. Denys at, vi., p. 20–23.

Rio del Oro, Africa, i., p. 15; de Gourgues makes it his rendezvous, p. 225.

Rio Perdido, Bienville at, vi., p. 56.

Rio de la Plata discovered, i., p. 30; entered by Sebastian Cabot, 34.

Rio de la Santa Cruz, now Edisto, or the Broad, i., p. 136, n.

Rio de Solis, i., pp. 30, 34.

Riqueronon, Iroquois name for the Eries, ii., p. 266, n.

Risingh, John, Governor of New Sweden, surrenders to Dutch, i., p. 56.

Riter, Sergeant, killed by Chickasaws, vi., p. 70, n.

Rivau, (Durivault,) Chevalier Amator Huet, Seigneur du, said to have accompanied Montortier and Desnos, iii., p. 255.

Rivaux, Henault des, mentioned as Governor of Montreal, iii., p. 255, n.

Riverin, Sieur Dennis, projects sedentary fisheries on the St. Lawrence at Mont Louys, v., p. 74; his failures, 75, 112.

River of Dolphins, i., p. 135; called St. Augustine, by Menendez, 188.

River of the Iroquois, now Sorel, ii., p. 12.

Riviere du Lievre, iv., p. 218.

Riviere Verte, see Blue Earth River.

Roanoke Island settled, i., p. 45.

Robbe and La Martiniere, errors of, i., p. 68.

Robert, Mr., Counsellor of State, appointed first Intendant of New France, but never came, iii., p. 67.

Roberval, John Francis de la Roque, Sieur de, called by Francis I. le Petit Roi de Vimeu, i., p. 129; obtains commission to continue American exploration, ib.; extent of grant, ib.; sends out Cartier in 1541, ib., 130, n.; followed in 1542, ib.; Cartier builds a fort on St. Lawrence, ib.; settles on Cape Breton, i., p. 39, 130, but see note; sends Alphonse to seek western passage to China, 130; detained in France by war, 131; returns with his brother, 131; both lost at sea, ib.; according to Thevet he was killed in Paris, 131, n.

Robeyre, (Rabeyre, Raberre, Robesle, l'Arabelle,) Lieut. de la, wounded and taken by Iroquois in Fort Roland, Montreal Island, iv., p. 30.

Robineau, Peter, member of Company of a Hundred Associates, ii., p. 169.

Robineau, René. See Bekancourt, Baron de.

Robineau, Peter. See Portneuf.

Robineau, Daniel. See Neuvillette.

Robineau. See Villebon, Menneval.

Roche, Troilus de Mesgouat, Marquis de la, Henry III. and IV. renew Roberval's grant to, i., p. 48, 241; lands a party on Sable Island, 48, 243; explores Acadian coast, 243; misfortunes and death, 244; errors as to his imprisonment, 244, n.

Roche Allard, Countess de, daughter of Francis Mary Perrot, iv., p. 163.

Roche de Jaques Cartier, i., p. 120.

ROCHEFERRIERE, SIEUR DE LA, French gentleman sent with malcontents to explore in Florida, i., p. 166 ; penetrates nearly to Apalache Mts., 170.

ROCHEFORT, v., p. 71.

ROCHEFOUCAULD LIANCOURT, Madame de Guercheville, wife of Duke de la, i., p. 263, n.

ROCHELLE, James Ribaut at, i., p. 206, n.; de Gourgues at, 236; merchants of, form association, ii., p. 25 ; illegal traders from sell arms at Tadoussac, p. 32; Louis XIII. in camp before decrees establishment of Canada Co., 43; d'Iberville sails from, iv., p. 227 ; de Nesmond at, v., p. 71.

ROCHER, CORPORAL DU, repulses Iroquois at Fort Richelieu, ii., p. 133.

ROCHES, CHEVALIER DES, commandant at Yazoos in Codere's absence, killed with all the French, vi., p. 85.

ROCK, ILLINOIS OF THE, remove to the Mississippi, vi., p. 71.

RODINUNCHSIOUNI, Colden's form of name of Iroquois, ii., p. 189, n.

ROENSA, Kaskaskia chief, removes village to Mississippi, v., p. 152, n.

ROGNOUSE, (RANOUS,) English port in Newfoundland, taken by de Brouillan, v., p. 37 ; called Renowes on modern maps, 40, n.

ROHAULT, RENÉ, son of Marquis de Gamache, founds College of Quebec, ii., p. 87.

ROHAUT, NICHOLAS, MARQUIS DE GAMACHE, ii., p. 88, n.

ROJAS, DIEGO DE, Spaniard, discovers Tucuman, i., p. 40.

ROLDAN, JUAN MANUEL, endeavors to prevent Chateauguay's occupation of St. Joseph's Bay, vi., p. 42; induces French soldiers to desert, ib.

ROLFE, REV. MR., of Haverhill, killed, v., p. 206.

RONDE, SIEUR DENYS DE LA, Canadian gentleman, naval ensign, heads Port Royal settlers during siege, v., p. 192 ; volunteer in attack on St. John, 212.

ROQUE, FRANCIS DE, see ROBERVAL.

ROQUE, Spanish officer, induces French soldiers to desert, vi., p. 42, n.

ROQUEMONT, CLAUDE DE, SIEUR DE BRISON, one of the Hundred Associates of New France, ii., p. 39 ; attacks English and is captured with all his squadron, p. 45.

ROSALIE, a fort built by Bienville at Natchez, so called in honor of the Countess de Pontchartrain, v., p. 126 ; vi., p. 31.

ROSSIGNOL, PORT, in Acadia, origin of name, i., p. 251.

ROUEN, Archbishop of, appoints Abbé de Queylus, Vicar General of Canada, iii., p. 20, n.; protests against consecration of Bp. Laval, ib.; claims jurisdiction in Canada; ib., 21, n.; Jesuits act as Vicars General of, 23, n.

ROUEN, Gamart of, Aubert's pilot, i., p. 106, n.; merchants of, form company, ii., p. 25.

ROUTINE, LA, a Temiskaming chief, leads his tribesmen at La Prairie, iv., p. 203 ; repulsed, 206, n.

ROUVILLE, JOHN B. HERTEL, SIEUR DE, joins Abénaquis with his four brothers, success, v., p. 161 ; wounded, ib.; commands a large party against New England, 205 ; speech to French before attacking Haverhill, 205 ; sent by Vaudreuil towards Lake Champlain, 216 ; attacks Deerfield, ib., n.; Sabrevois sent to meet him, 218 ; why sent to Boston, 234 ; Vaudreuil's praise of, ib.; sent on a scout towards English, 246.

RU, FATHER PAUL DU, Jesuit, erects cross on Mississippi, v., p. 125, n., 129 ; ordered to leave Louysiana, 129.

RUA, ALONZO PEREZ DE LA, begins discovery of Peru, i., p. 29.

RUPERT'S RIVER, Hudson Bay, i., p. 56.

RUTER, Breton sailor deserts La Sale, 101 ; comes to Joutel, 100 ; gives him information, 101; kills Liotot, 103; loose living keeps him among the Cenis, 107 ; his son, 117, n.

RUYZ, FATHER AUGUSTINE, Franciscan, enters New Mexico, i., p. 44.

RYDDEL, CAPT WALKER, of the Falmouth at Port Royal, v., p. 227, n.

SA, FRANCIS, Portuguese, i., p. 35.

SAAVEDRA, ALVARO DE, said to have discovered New Guinea, i., p. 35.

SABLE, CAPE, in Acadia, English repulsed at iii., p. 126.

SABLE ISLAND, described, i., p. 243 ; Baron de Lery's colony on, 10, 243, n.; Marquis de la Roche's, 243 ; settlers taken off by Chedotel, 244; cattle on, ib.

SABLE RIVER AND FORT, situation, iii., p. 285 ; Irondequois Bay, ib., n.

SABLONNIERE, MARQUIS DE LA, Lieutenant in the Infantry, volunteer on la Sale's last expedition, carried off by Indians, iv., p. 69 ; rescued, ib.; escapes at wreck of frigate, 86 ; probably killed at Fort St. Louis, 89.

SABOUET, or TABOURET, member of Company of 100, ii., p. 169 ; vi., p. 124.

SABREVOIS, JAMES CHARLES DE, Capt., sent to meet de Rouville, v., p. 218; commands a company under de Ramezay, 219 ; died Major of Montreal, ib., n.

SACCARDIE, SIEUR, King's engineer at Port Royal, iv., p. 159 ; taken by English, 161.

SACO, Abénaquis murdered at, iv., p. 273.

SACRIFICIOS ISLAND, i., p. 30.

SACS, Western tribe, Allouez preaches to, iii., p. 105, 120, n.; note as to, ib.; meet St. Lusson, 166; with La Motte Cadillac, v., p. 67 ; send delegates to peace, 142 ; some join us and some the Foxes at Detroit, 258, 263 ; desert the Foxes, 263 ; their report, ib.

SAGADAHOC BAY, v., p. 273, n.

SAGAMOS, Acadian chiefs, authority of, i., p. 265 ; polygamy permitted to, ib.; haughtiness to French, 269.

SAGEAN, MATTHEW, pretended discoveries of, iv., p. 117, n.

SAGET, La Salle's valet, iv., p. 89 ; murdered, 91.

SAGHARD, BROTHER GABRIEL, Recollect lay brother, ii., p. 35, n.; 59, n.; Chevalier's ignorance as to, ib.; author of Histoire du Canada, i., p. 78 ; goes to Huron country, ii., p. 35 ; Huron Dictionary of, 59.

SAGOCHIENDAGUETE, Atotarho or head sachem of Iroquois, ii., p. 264, n.

SAGUENAY, name applied first to a country reached by the river, i., p. 124.

SAGUENAY RIVER, Canada, when discovered, i., p. 37 ; Cartier enters, 115 ; Roberval enters, 133 ; Champlain's plan of mouth of, 246, n.; ships take refuge in, iv., p. 189.

SAGUIMA, Ottawa chief, defeats Mascoutins, v., p. 257 ; wife taken from, by Foxes, 258 ; leads his tribesmen to attack Fox fort, 260 ; delivers her, 261.

SAGUINAM, bay in Lake Huron, Iroquois attack Ottawas at, iii., p. 264.

SAIGNON, a Huron taken to France by Champlain, ii., p. 23.

SAILLANT, Naval Ensign ANTHONY DE, valor of, at siege of Port Royal, dies of wounds, v., p. 199–200.

SAILOR'S LEAP, rocks at Quebec, iv., p. 168 ; origin of name, ib., n.; batteries at, 178–9.

SAINT AMOUR, (PETER PAYET, called) Quebec (Montreal) settler taken by Iroquois, exchanged for an Oneida, iv., p. 238.

SAINT ANDRÉ AUX BOIS, Abbot of, projects a Premonstratensian house in Acadia, v., p. 156.

SAINT ANGE, SIEUR DE, officer in Illinois, defeats Foxes, vi., p. 71 ; stationed at Vincennes, which was also called by his name, 122, n.

SAINT ANGE, JR., SIEUR DE, burnt by Chickasaws, vi., p. 122, n.

SAINT ANNE. See QUITCHITCHOUAN.

SAINT ANNE. See PORT DAUPHIN.

SAINT ANNE DE LA PERADE RIVER, ii., p. 8, n.

SAINT ANTHONY'S FALLS, discovered and named by Hennepin, iii., p. 206.

SAINT AUGUSTINE, MOTHER CATHARINE DE, Hospital nun, Quebec, dies in odor of sanctity, iii., p. 112 ; life of, by Father Ragueneau, 113, n.

SAINT AUGUSTINE RIVER, so called by Menendez, called by French, Dolphin River, i., p. 188 ; Menendez at, 192 ; he takes possession, 194 ; puts Bartholomew Menendez in command at, 197.

SAINT AUGUSTINE founded by Menendez, i., p. 194.

SAINT BARBARA, la Sale's design on mines of, iv., pp. 115–6.

ST. BERNARD'S BAY, La Sale enters without knowing it, iv., p. 68; situation, ib.; called St Louis by la Sale, ib., n.; Bienville attempts to occupy, vi., p. 66; Spaniards settle at, ib.; Espiritu Santo of Spaniards, iv., p. 82 ; vi., p. 66, n.

SAINT CASTIN, BARON JOHN VINCENT DE, sketch of, iii., p. 294, n.; ensign, not captain in Carignan-Salieres regiment, appointed by Grandfontaine his lieutenant, 211, n.; summoned by English to

SAINT CASTIN, BARON J. V. (*continued.*) surrender Fort Pentagoët, 294; calls on Denonville for aid, ib.; report of, ib.; establishment pillaged by English, iv., p. 15; marries an Indian wife, 211; report to Frontenac, ib.; English attempt to assassinate, 236; leads 200 Indians at siege of Pemkuit, v., p. 25; exploit at siege of Port Royal, 193; Subercase attributes its deliverance to, 194; ambuscades English and attacks their works, 198; wounded, 199.

SAINT CASTIN, BARON ANSELM DE, son of preceding, commandant at Pentagoët, v., p. 235; sent to Vaudreuil to report surrender of Port Royal, v., p. 233; entertains Livingston at Penobscot, ib., n.; saves his life, ib.; appointed commandant in Acadia, 235; and lieutenant, 274, n.; treacherously carried off by English, 273; interrogated as a criminal at Boston, 274; Vaudreuil demands release of, 275; set at liberty and goes to France, ib.; prevented Abénaquis joining English, 302; marries Charlotte d'Amour, 274, n.

SAINT CATHARINE, port in Newfoundland, discovered and named by Cartier, i., p. 37.

SAINT CATHARINE'S CREEK, Natchez fort near, besieged by Loubois, vi., p. 97.

SAINT CHARLES RIVER, i., p. 50; English propose to attack Quebec at, iv., p. 175; fortifications at, 168; battery at, 169.

SAINT CHRISTOPHER'S, occupied by French and English, i., p. 54; Montmagny said to have died at, ii., p. 204, n.

SAINT CIRQUE, CAPTAIN DE, commands regulars in Denonville's expedition, iii. p. 282, n.; commander at battle of La Prairie, iv., p. 204; mortally wounded, but refuses to leave the field, 205.

SAINT CLER, SIEUR DE, French gentleman, left in command at Caroline, i., p. 193.

SAINT CÔME, REV. J. F. BUISSON DE, missionary, v., p. 130, n.; goes to Mississippi with Montigny, ib.; labors among Natchez, ib.; killed, ib.

SAINT CÔME, a Natché, son of the Woman Chief, presumptive successor of Great Sun, supposed to be son of a Frenchman, proceeds to French camp to negotiate, vi., p. 110; Perrier's terms to, 111; returns to his fort, ib.; brings in Sun and another chief, ib.; endeavors to exculpate Great Chief, ib.; arrested, ib.; fails to escape, 112; sold as a slave in St. Domingo, 114, n.

SAINTE CROIX ISLAND, De Monts settles at, i., p. 251; inconvenient 252; abandoned, 253; ruined by English, 283; taken by Kertk and Stirling, ii., p. 59, n.; English claim to, iii., p. 294.

SAINTE CROIX RIVER, discussion as to, i., p. 116.

SAINT DENYS, NICHOLAS JUCHEREAU, SIEUR DE, Seigneur of Beauport, ennobled for gallantry and wounds at defence of Quebec, iv., p. 177.

SAINT DENYS, LOUIS JUCHEREAU, SIEUR DE, son of preceding, notice of, vi., p. 12; uncle of Iberville's wife, ib.; put by latter in command of Fort Micissipi, 12; his adventurous journey to Mexico, 19; brings Biloxi Indians to relief of Dauphin island, 52; brings Indians to dance calumet to Champmêlin, 62; made Capt. and Knight of St. Louis, 64; marches with reinforcement for Fort Natchitoches, 65; secures their fidelity, 91; besieged by Natchez, 117; asks aid from Perrier and then sends to announce victory, 118.

SAINT DOMINGO, discovered, i., p. 19 French prisoners sent to, vi., p. 46.

SAINT EUSTATIUS, settled, i., p. 54.

SAINTE FOY, formerly NOTRE DAME DE FOYE, iii., p. 154, n.

SAINT FRANCIS DE SALES, Abénaqui mission, founded, iv., p. 44; Algonquins from, on Hertel's expedition, 132; on Portneuf's, 133.

SAINT FRANÇOIS XAVIER DU SAULT, MISSION OF, see SAULT ST. LOUIS.

SAINT GEORGE, one of the Azores, i., p. 16.

SAINT GEORGE, FORT, New London, or Wilton on the Edisto, i., p. 136; Spanish armada against, vi., p. 46.

SAINT GEORGE RIVER, (Maine,) limits between New France and New England fixed at, in 1700, v., p. 93.

SAINT GERMAIN EN LAYE, Canada restored to France by treaty of, ii., p. 58.

ST. HELENA ISLAND discovered, i., p. 24.

ST. HELENE, JAMES LE MOYNE, SIEUR DE, sketch of, iii., p. 270, n.; volunteer on Hudson Bay expedition, 270; takes

Fort Rupert by assault, 271 ; attacked near Tonihata, 302 ; bears Gov.-Gen's. orders to d'Iberville, iv., p. 39 ; one of commanders on Schenectady expedition, 122 ; ready to defend Jesuits, 179 ; wounded, 180 ; dies, ib.; eulogy, ib.; cause of death, 185 ; Onondagas send to bewail, 199.

St. Helen's Island, in the St. Lawrence, named by Champlain in honor of his wife, ii., p. 23 ; Denonville's army at, iii., p. 282.

St. Ignatius, Huron town, hunters of, surprised, ii., p. 210 ; destroyed by Iroquois, 218.

St. Ignatius, Michilimakinac, founded by Marquette, iii., p. 180, n.

St. James and St. Philip, i., p. 17.

St. Jean de Luz, i., p. 215.

St. Jean, Chevalier, commands at Sorel, iv., p. 236.

St. Joachim, pupils of industrial school at, volunteer, iv., p. 182.

St. John, chief English post in Newfoundland, de Brouillan fails to take, v., p. 37 ; French march on, 42 ; forts at, taken, 43 ; English surrender, 44; burned and abandoned, 45; English fortify, 73; failure of French attack on, 173 ; taken by St. Ovide, 313 ; deliberation as to preservation of, 214–5.

Saint John the Baptist, see Presidio del Norte.

Saint John the Baptist, Huron town, submits to Senecas, ii., p. 236.

Saint John the Evangelist, Tionontate town, surprised and destroyed by Iroquois, ii., p. 228 ; called by Indians, Oharita, ib., n.

St. John's Island, now Prince Edward's Island, situation and advantages, projected settlement on, v., p. 299.

St. John's River, the May of Ribault, i., p. 136.

St. John's River, one of bounds of Etchemins, i., p. 249; discovered and named by de Monts, p. 252; Indian name Ouygoudy, ib., n.; exploits of Indians of, iv., p. 43; Villebon meets Iberville at, v., p. 24.

Saint Joseph, a Huron town so called, ii., p. 77 ; the first mission station, ib.; surprised by Iroquois, 193 ; massacre of Father Daniel and flock, ib.; see Ihonatiria, Carragouha.

Saint Joseph, Island of, situation, ii., p. 226 ; Indian and modern names, ib., n.; Hurons fly to, ib.; famine at, 227; abandoned, 233.

Saint Joseph's Bay, Florida, abandoned by Spaniards, vi., p. 41 ; Chateaugué takes possession of, 42 ; Gousy left in command, 42, n.; evacuated, ib.; Spaniards escape to, 59 ; de Saujon proposes to occupy, 63.

Saint Joseph's River, Miami mission at, founded by Allouez, iii., p. 203 ; Mohegans at, iv., p. 242 ; necessity of retaining post on, v., p. 65; Courtemanche defeats Iroquois on, iv., p. 270 ; meets various tribes on, v., p. 141.

Saint Laurent, Chevalier de, Lieutenant-General of the West Indies, and Commissary at St. Domingo, treats La Salle well, iv., pp. 66–7.

Saint Laurent, Newfoundland, destroyed by Sir John Leake, v., p. 162.

Saint Lawrence, Gulf of, named, i., p. 115.

Saint Lawrence River, called Great River of Canada, i., p. 115 ; origin of present name, ib.; sometimes called River of the Great Bay, 242 ; called France Prime, 130, n.

Saint Louis, Huron town, destroyed by Iroquois, ii., p. 218 ; its position, 219, n.; held for a time by Atinniaoenten Hurons, 220, n.

Saint Louis, name given by la Sale to a bay in Texas, iv., p. 68, n.; called St. Bernard's by Charlevoix, iv., p. 68 ; the Espiritu Santo of the Spaniards, ib., n.; vi., p. 66, n.

Saint Louis, Fort, established by la Sale in Texas, iv., p. 72 ; Joutel and Moranget left in command of, ib.; described, ib, n.; second fort, 82, n.; la Sale's final departure from, 89 ; Spanish account of destruction of, 113 ; generally said to have been on the La Vaca, p. 73, n.; but Spanish fort of Santa Maria de Loreto, said to have been on site of, 82, n.

Saint Louis, Illinois, see Fort St. Louis.

St. Luke's Bay, Port au Mouton so called by Stirling, ii., p. 59.

St. Lusson, Francis Daumont, Sieur de, Talon's subdelegate, iii., p. 166, n.; takes formal possession of the northwest, 168; visits Acadia, 170; warns English off Kennebec, ib.

Saint Malo, Massé carried to, i., p. 281; des Prairies from, ii., p. 22; merchants of, annoy Champlain, 24; merchants of, form association, 25; eight ships of, with de Brouillan, v., p. 35; they complain of him, 38.

Saint Martin, Joseph Alexander de l' Estringan, Sieur de, reduced captain, commands Quebec militia in Frontenac's expedition, v., p. 13; and a company in de Ramezai's, 218–9.

Saint Mary, chief mission station in Huron country, ii., p. 220; besieged by Iroquois, ib.; wonderful deliverance, 221; abandoned, 227, n.; situation of, 226, n.

Saint Mary, Santa Maria de Galvé, Spanish name for Pensacola Bay, vi., p. 43

St. Mary's, Newfoundland, destroyed by Sir John Leake, v., p. 162.

St. Mary' Bay, Newf., v., p. 212.

Saint Mary's River, Champlain at, ii., p. 8.

St. Mary's of Ganentaa, mission station at Onondaga, ii., p. 264, 277; de Lauson grants land for, ib., n.; site of, iii., p. 17, n..

St. Mathias, or Ekarenniondi, Tionontate town, ii., p. 228, n.

St. Matthew, Huron town, conspiracy against missionaries in, ii., p. 231.

St. Matthew's Island discovered by Garcias de Loysa, i., p. 33.

Saint Michael, Gulf of, i., p. 29.

Saint Michael, in Culuacan, Friar Mark starts from, i., p. 38.

St. Michael, Hurons of, surrender to Senecas, and form town of Gandougarae, ii., p. 236; iii., p. 12.

St. Michael, Chagoimegon, iii., p. 49.

Saint Michel, Sieur de, sent to Michilimakinac, falls back twice to Montreal, iv., p. 218; accompanies an Ottawa convoy, ib.; taken by Iroquois, 219; account of martyrdom of an Iroquois woman, 300; escapes when condemned to the stake, ib.; his report to Frontenac, p. 239.

Saint Nicholas, Port, description of, i., p. 115; discovery, ib.

Saint Ovide, sketch of, v., p. 36; nephew of Mr. de Brouillan, takes two English forts in Bay of Bulls, ib.; St. John expedition, 212; notifies court and Costebelle of his success, 214; ordered to demolish St. John, 215; on the Valeur, 232; King's Lieutenant on Cape Breton, 296; Governor, ib.; sent to obtain Acadians, 296, n.; advice to them, 298; arranges for their withdrawal, 299.

Saint Ours des Chaillons, see Chaillons.

Saint Ours, Captain Pierre de, at the Rat's funeral, v., p. 147; land grant to, iii., p. 112, n.

St. Ours, Mary Anne de, and Mary Barara de, v., p. 13, n.

Saint Paul's River, Labrador, iii., p. 145.

Saint Pere, (Pair,) John de, killed by Oneidas, iii., p. 14.

Saint Peter's Island, discovered by Magellan, i., p. 31.

Saint Peter's Islands, see St. Pierre.

Saint Pierre, Newf., destroyed by Leake, v., p. 162, n.

Saint Pierre, Paul le Gardeur de, (called by Charlevoix in his Index, Tilly de,) son of Peter le Gardeur de Repentigny, v., p. 237, n.; notice of, ib.; sent to Michilimakinac, iv., p. 217; warns Indians, 221; sent to Detroit, v., p. 189; accompanies Ottawas to Michilimakinac, 190; brings down a large body of Indians, 237; negotiates with Foxes, v., p. 308, n.

Saint Pierre, son of preceding, serves in Chickasaw War, on Lake George and on the Ohio, v., p. 237, n.

Saint Pierre Islands, iii., p. 142; sole remnant of French power, ib.; Parat retires to, iv., p. 165; held by French, v., p. 161; Leake's squadron off, ib.; Port Toulouse, or St. Pierre, between them and Petit St. Pierre, 284.

Saint Pierre, Count de, at head of a company to settle St. John's Island, v., p. 299; obtains grants of it and of Miscou, &c., ib.; cause of failure, 300.

St. Pol de Leon, F. Jogues lands at, ii., p. 160, n.

Saint Sauveur, or Savior's, Mme. de Guercheville's colony on Mount Desert Island, i., p. 277; its position, ib., n.; destroyed by English, 279.

SAINT SAUVEUR LE VICOMTE, iii., p. 112.

SAINT SIMON, PAUL DENYS, SIEUR DE, nephew of Richard Denys de Fronsac, Canadian, sent to Hudson Bay to take possession, i., p. 57 ; iii., p. 231.

SAINT SULPICE, SEMINARY OF, Island of Montreal ceded to, iii., p. 23; takes possession, ib.; founds an hospital, 27; surrenders judicial power, 69; underdertakes to frenchify Indian children, and fails, 97; Indian missions of, 109, 117, 122 ; iv., p. 26, &c.; right to nominate and appoint Governor, 123.

SAINT SULPICE, seigneury owned by La Salle, iii., p. 122, n.

SAINT SULPICE, or REPENTIGNY, Oneidas defeated at, iv., p. 194.

SAINT TERESA BAY, on Lake Superior, origin of name, iii., p. 48; Guerin at, p. 51.

SAINT TERESA RIVER, so named by de Groseiller after his wife, i., p. 60 ; iii., p. 234; his operations at, 234-5; remarks as to capture of fort on, 269; granted to Northern Company, iii., p. 270, n.; Iberville at, v., p. 57.

SAINT THOMAS, Africa, discovered, i., p. 18.

ST. THOMÉ, Meliapor, i., p. 33.

SAINT VALIER, JOHN BAPTIST DE LA CROIX DE CHEVRIERES DE, Bishop of Quebec, sketch of, iii., p. 258, n.; arrives in Canada, ib.; visits it as Vicar General, ib.; his "Estat Present," i., p. 85 ; iii., p. 258, n.; he cites Fronsac not Le Clercq as to Portecroix, ii., p. 120; endeavors to obtain Benedictines or Premonstratensians for Acadia, v., p. 156; captured, 174; held as a hostage, 175.

SAKIS, Allouez preaches to, iii., p. 105.

SALAZAR, DON JOSEPH DÉ, Notice of his Chrysis del Ensayo Cronol., i., p. 92.

SALDANHA, A. DE, discoveries, i., p. 25.

SALE, (SALLE,) ROBERT CAVELIER, SIEUR DE LA, iii., p. 197; comes to Canada, ib.; projects, ib.; character, ib.; period of arrival, 198, n.; obtains seigneury of St. Sulpice, iii., p. 122, n., 198, n.; joins Dollier de Casson, ib.; proceeds to Seneca country, ib.; abandons them and returns, ib.; his Ohio voyage, 198, n.; meets Joliet, 198; at Onondaga, 199, n.; denounces Fenelon, ib.; Commandant of Catarocouy, ib.; undertakes to discover the Micissipi, 199; lays plans before Seignelay, 200; supported by Prince de Conti, ib.; joined by Tonti, ib.; embarks, ib.; restores Catarocouy and builds barks, 202; trials and perils, 203; firmness, 205; hauteur, discovers upper Micissipi, i., p. 57; iii., p. 206; new excursions, builds two forts, p. 208; down the river to the gulf, i., p. 58; iii., p. 213; takes possession, p. 213; Charlevoix's account meagre, ib., n.; details, ib., n.; two accounts of voyage, ib., n.; falls sick, 215; in France, ib.; la Barre writes against him, 222; consequence, 224; Seignelay's decision, ib.; Fort Catarocouy seized, p. 243; restored to, 259; misunderstanding with de la Barre causes Iroquois War, 310; good and bad qualities, iv., p. 61; project, ib.; accepted by Minister, ib.; extent of commission, 62; preparations, ib.; soldiers and mechanics badly selected, ib.; sails, 64; quarrels with de Beaujeu, 65; result, ib.; vessel taken by Spaniards, 66; sick, ib.; error, ib.; misses mouth of Micissipi, 67; at St. Bernard's Bay, 68; lands his force, 69; loss of ship, ib.; new opposition of Beaujeu, 70; ascends river, 72; builds fort, ib.; returns, ib.; second fort, 73; sees error in selecting men, 74; loses men, ib.; plans fort, ib.; exasperates men, 75; new misfortunes, 83; loses men, 84; said to have reached the Mississippi, 85, n.; Cenis, 88; sick, 89; wishes Joutel to go, ib.; sets out, ib.; ingenious way of crossing rivers, 90; uneasy about Moranget, 92; assassinated, 93; calumnies against, 95; ill-treatment of body, 96; reflections, 115; Tonti's letter for, at mouth of Micissipi, vi., p. 123.

SALE, MR. DE LA, navy officer, ordered by Iberville to man a prize, iv., p. 56.

SALIERES, HENRY DE CHAPELAS, SIEUR DE, Colonel of the Regiment Carignan-Salieres, brings part of the regiment to Quebec, iii., p. 81; builds fort, ib.

SALINAS, DON GREGORIO DE, sails to St. Josephs, vi., p. 42, n.; asked for aid, 44; report of, 47.

SALMON FALLS, (SEMENTELS,) taken by a Three River party, iv., p. 130; now Berwick, 131, n.; Indian name, ib.

SALMON, MR. DE, Commissaire Ordonnateur in Louysiana, takes possession for the King, vi., p. 120.

Salmon River, N. S., i., p. 259.
Salmon River, N. Y., iii., p. 254, n.
Salmon River, Vt. fatal encounter of two French parties near, iv., p. 128.
Salvaye, Peter de, sent to Dongan, iii., p. 248, n.
Salvaye, Madame and daughter captured by Mohawks but restored, v., p. 50.
Samal, one of the Pintados, i., p. 60.
Sanata Adivia, Chieftainess of the Texas Indians, iv., p. 80, n.
Sanders Glen. See Coudre.
San Domingo, Archbishop of, primate of all Spanish America, i., p. 31.
San Juan, New Mexico, founded, i., p. 48.
San Juan, mines of, discovered, i., p. 41.
San Juan de Piños, Florida, English settle near, i., p. 45.
San Juan de Ulua, island, i., p.30.
San Mateo, or Matheo, name given by to French fort Caroline 207; Villaroel made Commandant, ib.; fire at, 208; two forts at, 229; three forts taken by de Gourgues, 229-234; destroyed, 234.
San Miguel, one of the Azores, i., p. 16.
San Pelayo, Spanish galleon fitted by Philip II., i., p. 185; sent to Spain or St. Domingo, 194; run into Denmark, 208.
San Sebastian de Buenavista, i., p. 27.
San Vicente, John de, opposed to attacking French, i., p. 187; sent to occupy St. Augustine, 194; mutinies, 197–8.
San Vitores, Father Diego Luis, Jesuit, death of, i., p. 59.
Santa, port of, i., p. 35.
Santa Barbara, mines of, discovered by Francis de Ybarra, i., p. 41; la Salle's idea of taking iv., p. 115.
Santa Cruz. See Rio de la Santa Cruz.
Santa Cruz de la Sierra, i., p. 41.
Santa Cruz Islands, i., p. 47.
Santa Cruz, Marquis of, defeats Dom Antonio, i., p. 16.
Santa Maria, one of Azores, i., p. 16.
Santa Maria, in Darien, first Episcopal See on American continent, i., p. 27.
Santa Maria de Loreto de la Bahia del Espirtu Santo, Spanish fort and mission on the site of La Sale's fort, iv., p. 82, n.
Santa Maria de Galve, Spanish name for Pensacola bay, vi., p. 43.
Santa Rosa Island, at the mouth of Pensacola harbor, Fort Siguenza built on, vi., p. 43, n.
Saonchiogoua, Louis, Cayuga chief, brings prisoners, iii., p. 162; baptized, ib.
Saouandaouaskouay, Huron chief of Tondakhra, ii., p. 107, n.
Saraba, the Somme, i., p. 229, n.
Sarabay River, Florida, i., p. 229, n.
Saravia, Anthony de, takes possession of Marian islands, i., p. 59.
Sarmiento, Pedro de, sent against Drake, i., p. 45; discoveries of, 46.
Sarreslop, i., p. 63.
Sassafras, virtues of, i., p. 141.
Saturiova, or Saturioua, or Saturiba, Florida chief, welcomes Laudonniere, i., p. 149; obtains French aid, 151; marches against Timagoa, 159; defeats enemy, 161; quarrel with Laudonniere, ib.; dissembles, 162; asks to go to war, 172; meets de Gourgues, 227; gives him a Frenchman and hostages, 228; ib.; regrets his departure, 236.
Saujon, Chevalier de, Commodore, in Louysiana, vi., p. 63; projects capture of St. Joseph, ib.; sails back, ib.; ships of, ib., n.
Sault au Matelot, see Sailor's Leap.
Sault au Recollet, Father Viel lost at, ii., p. 37; Iroquois of Mountain retire to, iii., p. 117, n.; Schuyler tampers with Indians of, v., p. 166; mission, transferred to Lake of the Two Mountains, v., p. 308, n.
Sault St. Anthony, on the Micissipi, discovered by Hennepin, iii., p. 206.
Sault St. Louis, (Caughnawaga,) situation, Champlain at, i., p. 246; ii., p. 25, n.; Iroquois repulsed at, 32; Christian Iroquois of La Prairie remove to, iii., p. 117, n., 164, 191; iv., p. 123; Iroquois attack, 216; site of first village, p. 290, n.; Catharine Tehgahkouita at, ib.; La Salle has a seigneury opposite, 122, n.; Indians of, with de la Barre, iii., p. 249; declared enemies by the cantons, iv., p. 297; deceived, iv., p. 196; suspected, 197; prove fidelity, 199; not at La Prairie, 208; attempt to surprise, 215; some pursue enemy, 216; defence of, 232; march against Mohawks, 233; defeat expedition, 234; with Serigny at Hudson Bay, 252; chief of, expelled 264; complain of Frontenac, v., p. 20; offer to pursue Iroquois declined, 51; English tampering with, 83; relaxation caused by liquor, 203;

Schuyler persuades them to neutrality, ib.; leave a war-party, 205; their promise to Schuyler discovered, 208; Vaudreuil's action, 209; they atone for error, ib.; zeal, 240; see IROQUOIS.

SAULT STE. MARIE, rapid at mouth of Lake Superior, visited by Jesuits, ii., p. 137; iii., p. 101; Sulpitians at 122, n.; mission centre, 158; meeting of Western tribes at, iii., p. 166; formal possession taken of West at, ib., p. 168; rocks at pierced by water, 172; fight at, between Sioux and Algonquins, 196, n.

SAULTEURS, or CHIPPEWAYS. See SAUTEUX.

SAUSSAYE, M. DE LA, sent out in charge of Mad. de Guercheville's colony, i., p. 275; at Port la Haive, ib.; settles on Soames' Sound, Mt. Desert Island, ib., n.; calls it St. Sauveur, ib.; neglects to fortify, ib., n.; attacked by Argall, 279; robbed of his commission, ib.; taken to England, 281; sent to London by Mad. de Guercheville to demand redress, 285; Charles Lalemant with, ii., p. 35.

SAUSOY, DU, Commissary sent to Louisiana, vi., p. 69, n.

SAUTEUX, (PAÜOIRIGOÜEIEUHAK,) Algonquin tribe at Sault St. Mary, solicit missionaries, ii., p. 137; Jogues and Rainbaut go, ib.; what prevented conversion, ib.; gain some advantages over Mohawks and Oneidas, iii., p. 65; attire and speech of deputy at Congress, v., p. 151. See CHIPPEWAS.

SAUVOLE, MR. DE, with Iberville seeks mouth of Micissipi, v., p. 120; left in command of Fort Biloxi, vi., p. 12; dies, 15, n.; leaves journal, ib.

SAVAGE, CAPT. EPHRAIM, bark of, grounds in the St. Charles, iv., p. 175.

SAVAGE, MAJOR, at siege of Quebec, iv., p. 180, n.

SAXUMA, kingdom in Japan, i., p. 40.

SCALVE, JOHN, a Pole, discovery of Labrador and Estotiland attributed to, i., p. 18, 105; his real name Ivan w'Kolna, John of Kolno, 105.

SCARBOROUGH, ravaged, v., p. 161, n.

SCATARI, an island near Cape Breton, v., p. 284.

SCHENECTADY, town in New York, ii., p. 11; called by French, Corlar, ib.; de Courcelles' action with Mohawks near, iii., p. 89, n.; de Courcelles induces Dutch not to aid Mohawks, 88; described, iv., p. 124; attacked and burnt by French, ib.; effect of this blow, 127; alarm at, v., p. 221.

SCHODAC, French surrender to people of, v., p. 49, n.

SCHOOLCRAFT, HENRY R., invents absurd name, Itasca, iii., p. 207.

SCHOUTEN, WILLIAM, Dutchman, discovers Ascension Island, i., p. 52.

SCHUYLER, ABRAHAM, at Montreal, v., p. 80, n.; said to have been sent to Onondaga to prevent Cantons sending ambassadors to Montreal, p. 138; at a council, ib.; visits cantons to excite them against us, p. 239; his intrigues with our Indians baffled, p. 240; called by Charlevoix a brother of Peter, but erroneously, ib., n.

SCHUYLER, DAVID, sent to Onondaga, v., p. 138, n.

SCHUYLER, CAPTAIN JOHN, sent out by Fitz John Winthrop, iv., p. 147, n.; attacks La Souche, (Fourche,) 149, n.; at Onondaga, v., p. 166, n.

SCHUYLER, PETER, son of Philip P., v., p. 240; leads Mohawks and Albany volunteers to Wood Creek, in 1690, iv., p. 146, n.; attacks La Prairie with English Indian force, p. 202; pursues and engages Manteht's force, 235, n.; Major and Governor of Albany, brings back French prisoners with letter, v., p. 81; sent to dissuade Iroquois from treating with de Callieres, p. 102; incites Iroquois to war on us, and tampers with Christian Iroquois, 164; success with latter, ib.; at Onondaga, 166, n.; warns New England of French raids, p. 206, n.; boasts of controlling Christian Iroquois, p. 208; Vaudreuil writes to, 209; his reply, ib.; inconsistency of, 210; receives Father de Mareuil kindly, 216; draws Mohawks to Albany, 223; incites Iroquois to arm against us, 240; his intrigues disconcerted, ib.

SCOTCH left at Port Royal killed by Indians, iii., p. 128, n.; several lost at Sir Hovenden Walker's wreck, v., p. 247.

SCURVY, remedy for, employed by Cartier, i., p. 121.

SEBALD'S ISLANDS, i., p. 62.

SECON, Huguenot engineer on Barr's vessel, makes proposals, v., p. 126, n.

SEDENTARY FISHERIES, at Camceaux and Chedabouctou, iv., p. 15.

SEDGEWICK, ROBERT, with Captain Leverett, commands N. E. troops, raised to reduce New Netherland, iii., p. 134, n.; sent against Acadia, ib.; reduces fort on St. John and Port Royal, 134, 132, n.

SEIGNELAY, MARQUIS DE, succeeds his father, Colbert, in the Navy Department, iii., p. 200; favors la Sale, ib.; decision after de la Barre's letters, 224; approves plan for conquering New York, iv., p. 36; measures, ib.; asks Denonville for a report, 44; advice as to true course for Canada during war, 46; welcomes la Sale, p. 61; accepts his project, ib.; succeeded by Pontchartrain.

SEIGNELAY RIVER, Illinois so called, iii., p. 213, n.

SEINE RIVER, in Florida, discovered and named by Ribaut, i., p. 136; Laudonniere at, 152; de Gourgues at, 227; its Indian name Tacatacourou, 227, n.

SEINE, THE, a royal storeship, taken by English, v., p. 174.

SEMENTELS, English town, taken by Hertel, see SALMON FALLS, iv., p. 130; inquiry into name, ib., n.

SEMINARY OF THE FOREIGN MISSIONS, iii., p. 24.

SEMINARY AT QUEBEC, founded by the Seminary of Foreign Missions, Paris, iii., p. 24; burned, v., p. 181, n.

SEMINARY AT MONTREAL, founded by Sulpitians, iii., p. 23.

SENAT, FATHER ANTONINE, Jesuit, burned by Chickasaws, vi., p. 121-122.

SENECAS, one of the five Iroquois nations, ii., p. 28, n.; whether the Entonohonorons discussed, ib.; Indian name Sonontouaronons, Chonontouarouon, Sontouhoironons, ib.; Joseph, a Seneca, baptized by Brebeuf at Tondakhra, 107; canton described, 190; attack St. Ignatius, a Huron town, p. 210; attack the Aondironons, ib., n.; two Huron towns remove to, 231; Neuters form part of, 271, n.; many converted by Huron captives, iii., p. 12; ask peace and a French post, p. 43; ask peace from de Tracy, 85; Father Fremin sent at their request, p. 110, n., 116; attack Pottawatamies, 161; reply to de Courcelles, 162; incorporate Andastes and Shawnees, p. 175; Seneca chief killed by Illinois, 218; consequence, ib.; project of attacking them, 241; de la Barre wishes to destroy, ib.; attack Ottawas and Hurons, ib.; force of Senecas and Cayugas, ib.; de la Barre marches against, 250; they massacre 26 English in Maryland, 248; haughtiness of deputies at Famine Bay conference, 254; do not fulfill treaty, 257; distrust French and are distrusted, ib.; promise to send deputies to de la Barre, 254; invite English to Niagara, 266; favor their commerce with our allies, ib.; Denonville determines to make war on, ib.; they march against the Illinois, but fall back, 280; Denonville's campaign against them, 285; surprise French army, 287; repulsed at Dyagodiyio, near Boughton's Hill, and their canton ravaged, ib.; Denonville takes possession by right of conquest, 288; Ottawa negotiations with, iv., p. 53; fifty Senecas defeated at Tonihata, 217; three hundred posted on Ottawa to intercept French, 218; defeat a French escort and capture officers, ib.; deputies at Quebec embarrassed by Frontenac's questions, 253; his declaration to them, ib.; two Senecas of the Mountains desert from Frontenac's army and warn enemy, v., p. 16; why they do not support Onondagas, ib.; many killed by our allies, 68; four deputies at Montreal, 101; their conference with de Callieres, 102; Joncaire negotiates with, 105; deputies at Montreal, 108; totem of, 111; Joncaire negotiates successfully with, 139; Vaudreuil makes much of some Seneca chiefs, and sends Joncaire with them, he brings back a chief, 159; complain of Ottawa hostilities, 164; why he wished them to attend a conference at Albany, 165; they wish to include English in neutrality, Pontchartrain's opinion, 167; satisfaction for Ottawa insult, 169; do not join other cantons against us, 216; Joncaire well received, and brings deputies to Montreal, 236; how Vaudreuil treats with them, 239; permit French to erect fort at Niagara, v., p. 266.

SENECAS, BAY OF THE, Denonville near, iii., p. 288.

SENECHAL, jurisdiction of the Great Seneschal in Canada, iii., p. 66.
SENEGA or SANEGA, a negro of rank, i., p. 16.
SENEGAL RIVER, i., p. 16; origin of name, ib.
SERIGNY, JOSEPH LE MOYNE, SIEUR DE, at Montreal, iv., p. 251; Frontenac appoints to command Hudson Bay expedition, 252; success, 259; King orders him to Hudson Bay, 275; at Placentia, v., p. 48; returns to France unable to succor Fort Bourbon, 52; at Placentia with royal orders, 53; with Iberville attacks Port Nelson, 57; in Louysiana, vi., p. 14; brings news of war with orders to take Pensacola, 43; prepares for siege, 44; takes it, 45; defends Isle Dauphin, 50; reply to Spaniards, 51; report to Champmêlin, 55; sounds Pensacola Bay and engages to take fleet in, 57; dissuades Saujon from attacking St. Joseph's Bay, 63; sails for France, ib.; made captain, ib.
SERRANO, FRANCIS DE, discovers the Moluccas, i., p. 28.
SERROPÉ LAKE, Florida, i., p. 172; perhaps Lake Ware, ib.
SESEMBRE, i., p. 281, n.
SEVEN ISLANDS, Walker's fleet wrecked near, v., pp. 247, 252.
SEVERN RIVER, ii., p. 28, n.
SHARP, CAPTAIN, Hollander, discoveries of, i., p. 58.
SHAWNEE RIVER, i., p. 136.
SHAWNEES, defeated by Iroquois, iii., p. 174; said to have been met by la Salle, iv., p. 85, n.
SHIP ISLAND, Isle Surgere, vi., p. 15, n.
SHIPS,
Achille, vi., p. 63,n.
Aigle, vi., p. 16, n.
Aimable, iv., p. 64.
Albans, iv., p. 224.
Amazon, vi., p. 63, n.
Amphitrite, v., p. 69, n.
Annibal, v., p. 201, n.
Arundel, v., pp. 27, 30, n.
Assumption, i., p. 61.
Avenant, v., p. 113.
Badine, v., p. 117.
Baron de la Fosse, vi., p. 18, n.
Belle, iv., pp. 64, 67, 86.
Bot, i., p. 46.
Bouffonne, v., p. 160, n.
Brezé, iii., p. 81, n.
Castricoom, i., p. 56.
Chameau, v., p. 36, 309.
Charante, iv., p. 259.
Chateaufort, iii., p. 134.
Chatham, v., p. 247, n.
Chester, v., p. 227, n., 252, n.
Christo, iv., p. 114.
Colchester, v., p. 247, n.
Comte de Toulouse, v., p. 35; vi., p. 44, n., 61, 64.
Content, v., p. 247, n.; vi., p. 63, n.
Dauphine, i., p. 108.
Delight, iii., p. 140, n.
Deptford, v., p. 191.
Dering, v., p. 56.
Diamond, v., p. 35.
Dominus Vobiscum, iii., p. 140, n.
Dragon, iv., p. 275; v., p. 52, 225, 227, n.
Dudlow, vi., p. 38.
Duke de Noaille, vi., pp. 60, 63.
Edgar, v., p. 253, n.
Elizabeth, vi., p. 67, n.
Embuscade, iv., p. 27.
Emerillon, i., p. 117, n.
Envieux, iv., p. 227, 274, 275.
Falmouth, v., pp. 225, 227, n.
Faulcon, i., p. 148, n.
Feversham, v., pp. 225, 227, n., 252, n.
Fleur de Mai, iv., p. 189, n.
Flying Horse, iii., p. 188.
Fourgon, iv., p. 27.
François, v., p. 117, 121.
François Xavier, iv., p. 189, n.
Frankland, v., p. 195, n.
Galere, iv., p. 224.
Gironde, v., p. 69, n., 124, n.
Glorieux, iv., p. 189, n.
Golden Hind, iii., p. 140, n.
Gosport, v., p. 170.
Gran Diablo, vi., p. 50, n., 59, n.
Grande Holandesa, vi., p. 65, n.
Great Hermine, i., p. 114.
Griffin, iii., p. 202.
Hamshier, v., p. 55.
Harcour, v., p. 35, n.
Hardy, v., p. 52.
Henry, vi., p. 64.
Hercules, vi., p. 54, 62, n.
Heros, v., p. 181, 246.
Hudson Bay, v., p. 55.
Incarnation, i., p. 62.
Isabella Anne Katherine, v., p. 247, n.

SHIPS, (*continued.*)
Jane, iii., p. 211.
Jardin de Hollande, iii., p. 82, n.
Jersey, v., p. 170, n.
John and Thomas, iv., p. 178, n.
Joli, iv., p. 63, 64, 66, 67.
Joseph, v., p. 252, n.
Justice, iii., p. 82.
Leostaff, v., p. 225, n., 227, n.
Levrier, i., p. 205, n.
Ludlow, vi., p. 38, n.
Maréchal de Villars, vi., p. 44, n, 55, 61.
Marie, vi., p. 40, n., 55, n.
Marin, v., p. 117.
Marlborough, v., p. 247.
Mars, vi., p. 55, n., 61, 62, n.
Mary, v., p. 155, 252, n.
Maurepas, i., p. 60.
Mercure, vi., p. 63, n.
Mercury, i., p. 46.
Mutine, vi., p. 63, n.
Nathaniel and Elizabeth, vi., p. 247.
Neptune, v., p. 252, n.
Neptune, vi., p. 40.
Newport, v., p. 24.
Normande, i., p. 108.
Normandy, iii., p. 81, n.
Nuestra Señora de Vicuña, vi., p. 51, n.
Oxford, v., p. 27, n., 28.
Palmier, v., p. 56; vi., p. 14, n.
Paon, vi., p. 38, n., 39, n.
Pearl, i., p. 206, n.
Pelican, v., p. 35, 59.
Pembroke Galley, v., p. 169, n.
Pensée, i., p. 107, n.
Petit Breton de Dieppe, i., p. 148, n.
Philippe, vi., p. 40, 44, n., 50, 51, n., 55, n.
Philippeaux, v., p. 35.
Plymouth, iv., p. 224.
Poli, iv., p. 227, 259.
Postillon, v., p. 37.
Profond, iv., p. 275; v., p. 25, 56, 59, 172, n.
Province Galley, v., p. 30, n., 191, n., 227, n.
Province Snow, v., p. 170, n.
Province Tender, v., p. 24.
Renommée, v., p. 117; vi., p. 14, 17.
Rochfort, v., p. 227, n.
Rose Frigate, iii., p. 211; iv., p. 15.
Saint François, iv., p. 64.
St. François Xavier, iv., p. 27.
St. Jean Baptiste, i., p. 61.
St. Louis, i., p. 61.
St. Michael, v., p. 90.
St. Sebastian, iii., p. 82, n.
Samuel and Anne, v., p. 247.
San Pelayo, i., p. 185, 208.
Santo Christo del Buen Viage, vi., p 51, n.
Sapphire, v., p. 36.
Sauveur, i., p. 281, n.
Seignelay, v., p. 296.
Seine, v., p. 174.
Severn, iv., p. 178, n.
Six Friends, iv., p. 178, n.
Smyrna Merchants, v., p. 247, n.
Society of Pool, v., p. 169, n.
Soldat de Prise, v., p. 36.
Soleil d'Afrique, iv., p. 215.
Somme, vi., p. 106.
Sorlings, iv., p. 274; v., p. 24, 27, n.
Squirrel, iii., p. 140, n.
Subtile, vi., p. 66, n.
Swallow, iii., p. 140, n.
Swan of Veer, i., p. 46.
Teron, iii., p. 82, n.
Trinidad, i., p. 32.
Triton, vi., pp. 55, n., 62, n.
Union, iv., pp. 27, 161; vi., p. 55, 62, n.
Valeur, v., p. 232.
Vendome, (Vendange,) v., p. 35, n.
Venus, vi., p. 69.
Vitoria, i., p. 32.
Wasp, v., p. 22, 37, 56, 59, 118, n., 172.
Ysabeau of Harfleur, i., p. 148, 157, n.
Zephyr, (Sapphire,) v., p. 36.
SHUTE, Gov., declares war against Abénaquis, v., p. 277, n.
SIAM, Ambassadors of, i., p. 28; Maladie de, v., p. 241, n.
SIGOGNE, MR. DE, Governor of Dieppe, ordered by Queen Mother to see to embarkation of Jesuits, i., p. 262; is disobeyed, ib.
SIGUENÇA, FATHER CHARLES, on Spanish fleet at Pensacola, vi., p. 43.
SIGUENÇA POINT, on Santa Rosa Island, abandoned by French, vi., p. 48; Spanish fort at, 53; demolished by French cannon, 58.
SIKIK, (KIGGINS,) English captain besieges Naxoat, v., p. 30. See KIGGINS.
SILLERY, COMMANDER NOEL BRULART DE, Knight of Malta, aids Jesuit missions, ii., p. 97; founds a settlement for Christian

Indians, 98; connected with Villegagnon, ib., n.; sketch of, ib.

Sillery, Indian town, founded by preceding, ii., p. 98; first settlers of, ib., n.; fervor at, 167; iv., p. 306; reduced to extremity, ii., p. 167; walled, 245; Bro. Liegeois killed at, 260; precautions against intoxication, iii., p. 55; Sillery Algonquins defeat Mohawk Oneidas, 64; people carried off by smallpox, 154; iv., p. 44, n.; depopulated by measles, iii., p. 295, n.; iv., p. 44, n.; Abénaquis at, ib.

Silver, Adelaide, of New England, an Hospital nun, v., p. 303, n.

Silvy, Father Anthony, Jesuit, sketch of, iii., p. 270, n.; on Hudson Bay expedition, ib.

Sinagaux, Ottawa tribe, iii., p. 218, n.

Sioux, Indian tribe in Canada, Dacotas called by Algonquins, Nadwechiwec, iii., p. 31, n.; insulted by Ottawas and Hurons, ii., p. 271, n.; iii., p. 31; their country, p. 32; peculiarities, ib.; visited by Marest and Guignas, ib.; render honors to some articles of Father Mesnard, 50; speak to Allouez of countries beyond them, 106; fight with at Sault St. Mary's, 196, n.; take Dacan and Hennepin prisoners, 206; directed to leave our allies in peace, 280; le Sueur sent to, iv., p. 242; ask Frontenac's protection, 272; their condition, ib.; trade with, ib.; defeated by Miamis, v., p. 64; repulse them in turn, ib.; de Callieres censures Ottawa attack on, 101; village carried off by Ottawas, 111; de Courtemanche prevents war on, 142; Bourgmont proposes general war on, 184; join Foxes against us, 305.

Siquyera, Diego Lopez de, discovers Sumatra, i., p. 27.

Sir Thomas Roe's Island, i., p. 54.

Sisters of the Congregation, Montreal, founded by Margaret Bourgeoys, iii., p. 28; ii., p. 250; court wishes them to become nuns, iii., p. 28; at Louisbourg, v., p. 296, n.

Skanchioe, Neuters flee to, ii., p. 271, n.

Skaouendes, Mary Magdalen, a Mohawk oyender, emigrates to Lorette, iii. p. 163.

Skiae Rapid, or Sault St. Mary's, ii., p. 271, n.

Slavery recognized in Canada, v., p. 224.

Small Pox, ravages among Iroquois, iii., p. 153; destroys Sillery, 154.

Smith, Capt. John, explorations and settlements of, i., p. 50.

Smith, William, historian of Canada, had F. Jogues's Journal, ii., p. 186.

Smit's Jan, English name for Flemish Bastard, which see.

Société de Montreal, Motifs de la, noticed, i., p. 82; island granted to, by de Lauson and New France Co., ii., p. 130.

Socotora, discovered, i., p. 35.

Sofala, discovered, i., p. 20, 25.

Soissons, Charles de Bourbon, Count de, Viceroy of New France, ii., p. 23; makes Champlain his lieutenant, 24; dies, ib.

Sokokis, Sokokinois, Indians of New France, origin of name, ii., p. 156, n.; position, 155; two freed by Montmagny in order to deliver F. Jogues, ib.; kill Christian Montagnais, 185; French ask New England to defend, 215; some on Hertel's expedition, iv., p. 130; on Mohawk expedition, 233; on Frontenac's, v., p. 13; promise to send deputies to General Congress, 141; Courtemanche finds some on the St. Joseph's, ib.

Soleil d'Afrique, fast French ship, iv., p. 215.

Solis, Juan Diaz de, discovers Yucatan, i., p. 26; explores Brazilian coast, 27.

Solis de las Meras, chaplain to Menendez, his Narrative of the Expedition, i., p. 72.

Solomon's Islands discovered, i., p. 43; names of, ib.

Somme River, Florida, Laudonniere at, i., p. 152; Indian corn obtained from, 177; de Gourgues at, 229; called Saraba and Halimacani, ib, n.

Sorel, Pierre de Saurel, Sieur de, captain of the Carignan-Salieres regiment, erects Fort Sorel on the Richelieu, or Sorel, iii., p. 82; takes the field, 87; commands Tracy's van, 90; land grants to, 112, n.

Sorel, Fort, built by Captain Sorel, iii., p. 82; menaced, iv., p. 232; repaired, 236; Mme. Salvaye taken near, v., p. 50.

Sorel River, its names, ii., p. 12; Champlain ascends, ib.

Soto, Fernando de, his Florida campaign, i., p. 38; death, 134, vi., p. 11; body thrown into the Mississippi, iii., p. 214,

SOTO, F. DE, (*continued.*) n.; battle with Indians at Maubile, v., p. 119.

SOUART, REV. MR., Sulpitian, arrives, iii., p. 23.

SOUCHE, LA, Charlevoix's misprint for FOURCHE, LA, iv., p. 149, n.

SOUDRIC, English commissioner to settle limits, v., p. 93.

SOUEL, F. JOHN, Jesuit, arrives in Louisiana, vi., p. 76, n.; missionary at the Yazoo, 85; killed, ib.; the cause of his death, b.

SOURDIS, MADAME DE, aids F. Biard, i., p. 262.

SOURIQUOIS, Acadian Indians, included in Abénaki nations, i., p. 264. See ACADIANS, MICMACS, GASPESIANS.

SOUTHACK, CAPT. CYPRIAN, of Province Galley, at Port Royal, v., p. 30, n., 191, n., 227, n.

SOUTHWICK, CAPT., relieves Casco, v., p. 161, n.

SPANBERG, CAPT. discovers islands north of Japan, i., p. 64.

SPANIARD BAY, Chevalier du Palais at, iv., p. 222; Iberville at, v., p. 24.

SPANIARDS, account of two captives in Florida, i., p. 171; information given to Laudonniere by them, ib.; under Menendez found St. Augustine, 194; destroy French colony, 201, &c.; surprised at San Matheo by de Gourgues, 230; hated by Indians, ib.; how treated by de Gourgues, 236; set out to expel la Sale, iv., p. 113; find his fort in ruins, ib.; subsequently plant a fort and mission there, 82; settle Pensacola, v., p. 118; among Assinais, vi., p. 20; found a post there, 31; war declared against, 43; Pensacola taken from, ib.; recapture Pensacola, 49; besiege Dauphin Island, 53; lose Pensacola, 58; aid St. Denys against Natchez, 118.

SPINOLA, AUGUSTINE, brings tidings of peace vi., p. 66.

SPURWINK, ravaged by Abénakis, v., p. 161, n.

SQUIRREL TRIBE, near the Nekouba, iii., p. 40.

STAATS, LIEUT. BARENT, nephew of Mr. Schuyler, exchanged for F. Mareuil, v., p. 221.

STADACONÉ, Donnacona's town, i., p. 117, n.; its site in the present city of Quebec, ib.

STARKY, killed by Canibas, iv., p. 41, n.

STARVED ROCK, site of La Salle's fort, iii., p. 208, n.

STATEN LAND, discovered and named by le Maire and Schouten, i., p. 52.

STEENWYCK, CORNELIUS, Dutch Gov. of N. Scotia and Acadia, iii., p. 188.

STERLING, WILLIAM ALEXANDER, EARL OF, James I. grants Acadia and all wrested from France to, i., p. 249; iii., p. 125; divides grant, ib.; neglects and abandons it, ii., p. 59; reduces it by Kertk's aid, ib.; wins over la Tour, iii., p. 125, n.

STOUGHTON, WILLIAM, Lieut. Gov. of Massachusetts, conduct towards Abénaquis, iv., p. 273; sends Cary to exchange prisoners, v., p. 76, n.

STRAITS OF LE MAIRE, i., p. 52.

STUKELY, captain of Deptford, v., p. 191.

STUNG SERPENT, I., Natché chief, vi., p. 29; compels Apple and other villages to make reparation, 72, n.; death of, 112, n.; II. in Perrier's hands, 112, n.; apparently sold, 114, n.

STUYVESANT, PETER, Governor of New Netherland, reduces New Sweden, i., p. 56.

SUBERCASE, DANIEL AUGER DE, Captain on Isle Orleans, iv., p. 186; Major Gen. in Frontenac's expedition, v., p. 13; draws up army, 16; Governor of Placentia, 161, n.; gives English no rest, 161; Gov. of Acadia after Brouillan, 172, n.; Newfoundland expedition, 172; why not a complete success, 174; twice compels English to raise siege of Port Royal, 191; 200; projects for a solid establishment, 201; prepares for defence, 225; projects settlement at La Héve, ib.; warned of attack makes no preparation, 226; soldiers and settlers ill-disposed, 226; attacked, 227; surrenders, 231; conditions, 231; sends capitulation to Vaudreuil, 233; court martialled at Rochefort, 231, n.

SUEUR, MR. LE, notice of, iv., p. 273, n.; vi., p. 13, n.; sent to establish post at Chagoimegon, and renew alliance between Chippewas and Sioux, iv., p. 242; brings down convoy, 272; Iberville sends

him to found a post at Copper mine in Sioux country, v., p. 134 ; vi., p. 12 ; visits Choctaw country to sound them, p. 93 ; attacks Natchez at head of Choctaws, 96 ; leads the van in Perrier's Natchez War, 107; guards Natchez chiefs and prevents escape, 112 ; prisoners on galley of, 114 ; report of, 115 ; not permitted to pursue fugitives, ib.

SUEUR, MR. LE, land grants to, iii., p. 112, n.

SULPITIANS, Montreal ceded to, iii., p. 23 ; begin missions on Lake Ontario, 109 ; explore Lake Erie, 122, n.; see MOUNTAIN, SAULT AU RECOLLET.

SUMATRA discovered, i., p. 27.

SUN, THE GREAT, Natché chief, meets Bienville, vi., p. 29 ; surrenders to Perrier, 111 ; sold as a slave in St. Domingo, 114 ; seen there by Bienville, 114, n.

SUN, THE LITTLE, goes to obtain murderers, vi., p. 29 ; sold as a slave, 114, n.

SUPERIOR COUNCIL, formally established, iii., p. 67 ; how constituted, ib.

SURGERES, CHEVALIER DE, reply of Governor of Pensacola to, v., p. 119 ; arrives again in the Gironde, 124, n.

SURINAM, ceded to Holland in exchange for New Netherland, ii., p. 11 ; iii., p. 73 ; v., p. 91.

SUSANNA, an Oneida woman, comes to see Frontenac, iv., p. 244–5 ; account of, ib.

SUSE, peace concluded at, before capture of Quebec, ii., p. 55, n.

SUSQUEHANNAS, identical with Andastes, Minquas, &c., ii., p. 72, n.

SWANSEA, Laudonniere at, i., p. 206, n.

SWEDEN, NEW, Swedish colony, situation, origin and history of, i., p. 55; ii., p. 11.

WEDES, settle on Delaware, i., p. 55 ; ii., p. 11 ; conquered by Dutch, 56 ; iii., p. 73, n.

SWISS, a company of, in Louysiana, desert and reach Carolina, vi., p. 67.

SYRESME, FATHER JAMES DE, Jesuit, succeeds Rale at Norridgewalk, v., p. 281, n.

SYDNEY HARBOR, BAIE DES ESPAGNOLS, Cape Breton, v., p. 285.

SYLLERI, see SILLERY.

TACAMES, TECAMENEZ, THECAMES, Texas Indians, mission among, iv., p. 78, n.

TADOUSSAC, port on the St. Lawrence, Pontgravé at, i., p. 245 ; Chauvin leaves men at, 246; his house at, ib.; de Monts trades at, 248, 259 ; Champlain sails from, ii., p. 19, n.; arrives at, 20; Kertk at, 44 ; trading centre for Indians, 119 ; missions at, ib., 166 ; intoxication at, 242 ; shower of ashes at, iii., p. 61 ; Talon nearly wrecked at, 149 ; abandoned by Indians, 153; Charlevoix sees whales at, iv., p. 18 ; Phipps at, 153.

TAENSAS, Louisiana tribe, receive La Salle well, iii., p. 214, n.; Mr. Montigny establishes mission among, v., p. 130, n.

TAHONTAENRAT, Neuter chief, defeats Iroquois, ii., p. 271, n.

TAIGNOAGNY, Canada Indian, visits France with Cartier and returns, i., p. 118.

TAILER, COLONEL, at Port Royal, v. p. 230, n.

TALBOT RIVER, ii., p. 28, n.

TALLARD, MR. DE, Boundary Commissioner, fixes limits of Canada at the St. George, iv., p. 93.

TALLIGEU, or TALLIGEWI, surmise as to, iii., p. 31, n.

TALON, JOHN, sketch of, iii., p. 176 ; Intendant of Canada, iii., p. 67 ; instructions to, 81; regulates tithes, iii., p. 24, n.; arrives, p. 82, n.; conduct towards de Mesy, 84 ; studies country, ib.; report to Colbert, ib.; opinion of Courcelles, Tracy and West India Company, 84 ; wishes to frenchify Indians, 97; encourages commerce, ib.; deceived as to silver-mine at Gaspé, 98 ; iron-mines, ib.; encourages manufactures, ib, n.; lays aside prejudice as to Jesuit management, ib.; returns to France, 120 ; niece of, wife of Perrot, Governor of Montreal, 123 ; brings back Recollects, 148 ; shipwreck, ib.; at Quebec, ib.; godfather of Cayuga chief, 162; projects taking possession of northwest, p. 165 ; sends de Lusson and Perrot, 166 ; zeal and activity, 176 ; solicits recall, ib.; sends to explore Micissipi, 179 ; visits Acadia, 187 ; sends to take possession of Hudson Bay, 231.

TALON, LUCIEN, Canadian, with family joins La Sale's last expedition, iv., p. 62 ; with la Sale on last expedition, 89 ; adventures of two sons, 113–4.

TALON, PETER, among Cenis, iv., p. 94, n.; taken by Spaniards, 113 ; narrative cited, 89, 93, n.

TALON, Indian chief, see BLANC, JOHN LE, v., p. 189.

TAMAROAS, Illinois tribe, passed by la Sale, iii., p. 214, n.; mission among, v., p. 130, n.

TANESTHIONI, Seneca chief, taken by Ottawas, v., p. 135.

TANGIBAOS, or White Corn Indians, Louisiana tribe, iii.,p. 214, n.; destroyed by Quinipissas, v., p. 123.

TANNER, FATHER MATHIAS, Jesuit, Notice of his SOCIETAS MILITANS, i., p. 82.

TANNERY successfully established, iii., p. 99.

TANUXIMA, island in Japan, i., p. 40.

TAONDECHOREN, JOSEPH, a Huron taken with Jogues, ii., p. 163; zeal and noble answer of, ib.

TAOUACHAS, Louisiana tribe, sing calumet to l'Epinai, vi., p. 39.

TAPIA, i., p. 41.

TARBELLS, taken at Groton, chiefs at Sault St. Louis, v., p. 161, n.

TAREHA, Oneida chief, brings proposals of peace to Frontenac, iv., p. 238 ; Governor's reply, 239 ; insolent proposals on next visit, 244 ; his reception, 245 ; returns to Quebec and is ill-received, 254.

TARTARIN, F. RENÉ, Jesuit, arrives, vi., p. 76, n.

TAST, CAPT. DU, sent to Catarocouy with convoy, iii., p. 249.

TAST, CAPTAIN DU, arrives at Quebec with a convoy of 14 vessels, iv., p. 200 ; does not follow chief orders, but cruises off Gulf of St. Lawrence, 201.

TAST, ENSIGN DU, midshipman serving as ensign, under d'Iberville, dies of pleurisy from exposure at Pemkuit, v., p. 28.

TATAHWISSERE, Oneida of Sault St. Louis, his report, v., p. 49.

TATEGUENONDAHI, Seneca chief, defeated on Ottawa, iv., p. 217, n.

TAWERAHAT, Colden's form for OUREOUHARÉ, which see.

TAXOUS, Abénaqui chief, takes Groton, iv., p. 257 ; taken, kills some and escapes, v., p. 23.

TAZMAN, ABEL, discoveries of, i., p. 56.

TAZMANIA discovered, i., p. 56.

TCHACTAS, see CHOCTAWS.

TEANANSTAYAE, or ST. JOSEPH'S, Huron town, destroyed by Iroquois, ii., p. 210.

TEAONTORAI, perhaps Noquet Islands, ii., p. 271, n.

TEAOS, Texas tribe, iv., pp. 78, n., 90, n.

TEBACHI, Indian hostage, ii., p. 31, n.

TECHOUEGUEN, or CHOUGUEN, the Oswego, iii., pp. 218, 219, n.

TEGAHKOUITA, CATHARINE, Iroquois virgin, iii., p. 117; famous for miracles wrought at her tomb, iv., p. 295 ; her life, 283 ; known as La Bonne Catherine, p. 283, 296.

TEGANANOKOA, STEPHEN, sketch of, iv., p. 296.

TEGANEOUT, Iroquois chief, seized by de la Barre, iii., p. 249 ; did not speak at la Famine, 254, n.; speech at general congress, v., p. 144.

TEGANISSORENS, Onondaga chief, at Montreal with deputies of the Five Nations, iii., p. 221 ; sent to blind French, ib.; ambassador for peace, taken on way by Le Rat, but released, iv., p. 13; Frontenac confides in, 52 ; died a Christian, 247 ; useful to colony, ib.; at Quebec with eight deputies, 250; presents Frontenac a belt from Garakonthié, ib.; Frontenac's courtesy to, ib.; proposes restoration of Fort Frontenac, 251; Frontenac shows irritation at his not returning, 253 ; his reception of French ambassadors at Onondaga, v., p. 103 ; con duct at a council of Five Nations, to English and French envoys, 105; undertakes to bring in all French prisoners, 108 ; complains to de Callieres of an Ottawa hostility, 135 ; interview, 136; returns to Onondaga with French envoys, 138 ; speech to them and English, 140 ; unable to restore prisoners, ib.; promises to labor for neutrality during war between France and England, and to retain missionaries, 160; advice to Vaudreuil, 239; died at Sault St. Louis, 247.

TEGARETOUAN, chief of Iroquois of the Mountain, killed in Denonville's Seneca battle, iii., p. 289, n.

TEGUAIAGUENTA, MARY TERESA, iv., p. 290.

TEHARONHIAWAGON or AGRESKOUÉ, great Iroquois deity, iii., p. 157.

TEISSIER, or TESSIER, or TEXIER, pilot of the Belle, iv., p. 83, n., 86, n.; goes with la Sale, 89; approves of Moranget's death,

91; sent to Cénis for food, 98; starts for Illinois, 107; abjures Calvinism at Montreal, 111.

TELLO, FRANCIS DE, Spaniard sent to explore California, i., p. 38.

TEMISKAMINGS, Algonquin tribe at la Prairie, iv., p. 203.

TEMPLE, SIR THOMAS, English, pretensions over Nova Scotia, iii., p. 132; signs a document at Boston restoring Acadia and adjacent shores to France, 138; unwilling to surrender Pentagoët, ib.; surrenders to Grand Fontaine, 139; its value to him; his intention of joining French, 187; leaves his property to his nephew Wm. Nelson, 187.

TENAOUTOUA, Seneca town, Dollier de Casson winters at, iii., p. 122, n.

TEONNONTOGUEN, Mohawk town, not Fort Hunter, iii., p. 109, n.; iv., p. 234, n.; corrected, vi., p. 125.

TEOTONHARASON, an early Onondaga convert, ii., p. 265.

TE OTONDIATION, Neuter town, taken by Iroquois, ii., p. 271, n.

TEQUENONKIAYE, Huron town, ii., p. 210.

TERAN DE LOS RIOS, DOMINGO, Governor of Coahuila, iv., p. 114, n.

TERCEIRA, one of the Azores, i., p. 16.

TERESA, Iroquois woman, conversion of, friend of Catharine Tehgahkwita, iv., p. 290.

TERNATE, discovered, i., p. 28.

TERRA AUSTRAL DE ESPIRITU SANTO, discovered, i., p. 49.

TERRA CORTEREALIS, early name for Labrador, i., p. 23.

TERRA DEL FUEGO, discovered, i., p. 32.

TERRISSE, SUB-LIEUT., left at Pensacola, vi., p. 62, n.

TESSERIE, JAMES DESCAILHAUT, SIEUR DE LA, opinion of, as to Bay St. Paul iron mines, iii., p. 98.

TESSERIE, LA, interpreter, iii., p. 87, n.

TESSOUAT or TESSWEHAT, chief of the Algonquins de l'Isle, or Kichesipirini, iii., pp. 24, 163; converted, 164.

TETINCHOUA, Great Miami chief, Perrot's account of, iii., p. 166; reception of Perrot, 167; represented by Pottawatamies at Sault St. Mary's, 168; Dablon said to have met, 184.

TEXAS, Indians of, v., pp. 75, 78, n.; animals, 76; production, 77.

TEXAS, tribe of Indians, account of, iv., p. 80, n.

TEXEYRA, PEDRO, explores Amazon, i., p. 55.

THEMINES, PONS DE LAUSIERE THEMINES CARDAILLAC, MARSHAL DE, King's lieutenant in New France during imprisonment of Prince of Condé, the Viceroy, ii., p. 31, n.

THET, BROTHER GILBERT DU, Jesuit, killed at St. Saviour's, Mount Desert Island, i., p. 280; de Laet on, ib.

THEVET, ANDREW, Cosmographie Universelle, i., p. 67.

THIBET discovered, i., p. 54; visited, 62; names of, 63.

THIONONTATEZ, see TIONONTATEZ.

THOU, JAMES AUGUSTUS DE, implicates French court in Spanish massacre in Florida, i., p. 213.

THREE RIVERS, post and city in New France, ii., p. 58; settled, 30; trade, 34; northern tribes trade at, 86; Chevalier Brasdefer, Governor, p. 91, n.; de Lisle, Governor, 91, 123; Hurons taken near, 96; missions at, 118, 166; de Champflour, Governor, 123; Governor-General gives public audience to Iroquois at, 173; Father de Noue at, 184; d'Ailleboust erroneously called Governor of, 203, 4; religious triumphs among Indians at, 243; blockaded by Mohawks, 252; Mohawks driven off, ib.; jurisdiction, iii., p. 69; almost abandoned by Indians, iii., p. 55, 153; militia of, iv., p. 176; mines near, iii., p. 99, n.; sends out expedition against Salmon Falls, iv., p. 130; Sieur de la Chassaigne, Governor, p. 142; Indians from, against Mohawks, 233; militia of, v., p. 13; Ursuline convent at, p. 80, n.; Indian name of, vi., p. 125.

THUNDER, extraordinary, i., p. 162.

THUNDER BAY, Ottawas at, ii., p. 270, n.

THURY, REVEREND PETER, Canibas missionary, sketch of, iv., p. 40, n.; praised, 40; at Pentagoët, 40-3; induces Indians to break off negotiations with English, 256; encourages Indians, 258.

TIBIERGE, agent of Acadia Company, supports Villebon in defence of Naxoat, v., p. 31.

TICONDEROGA, Champlain engages Iroquois near, ii., p. 16.

TICONNONDADIHA, Iroquois, deserts to English, v., p. 216, n.

TIDOR discovered, i., p. 28.

TILLY, see LE GARDEUR.

TILLY DE COURTEMANCHE, see COURTEMANCHE.

TILLY, LIEUTENANT DE, dies of scurvy a Port Nelson, iv., p. 262.

TIMAGOA, Florida chief and tribe, enemy of Saturiova, i., p. 151; tribe called also Thimogona, and by the Spaniards Timuqua, Tinqua, ib., n.; works on language of, ib., n.; town of, taken by Saturiova, 161; subject to Outina, 162.

TIMOR discovered, i., p. 28.

TINNSALS, Louisiana tribe, sing calumet to l'Epinai, vi., p. 39, n.

TIOSKATIN, Sioux chief, asks Frontenac's protection, iv., p. 272.

TIONNONTATÉS, called by Charlevoix real Hurons, not regarded as such, really the Petuns, ii., p. 71, n., 228; their country, 228, n.; defeated through rashness, ib.; their wanderings, p. 271, n.; with the Sioux, iii., p. 31; on Black River, ib.; at Michilimakinac, ii., p. 271, n.; iii., p. 170; excite Iroquois against Kiskakons, 222; Rat, chief of, v., p. 110; see HURONS OF MICHILIMAKINAC, QUIEUNONTATERONONS, PETUNS, DINONDADIES.

TIONONTATEZ, LE CIEL DES, chief killed in battle in Seneca country, iii., p. 289, n.

TIOUX, Indian tribe, allied to Natchez, endeavor to excite Tonicas to attack French, vi., p. 95; exterminated by Arkansas, 102.

TISNÉ, SIEUR DU, Louysiana officer, marches against Natchez, vi., p. 28; stationed at Rosalie, p. 31; sent to build fort in Natchitoches Island, ib.; information from Spaniards, ib.; marches to aid Illinois, p. 71, taken and burned by Chickasaws, 122, n.

TITHES, regulation as to, iii., p. 24.

TLASCALA conquered, i., p. 31.

TOANCHE, Huron town, ii., p. 27, n.

TOBASCO, i., p. 30.

TOGINGA, Arkansas tribe, iv., p. 109, n.

TOHONTAENRAS, Huron tribe, ii., p. 108; remove to Seneca country, ib.

TOLEDO, ANDREW DE, Jesuit, explores Amazon, i., p. 55.

TOLEDO, FRANCISCO DE, Viceroy of Peru, i., p. 45.

TOMÉS, Louysiana tribe, kill an English officer, vi., p. 24; sing calumet to l'Epinai, 39.

TONATAKOUT, Seneca deputy, v., p. 101, n.

TONARENGUENION, Seneca deputy, v., p. 101, n.

TONDAKHRA, Huron town, Brebeuf baptizes a Seneca at, ii., p. 107, n.

TONDIHARON, chief of the Iroquois of the Mountain, killed, iv., p. 193, n.

TONICAS, Louysiana Indians, Rev. Mr. Foucault killed among, v., p. 124; Davion's mission to, 130; follow St. Denys to Natchitoches, vi., p. 19; refuse to join Natchez, 27; chief's reply, ib.; Chickasaws fear, 79; attached to French, 86; French army at Tonica Bay, 88; sounded by Tioux, 95; to be depended on, 102; Head Chief asks Perrier's permission to receive some Natchez, 115; murdered by them, 116; a Christian, 117, n.

TONIHATA ISLAND, in the St. Lawerence, French attacked near by Iroquois, iii., p. 302; Iroquois party defeated at, by de Beaucourt, iv., p. 217.

TONTI, CHEVALIER HENRY DE, work of, i., p. 90; criticised, v., p. 121, 125; son of Lorenzo, inventor of Tontines, iii., p. 200, n.; his early career, ib.; Prince de Conti gives him to la Sale, ib.; builds fort at Niagara, 202; at St. Joseph's River, 203; wins Illinois over to la Sale, 205; unable to save them from Iroquois defeat, 211; driven from river, winters at Green Bay, 212; sent to build Fort St. Louis, 213; descends Mississippi, 214; sent to Michilimakinac, 215; disavows Relation, 207, 214; repulses Iroquois at Fort St. Louis, 244; descends Mississippi and sends Couture and Delaunay to Arkansas, iv., p. 108; to await la Sale, iii., p. 279, n.; ordered to collect large Illinois force for Seneca campaign, 279; able to bring only eighty to Detroit, 280; on Denonville's expedition, iv., p. 110; gives Cavelier a draft, ignorant of la Sale's death, 111; sent to Michilimakinac with a French party, 242; allowed to retain Fort St. Louis on conditions, 276; letter of, to La Sale, found by d'Iberville, v., p. 122; joins Iberville, 125; firm-

TONTI, HENRY DE, (*continued.*)
ness of, retains Illinois, 131 ; death, iii., p. 200.

TONTI, ALPHONSUS DE, BARON DE PALUDY, captain, brother of preceding, commandant at Detroit, his house burned, v., p. 164 ; attacks Ottawas, 168 ; superseded by de Bourgmont, 184 ; indiscreet remark of, ib. ; brings down a great many Indians, 237.

TONTI, MR. DE, taken and burned by Chickasaws, vi., p. 122, n.

TORCAPEL, REVEREND MR., arrives, iii., p. 22, n.

TORIMAN, Arkansas village and tribe, iv., p. 109.

TORRE, DON ALPHONSO CARRASCOSA DE LA, commands fleet intended to attack Carolina, sent to retake Pensacola, vi., p. 45; takes two French ships, 46; besieges and takes Pensacola, 48; reinstates Matamoros as Governor, 49 ; solicits aid of Viceroy of Mexico, ib.; appeases a mutiny, 50; attacks Dauphin Island and summons Serigny, 51; fortifies and provisions Pensacola, 53 ; prepares to defend himself against French fleet, 55; surrenders to de Champmêlin, 58.

TORSKIM, Nephew of Grande Gueule, Onondaga envoy, iv., p. 249, n.

TORTOISE, one of the three families of the Mohawk tribe, opposes Jogues' death, ii., p. 195.

TOTATHIRON, chief of the Iroquois of the Mountain, killed through mistake by a French party, v., p. 49.

TOTIRI, STEPHEN, a Huron, endeavors to convert Neuters, ii., p. 163.

TOUCHARONTION, at the mouth of Detroit river, iii., p. 284–5.

TOUCHE, JOSEPH DE LA, son of Seigneur of Champlain killed at Quebec, iv., p. 177.

TOUDAMANS, probably Iroquois, i., p. 113, n.

TOULLE, BAY OF, Charlevoix's misprint for Bay of Bulls, an English post in Newfoundland, v., p. 40.

TOULON, squadron from, vi., p. 64.

TOULOUSE, COUNT DE, directs Canadian affairs, v., p. 307, n. ; praises Father Laval, vi., p. 64.

TOUR, CHARLES TURGIS DE ST. ETIENNE, SIEUR DE LA, proprietor of part of Acadia, captured on one of de Roquemont's vessels, iii., p. 125, n. ; marries in England, 125 ; made Baronet of Nova Scotia, not Knight of the Garter as Charlevoix supposes, p. 126 ; undertakes to put English in possession of Cape Sable, ib. ; correspondence with his son, ib. ; fears to return to England, 127 ; generosity of his son, ib. ; noble reply of his wife, ib. ; he retires with Scotch to Port Royal, 127, n. ; house built for, by son, 128.

TOUR, CHARLES AMADOR DE ST. ETIENNE, SIEUR DE LA, son of preceding, part of Acadia bequeathed to by Biencourt Poutrincourt, iii., p. 125, n. ; holds Fort St. Louis at Cape Sable against his father, 127 ; relieved by Marot, ib., n. ; made Lieutenant-General of Acadia, ib. ; urges father to leave English, and builds a house for him, 128 ; extent of grant to, ib. ; supposed agreement with de Razilly, 129; founds settlement on St. John's, ib., n. ; seeks aid from Massachusetts, p. 131 ; his fort defended by his wife against de Charnisé, 130–1 ; de Charnisé's disloyalty, 131 ; retires to Newfoundland and Quebec, 131, n. ; made Governor and Lieutenant-General, 132, n. ; marries de Charnisé's widow, 132 ; surrenders to English, 134; obtains grant from Cromwell, 132, n. ; dies, ib.

TOUR, CAPTAIN LE BLOND DE LA, takes possession of Fort Alibamon, vi., p. 25 ; lays out New Orleans, 68, n. ; builds fort at Balize, 70, n. ; dies soon after, ib. ; ordered to assume command of colony till de Boisbriand arrived, 75, n.

TOUR, MADAME DE LA, defends Fort St. Louis, iii., p. 130–1 ; dies soon after, ib., n.

TOUR, SIEUR DE LA, French officer, dangerously wounded at Port Royal, v., p. 229.

TOURMENTE, CAPE, English ravages at, ii., p. 44.

TOURVILLE, COUNT ANNE HILARION DE COTENTIN DE, defeats English and Dutch fleets in the Channel, iv., p. 188.

TOWNSEND, COLONEL, at siege of Port Royal, v., p. 196, n.

TOYA, Floridian deity, festival in honor of, i., p. 143.

TRACY, ALEXANDER DE PROUVILLE, MAR-

QUIS DE, Lieutenant-General of the King's armies, sent with power and commission of Viceroy, iii., p. 81 ; arrives, 82 ; regulates tithes, iii., p. 24, n.; instructions, 80 ; at Quebec, 81 ; erects forts on the Richelieu, 82 ; a better course, 83 ; receives Garakonthié, 85 ; punishes a Mohawk chief, 88 ; Mohawk expedition, 89 ; why he erected no fort there, 92 ; why he did not punish Oneidas, 93; hangs some Mohawks, ib.; puts West India Company in possession of estates of Hundred Associates, 94; returns, ib.; eulogy, ib.; does not approve frenchifying Indians, 97.

TRAVERSY, JOHN L'AUMONIER DES, ensign, surprised by Iroquois, iii., p. 87, n.

TREATY of Suse, ii., p. 55, n.
- of St. Germain en Laye, ii., p. 58; iii., p. 128, n.
- of Norman's Kill, ii., p. 75, n.
- with Iroquois, Montmagny's, ii., p. 178.
- with Iroquois, Dec. 13, 1665, the first formal one, iii., p. 86, n.
- of Breda, iii., p. 94, 124, 135; territories restored by, iii., p. 138, n.; iv., p. 15.
- of Nimeguen, iii., p. 188, n.
- of neutrality with England, iii., p. 273.
- of Ryswick, v., p. 80, n.
- with Abénaquis at Mare Point, v., p. 98, n.
- at Montreal, v., p. 111.
- of Utrecht, v., p. 267.
- at Portsmouth and Arrowsick Island, v., p. 267, n.

TRENCHANT, French pilot, forced by Caroline mutineers to join them, i., p. 168 ; brings some back, 169.

TRENT RIVER, ii., p. 28, n.

TREPASSEY, N. F., destroyed by Leake, v., p. 162.

TRINIDAD discovered by Columbus, i., p. 21.

TRISTAN NUÑO discovers Cape Blanco, i., p. 15 ; Cape Verde, 16.

TROCHE, RODERIC, plants Spanish flag on Carolina, i., p. 203.

TROUVÉ, REVEREND CLAUDE, sent by Bishop of Petræa to Iroquois at Kenté, iii., p. 110; taken prisoner to Boston, iv., p. 157, n.; 159 ; on Phips' fleet, 187 ; exchanged, ib., n.

TROYE, CHEVALIER PETER DE, captain, on Hudson Bay expedition, iii., p. 270 ; commands regulars in Denonville's campaign, 283, n.; commandant at Fort Niagara, 290 ; perishes with all the garrison, 291.

TRUDEAU, Canadian, repulses Spaniards at Guillory Island, vi., p. 52.

TUBERONES ISLANDS, i., p. 31.

TUCUMAN discovered, i., p. 40; settled, 41.

TURGIS, FATHER CHARLES, Jesuit, dies of his labors at Miscou, ii., p. 119 ; printed in Charlevoix, TURSIS.

TURNELL, CAPTAIN, English, carries Father Biard and two other Jesuits to England, i., p. 283 ; their noble conduct toward, 284.

TURSIS, see TURGIS.

TYAKAPPANS, Texas tribe, iv., p. 90, n.

ULÉE, island near Ladrones, i., p. 63.

ULPIUS, EUPHROSYNUS, globe of, ii., p. 20, n.

UMBRIA, GONZALO DE, explorations of, i., p. 32.

UNDERDOWN, CAPTAIN, of the Frankland, v., p. 195, n.

UNIVERSITY LAVAL, origin of, iii., p. 97, n.

URFÉ, REVEREND FRANCIS SATURNIN LASCARIS D', Sulpitian missionary, iii., p. 110.

URSINS, MR. DE LA LOIRE DES, killed at Natchez, vi., p. 82 ; see LOIRE.

URSINS, M. DES, at Quebec with intelligence from de Nesmond, his orders, v., p. 69, 73.

URSULINES, proposed for Canada, ii., p. 100 ; object of introducing them, ib.; their foundress, 101 ; reception at Quebec, 102 ; fervor, courage and charity during smallpox, 104 ; site of first convent, 103, n.; services to Canada, iii., p. 28 ; give up Indian pupils, 29 ; leave convent by night for fear of Iroquois, iii., p. 34; Reverend Mr. Vignal, chaplain of, p. 46, n.; convent burnt, 261, n.; during siege of Quebec, iv., p. 178, n.

URSULINES AT THREE RIVERS, foundation of house, v., p. 80, n.

URSULINES AT NEW ORLEANS, establishment of, vi., p. 76–77, n.; receive Natchez orphans, p. 100, n.

URUGUAY RIVER, i., p. 30.

UTRECHT, negotiations at, v., p. 265.

UXELLES, NICHOLAS CHALON DU BLÉ, MARQUIS AND MARSHAL D', informed by English envoys at Utrecht that the settlement of Louysiana annoyed them, vi., p. 36.

VAILLANT DE GUESLIS, FATHER FRANCIS, Jesuit, sent by Denonville to Dongan, iii., p. 300 ; not allowed to pass through Mohawks, 303 ; at Catarocoui, 303 ; at Detroit in 1701, v., p. 154, n.; sent to Senecas, 155, n.; reports Schuyler's propositions to Iroquois, 164.

VALDEZ, DIEGO FLORES DE, Admiral, i., p. 217.

VALDEZ, DON PEDRO, Maestro de Campo and son-in-law of Menendez, advises sudden attack, i., p. 187 ; sent to obtain information, 188; ordered to lead attack on Caroline, 198 ; advises attack, 200 ; takes a prisoner, 201.

VALDIVIA, PEDRO DE, Spaniard, explores Chili, i., p. 39.

VALERO, BALTASAR DE ZUÑIGA, MARQUIS DE, Viceroy of New Spain, orders of on receiving intelligence from Pensacola, vi., p. 46–7 ; learns recapture and order expulsion of all French from gulf, 49.

VALLETTE, LAUDUN, CAPTAIN DE, in Cafaro's squadron, takes command of the Comte de Toulouse, vi., p. 64 ; describes the voyage, ib., n.

VALLIERE, MR. DE LA, attacked on Cape Breton by English, iii., p. 93.

VALLIERE, MR. DE LA, Commandant at Port Royal, unable to prevent settlers surrendering to English, iii., p. 211; robs settlers, ib., n.

VALLIERE, MICHAEL LE NEUF, SIEUR DE LA, Capt. of Frontenac's guards, father of Alex. le Neuf, Sieur de la, at Beaubassin, v., p. 160, n.

VALLIERE, MR. DE LA, Major of Montreal, sent to Boston, v., p. 98.

VALRENES, CLEMENT DE VUAULT, notice of, iv., p. 203, n.; commands regulars in Denonville's expedition, iii., p. 283, n.; iv., p. 203, n.; distinguished in the Seneca battle, iii., p. 287, n.; commandant at Catarocouy, ordered to evacuate and dismantle, iv., p. 32 ; obeys, 34 ; at Montreal, ib.; advises hanging Phips' messenger, 172 ; sent with 200 men to defend Chambly, 203 ; defeats English, his gallantry, 205.

VALTERYE, or VALTRIES, SERAPHIN MARGANE, SIEUR DE LA, commands militia in Denonville's expedition, iii., p. 283, n.; see iv., p. 237, n.

VALTRIE, ENSIGN DE LA, attacked and killed by Iroquois, iv., p. 238, n.

VALUOT, CAPTAIN, visits Laudonniere, i., p. 205, n.

VAN CORTLAND, Letters of, show English complicity in Lachine massacre, iv., p. 31, n.

VAN CURLER, ARENDT, tries to save Jogues, ii., p. 148, n.; governors of New York called Corlar, after him, iii., p. 88, n.; Schenectady known in Canada as Corlar, a corruption of his name, ii., p. 11 ; iii., p. 88, n.

VAN DIEMAN'S LAND discovered, i., p. 56.

VANNES, Mother Jane Thomas of St. Agnes, Hospital nun of, comes to Quebec, iii., p. 114, n.

VARENNES, RENÉE DE, marries Christopher Dufrost de Lajemmerais, iv., p. 139, n.

VARENNES, RENÉ GAUTHIER, SIEUR DE, v., p. 310, n.

VARLET, SIEUR, officer, mortally wounded at Laprairie, iv., p. 207.

VASSEUR, MICHAEL AND THOMAS LE, Laudonniere's pilots, i., p. 149 ; one sent to a Florida chief, 158, 162 ; mutineers at Caroline take flag from, 167 ; Michael (or Thomas) sent by Ribaut to reconnoitre Fort Caroline, i., 209.

VASSEUR, MR., engineer, v., p. 13 ; builds fort where Frontenac lands, 15.

VASSEUR, Major of Fort Biloxi, v., p. 124, n.

VAUDREUIL, CHEVALIER DE, sketch, iii., p. 282, n.; at Quebec, commandant of forces, 282 ; on Denonville's expedition, ib.; leads convoy to Catarocouy, 306 ; to command New York expedition, iv., p. 25 ; reconnoitres and annoys English fleet, 167–9 ; defeats Iroquois at St. Sulpice, 194; marches against Iroquois war parties, 199, 220 ; defeats Black Kettle, ib.; reinforces de Callieres, 240; on Frontenac's expedition, v., p. 12 ; commands van and rear, 13; commands debarkation, 14 ; on right, 15 ; sent to Oneida, 18 ; lays it waste, 19 ; brings in French prisoners and chiefs, ib.; to replace Frontenac on New England expedition, 71 ; Governor of Montreal,

97; praised, ib.; at Rat's funeral, 147; with de Callieres at Great Indian Council, 152; smokes great pipe of peace, 152; unanimously desired as governor, 158; appointed, 159; favors Senecas, ib.; a chief gives investiture of canton, 159; secures Tegannissorens, 160; labors for neutrality, ib.; aids Abénaquis, ib.; uneasy as to Upper Indians, 163; and Iroquois, 164; Senecas complain to, of allies, 165; averse to Detroit, ib.; advises Senecas to attend Albany Council, 166; aids Abénaquis, 166; Indians at Bekancourt, 167; his design, ib.; Senecas to be Mediators, 168; exchange of prisoners proposed by English, 175; leaves New York unmolested, 179; reconciles Iroquois and Ottawas, ib.; prevents war, 180; wise course in Detroit troubles, 187; Ottawa chiefs make reparation, 188; speech of chief, 189; his opinion as to, 189; sends war party to New England, 204; treatment of domiciliated Iroquois, 209; complains of Schuyler's tampering with Indians, ib.; Schuyler's reply, ib.; deceived by Iroquois, 215; undeceived and acts with vigor, 216; will not let Ramezay take the field, 218; sends him out, ib.; encamps at Chambly and sends out detachments, 220; receives deputies, 222; report to Pontchartrain on Manteht's Hudson Bay expedition, 224; promises Iroquois redress, 225; reinforces de Subercase, 226; capitulation of Port Royal sent to, 233; correspondence with Nicholson, ib.; sends two officers to Boston, 234; appoints Baron Anselm de St. Castin commandant in Acadia, 235; Acadians ask aid, ib.; urges missionaries to retain Indians in fidelity, ib.; sends officers to bring down Upper Indians, 236; at Montreal, ib.; sends officers to Iroquois, ib.; informed of English preparations, 237; orders Beaucourt to complete defences of Quebec, ib.; orders the Marquis d'Alognies to Acadia to aid in operatons against Port Royal, 238; obliged to recall him, ib.; council with Western and Iroquois deputies, 239; finds allies well disposed and retains some, 240; labors with missionaries to baffle Schuyler's intrigues, 208; diligence on Quebec works, 216; places Count de Vaudreuil, his son, in the post of danger, 245; at Montreal, ib.; encamps at Chambly 246; sends Rouville on a scout, 246; sends barks to scene of Walker's wreck, 247; gains over Iroquois, 256; Abénaquis send deputies to ask whether King has ceded their country to the English, 270; his reply, 270; demands release of St. Castin seized by English, 275; renews alliance with Iroquois, 300; project for increasing population, 301; in France, 303, n.; returns, 307; unites almost all our allies against Foxes, 305; his orders to Louvigny how to treat them, ib.; Foxes break their pledge, 309; death and eulogy, 310.

VAUDREUIL, MADAME, captured by English, v., p. 216, n.

VAUDREUIL, LOUIS PHILIPPE, COUNT DE, son of Governor-General, placed by him in position of danger, v., p. 245; services of, ib., n.

VAUDREUIL, LOUIS PHILIPPE, MARQUIS DE, son of preceding, services of, v., p. 245, n.

VAUDREUIL, MARQUIS DE CAVAIGNAL, iii., p. 228.

VAZ, TRISTAN, discovers Porto Santo Island, i., p. 14; and Madeira, 15.

VEGA, GARCILASO DE LA, account of his Florida, i., p. 73.

VELASCO, Spanish captain, said by Vincent le Blanc to have first ascended St. Lawrence, i., p. 106.

VELASQUEZ, DIEGO, Governor of Cuba, i., pp. 28, 30.

VELLO, GONZALO, commander of Almouros, explores the Azores, i., p. 16.

VELSERS, Augsburg merchants, obtain grant of Venezuela, i., pp. 35, 41.

VENEZUELA, or LITTLE VENICE, discovered, i., p. 21; explored, 35.

VENTADOUR, HENRY DE LEVI, DUKE DE, becomes a priest, ii., p. 35; object in purchasing Viceroyalty of New France, ib.; sends over Jesuits, ib.; rebukes William de Caen for ill-treating them, 38; resigns office to King, 43; Point Levi named after, ii., p. 35.

VENTE, ABBÉ DE LA, arrives in Louisiana, vi., p. 16, n.

VERA CRUZ, i., p. 30; founded, 31.

VERAGUAS discovered by Columbus, i., p. 25; Louis Columbus made Duke of. ib.;

VERAGUAS, (*continued.*)
title descends to other houses, ib.; Nata in, 30.

VERAZANI, (VERASSENS,) JOHN, a Florentine, said to have commanded one of Aubert's ships in 1508, i., p. 106, n.; date of his first voyage to America, i., 33, 107; second and third, 33-4, 108; Ferland reduces the three voyages to one, 108, n.; touched Newfoundland or Cape Breton, 33, 111; embarks again, his fate unknown, 111; first landing, 109; adventure of sailor, ib.; takes possession of discovered lands, ib.; not taken and hanged, 34, 108; last voyage mentioned by Thevet, i., p. 111; by Belleforest, vi., p. 123; authenticity of voyages discussed by Smith, i., p. 107, n.

VERCHERES, MR. DE, land grant to in 1672, iii., p. 112, n.

VERCHERES, SIEUR DE, officer, killed on Hewreuil expedition, v., p. 207.

VERCHERES, MARY MAGDALEN DE, her defence of fort, v., p. 207, n.

VERCHERES, burnt by Mohawks, iii., p. 299, n.

VERDERONNE, or LA BOULARDERIE ISLAND, near Cape Breton, v., p. 282.

VERLIER, JOHN, member of Company of 100, ii., p. 169; vi., p. 124.

VERDIER, CAPT. NICHOLAS, in Ribaut's squadron, sent to governor of San Matheo, i., p. 210.

VERDURE, CAPT. DE LA, Commandant at Port Royal and guardian of d'Aulnay's children, iii., p. 134, n.

VERENDERYE, PIERRE GAULTIER DE, explorations of, v., p. 310, n.

VERNEUIL, MARCHIONESS OF, liberal to Acadian missionaries, i., p. 262.

VERRAZANA, New France so called on Ulpius' Globe, ii., p. 20, n.

VESCHE. See VETCH.

VESPUTIUS, AMERICUS, ship's husband to Ojeda, i., p. 21; publishes an account, ib.; probably ignorant of the use of his name, 107, n.

VETCH, SAMUEL, notice of, v., p. 217, n.; neutrality proposed through, 18; sounds the difficult points on the St. Lawrence, 176; 217, n.; urges preparations against Montreal, 217; governorship of New France promised to, ib.; failure to attack Chambly ascribed to, 220; adjutant general in Port Royal expedition, 227, n.; Commandant at Port Royal, illtreats French, 235; returns to England and dies, 217, n.

VIDARETA, ANDREW DE, Spaniard, discovers New Guinea, i., p. 35.

VIEL, FATHER NICHOLAS, Recollect, goes to the Hurons, ii., p. 35; drowned on his way back in the Saut au Recollet, but not accidentally, 37, 69.

VIELE, ARNOLD CORNELISON, of Albany, interpreter, sent by Dongan to Onondaga, iii., p. 251; sets up Duke of York's arms, ib.; address of a chief to, ib.; reports failure of Western Iroquois, iv., p. 145, n.

VIENNE, CAPTAIN DE, of the Triton, vi., p. 54, n.; sounds entrance to Pensacola Bay, p. 55.

VIEUX FORT, or BREST, Labrador, iii., p. 145.

VIEUXPONT, FATHER ALEXANDER DE, Jesuit, wrecked, retires to Cape Breton ii., p. 46.

VIGNAU, NICHOLAS DE, deceives Champlain, ii., p. 24, n.

VIGNE, SIEUR DE LA, French gentleman, left on guard at Caroline, i., p. 193; unwittingly contributes to its capture, p. 201

VIGNE VOISIN, captain, builds fort at Mobile, vi., p. 15, n.

VIGNOL, (VIGNAL,) REVEREND WILLIAM, Sulpitian, sketch of, iii., p. 46, n.; missionary on Cape Breton, ib.; chaplain of Ursulines, ib.; joins Sulpitians, ib.; killed by Mohawk-Oneida party, p. 45-6.

VIGNON, ARNAUD DE, deserter, iv., p. 229 taken and executed, 231.

VILESCAS, DON PEDRO, commandant at Presidio del Norte, receives de St. Denys well, vi., p. 20; sends him to Caouis, 21; St. Denys renders him a great service, 23; marries his daughter, ib.; better authorities call this person DON DOMINGO RAMON.

VILESCAS, DON JUAN, brother of preceding, accompanies St. Denys to Maubile, vi., p. 24.

VILINVILLE, SIEUR DE, exploit of, vi., p. 50; reinforces de Serigny, 52.

VILLAGAS, JOHN DE, Spaniard, discovers New Segovia, i., p. 41.

VILLALOBOS, RUY LOPEZ DE, Spaniard, discovers Luzon, i., p. 39.

Villarica de la Vera Cruz, or Old Vera Cruz, i., p. 31.

Villaroel, Spaniard, discovers mines of Potosi, i., p. 40.

Villaroel, Gonzalo, sergeant-major, distinguished at Caroline, i., pp. 197, 198, 201 ; Governor of San Matheo, 207.

Villebon, Robineau, Chevalier de, captain, son of Baron de Bekancourt, iv., p. 158 ; on de la Barre's expedition, iii., p. 249 ; hears of capture of his brother, Manneval, iv., p. 158 ; loses ship and two ketches, 161 ; at Jemset, 162; reply of the Abénaquis to, 163 ; goes through to Quebec, 167; at siege, ib.; in France, 214 ; Commandant of Acadia, 213–4 ; at Quebec, 215 ; returns to Port Royal, ib.; Governor of New England tries to carry him off, 226 ; urges Frontenac to take Pemkuit, 227 ; failure of plan arranged with Bonaventure and Iberville, reports to Frontenac, 244 ; warns Iberville of English fleet, v., p. 24 ; meets him at the St. John's, ib.; supposed by Charlevoix to have been captured, 28 ; Villieu really taken, ib., n.; learns that an English squadron menaces Fort Naxoat, 29 ; preparations for defence, 30 ; speech to men, 31 ; conduct during siege, ib.; Indians pursue English, 33 ; King orders Nesmond to give him all the aid he requires, 72 ; report to Pontchartrain on disposition of Indians and English, 92; unable to do more than defend Fort Naxoat, 113; death of, ib., n.

Villedonné, Stephen de, Sieur de, French lieut. taken prisoner by Iroquois, iv., p. 30 ; escapes, reports to de Callieres, 220 ; announcing speedy arrival of deputies of Upper Tribes, v., p. 139 ; distinguished in Newfoundland, 174.

Villegagnon, Nicholas Durand de, Knight of St. John of Jerusalem, Vice-Admiral of Britanny, his expedition to Brazil, i., p. 41, 132 ; returns to Roman Church, 133 ; goes back to France, 42, 133.

Villemande, name said to have been given by Menendez, i., p. 214.

Villemonte, French officer, pursues and slaughters mutineers, of Fort Toulouse, vi., p. 68, n.

Villeperdry, Sieur de, one of La Sale's party, orders to, iv., p. 73 ; death, 74.

Villeray, Louis Rouer de, Councillor in Superior Council, removed and sent to France by de Mesy, iii., p. 74.

Villieu, Lieut. Sebastian de, exploit of, at siege of Quebec, iv., p. 181; at Cape Tourmente to hold English in check, 186 ; baffles New England negotiations with Abenakis, 256 ; leads Indians against English, ib.; takes Oyster river, ib.; encourages Indians intimidated by English goveror, 256; takes chiefs to Quebec, 259 ; at siege of Pemkuit, v., p. 25; takes it, ib.; captured by English, 28 ; Charlevoix confounds him with Villebon, ib.; Frontenac complains of his ill-treatment, 82 ; on the part of France co firms boundary regulation of New France, 93.

Vimond, Father Bartholomew, Jesuit, at Cape Breton, ii., p. 46 ; Sup. General of Missions of New France, ii., p. 102 ; receives vows of Mother St. Augustine, iii., p. 114 ; brings over missionaries, Ursulines and Hospital nuns, ii., p. 102 ; iii., p. 114 ; says first Mass at Montreal, ii., p. 127 ; baptizes an Algonquin chief, 164 ; attends Montmagny's, audience of Iroquois deputies, 178.

Vimont, Father, Jesuit, on Cape Breton island, ii., p. 46.

Vincelotte, Sieur, bearer of royal dispatches to Frontenac, lands near Pentagoët, v., p. 51; sent to France by Champigny, 96, n.

Vincennes, John Baptist Bissot, Sieur de, Canadian gentleman, brings down Ottawa deputies to Vaudreuil, iv., p. 180; defeats Ottawas and rescues prisoners, v., p. 169 ; announces coming of Ottawa envoys, 180 ; pursues Foxes, 264, n.; heroic death, vi., p. 121.

Vincennes, French post, founded by Mr. de Vincennes, vi., p. 122, n.; called also St. Ange and Ange Gardien, ib.

Virginia, named in honor of Queen Elizabeth, i., p. 55.

Viseu, Henry, Count of, Canaries ceded to, i., p. 14.

Vitelleschi, F. Mutius, General of the Jesuits, accepts foundation of College of Quebec, ii., p. 88.

Voisin, Sieur, young officer of fifteen conducts retreat from Chickasaw country, vi., p. 121.

VREDEMAN, NICHOLAS, German, discoveries of, i., p. 38.

VRIEZ' STRAITS, i., p. 56.

WAEIGATZ STRAITS discovered by Barrow, i., p. 42; visited by Patt and Jackman, 44.

WAINWRIGHT, COLONEL, on Port Royal expedition, v., p. 191; March turns over command to, 196, n.

WAINWRIGHT, CAPTAIN, killed at Haverhill, v., p. 206, n.

WALCOP, see WAUCHOP.

WALKER, SIR HOVENDEN, notice of, v., p. 253, n.; commands fleet against Quebec, 247; its wreck, 247, 253; loses more ships on Cape Breton, 252; takes possession of island, 253; removes to Carolina, ib., n.; dies in Barbadoes, ib.

WALLEY, JOHN, commands forces in Phips' Quebec expedition, sketch of, iv., p. 183, n.; lands at la Canardiere, 176, n.; thrice repulsed, 177, 179, 181; abandons artillery and retires, 183.

WALTON, COLONEL, at Port Royal, v., p. 228.

WAMPUM, called by French Porcelaine, ii., p. 254, n.

WATTEAU, FATHER MELITHON, Recollect, iii., p. 203.

WAUCHOP, CAPTAIN ALEXANDER, Scotch officer, in Spanish navy, brings over treaty of peace to Pensacola, vi., p. 65, n., 67.

WEAS, see OUYATONONS, MIAMIS.

WEEMS, CAPTAIN (JAMES,) Commandant at Fort Pemkuit when taken by Canibas, iv., p. 41–2, n.

WELLS, attacked, iv., p. 227.

WELLS, LIEUTENANT JOHN, of Northampton, killed, v., p. 219, n.

WENRON, Indian tribe, ii., p. 84; see OUENRONRONON.

WESSELS, DIRCK, at Onondaga, v., p. 166, n.

WESTBROOK, COLONEL, destroys Penobscot town, church, &c., at Passadumkeag, v., p. 277, n.

WEST ENGLAND discovered by Frobisher, i., p. 44.

WEST FRISELAND, reconnoitred by Frobisher, i., p. 44; see ZANI.

WEST INDIA COMPANY, New France included in grant to, iii., p. 79; Tracy puts in possession, 94; ill success of, ib.; commission Denys to colonize Cape Breton, 132; overreached by la Giraudiere, 136; drives fur trade to English 216.

WESTERN COMPANY, (LAW'S,) vi., p. 37; obtains grant of Louisiana, ib.; Spaniards seize negroes of, 50; result of government of, 67, 69.

WHALES found in Sea of Corea, with Greenland harpoons, i., p. 48; seen above Tadoussac, iv., p. 18; fishery, 17.

WHEELER, SIR FRANCIS, attacks Martinique, iv., p. 241, n., 244, n.

WHEELWRIGHT, ESTHER, an Ursuline, v., p. 303, n.

WHITE'S NEWFOUNDLAND noticed, i., p. 89.

WICHE'S ISLAND, north of Greenland, i., p. 52.

WILD PIGEONS, ii., p. 192.

WILLIAM III., sends to de Callieres a duplicate of letter to Governor of New England, v., p. 99, considers Iroquois subjects, 100; wishes to send French refugees to Louysiana, 126.

WILLIAMS, ADMIRAL, English, besieges Placentia and summons Governor, raises siege, iv., p. 244.

WILLIAMS, REVEREND JOHN, taken at Deerfield, v., p. 161, n.

WILLIAMS, EUNICE, daughter of Reverend John, taken at Deerfield, v., p. 161, n.

WILLIAMS, ELEAZAR, descendant of Eunice, pretends to be Louis XVII., v., p. 161, n.

WILLOPS, or WILLOUGHBY'S LAND, i., p. 41.

WILLOUGHBY, SIR HUGH, English, dies in Lapland, i., p. 41.

WILTON, FORT ST. GEORGE or NEW LONDON, menaced by Spaniards, vi., p. 46.

WINDRESSE'S REGIMENT, loss of, in Walker's shipwreck, v., p. 247, n.

WINNEBAGOES, call themselves Otchagras, called by Algonquins, Ouenibégouc, or Men of the Fetid (i. e., salt) Water, called by French, Puants, iii., p. 31, 106, n., 120, n.; meet de St. Lusson, p. 166.

WINSLOW, JOHN, ii., p. 203, 214, n.

WINTHROP, JOHN, ii., p. 213, 214, n.

WINTHROP, GOVERNOR, of Massachusetts, La Tour seeks aid from, iii., p. 131, n.

WINTHROP, FITZ JOHN, sketch of, iv., p. 147, n.; appointed to command New York and Connecticut force against Montreal, 145–6, n.; arrested by Leisler on

charge of cowardice, 147; Governor of Connecticut, ib.

Wolf family of Mohawks, opposes Jogues' death, iii., p. 195.

Wolf, or Loup, see Mohegan.

Wood Chuck, ii., p. 72, n.

Wood Creek, Fitz John Winthrop's force at, iv., p. 146, n.; Nicholson to march to, 220, n.; see 246, n.

Wouverdelik, Swiss captain in Louisiana, mutiny and escape of company, vi., p. 67, n.

Wright, Captain, of Northampton, defeated, v., p. 219.

Wyandots, name now assumed by Tionontatez, ii., p. 71, n.; various forms of name, ib.

Wye, St. Mary's on the, ii., p. 226.

Xaguana, called by Charlevoix Yaguana, i., p. 168.

Xavier, St. Francis, at Goa, i., p. 39.

Ximenez, Francis, pretends to make salt water fresh with sassafras, i., p. 142.

Yaguana, or Xaguana, ancient city in St. Domingo, i., p. 168; Florida pirates plan pillage of, ib.

Yalaas, Louisiana tribe, sing calumet to l'Epinai, vi., p. 39.

Yanekey's and Jacob's Piratical Company, iv., p. 15.

Yazoos, Louisiana Indians, English seek trade with, vi., p. 24; encouraged by English to obtain slaves, ib.; great Natchez chief calls them perfidious, 27; Frenchman, escaping from Natchez, received and taken to Orleans, 84; assure Perrier of their fidelity, ib.; kill their missionary and all the French, 85; cause of missionary's death, ib.; Yazoos attack Father Doutreleau while saying Mass, 87; almost destroyed by Arkansas, 102; some join Natchez, ib.

Ybarra, Francis de, Spaniard, discoveries of, i., p. 41.

Ydalgo, Father, Recollect, among Asinais, vi., p. 19, n.

Yendat, ii., p. 71; given for Wendat.

Yesso, Strait of, i., p. 44; visited by Father de Angelis, 53; Japanese send to, 60.

York, destroyed by Indians, iv., p. 227.

Yost, Thomas, (Yeo, or Yow,) opens trade between New England and Canada, ii., p. 216, n.

You d'Youville, Madame, foundress of the Sœurs Grises, iv., p. 140, n.

Ysbrandtz, Brandt, discoveries of, i., p. 46.

Yucatan discovered, i., p. 26, 30; reduced, 35.

Yvetot, see Larchevêque.

Zani, two noble Venetians, brothers, fable as to Estotiland, i., pp. 44, 105.

Zarco, John Gonzales, discovers Porto Santo Island, i., p. 14, and Madeira, 15; takes surname of Cambra, ib.

Zechaen, pretended discoveries of, i., p. 56.

Zeno, see Zani.

Zimotto, Diego and Francisco, Spaniards, enter Japan, i., p. 39.

Zipangu, Japan so called by Marco Polo, i., p. 40.